Glad Adventure

Author: Experiments in International Administration (1919); Cases on Labor Law (1922); Cases on Criminal Law (1927), abridged edition (1930); Siam, Treaties with Foreign Powers (1928); Cases on the Law of Admiralty (1929); America Must Act (1936); The Way Forward: The American Trade Agreements Program (1939); The Protection of American Export Trade (1939).

Francis Bowes Sayre

Glad Adventure

FRANCIS BOWES SAYRE

THE MACMILLAN COMPANY · NEW YORK

1957

© FRANCIS B. SAYRE 1957

FIRST PRINTING

PRINTED IN THE UNITED STATES OF AMERICA

LIBRARY OF CONGRESS CATALOG CARD NUMBER: 57-7213

To

ELIZABETH EVANS SAYRE

dear comrade
through the years

"Lord, take my lips and speak through them; take my mind, and think through it; take my heart, and set it on fire."

Foreword

As each of us looks back over his life the conviction must grow that the real satisfactions—the memories that sing—come out of struggle and often of suffering, and not from days of ease or physical delight. The dynamic that gives to life its real glory, its matchless harmonies, is not, when all is said and done, the reaching out after comfortable living, the effort to scale successfully some professional ladder, the hunger for the plaudits of the crowd. It is rather the determination, cost what it may, to give truly of oneself to help brighten or lift other lives. Again and again, whatever be one's creed, one is forced back to the practical and undying truths that radiated from a Life nineteen hundred years ago. My own life's experiences, so far as I can understand them, keep emphasizing the utter and inescapable truth of the things He taught.

Measured by such a standard much of what I must here set forth is failure. Yet the Christian dynamic does not allow one to be disheartened by failure. Out of failure must come understanding and out of past forgiveness present hope.

Unskilled as I am in the art of writing, I have had to turn for helpful criticism to many of my friends to whom I feel deeply grateful. I desire to express particular appreciation to our son, Ralph Graves, for his generous help, to my brother, Nevin Sayre, to my former colleague, Zechariah Chafee of the Harvard Law

School, to Harry Hawkins and Benjamin Gerig, coworkers with me in the Department of State, to Frank Loveland who helped me to fight crime in Massachusetts, to Woodbury Willoughby who shared with us the Manila days, our life on Corregidor and our submarine escape, to Kenneth Heim who was with me in Japan, and to those others who along the way have made helpful suggestions.

To publishers who have kindly given me permission to use material already published in former magazine articles I desire to express my particular appreciation. Especially I owe grateful acknowledgment to *The Atlantic Monthly, Harper's Magazine, Life,* and *Foreign Affairs.*

Washington, D.C.
July 1956

Contents

Illustrations

I

With Grenfell in Labrador

It was June, 1908. All spring Douglas Palmer and I had been living in anticipation of the summer. Now at long last our junior year at Williams College was over, and reality began to take the place of dreams. We were actually aboard the little mail steamer bound for Labrador to join Dr. Wilfred T. Grenfell, the great medical missionary of the North.

For two days our small vessel, the *Home,* had been coasting along the large northern peninsula of Newfoundland, putting into lonely harbors along the way.

"Gosh! What a different world this is!" exclaimed Doug, as we idly stood at the ship's rail, watching the small boats from some isolated fishing settlement gathering alongside to receive their mailsacks and meagre supplies.

A different world it certainly was. Already we were getting into the North with its long stretches of summer twilight. At ten o'clock in the evening we could still sit on deck and read. Listening to the howling of the Eskimo dogs on the rocky shore, we began to feel the desolation, the loneliness, and the challenge of the North.

We tied up for a few hours at Port Saunders, one of the larger settlements. Walking ashore, Doug and I were accosted by a bearded fisherman.

"Be ye one of Doctor Grandfield's helpers?" he asked anxiously.

1

"There's a b'y lyin' in the bunkhouse here who sure needs help."

We found a young fisherman who had broken his hip two weeks before, falling from the high rigging of his schooner. The crew, unable to care for him, had brought him ashore before sailing north to the fishing banks.

As we spoke with the stricken youth, stretched out on a dark bunk, utterly helpless and suffering agony, our hearts sank. If only *we* were Grenfell! But we could do nothing. The news of his death some ten days later haunted us through the summer.

As we headed from Flower's Cove, our last port of call in Newfoundland, across the Strait of Belle Isle toward Bonne Esperance on the Labrador coast, the chill in the air sharpened. Here and there we could see icebergs floating in the distance, and soon we began to make out the coast to the north with scattered patches of snow. Suddenly we caught sight of a little steamer far ahead.

"That's the *Strathcona*," our skipper called from the pilot house. "Dr. Grenfell must be making for Bonne, too."

Our excitement mounted. Labrador at last!

"I can't believe it's real!" muttered Doug, half under his breath.

An hour later we entered Bonne harbor, passing close by the small eighty-ton steamer, the *Strathcona*, already anchored in the bay; and eagerly we jumped into the small boat and were rowed ashore. No sooner had we landed than we saw a knot of fishermen in animated conversation on one of the fishing stages over the water. In the center of the group, joking and laughing, stood a man of moderate stature in rough sweater and seaboots, ruddy-complexioned, bareheaded, with rumpled hair and sandy mustache. At once I recognized Dr. Grenfell. He caught sight of us and jumped forward to meet us.

"Well, Frank, so you're really here at last. I'm so glad. And Douglas Palmer, too. How jolly! You, Doug, are to take the mail boat south from Battle Harbour to our headquarters at St. Anthony. And for you, Frank, we have saved a bunk up forward on the *Strathcona*. Get your things off the *Home* and come right aboard. We'll be sailing at nine tonight."

Within half an hour the Doctor and I were being rowed out to the *Strathcona*. Actually to board her and walk her crowded deck was like a dream come true. Here was the hospital ship which the intrepid doctor drove every summer, as long as open water lasted, through storm and fog and ice along the entire length of the Labrador to bring medical and other help to the isolated settlements along that desolate coast and to the fishing fleets sailing north from Newfoundland every spring in the search for cod.

I had read much about him; and so virile and winning a worker for Christ, I had wanted to know. During my junior year at Williams College he was raising money in the States on a lecture tour, and I had invited him to speak to our student body. He had come; and the day of his address I took him for an all-afternoon tramp through the woods and into the hills. It was plain that he loved the out-of-doors; and his enthusiasm for his work was so contagious that I longed to have some small part in it. No one I had ever met had impressed me so deeply. As a result of his talk to the college that evening we students set to work raising money for his mission, and it was then that I had promised to join him on the coast.

Now at last that June evening I stood on the deck of the *Strathcona* beside him, prepared to share in his work. No one would guess, seeing him as I saw him then, hatless, garbed in old clothes and seal-skin boots, that he was skipper of the ship, helmsman, physician, the King's magistrate, head of an international Mission, director of four hospitals, preacher of the Word and friend of all. I heard him call down to the engineer below; and shortly thereafter we were heaving up anchor and then threading our way through the fishing fleet where the men were still on deck cleaning cod by torchlight. Soon we were clear of the harbor, plunging through the open sea.

A soft light pervaded the sky even at midnight. At 2:30 A.M. I took a turn at watch on the bow, scanning the sea for ice. Several times we passed great icebergs. Very early the sun rose in its glory, painting the rocky coast line a riot of color. All that day we steamed west along the Canadian Labrador for Harrington, where was located one of the four Grenfell hospitals.

The *Strathcona* was admirably fitted for its purposes. Amidships below was a small hospital for carrying the seriously sick to one of the Grenfell hospitals; adjoining was the sickbay where lines of fishermen and "livyeres" (i.e. "live here") gathered for treatment whenever the little ship put into port or came to anchor. On the decks was all manner of cargo, being carried from place to place. Up forward were the wheelhouse and chartroom. Here Dr. Grenfell could generally be found, standing at the wheel or, when the ship lay to, sitting at work at his writing desk, or talking with fishermen who kept bringing to him their never-ending problems.

The first thing I saw on the wall as I entered the chartroom was the verse:

> So many gods, so many creeds,
>   So many paths that wind and wind,
>   When just the art of being kind
> Is all this sad world needs.

The *Strathcona* was the fascinating workshop of a man who at every turn was making his life count. "My own principle has always been where two paths are open to take the more venturesome," he once had said. He was emphatically a man of action. Furthermore he was consecrating his life to the joyful service of Jesus Christ. To him, his work and his religion were one.

Perhaps it was the pioneer blood I inherited from my father that responded to the magnetism of this man. My father, Robert Heysham Sayre, also had been a man of action and a builder. Born in 1824, self-made, with only a lower-school education, he had gone to work at sixteen to earn his living. Learning railroading from the bottom up, he became one of the pioneer railroad builders in his home state, Pennsylvania. He was an early advocate of iron railway bridges and began the use of steel rails in 1864. He became chief engineer, then second vice president and still later assistant to the president of the Lehigh Valley Railroad. Much of his life was given to building and operating this railroad.

Among my earliest boyhood memories is a trip in his special car, speeding to the point where a freshet in the Lehigh River had caused a washout and carried away a bridge. My father examined the situation and then organized and directed emergency work, until trains could once more be gotten through and running again.

Ours was a railroading family. During our childhood, my father had had made for my brother and me two small flat-topped steel cars on which we could ride; and some of our happiest boyhood days were spent building and running a small gravity railroad on our grounds with switches, curves, small embankments, and even a roofed station. It meant to us countless days of creative activity and endless joy.

Steel was coming into increasing use throughout the country; and my father, realizing this growing demand, was one of the small group who helped to organize in Bethlehem, Pennsylvania, a plant for the making of steel. He became director of the resulting Bethlehem Iron Company in 1862, general manager in 1886, and vice president in 1891; later the Bethlehem Iron Company became the Bethlehem Steel Company.

In South Bethlehem on a hillside overlooking the Bethlehem ironworks and within sight of the Lehigh Valley Railroad station my father built his rather imposing Victorian house surrounded by spacious grounds and gardens. This was my childhood home. Here we lived as the privileged used to live in those Victorian days.

When I was born in 1885 my father was sixty and had already made his place in the world. He had won success in his work and the deep respect of the whole community. In other words, I did not know him in his days of struggle when the going was hard and the comforts few. At one time, because of his lack of technical schooling, he had despaired of being able to carry on his work of superintending and pushing forward his railway building. When I came upon the scene these dark days had passed. My boyhood environment was not among the toiling, struggling mass of men and women, cramped for money and dependent for daily food often upon humdrum work. I realize now, as I did not then, that privilege can constitute a serious handicap to a boy and is not the ideal preparation for life.

Always my father was a builder. In the midst of his railroad and his Iron Company activities he was continually building up the community of South Bethlehem: the handsome stone Church of the Nativity, where he served as senior warden; Lehigh University with its outstanding courses in science and engineering, where he served as chairman of the Board of Trustees; the imposing St. Luke's

Hospital, where the growing population and the Lehigh Valley Railroad's personnel could get the most modern treatment. As South Bethlehem grew and developed it was always to my father that the community turned.

Many of the Bethlehem people of those early days still vividly remember my father's annual Flag Raising on the Fourth of July. In response to engraved invitations scores of friends with their families would assemble on our lawn around a seventy-foot flagpole which he had erected; and as a brass band burst forth with patriotic music, promptly at nine o'clock a huge American flag would be unfurled and hauled aloft by the children and grandchildren, with all the guests standing at attention. Then as the band continued its martial music great boxes of firecrackers were brought out from our barn; and we children, wild with excitement, proceeded to shoot off the firecrackers, while others inflated brightly colored paper balloons with hot air and sent them soaring aloft. In the midst of it all, distinguished by his white, flowing beard, my father was the life of the assembled multitude, greeting friends, pinning small American flags on some of the newcomers, seeing that everything went as it should. To this day old residents of Bethlehem speak of those unique Fourth of July celebrations. The evening was climaxed by elaborate fireworks; and we children went off to bed with skyrockets, Roman candles, and pinwheels dancing through our heads.

Courage and initiative were what built pioneer America. I never saw my father quail before a difficulty. His motto, underlying his entire life, was "Keep a-goin'!" When he was a boy of eight whittling a stick his knife had slipped, and the point had pierced his eye, so that for the rest of his life he was blind in one eye. But he never let this curb him in the slightest way. In fact with one eye he saw more than any one else I ever knew.

Aboard the *Strathcona* I saw the same virile qualities in Dr. Grenfell at his work. He, too, was a man of action, a leader to whom people naturally turned for help.

Moreover, Wilfred Grenfell had centered his whole life in Christ; this was to me his greatest appeal. From my mother I had gained a similar burning desire to center my life in Christ. Nearer to me in age than my father, gentle and self-effacing, she was my boyhood confidante and close companion. She came of a highly intellectual family, her father, John W. Nevin, D.D., having been a leading theologian in the German Reformed Church and, in later years, president of Franklin and Marshall College at Lancaster, Pennsylvania. I remember no cross or impatient word from my mother. Her own faith in God, she planted in me as a child; and this faith has undergirded my entire life.

So I saw in Grenfell the characteristics predominant in my two parents. He had had every promise of a brilliant career in medicine in London as associate and friend of Sir Frederick Treves, who later became the King's physician. But one night while he was house surgeon at the London Hospital, he strayed into a revivalist meeting led by Dwight L. Moody, the American evangelist. There he decided that either he must make Christianity a more vivid and telling force in his own life or he must renounce it. He could not renounce it; so he determined to devote his life henceforth unreservedly to the service of Christ.

Enlisting in the work of the Royal National Mission to Deep Sea Fishermen, he had sailed across the Atlantic in 1892 to assess the need in Labrador. In that adventurous summer he found such dire suffering with no medical help available that he determined to consecrate his life to meeting the need. In the entire length of the bleak Labrador coast there were no hospitals or medical aid of any kind to be found. If hands or feet were frozen there was nothing to do but cut them off with an axe. So to Labrador he came; and there he was giving his life to the challenging service of a people.

By 1908 when I first visited the coast he had built, with money he had himself collected in both England and America, four hospitals at strategic points along the coast, and a nursing station at Forteau. All were in hard use. But hospitals were not enough. To meet the rising costs of food he had organized and built cooperative stores for the people on the coast. Destitute children must also be cared for, so he built a substantial orphanage at his St. Anthony headquarters in northern Newfoundland. Every Sunday, wherever he happened to be, groups of fishermen and "livyeres" would gather to hear him preach the Word. Sometimes it was in a church; more often it was in the sunshine on the rocks looking out over the sea, for he refused to have any hand in the petty denominational

controversies that locally raged between the Methodists and the
Church of England. I loved to hear him tell about the appeal he
once made in a Presbyterian church in America for an artificial leg
for a Labradorman. "Through my Presbyterian appeal a good
Methodist was persuaded to give the necessary money; and when I
got back to Labrador I attached the Presbyterian leg paid for by
Methodist money to a Church of England man. So far as I could see
he walked all right with it."

Thoughts such as these—and of how much a single life can
achieve—kept crowding through my mind that June day as we
made our way westward along the rocky coast. Late in the afternoon
we reached Harrington, where the simple white frame hospital with
its limited ward was filled with patients. A Canadian doctor was in
charge, with a resident nurse assisting him. Here we spent the
night and the following day. I watched Dr. Grenfell talking with
the patients, always with a kindly sparkle in his eye, conferring with
the doctor and nurse, settling problems, determining policies, going
off to visit friends near by, ever alert and cheery and uplifting. He
seemed, indeed, to win every one by his utter simplicity and selfless-
ness, his sheer warmth and joy of heart. These people of the bleak
North responded to it as to the sunshine.

It was a crowded day, but time was pressing; and by late
afternoon we were off again in the teeth of a gale, this time steam-
ing back eastward for Red Bay, where patients were to be treated
and a cooperative store tangle waited to be straightened out. From
there, on along the Labrador coast to the important station of
Battle Harbour, where another Grenfell hospital was located and
various problems were waiting for decision. After a night at Battle
Harbour, we headed south for St. Anthony in northern Newfoundland, passing now and again towering bergs of ice drifting southward in the Arctic Current which washes the Labrador coast. Rocks
can be charted, but icebergs cannot; and as we watched these
mountains of ice and realized that eight-ninths of them were under
water, we began to understand why Dr. Grenfell, when the fog
descended, would call the mate to take the wheel and would himself take his stand on the bowsprit of the *Strathcona,* straining his
eyes for ice.

St. Anthony, the headquarters of the Grenfell Mission, was a fast-growing settlement. Here was the largest of the Grenfell hospitals, and also a Grenfell cooperative store and an orphanage housing some fifty children gathered in from various parts of the Labrador coast. Here were a bunkhouse for workers like myself and a little guest house for visitors. Mission boats lay to in the bay; and a stout wharf was piled high with lumber and building material. The Grenfell buildings formed the center of a lively community.

A few days later Dr. Grenfell departed on the *Strathcona* for his long summer trip down North.

The rest of that summer I was stationed at St. Anthony, working hard at a miscellany of jobs. I loaded and unloaded boats, shipped on a trip north as a schooner hand, went south to help dynamite a wreck, lent a hand at construction or in the hospital— even assisting at an operation or two—and one time played barber and clipped the hair off all the orphans, several heads being "infested." Doug Palmer was with me, and we tried to live by the Doctor's creed: "Wherever help is needed, try to give it." My greatest adventure came at the end of the summer.

Some five years before, as a boy at Lawrenceville School, immersed in school activities and planning to enter college in the autumn, I had suffered a physical breakdown and my doctor had ordered me out of school. It seemed like black disaster. But, as so often happens, the sentence, exiling me for a year or two to the out-of-doors in strange places, eventuated in one of the truly rewarding experiences of my life. It was not sunset but sunrise. So little, at the time, do we understand the great events—the challenges—of our lives.

It meant once I was well again going out West with my brother, travelling by stage across southern Wyoming, and a summer on the Shoshone Indian Reservation in the home of the Indian trader. A troop of United States cavalry was stationed near the trading post. No white settlers were admitted on the Reservation; the Indians, unarmed, roamed unmolested and still carried on something of their old life. Once a year the Shoshones held their ancient three-day sun dance; and we spent one weird night sitting in the circle with them, watching their painted, naked figures dancing back and forth in the torchlight.

Following our July days at Fort Washakie on the Shoshone Reservation, my brother and I had packed across northern Wyoming into the Yellowstone Park; and after my brother returned East in September I spent the fall and winter on a sheep ranch in Montana. Off the line of any transcontinental railway I was in pioneer country. The buffalo had already been shot off; but their whitening skulls and bones remained, dotting the prairie on every side. Cattle roamed the country, although here and there wire fences were beginning to mark off ranch properties. Ranches were few and far between; in many places the need of supplies or the mailing of a letter involved at least an all-day ride or drive.

It was one of the memorable experiences of my life. When I was not working with the sheep or engaging in other forms of ranch activity I lived in the saddle, riding through the country or visiting other ranches. Sometimes I was off on camping trips into the snowcapped Crazy Mountains high on our southwestern horizon or on hunting trips for deer or elk. In the surrounding country were quantities of big game: black-tailed deer; wapiti, or elk; brown and grizzly bear; and cougars, or mountain lion. On the hunt for these we used to go off with a pack horse for a week or two. Deer were to be found even near our ranch on Porcupine Butte. I enjoyed to the full roaming alone through the forest and climbing the mountains, following the trail of big game and coming back to camp at nightfall to sit around a blazing camp fire.

Life in the West in those days was rugged but happy. There was no inhuman poverty, and fortunately, in the bracing, pure air, there was little disease. Rank played no part whatever in the size-up of a man, and there were few extremes of wealth and poverty. It was an open, expansive life, and I always found far more of human comradeship in the West than in the East. Travellers were invariably made welcome; and if trouble came a rancher's neighbors and acquaintances were quick to respond with help, even from long distances. I liked the people. I liked their breadth of outlook.

In those Montana days I got something that has gone with me all through my life.

Thus, my breakdown at Lawrenceville School, which had seemed like disastrous tragedy, had opened up new vistas. It had meant building up at the critical period of growth lasting bodily strength and health, which have ever served me generously. It had brought new self-reliance and a growing love of adventure. It had enabled me to climb out of the cramping barriers of the privileged life I had known in the East and gain a livelier appreciation of human comradeship and brotherhood. My love for the infinitely beautiful and changing joys of nature deepened, and my whole spirit grew apace. As a preparation for life what I learned in the West gave me far more, I am convinced, than any year in school or college.

Without these experiences of the Far West I am sure I could not have undertaken this new adventure in the North which called upon the brawn and sinews of vigorous youth. With Scoville Clark, a student friend from Yale who had come North to work with Dr. Grenfell, I set out at the end of the summer to cross the great Northern Peninsula of Newfoundland, which is separated from Labrador by the Strait of Belle Isle. In the winter snow it is often crossed by dog team; in September, with bare ground and no marked trails, it was a venturesome undertaking. Sco and I left St. Anthony on the east coast with rifle, shotgun, a blanket, and a small supply of food on our backs, travelling due west by compass, hoping to shoot a caribou for food once we gained the interior. Unhappily the caribou had already commenced their annual migration southward; we saw plenty of tracks but no caribou or other game. Instead ravenous blackflies began devouring us; mosquito nets and face lotion were useless, and our faces streamed with blood. Perhaps, in the light of our intentions, we received only fair play from the animal world. With the food in our packs running low, with the trackless country becoming more and more difficult, with tangled growth and extensive marshland impeding our march, our prospects looked grim. A creek up along the bed of which we made our toilsome way one day, we appropriately named "Misery Creek"; and I remember how all that day and the next we trudged along in unison, chanting, "Misery Creek, she makes me sick." Never can I forget the gloomy night when, huddled close together under our single blanket, cold and shivering, we watched the brilliant northern lights shooting back and forth across the sky, and wondered if we could make it. Next morning I climbed a tree to scan the country. Ahead I could see nothing but almost impassable tangles of small trees and matted vegetation and stretches of open water. We knew that the country was more open to the north; and, fearing we could not make the coast to the west, we turned northward. As we proceeded the going became better. Finally we reached Cape Norman at the extreme northern tip of Newfoundland. There to our immense delight was a settlement and a small store, where we could buy food. As we came in sight of the settlement, almost without a word we sat down and ate our last can of food, rejoicing. From Cape Norman we decided to follow the coast southwestward to Flower's Cove, where we planned to board the steamship *Home* for the Bay of Islands.

Trudging southward late one afternoon we came to a little cabin of logs—as we supposed, deserted. We looked through the window and were startled to see an old man peering out. In this uninhabited and desolate country, who could he be? He beckoned to us, and as we entered he went almost without a word to his oven and lifted out two wild duck, roasted to a turn. He set them on the table before us. "It's too late to go any further this afternoon," he said. "I haven't seen anyone to talk to all these months. Ye must spend the night here with me."

We fell to on the duck; we had not had such a meal for days. We found that the old man lived by trapping and hunting. As the light faded he told us something of his life. His name was Tom Smith. English-born, he had shipped before the mast when he was a lad of ten, had sailed all over the world, and finally had been shipwrecked off the Labrador coast. Here he had settled down and married; and after his wife died he stayed on. He lived after the fashion of a hundred years ago. He carried an old muzzle-loading gun and powder horn.

As night fell Sco Clark, tired out, rolled up in his blanket and was soon fast asleep on the floor. But the old trapper would not let me follow suit. "I've had nobody to talk to all this time," he kept saying. "I want to talk. Will ye play a game of dominoes with me?"

"Of course I will," I said. He got out his meagre supply of oil, lit an old lamp, and placed before me a battered, greasy set of dominoes. As we played he told me of his life. And when next morning the time came for us to leave he said: "I have nobody on earth to write to. Will ye let me write to ye?" When I gladly assented, he asked me to leave him some self-addressed envelopes, which he said he could mail at the post office, some twelve miles south. I took his picture, and we left him in the door of his cabin waving us goodbye.

For some years I received from him long letters, which he travelled south in winter by dog team to mail. I tried to write interesting letters in return. When I was about to be married I sent him an engraved invitation to the wedding. Accompanying the invitation was a card asking that a reply be duly sent to the secretary of the President of the United States. That floored the old man. In his reply he appealed to me for help. Some months later I received a letter saying that on the day of the wedding, at the appointed afternoon hour, he had celebrated by giving a round of salutes on his trusty blunderbuss. A year or two later the letters stopped coming, and I never heard from him again. How he died, I do not know.

From Smith's log cabin Sco Clark and I made our way south along the coast; we finally reached the little village of Flower's Cove and caught the mail steamer south to Bay of Islands.

That summer in Labrador had proved a soul-satisfying experience. In the months that followed during my senior year at Williams, Dr. Grenfell and his work often filled my thoughts. Was Labrador the place where I could serve Christ best?

I completed my college work in three and a half years, and after a cowboy trip in Montana returned to Williams for graduation in June, 1909. Early in the year I had expressed the hope to the Williams trustees that they might confer upon Dr. Grenfell an honorary degree; and to this they had gladly agreed. Hence I found Dr. Grenfell attending my graduation to receive his honorary degree, and with him was his mother, recently arrived from England.

I had been chosen valedictorian, and at the conclusion of my address I remember my mother waving to me from the audience and sending up a little note of love and pride. Smiling and happy, Dr. Grenfell sat near me on the stage. After receiving his degree he was asked to speak. As always he sounded the deeply Christian note in his uplifting impromptu address; and I think all the audience fell in love with him.

Following the graduation exercises, I again turned my face northward, bound for Labrador, this time to spend the summer on the *Strathcona* with Dr. Grenfell, as his secretary and general assistant.

It was a summer of rare experience. Cruising northward from Battle Harbour along desolate rocky coasts and past drifting icebergs; avoiding many a sunken reef; often facing or riding out violent gales and storms; running up into Hamilton Inlet for a brief visit; touching at the Hudson's Bay post of Rigolet, to which the Montagnais Indians came from the interior with furs and deerskins to do their trading; on to Indian Harbour, where another Grenfell hospital was dispensing mercy in a very practical form; then on north to Eskimo country, stopping at Hopedale and Turnavik; coasting still farther north, past Nain, all the way to Okkak near Cape Mugford, along a coast line of dark massive rock rising sheer out of the water for several thousand feet; rejoicing in the very substantial help we were able to bring to the needy in every little settlement. We kept in the very pink of physical condition, sometimes beginning the day and thoroughly awakening ourselves by throwing a rope over the ship's side and jumping into the icy water, with bergs floating near, and, needless to say, immediately climbing back on board. Of Dr. Grenfell I was the constant companion, by his side in the chartroom, typing his letters or copying his manuscripts, helping when necessary in the dispensary, taking charge of the clothes box from which used clothing was dispensed, occasionally taking a turn on watch at the bow and straining my eyes to spot the low floating ice and the bergs. If ever we took a day off it would be to go ashore and climb the rocky coast, up into grassy hills above, and from the heights look over the magnificent wild Northland panorama spread out before us, rocks and cliffs and endless sea. On Sundays we stopped in port and customarily held open-air services, often on the rocks overlooking the sea. Again and again I was reminded of the Gospel stories of Christ talking to fishermen and disciples gathered around Him on the shore.

In mid-August we had to turn and start the journey homeward. By September we reached Battle Harbour. To our surprise we found it filled with craft quite different from the customary fishing boats. We were greeted with exciting news: Peary, the explorer, had just unexpectedly made his appearance, returning from the North Pole aboard the *Roosevelt,* which we could see anchored off shore. Most exciting of all, after years of brave but unsuccessful attempts, he had at last actually reached the North Pole.

Once the *Strathcona* was tied up Dr. Grenfell and I rowed out to the *Roosevelt*. Here was a ship altogether different from the small, steel *Strathcona*. It was considerably larger, more commodious, with high masts and full rigging. It was stoutly built, heavily timbered, and braced with great wooden beams to withstand crushing pressure from floating fields of ice. On its deck we examined the komatiks, or dog sledges, on which the Pole had been reached. In the rigging were the drying heads of musk ox. Men were cleaning up the ship, putting it in order after the long polar struggle.

Bob Bartlett, the skipper of the *Roosevelt,* gave us a hearty welcome and took us below to see Commander Peary. We found him in his cabin amidships—the man who had first in the history of the world reached the North Pole—tall, stalwart, large-featured, with blue eyes and heavy, blond mustache, his face still seamed and gaunt from the gruelling trip over the ice to the top of the world. In a blue sweater and dark faded trousers, he strode across the cabin to give us a welcoming hand. His personality inspired confidence. Indeed, he bore the marks of a natural leader, whom men would follow undoubting into dangerous places; his face was kindly and strong and transparently honest.

He was glad to meet people from the outside world; and we talked at length about current events and about his own return from the Pole. He told us that he had reached the Pole in April. He had planned to race back with his dogs to Baffin Land and spend the ensuing winter in northern Greenland, hemmed in by ice. But favorable weather had persuaded him to chance pushing out among the ice floes in Kennedy Channel and drifting south with the ice that very summer. This he achieved, so that he was reaching civilization almost a year in advance of expectations. At Battle Harbour he was in telegraphic touch with the outside world. Once the news of his discovery had flashed upon the world, reporters in chartered ships had rushed to Battle Harbour to obtain his story. So it was that jaunty reporters in straw hats and well pressed suits astonished the "livyeres" of southern Labrador by climbing over the rocks looking for non-existent restaurants or amusement houses.

"I expect to spend several more days here," said the Com-

mander, "cleaning up ship, completing my records, and preparing
for our re-entry into civilization."

He showed us the American flag made by Mrs. Peary in 1898
which he had carried on all his explorations, and out of which he
had cut pieces to leave at each of his "farthest north" stations suc-
cessively attained. Finally, at the North Pole he had left a strip cut
diagonally across the entire flag. Many of the pieces left on land
monuments were found and brought back by later explorers; the
North Pole strip, left on floating ice, was of course never recovered.

"If you want a good secretary to assist with your records and
help around the ship," Dr. Grenfell said, "here is Frank Sayre with
his typewriter, just about to leave for the States to enter the Harvard Law School next month, who I'm sure would be glad to help.
For a whole summer, I've managed somehow or other to get along
with him."

Breathlessly I awaited Peary's reply. He looked at me a little
quizzically and sharply. Then he expressed gratification and asked
me to come on board that afternoon. Here was fresh adventure
indeed.

And so two days later I sailed southward from Battle Harbour
aboard the *Roosevelt* with Peary. I was warmly welcomed by the
members of the expedition, including Captain Bob Bartlett, Donald
MacMillan, George Borup, and Dr. Goodsell, and helped Peary
with his records as we steamed south.

It was an exciting and happy trip. These men, after wrestling
against supreme odds for over a year with life or death at stake,
had won and were now sailing home. As we anchored for a few
hours off Belle Isle for the tide to turn, several rowed ashore.
Captain Bob Bartlett came back jumping with excitement. He
had taken off his shoes and waded through the long green grass,
and "My God, man," he cried out, "we've seen a cow!"

We put in at Sydney, where Mrs. Peary and the children were
waiting to welcome the Commander home; and there we stopped
a night for the first welcoming ceremonies, including a dinner
with enthusiastic speeches. While we were ashore throngs of
sightseers trooped on board the *Roosevelt*—and unhappily departed with many removable articles as North Pole trophies—
including my camera left in the bookcase in the messroom. I often

wonder if the taker is still telling his grandchildren: "This camera was at the North Pole with Peary."

From Sydney we sailed south; and, reaching Casco Bay in Maine, the Pearys and I were taken off in a small launch waiting for us off Eagle Island, where the Commander had his home. There in his distinctive cabin filled with polar trophies, we spent a day; and then we all went south by train from Portland to rejoin the *Roosevelt* at New York. Early in the morning we boarded the *Roosevelt* at anchor in the Lower Bay, and shortly thereafter the ship, gaily bedecked with flags and bunting, steamed triumphantly through the Upper Bay and into the Hudson River, escorted by a long line of welcoming ships, screaming their deafening salutes.

But Peary was robbed of his full triumph. Dr. Frederick A. Cook was making the startling and amazing claim that he was the real discoverer of the Pole and had reached it months before Peary.

To us Cook's claim seemed incredible. Once before, he had falsified a claim of exploration in Alaska. As a matter of fact Peary, who knew well the Eskimos of the region, had sought out and talked to those who had accompanied Cook the previous year and knew exactly where they had gone. They had been nowhere near the Pole,—had never even gotten out of sight of land, which is some four hundred miles distant from the North Pole. Sea ice with its huge pressure ridges is of a character altogether different from land ice; and most of Cook's pictures were of land ice. His claims seemed so preposterous that we could not believe they would be seriously accepted. Yet so few people knew polar work or were familiar with ice conditions that many accepted Cook's plausible and well-told story without serious question and welcomed him with open arms; and when Peary denied its truth he was accused of lying to rob a rival of his due deserts.

Here was real tragedy. Peary, a man of utter integrity, singularly free of falsity or indirection, was admired and trusted by the members of his party and all who knew him. He had given his life to training and equipping himself for his supreme ambition, the discovery of the Pole. He had made trip after trip, each time getting a little nearer to the Pole, learning to drive and handle dogs expertly and to live the Eskimo life. There were no planes in those days. There was not the wealth of canned food and portable stoves and gadgets we have today. You had to subsist on pemmican and seal meat and a little boiled tea. You had to live the life of the Eskimo and win their confidence and loyalty. You had to learn the perils of ice and the ways of Eskimo dogs. After years of struggle and successive expeditions he finally in 1909 attained the prize, only to have the reward stolen from him at the very moment of triumph by an impostor who had counted on his not reaching civilization for another year.

It was only after the records of each had been submitted and had been studied by learned societies that the truth came to be made known. The National Geographic Society and other groups recognized the facts and accorded honor to Peary. But by then the popular mind was absorbed in other issues.

On November 18, 1909, Dr. Grenfell was married. The story goes that, returning from England to New York, he met an unusually attractive American girl on the deck of the *Mauretania*, fell head over heels in love with her, and asked her to marry him. "Why, you don't even know my name," she exclaimed.

"That makes no difference to me," he replied. "I want to change it."

The ceremony took place in Chicago, and I felt particularly honored by being asked to be an usher and a member of the wedding party.

Almost exactly four years later he stood beside me as my best man in the East Room of the White House.

2

Harvard Law School
Student Days

In late September I entered Harvard Law School. My work at Williams College completed, I was eager to plunge into graduate study and prepare for my lifework. I chose the Law School not because I expected necessarily to practice law but because I was convinced, as I still am, that there can be no better basic preparation than the law for public service, toward which my mind was tending.

Harvard seemed to me the outstanding law school of the country. The professors made their main objective teaching students how to think rather than trying to cram into them an encyclopedic knowledge of law. If they could succeed in this they cared little whether or not a legal subject was covered in its entirety. For instance, in the courses on contracts or torts or criminal law the class seldom covered more than two-thirds of the subject—sometimes less. Students taking bar examinations at the end of the law course would have to cover the omitted parts by their own efforts—and also acquire by themselves a knowledge of the statute law in their own states. Harvard then troubled itself little with statute law. It concentrated rather on the uncodified English common law as it had developed by successive legal decisions through the centuries. It was on the principles and the development of the unwritten law that the teachers drilled their students, teaching them to think and accurately to express their thoughts.

Harvard used the system of law teaching developed by Christopher Langdell, one of the builders of the Harvard Law School. We used no textbooks. Instead we read particular judicial decisions assigned to us upon the subject at hand. The professors did not give us systematic lectures on the law, but engaged in a discussion of each case by means of question and answer. Was the particular decision a correct one? If yes, would such and such a result not be inevitable? How could it be reconciled with some previous decision? In rapid-fire questions and answers an intellectual tug of war developed between professor and students; and it was always the professor's aim, if a student chose a wrong tack, not to call his answer wrong but rather by questions to force him into an ultimately untenable position. It was a constant mental battle, and both professors and students were kept on their toes. At Harvard Law School, in a word, we concentrated not on learning laws, on "book-l'arnin'," but rather on how to think straight and to use our minds.

The classes were large, containing often two or three hundred men. In the classrooms no records were kept, no marks given, and no attendance checked. A student was free to attend classes or not as he pleased. Even if a student attended class, he was always at liberty to avoid entering the discussion by declaring himself "unprepared." A student might not be called on more than two or three times a year. On the other hand, any student was at liberty to jump into the mental scuffle and take part in the discussion. Thus certain keen minds moved to the fore.

Instead of having to take a room in a dormitory I was blessed during my Law School days with a real home. After my father's death in 1907 my mother had given up our home in Bethlehem, Pennsylvania. Now she took a house on Kirkland Street in Cambridge, and here with my warm friend Maynard Hazen, who had graduated from Williams College the previous year and was entering the Law School with me, we made our home.

My mother's coming to Cambridge helped to unite again our broken family; for my brother Nevin, a year older than myself, was studying for the ministry at Union Seminary in New York and

Martha Nevin Sayre   Robert Heysham Sayre

Francis B. Sayre
H. B. Eggert, Bethlehem, Pa.

Right. Grenfell on the lookout for ice on bowsprit of *Strathcona,* 1908

Below. Down North on the Labrador
Photos by F. B. Sayre

planned to take his last year at the Episcopal Theological School in Cambridge. My brother had always been very close to me. In our boyhood days we were inseparable. We played together and now and again fought together strenuously. But at night in bed before we went to sleep we used to ask each other's forgiveness; and he has meant to me throughout my life more than words can tell. To him I still turn, knowing that he will never fail me.

Work at the Law School was in striking contrast to that at college, where knowledge had seemed to be more or less cut and dried and was to be artfully rammed down into the student's mind. At the Law School education meant thinking *drawn out of* the student's mind.

The instruction was so fundamentally different from that at college that many if not most of us floundered hopelessly during much of the first year. Discussion followed discussion, and in the opening months no general underlying principles seemed to emerge. Nor in that day were we taught or advised how to pursue our work or direct our studies. It was a sink or swim, rough and tumble schooling.

Optional examinations were given in the middle of the first year to those who cared to try them. I took them; and in unhappy contrast to my college A's, I received only a C. I began to perceive that something was radically wrong, and that I must somehow evolve a better mode of study. I found, too, that I was clearly failing to find a place during that first year among the top-ranking men of my class. Was law after all my rightful field of work?

By the spring of my first year, after consulting with other students, I had worked out a careful system of study. It was built upon taking copious lecture notes, preparing weekly written digests of my notes and of the emerging legal principles, and checking these against textbooks in the library. All this meant unflagging home work and constant review beginning as early as November.

On the other hand, many easy-going first-year men, who conceived of the law course as requiring little more than attendance upon the classroom lectures, began to regard the school as a bed of roses. The unhappy consequence was that most of these found themselves thrown out at the end of the first year. At the beginning of my second year twenty per cent of my class failed to return. Never-

theless, the system of my day did teach a man, if he survived, how
to stand on his own feet and how to master difficulties.

Since that time, as a result of a careful selective admissions program and the appointment of Teaching Fellows to advise students
with regard to study problems, the percentage of first year failures
has been greatly reduced, being now considerably less than 10 per
cent. In June of 1956 it reached a new low of 6.3 per cent.

The only marks given at the school were on the four-hour examination in each subject at the end of each year. This was totally
unlike the ordinary college examination. It could never be answered
by the mere recitation of information. Each question would recite a
state of given facts and generally ask whether or not recovery (or
finding of guilty) should be allowed. Whether a student answered
yes or no was of little consequence. What mattered, and what his
marks were based upon, was the process of reasoning by which he
reached his result.

The Harvard Law School as I saw it during my first year was
not at the peak of its prime. Langdell, who had originated the case
system of teaching law had died. So had J. B. Thayer, one of the
outstanding law teachers of his generation. Dean James Barr Ames,
universally respected and admired, died during my first year. John
C. Gray ("Pop," as we all called him) was in his last years and spoke
so indistinctly that only the students in the front rows could hear
and understand him. "Jerry" Smith, teaching torts, was in his de-
clining years. The fire of earlier days had gone. A younger crop of
teachers was about to be brought in. Unfortunately my student days
came during the interregnum.

Of the older school, Joseph Beale and Samuel Williston were
still teaching and were still stimulating and outstanding. "Joey
Beale," as we called him, with round bald head and twinkling eyes,
had as nimble a mind as I have ever known. He would dart from
point to point, fencing as with a rapier. Sometimes one was inclined
to question how sound a path he was beating out. Perhaps his mind
was a little too nimble. But he was a teacher of first-rate ability; he
excited his students to think and to stand on their own intellectual
feet.

Samuel Williston, on the other hand, was of a much more
placid disposition. His mind was just as keen; but the principles he

sought to impart were developed out of sweet reasonableness rather than out of intellectual fencing. He had a profound mind; and his great treatises on the law of contracts and the law of sales became landmarks in the development of the law.

Then there was Professor Edward Warren—we called him "Bull"—a red-blooded, two-fisted professor who used to overpower his students by his caustic remarks and overbearing demeanor. His pedagogy was built on fear; and although he always had his students on their toes, I suspect that this is fundamentally not the best teaching. Indeed, I was for the Williston type of teacher.

Roscoe Pound, subsequently chosen dean, was then a newcomer. He had a unique mind. I believe that his mother taught him Latin, and I am told that he used to speak Latin when he was only about six or seven years old. He was a botanist of parts, too. He possessed an extraordinary gift of memory. He could quote by the page from books of English, of Latin, and of Norman-French. He had a comprehensive knowledge and a profound understanding of the long development of English law. He made his course in jurisprudence famous. He held his students not by his personality but by the sheer power of his intellect and his comprehensive grasp of the law. His teaching, however, was not in the tradition of Langdell. He seldom used the Socratic method of question and answer. Instead, he followed largely the lecture method, opening up his mind and pouring out a torrent of learning.

Apart from the classroom there was little direct contact between students and professors. That seemed a pity. So far as I remember I never was invited by any of the professors to visit in their homes. Perhaps the student body was too large. The faculty lived a life of their own. Every one was too hard at work.

We students all talked, ate, and slept law. Legal debates and controversies constantly absorbed us; unending legal discussions filled our days. Morning, noon, and night, we discussed the decisions and cases which we were studying. We lived in a rarefied atmosphere of law; seldom did we descend to the mundane level of attending actual trials in the courts.

The student body was an exceptional group of men. They came from every part of the country, attracted by the traditions and eminence of the Harvard Law School, bent upon hard work and determined to win a place in the legal fraternity. Among the members of my class who took a leading part and with whom I was closest were Charles E. Hughes, Jr., the son of Justice Hughes, Harold Burton, John Buchanan, and Henry Toll. Bob Taft was in the class following mine. Charlie Hughes and I at one time planned to room together in New York following Law School. Later he became Solicitor General of the United States. Harold Burton is today a member of the United States Supreme Court. John Buchanan is a leader of the Pittsburgh bar; Henry Toll is outstanding in Denver.

If the Harvard Law School of my day was open to criticism it was, it seemed to me, because the faculty were so absorbed in training men to think, that they seemed at times oblivious of the social and moral problems of the day. I think, for instance, of Professor Beale. In teaching criminal law he became absorbed in technical questions of legal cause and effect, in exactly what constitutes a *mens rea* or guilty mind, in the endless technicalities of criminal law as it had been worked out in English courts. Criminal justice to him was a fascinating, highly intellectual game. We students were not made to realize that it was an instrument of society which might make or break human lives. In Law School I heard very little about existing deep, social problems. Almost no mention was made of child labor or minimum wage laws. Juvenile courts were seldom mentioned. Discussions of the law controlling industrial relations were more or less incidental. In fact, some years later when I came to teach at the Law School, I introduced something entirely new, a course on industrial law.

Some students felt deeply this dehumanized atmosphere. Some even left and entered other fields of study because the law seemed to them to offer so little help in meeting the great human problems of the day. Unless the minds and the desires of students could be directed toward really serviceable ends, of what avail was it to teach them to think straight, to sharpen their intellectual weapons? Perhaps here we touch one of the profound problems of all education.

The ruling purpose of the Harvard professors of that day—be it said to their credit and in their defence—was to train able builders and technicians in the law. They realized that only upon a sound body of well administered law can civilization progress. No one can gainsay the tremendous part played by the law in the growth of a people. As the Roman law was among the greatest of Rome's contributions to humanity, the common law and English government are perhaps England's two greatest contributions to the world. The development and enforcement of a sound and just body of law is of infinite consequence to mankind.

From the arduous pursuit of law I often sought relaxation by occasional week-end visits of one kind or another. On many happy week ends I returned to Williams College, to see old friends, perhaps participate in fraternity activities, or revisit old haunts in the hills or countryside. More than once, by invitation, I visited Admiral Peary at his unique hideaway home in Casco Bay. There he lived amid his polar trophies, with his wife, his daughter, Marie, and his son, Robert, Jr. In the center of the living room was a large triangular stone structure composed of three fireplaces back to back; so that one could always build a fire and sit before it to leeward of whatever wind might be blowing. The windows were shaped like portholes, and the walls lined with charts. Looking out through the windows upon the blue Casco Bay waters one could well fancy himself on shipboard bound for the North.

Nine months of intensive study at the Law School made me eager once more for the great open spaces. So, at the conclusion of my first year of law school I set off for the North again, but this time for Alaska. It proved an exciting summer.

With my college friend Bennie Burton, I sailed up the magnificent Inside Passage from Seattle to Skagway. There we shouldered packs and rifles and, with an Indian guide, hit off into the mountains at Denver Glacier on a hunting trip for big game. Up and up we toiled over rocky ridges and mountain slopes until we seemed at the very top of the world. Snow and ice lay all around us. Suddenly our guide seized my glasses and gazed intently. "Goats," he exclaimed, pointing to a distant ridge of rock. Through the glasses I made out several Rocky Mountain goats feeding on the other side of a precipitous valley. We had to climb down and across and then make our way up a difficult ascent so as to remain out of view and yet not lose sight of the game. Finally we got within rifle shot, and I was lucky enough to bring down a beautiful head. We had pitched our camp at the base of a towering snowy peak, called Our Lady of the Snows, and we carried back sufficient meat to last several days.

We had hoped to get a bear but saw none. Nevertheless, the imposing Sawtooth Mountains, the snow and glaciers, the dizzy heights, the lonely, overpowering country, left vivid memories.

Upon our return we went over to see Dyea which had been the gateway to the Klondike Trail during the Gold Rush of 1897. Once a city of 10,000, it had been abruptly abandoned when the easier route via Skagway was opened. Now we found a ghost town, silent and deserted. The old wooden stores and saloons, still covered with signs, recalled the turbulent days of 1898; but the buildings were empty. Dyea was only a memory.

Before we left Skagway I arranged to have a gold claim staked out in the Klehini River country. Romance conjured up exhilarating possibilities, although I had no illusions about the claim.

Then, unlike the thousands of gold seekers who had toiled from hope to despair, packing their supplies on their backs over "Heartbreak Trail," we travelled the same route by railway train across the historic White Pass, and from there by a small wood-burning steamer down the Yukon to Dawson, once the fever center of the Klondike gold rush.

At Dawson we boarded an old Mississippi River stern-wheeler in whose pilothouse the Mississippi pilot licenses were still hanging. She was old-fashioned, but roomy and comfortable. We were fortunate to have as fellow passengers for a week two Cabinet officials, Attorney General George Wickersham and Secretary of Commerce and Labor Charles Nagel. In their good company we slowly steamed some two thousand miles down the Yukon; and from St. Michael on the coast we caught a seagoing boat to Nome. Nome boasted no dock in those days. Our boat anchored outside, and we transferred to a small barge in which we stood like cattle as it chugged toward the shore. From it we climbed into a swinging cattle crib strung on a cable, which carried us over the high surf and lowered us onto the beach.

From Nome I was anxious to cross Bering Sea for a look at Siberia; but every one told us it couldn't be done: "It would be crazy to try. No steamer ever goes across." That made me all the more eager. We roamed the waterfront and finally located a small fifteen-ton schooner which we succeeded in chartering. The skipper and I agreed to take with us a Russian trader who wanted to get across and was fluent in the Eskimo tongue. All set to go, we had to wait two days until the high pounding surf calmed down sufficiently to allow us to launch a rowboat and get safely to the schooner anchored in the harbor. Once aboard we set sail about two A.M. on a course west by north. I took the wheel the greater part of the day and the skipper took it at night.

For two days we sailed steadily westward, part of the time through fog—and still no sign of Asia! Finally on the second afternoon the fog lifted and we sighted land. Towering cliffs, highly colored and covered with patches of snow and ice, rose a thousand feet sheer from the sea. We sighted an Eskimo village and sailed into Plover Bay in sight of Vladimir, the trading post frequented by our Russian trader. Here we landed and walked about among throngs of wondering, primitive Eskimo. They welcomed us with friendly smiles and followed us wherever we went. They accepted us as coming from another world.

We found them living in underground igloos, subsisting on walrus, whale, seal, fish, and occasional polar bear. From these they secured not only all their food, but also their clothing, skins for making boats and needed implements for hunting. The custom of family gatherings for meals apparently was not for them; instead, individuals ate whenever hungry, cutting off slabs of raw meat and eating them with relish. Food was stored in the icy ground; if it chanced to be malodorous when dug up, it was still food and satisfied hunger.

Boarding our schooner once more we sailed from Indian Point north along the coast until we reached the Arctic Circle. Then turning back we sailed southeasterly toward the Diomede Islands, midway between Siberia and Alaska. Here we landed and visited the Eskimo, who through the summer lived in airy houses made of walrus-skin, stretched over props of whalebone.

What particularly interested me was the striking similarity of the Eskimo of Alaska and Siberia to the Eskimo I had seen in Labrador. Both used the same implements, apparently followed the same methods of whaling and sealing, and lived much the same kind of life. I was interested, too, in their pronounced Mongolian features and their skillful carving of walrus ivory. I kept asking myself whether these people were not Mongolians who in prehistoric days had strayed north into the Arctic and learned to live, as live they must, on whale and walrus and seal. From the East Cape in Siberia it is not many miles to Cape Prince of Wales in Alaska; Eskimos still cross and recross the strait in their whaleskin umiaks. From Alaska the Eskimo could have spread across the northern reaches of North America, all the way to Labrador. In any event, in the Eskimo of Siberia and those of Labrador, I saw unmistakably the same people; and they are just as different, as far removed, from the North American Indians as is day from night.

From the Diomedes we sailed for Nome, and found it very good to get back to civilization.

On our way home we stopped a few days in Montana at the Van Cleve ranch near Big Timber, where some seven years before I had lived the life of a rancher and cowpuncher, regaining my health and falling in love with the great open country. By the end of September I was back in Cambridge, ready for another year of intensive study of law.

My brother Nevin, who had been married the previous June, now came with his bride to Cambridge to study at the Episcopal Theological School and take his divinity degree. They found a house on Kirkland Street almost opposite our own, and that winter we spent many happy evenings together.

I had expected to spend the following summer in Montana, but the sudden and tragic death of my brother's wife in June, 1911, changed all plans. I wanted to be with him.

Accordingly, he and I took a summer trip together into western Canada, visiting Lake Louise, the Yoho Valley, and Vancouver Island. Throughout that summer my brother was struggling manfully to overcome the tragedy that had befallen him; and he found healing in the eternal beauty and peace of forest solitude and towering mountain. Toward the end of August he returned east to prepare for teaching at Princeton, and I decided to make a quick trip to Alaska to examine the gold claim which I had had staked out during the previous summer.

Taking with me my friend, V. V. Clark, a mining engineer whom I had met in Nome, we sailed from Seattle and disembarked at Haines, Alaska. From there we proceeded overland to the Klehini River, with snowy mountains on every side. During the next ten days we worked our way up into wild country, inhabited by Indians and also by enormous Kodiak bear, which weighed up to 1,100 pounds. In the summer nights they fattened by wading the streams and skillfully scooping the spawning salmon out of the shallow water. I spent one thrilling night on the bank of a stream alive with salmon, with my rifle across my knees, cocked and ready for any approaching bear on an instant's notice. The sudden swish of the jumping salmon now and again sounded exactly like an oncoming bear. Again and again I jerked my rifle to my shoulder straining my eyes and ready to shoot. But, perhaps luckily for me, no bear came along.

My gold claim was far up the Klehini River, and with Indians and a dugout canoe it took a toilsome two days to reach it. Once there we set to digging up dirt and panning it out. No gold. Perhaps the valley was too wide, or bedrock too deep below. In any event, unless extraordinarily rich, the claim was too far inland to pay for the costly transport of necessary supplies. I decided to abandon it.

The most exciting part of our trip was the canoe ride down the Klehini River back to civilization. Two skilled Indians took us, and much of the way was through white water boiling over and around the rocks. We did once slightly crack the canoe against a rock; but the crack was soon repaired, and we made it safely to the lower waters, and thence by easy stages back to Haines.

The next day I was on the steamer for Seattle; and ten days later, after a short stay at the Van Cleve ranch in Montana, I was back in Cambridge for my final year at the Law School.

I have often wondered whether those summers in the North were not every bit as important a part of my education as the winters in the classroom.

My last year of law study was perhaps the best. I had come to understand more clearly the underlying principles we were seeking to master and I had learned more effective ways of study. Whereas I had received only a C in the optional examinations in the middle of my first year, I raised this to a B at the end of the year and to an A during my second year. I graduated with an A *cum laude*.

And now my thoughts were centering more and more on which way to turn and where to go after graduation.

3

Choosing a Career

My father had hoped that I would follow in his footsteps and enter the field of engineering. He wrote to my brother and myself in 1901, when we were youngsters at school:

One of you should, in my opinion, become a mining engineer, metallurgist and chemist, so that you may direct and oversee the development of the properties you will succeed to, and the other become a lawyer and businessman. I want you to become useful men and not idlers in the world, to be a part of the community in which you may reside, to take an active interest in the development of the various enterprises you may engage in. "Make two blades of grass grow where one grew before!" Be loved and respected wherever your lot may be cast, and in a position and of a desire to aid the unfortunate. Remember that the talents you have and the accumulations that come from an intelligent use of them, are from God and should be so used as to make your fellowmen better and happier and be able to say when you come to leave this world, that they are glad you lived. Remember that you must give an account of your stewardship at the final reckoning. Remember that "the dead carry in their clenched hands only that which they have given away."

I did not mean to preach to you but the thought came to me of the great difference between your equipment and mine. I left school at sixteen years of age, and had not a dollar from anyone then or since but that gained by my own efforts. I married when I was twenty-one, and then came one after another of my children, who had to be fed, clothed and educated. Up to 28 years of age the highest salary I received was $750.00 per annum, so you can imagine the days of labor and hours of anxious thought I had, but I had faith and trust in God that faithful honest endeavor would bring its reward.

All these disadvantages you will escape, and when you leave college you will be better fitted to grapple with the world than I was at 30 years of age.

In accordance with my father's hope I had entered Williams College planning, after my degree in liberal arts, to take a technical course in mining or civil engineering. I presumed that my brother would take up law.

But during my college years I came to feel that I could make my life count for most in some humanitarian field or in public service. There were times when I thought of the ministry. But if I had talents they did not seem to be for writing sermons and conducting church services.

Once I considered medicine. I bear the name of my great-grandfather, Dr. Francis Bowes Sayre, who was born in Lancaster, Pennsylvania, and practiced in Philadelphia. Unhappily he died at thirty-two—as a fellow physician wrote, "a glorious martyr to his philanthropy." When yellow fever was raging in 1798 and thousands fled from Philadelphia to escape death, he had over one hundred patients under his care. He sent his young wife away, but himself remained to fight the deadly epidemic. I have his last letter to his wife, written on Aug. 30, 1798, only two days before death struck him down.

"I have been ill these past two days," he wrote, "but my physicians tell me I am better this morning. I feel abundantly more comfortable and expect to be with you in three or four days. You are not to come to Town."

At the bottom is written, in the hand of his bereft wife: "This is the last proof . . . of the unceasing affection of the best of men. Two days after writing it, God withdrew his spirit and my Francis died. . . . His memory will be ever dear to all who knew him."

Should I follow in his footsteps? Should I answer the call of medicine, perhaps by joining in the work of Dr. Grenfell?

By the time I completed my course at the Law School I had reached certain very definite conclusions. Life was too big to be

spent simply in seeking to accumulate this world's goods or in assisting other men or corporations to do so. Entering a large city law
office, or even undertaking to build up a remunerative private law
practice, did not appeal to me. This was not the way to the satisfactions and happiness which I wanted out of life. But where and
how were these to be found?

The Grenfell work kept calling. Dr. Grenfell had asked me to
share the direction of his work. From St. John's in early June of
1910, the year after I had sailed north with him, he had sent me a
characteristic hastily scrawled letter:

Dear Frank

4:30 A.M. We ran in here after a very rough voyage last night.

There is a heap of mail—and I have enough troubles and worries to
keep me awake anyhow. But as I can't sleep I'll work; and though I can't
write you at length I just want to say, among 100 letters *yours* gets first answer . . .

Dear old lad, your love and loyalty are worth everything, when one has
to stand as much alone in responsibility as I do. I *do* wish you were going to
join me as a colleague *altogether* with headquarters in charge at St. Anthony
—with a house alongside mine.

Won't you think this over? We could make the coast together, God
permitting. . . .

Ever your sincerest friend

My diary is filled with questionings. Should this be the work
to which I would devote my life?

I wrote to Dr. Grenfell of my uncertainties. In October, 1911,
he wrote again:

Dear old Frank,

A breeze from the old ship comes with your letter.

Here, dear lad, is the crux of the decision, I think. "Where can I be
most useful."

Little I thought when we let go the hawsers from Yarmouth wharf
in June 1892, God would have a work of any size for *me* out in these uttermost lonely parts.

I was for the more crowded centers. But God *can* use a lonely life for the world, and out of the wilderness and desert men have spoken to the world in a way they never would have been listened to otherwise. . . .

Personally I would just give almost my right hand to have you say, "I'll come." I can outline for you a work you could do with me that I can't do alone—or pay to get done . . .

There, I'm off on a selfish tack. I want you *so* badly I am a prejudiced debater. Let us *talk* it over,

Affectionately ever,

WILFRED GRENFELL

In the same strain was Dr. Grenfell's letter of November 8, 1911, written on his way to the States in reply to mine:

Dearly beloved Frank,

Yes, truly, Life, as God's best gift, *must* be put into the largest field where it will tell.

Only God can make plain where that is.

Why Jesus chose Galilee, and not Jerusalem, or Rome, who can say? . . .

I'll pray, dear lad—as all I can do—that you may be led to a right and unhesitating conclusion. . . .

It was indeed a hard decision. I could not but realize, however, that the Labrador work of Dr. Grenfell was largely a medical mission and I was not a doctor. Also, if the winning of other lives for service to humanity was the prime objective, was it fair to choose Labrador with its thousands rather than New York with its millions? This was the deep question I wrestled with during my later Law School days. In the end, after considerable soul-searching, I chose New York.

But in New York which of the many fields of service should I choose? Like most young men on the threshold of their lives, I wanted to make my life count. But how and where?

In my college days Theodore Roosevelt, completing his second term in the White House, was one of our popular heroes. As I look back, his actual achievements at Washington seem to have been extremely limited, and his judgment not always sound. In constructive domestic legislation there is comparatively little to show; and in the international field, while he achieved the building of the Panama Canal through a premature recognition of the Republic of Panama, his "big stick" policy did us immeasurable harm, especially throughout South America.

Nevertheless, Americans owe a debt to Theodore Roosevelt. He came to the White House at a time when profound social and industrial evils were rampant. Yet few people in America were prepared to take action. Here and there writers and public speakers pointed out the growing evils. Theodore Roosevelt, vigorous and always energetic, helped to awaken the American conscience to the necessity of action. The later impressive and outstanding achievements of Woodrow Wilson in domestic legislation were in part made possible by Theodore Roosevelt, who stirred the American people to break away from their apathy and complacency.

Theodore Roosevelt was a hero to the young men of my day. Perhaps that was one reason why my thoughts turned in his direction when I decided upon public service, preferably in New York. At that time another public figure appealing to youth was Charles S. Whitman, District Attorney of New York County. He had just sprung into sharp prominence as the successful prosecutor of corruption in New York's police force and was in the midst of his famous prosecution of Becker, a New York City police lieutenant. I felt that I could gain, in the New York County District Attorney's office, both an invaluable first-hand knowledge of conditions existing in New York and also a close contact with many personalities working in the field. From such a vantage point opportunities for public service were likely to open up.

I knew well Frank Baldwin, one of the editors of the *Outlook* magazine in New York; and Mr. Roosevelt himself, then retired from active political life, had become a contributing editor to the *Outlook*. Mr. Baldwin was kind enough to introduce me to him and tell him that I was just graduating from law school and was anxious to secure a position in the District Attorney's office. Mr. Roosevelt was interested; he wrote a personal note to his friend James Bronson Reynolds, former head of a settlement house in New York, who was now in charge of the Complaint Bureau in the District Attorney's office. Armed with Mr. Roosevelt's letter I called upon Mr. Reynolds and had a talk with him. The result was Mr.

Whitman's appointment of me as Mr. Reynolds's assistant in the Complaint Bureau.

The years of youthful study and preparation were now over. Certainly this first job of helping to round up the criminals of a great city had the making of exciting adventure.

To the Complaint Bureau would come men and women to complain against wrongdoers; as Mr. Reynolds's assistant it was my lot to hear whoever wished to charge another with crime or criminal activity and then to determine whether or not there was adequate evidence for the District Attorney to bring a prosecution. Murder cases were handled by a special bureau; but almost every other crime named in the New York Penal Code might come before us. Complainants trooped into the outer office, and our days were filled with an endless succession of conferences with them. If a case seemed to merit careful examination, we would send out subpoenas for the necessary witnesses for a preliminary informal examination in our office. If the evidence proved to be sufficient we would then send the case up to a Magistrate's Court for hearing and trial.

Ours was an intensely human kind of work. Accusations of almost every imaginable crime were brought before us, including larceny, embezzlement, rape, criminal assault, robbery, receiving stolen property, forgery, and arson. Our task was to sift out the genuine from the trumped up cases, those with sufficient supporting evidence, those which fell within the corners of some specific crime named in the New York Penal Code. All this required the nicest kind of judgment.

I soon came to realize that common sense was quite as important in my work as a profound knowledge of the New York criminal law. We learned to distinguish truth-tellers from holders of grudges. Many of our clients were mental cases or paranoiacs convinced that others were plotting against them. It was most difficult to draw the line between persons who were more or less mentally deranged—what my doorkeeper irreverently designated as "bugs"—and persons who were not. I recall one woman who stated that a certain relative was trying to poison her. To prove her statement she produced the actual box of poisoned candy. Convinced that she was a mental case —I blush to think of it—I foolhardily took a piece of the candy and ate it—to her utter horror. I did not drop dead. I hope I convinced her that her suspicions were unjustified, but I do not know. I never saw or heard of her again.

I often found that I could do more to help the complainants through advice based on common sense than through the intricate processes of the law.

The experience that came to me that year helped to build in me a better understanding of humanity; and this has remained with me all through life. With the crime and the evil were inextricably interwoven nobility of character and the willingness to endure suffering for another. I learned definitely and positively that humanity is not composed of good men and bad men. There is sordid evil in the very best of us and genuine good in the very worst. The real task is to win the good and bring it out on top.

As I look back over this part of my life I realize that Republican influences weighed large. Theodore Roosevelt helped me to get my first job, and I served under another Republican, Charles S. Whitman, who later became the Republican Governor of New York. My father, general manager of the Bethlehem Iron Works and builder of the Lehigh Valley Railroad, lived in a strongly Republican district in Pennsylvania and was a staunch Republican. He and his associates devoutly believed that the Republican was *the* party, the only party. So did I until I went to college.

But during college days the study of tariff history and other national issues changed my party beliefs. I became convinced that the Democratic party by and large was more genuinely concerned than the Republican with the welfare of the American people as a whole. The underlying objective of the Republican party seemed to be to protect the financial and other special interests. High tariffs, advocated by the Republicans, meant special privileges for the large moneyed interests. I myself believed in a party fighting, not for privileged groups, but for the great mass of humanity—for the protection of their rights and the advancement of their welfare.

During this year in New York I came more vitally to realize and understand something of the national struggle then facing the country. When I entered the District Attorney's office Mr. Taft was completing his term in the White House. The Republicans were in full control. But Woodrow Wilson was preaching "the new freedom." As Governor of New Jersey he had come out courageously and firmly for the rights of the common man and against special privileges for big business. He had inaugurated far-reaching reforms. Now, as the chosen candidate of the Democratic party for the Presidency, he was electrifying the country by his speeches, calling upon the voters to have done with complacency and stand-patism and to seek new life for the forces of genuine democracy.

Speaking of the distinction between reactionaries and progressives, he had said: "A reactionary is a man who looks at public affairs through spectacles of his own; a progressive looks without regard to his own interests, with the purpose and hope that he may be privileged to serve the country by some touch of self-sacrifice, some consideration of those things which are larger and greater and more permanent than himself."

I believed with all my heart in the things for which Mr. Wilson stood. So did millions of other Americans, aroused not only by him but also by the speeches and efforts of others who had preceded him, convinced that true democracy meant something very real. I was one of the little ones marching in Woodrow Wilson's growing army.

The election in early November, 1912, was momentous in what it spelt for American democracy. The forces of progressive liberalism were coming into their own. Crucial problems were pending: a mounting American tariff which cut us off from normal international trade and seriously endangered our economic welfare; the critical need of a reformed banking and currency system; the growing injustices in our industrial life and the consequent increase in strikes and disruptions; a national agriculture "never yet given the efficiency of great business undertakings"; the wastage of natural resources, and the need of a nation-wide development of water power and watercourses.

Mr. Wilson concluded his inaugural address on March 4, 1913, with these historic words:

This is not a day of triumph: it is a day of dedication. Here muster, not the forces of party, but the forces of humanity. Men's hearts wait upon us; men's lives hang in the balance; men's hopes call upon us to say what we will do. Who shall live up to the great trust? Who dares fail to try? I summon all honest men, all patriotic, all forward-looking men, to my side. God helping me, I will not fail them, if they will but counsel and sustain me!

I continued hard at work helping to fight crime in New York City. My days were filled to overflowing with the unending stream of cases—situations of every kind where evil threatened havoc in human lives. In the odd moments when I could get away from the office there were meetings and gatherings to rally the growing liberal and progressive forces of the city.

In the field of prison work Thomas Mott Osborne was opening men's minds to the human problem of prison reform. I became absorbed in such books as Henry George's "Progress and Poverty" and Jacob Riis's "How the Other Half Lives." There were calls for help from a growing number of organizations to serve special needs —the Young Men's Christian Association, the Big Brother Movement, probation and parole committees, prison reform associations, the Child Labor Committee, various juvenile organizations, city settlement houses. In America the times were charged with hope— for great things to come.

4

White House Wedding

Some of my earliest memories cluster around my mother's gifted sister, Blanche Nevin, one of the most colorful figures of my little-boy life. I remember her of an evening by my bedside, strumming her guitar and singing to me before I wandered off into the land of dreams:

"Hi, Nellie, ho, Nellie,
Listen now to me,
I'll sing for you, I'll play for you,
A dulcet melody."

Back in another world, it seems—those fragrant tunes and Negro lullabies and the loved sound of her guitar.

She herself was full of charm and rare distinction. She was different from all others. She never married, but her life was filled with varied and interesting friendships and with adventurous travel in many countries. She was imaginative, creative, artistic. In her clothing and her personal adornment she followed her own unconventional tastes; current fashion, she never deigned to notice. Her dress expressed her artist's love of color and dramatic sense. If it suited her mood and her fancy she would wear an evening dress at noon, and carry it off with both humor and wit. Her necklaces and bracelets clinked as she moved; often she used to wear a silver snake necklace, its long coils reaching below her waist. She modeled, she sketched, she painted, she told fascinating stories, she wrote poetry. I can still hear her softly whistling as she worked. She fascinated and she charmed young and old alike.

While Aunty Blanche was in Bermuda in 1910 she met Governor and Mrs. Wilson visiting there; and, impelled by her sense of the strong character and vigor expressed in his head, she modeled a bust of him. Meanwhile the Wilsons spoke often of their children and especially of Jessie, "the angel of the family," and Aunty Blanche talked about "a favorite nephew" named Frank Sayre. After her return Aunty Blanche had told me something about Jessie. And several letters, it must be confessed, were exchanged between Jessie and me before we ever met.

Aunty Blanche lived in a dreamy old house called "Windsor Forges" at Churchtown in Pennsylvania. On the place, acquired by patent in 1742, had been erected an iron forge and a mansion house, the eastern part of the present building. The western part had been built in 1765. Here for generations my ancestors had lived and married and died. From the old house, stately and beautiful, the gardens still sloped gracefully down to the Conestoga Creek; but the iron forges, now silent, and the slave house, deserted, were mute witnesses of another age.

Here Aunty Blanche made her home. To the ancient mirror hanging in the hall she had written:

> Sagacious mirror, thou dost know
> Such histories of joy and woe—
> Thou awest and thou bafflest me.
> Why is it that I cannot see,
> Strain as I will, the ghostly faces
> Thou holdest deep in thine embraces?
> The faces in their life and laughter,
> The ancestors I follow after? . . .

My aunt had made "Windsor Forges" live again. The architecture, she wisely left unchanged. The large, simple rooms with deep window seats and open fireplaces, she made beautiful with heirlooms and old family pieces of furniture. In the dining room was a spacious fireplace, so large that I have often stood inside even while a fire was burning. The original iron crane on which kettles and pots were hung for cooking, and the old bake oven on the side, were still intact.

Into this ancestral home Aunty Blanche invited Jessie; and strangely enough the invitation coincided with the date for my visit to Windsor during spring recess at the Law School.

But it needed no dreamy ancestral home for such a meeting. When Jessie and her sister Nell stepped off the train I was there to meet them with horse and buggy and drive them to "Windsor Forges." As I greeted her I saw a rarely beautiful girl, gracious and winning, of medium height, with radiant blue eyes, clusters of golden hair wound around her delicately shaped head, her countenance beaming with health and beauty. Her face was strong-featured and firm, yet withal of ethereal loveliness.

Three happy days we spent at "Windsor Forges" in the full charm of the oncoming spring. We walked over the country roads, drove up to Lancaster one day and there saw Buffalo Bill's Wild West Show. We sat fortunately under cover and watched the show carried on in a torrent of rain. But somehow the downpour could not dampen our enjoyment. We talked about many things. When we parted, God had planted, perhaps without our full realization, something rich and rare.

After that letters followed; but Jessie was working hard at a settlement house in Philadelphia and I was at the Law School. During the following summer when my brother needed me I went West with him and later to Alaska. Jessie and I could meet but rarely.

Shortly after my return from Montana in October, 1912, after I had won a position in the New York County District Attorney's office, I invited Jessie for a Sunday afternoon drive through the lovely autumn countryside surrounding Princeton where the Wilsons were living. As I called at the Wilson house at 25 Cleveland Lane and entered the front door, Governor Wilson, whom I had never met, was descending the stairs. I gave him my name and asked if Jessie was in. "Oh, no," he replied; "she's not at home. She's off teaching her Sunday School class, which she has every Sunday afternoon. I'm sorry she's not in." At that moment Jessie, expecting me, descended the stairs. All three of us laughed and enjoyed the humor of the situation.

That afternoon Jessie and I drove out into the peaceful country behind a very understanding horse. Again, we talked of many things; and off by ourselves in the quiet of the October afternoon, I told her that I believed that God had made us for each other and had brought us together; and I asked her to share my life. Taken aback, she asked for time to think it over. On the following Tuesday evening I was back in Princeton and called at the Wilson house. Jessie met me at the door, threw her gray cloak about her, and led the way out into the foggy, deserted street and down a dark pathway. Then, almost without a word she raised her face to mine and put herself into my arms. Our hearts beat close together, and Heaven that night touched earth. Under the misty moon we plighted our troth. The evening of October 29 will always be a holy time for me.

As I grew to know her and to feel ever more deeply her rare charm, her mastery of life, her loftiness of soul, my life was lifted and my horizons widened. As I wrote to one of my intimate friends after our engagement was announced: "She is very wonderful; she has changed all the world for me. . . . I still cannot understand why God has brought such a wonderful gift into my life. And yet, who deserves the flowers, or the stars, or the love of a crucified Christ?"

Mr. Wilson was elected President a week later. Thereafter a secret service official was on constant watch in front of the Princeton house; and reporters were omnipresent. Jessie and I played a constant game to escape and elude reporters. Our salvation was the resemblance of my features to those of Mr. Wilson. I was generally accepted among the gentry of the press as a Wilson cousin. That helped us; and, in spite of the many times when I took the five o'clock train from the Pennsylvania Station at New York for Princeton and returned late the same evening, I was never caught or suspected.

Jessie, in order to spare her father, did not tell him of our engagement until the day after his election; and that evening at dinner I was welcomed into the family circle with a warmth which I can never forget. It was a family closely knit together with rare love and depth of affection; and Mr. Wilson's simple, unaffected warmth of heart contrasted sharply with the shyness and aloofness sometimes attributed to him. Into this haven of home Mr. Wilson could always retire out of the maelstrom of public life; without this his spirit must have surely broken under the terrible strain of later days.

Early in the spring of 1913 the loved home in Princeton had to be given up, and the Wilsons almost with a sense of regret boarded their special train for Washington, realizing that the quiet home life of the Princeton days was gone probably forever. To escape detection I avoided attending the Inauguration or the attendant ceremonies on March 4; and during subsequent visits that spring to Washington to see my fiancée I was always accepted by stray newspapermen as a Wilson cousin.

Thus we completely escaped detection or even suspicion during the eventful winter and spring months when the eyes of all the country were fixed upon Washington and the incoming Administration. Finally on July 2 President and Mrs. Wilson announced to the press the news of our engagement, and we could feel thenceforth less like fugitive criminals.

The Wilsons to escape the deadly summer heat of Washington had rented "Harlakenden House," in Cornish, New Hampshire, the summer home of Winston Churchill, the novelist; and here in this quiet retreat and painter's paradise, with Maxfield Parrish our nearest neighbor, I was privileged to spend part of the summer learning to know and to love the Wilsons.

Both Jessie and I were fond of the out-of-doors; often we went on all-day walks through the countryside, carrying a picnic lunch. Sometimes we went horseback riding; occasionally we resorted to a small electric runabout, one of the White House cars. On one horseback ride Jessie's horse suddenly shied and lurched, throwing her off; and as I anxiously jumped to her side and knelt over her by the roadside, a country doctor came driving by. She was shaken but happily uninjured, and we all returned to "Harlakenden House" together. The worst of the episode was the story which the doctor next day told to eager reporters of how, driving along on a sick call, he had found a girl lying by the roadside, and the girl turned out to be the daughter of the President of the United States! No mention whatever was made of me. So far as appeared in the newspapers, although we had set forth together I had disappeared from the scene; and readers were left to believe that I had ridden happily away and done nothing to help. Editorials in several papers commented on the loss of gallantry among American youth in these degenerate days—all of which were hard to take.

The whole Wilson family enjoyed the Cornish retreat. Drives, picnics, long walks, family readings together in the evenings, filled our days. Mrs. Wilson fitted up a studio and went back to her painting as at Princeton. Margaret was busy with her singing and voice-training.

President Wilson could be with us only part of the time; his leadership and driving force were imperatively needed while his first Congress was in session to help crowd through an impressive list of history-making bills. But when he could he hurried to his family in Cornish. There he could relax on the golf course, take long drives with us in the country, or share in family picnics. Here, as in Washington, through Mrs. Wilson's thoughtful love the family would forgo discussing national problems or political issues at the dinner table. In our circle he cast aside all anxious and racking thoughts; he joked, recited limericks, and led us to thought-provoking conversation. In the evenings he would often read to us—perhaps from Wordsworth or some other favorite author. Sometimes we played family games, such as "Twenty Questions."

Jessie had been working in a settlement house on Lehigh Avenue in Philadelphia since her graduation at Goucher College in Baltimore in 1908. She was particularly interested in the Young Women's Christian Association, and after our marriage became an active member of its National Board. She often spoke at college girls' conferences, and penetrated deep into their lives; years later often I would find some of her "Y" girls still depending upon her for advice and help.

Jessie and I were sinking deep into each other's lives; and those quiet days in the country together gave us the chance to talk over many plans. As I came to know her, I came to appreciate ever more deeply the profundities of her spirit. Rufus Jones in "The Luminous Trail" wrote about "luminous spirits" he had known. One who knew Jessie well, wrote to me after her death: "I have always felt that Jessie was one of them, and to me she will always live, her face transfigured with that light of love as it has stamped itself in my memory. . . . They continue to help us to see our way in times of darkness."

"My associations with Jessie Sayre," wrote a fellow worker in the Boston Student Y.W.C.A. after she left us, "have always had a halo of radiance about them; for I was never with her, even for short meetings on the Cambridge trolley or the subway train, without getting something joyful and beautiful to treasure. Always there was the lighting up of her lovely face, the happiness of touching a truly glowing spirit, the expression in look and word of a completeness of beauty and love that made my life forever richer."

" 'No life can be pure in its purpose and strong in its strife, and all life not be purer and stronger thereby.' Was there ever a purer purpose, a more ardent and courageous striving, than Jessie Sayre's?" wrote another. "The unusual beauty of her face bespoke the beauty of her soul. It was indeed the beauty of holiness. Such lives shine like the stars to guide us on our way."

Yet, withal, Jessie was full of play and fun, and she had the quiet deep humor of her father. She was utterly unique. I wonder sometimes if in all history there was ever another quite like unto her.

That summer in Cornish we talked over our wedding plans. Both of us were anxious to have Dr. Wilfred Grenfell at our wedding; I hoped he would be my best man. A letter from Labrador told us that he would be able to come to Washington for our wedding in the late autumn. We wanted the wedding on a Tuesday, the day of our engagement, which to each other we always called "Happy Day." The Wilsons finally chose November 25 for our wedding, provided no national catastrophe intervened.

We also looked ahead to the planning of our future life. In the rough-and-tumble work of the District Attorney's office, I had gained rich experience; but clearly I should want sooner or later to move on to other things. President Harry Garfield of Williams College was urging me to come to Williams as Assistant to the President and Instructor in Government. He made the offer very attractive; and the chance to be of real influence in the lives of young students at my Alma Mater had strong appeal. Jessie and I talked it over carefully together and with her father; and I decided to accept the offer. I therefore resigned from the District Attorney's staff in October, 1913.

Much as we should have liked to have a small and informal wedding, it proved quite impossible. There were Senators and Representatives who could not be omitted from the wedding list; there were members of the Supreme Court; there was the diplomatic list; and there were hosts of friends of both Jessie and myself, many indeed from humble walks of life, whom we wanted to include.

So the wedding list grew; ultimately it was limited only by the size of the East Room of the White House, where we were to be married. It was to be the thirteenth wedding in the White House, and that interested us, too, for the Wilsons had always regarded thirteen as their lucky number.

My ushers' dinner was given on the President's yacht, the *Mayflower*, while Jessie gave her bridesmaids' dinner at the White House. Her sister Margaret was her maid of honor; Dr. Grenfell was my best man. Our ushers were Charlie Hughes, the son of Justice Hughes and my classmate at the Law School, Dr. Gilbert Horrax, one of my classmates at Williams College, Dr. Scoville Clark who had been with me in the Labrador work and packed across northern Newfoundland with me; and Bennie Burton of Williams College who had accompanied me to Alaska and to Siberia.

Dr. Beach, the Wilsons' minister at Princeton, and my brother Nevin, recently returned from China, we asked to perform the ceremony.

Following an old custom, Jessie and I did not see each other the day of the wedding until the ceremony. Instead I went for a walk with Dr. Grenfell, over the Fourteenth Street Bridge and into Virginia. We talked of Labrador and of his future plans.

At four o'clock I motored from Justice Hughes's home where I had been staying to the White House, and found the front gate closed and guarded by the police.

"Sorry, sir. No one is allowed to enter by the front gate this afternoon." The officer was firm, and his stiff and polite finality brooked no discussion.

Here was a pretty how-do-you-do. I carried no card of identification nor ticket of admission. Was I to be excluded from my own wedding?

"But, officer," I expostulated, "you would not wish me to be late for the wedding. I am the groom."

He looked completely unconvinced. After all, lots of cranks and crooks try daring ruses. He wasn't going to be fooled—not he.

"You'll have to tell that to the Captain," said he. "I have my orders, and this is a very special White House occasion."

At my request he called the Captain out of the sentry box, while I stood waiting under his stern eye.

When the Captain walked up I was ready.

"You see, officer, I am Francis Sayre. If you can't see your way to letting me in I guess there won't be any wedding; for I am the groom."

Perhaps my honest embarrassment convinced him. With a twinkle—or *was* it a slight wink—he gave me entrance.

In the White House all was excitement. The Marine band in gorgeous scarlet uniforms were assembling in the large entrance hall. For the occasion they played not only the "Lohengrin" wedding march but also poignant wedding music written by Ethelbert Nevin, my mother's first cousin. Gathering in the East Room were a great company—high officials, diplomats, chosen Senators and Congressmen, and, more important to us, Jessie's and my close relatives and intimate friends. Among these were my mother and Aunty Blanche.

Just before half-past four Dr. Grenfell, my ushers, and I descended the stairway and walked into the East Room where Dr. Beach and my brother Nevin waited. At a sudden hush I looked up to see Jessie entering the room on her father's arm. I suppose I know now that she was wearing a satin dress and veil and that her bridesmaids preceded her. But at the time I saw only Jessie's face, aglow with happiness and with a beauty not of this world.

And then in the deep silence which followed, "in the sight of God and in the face of this company" Jessie and I pledged each to the other "to have and to hold, from this day forward, for better for worse, for richer for poorer, in sickness and in health, to love and to cherish, till death us do part." God was very close to us that afternoon, uniting forever our hearts and our souls; and our lives were henceforth buttressed with new foundations of love and power.

We knew that our getaway that November day would be difficult. As we later learned, a reward of $1,000 had been promised to any newspaperman who could follow us or report on our whereabouts. Reporters were watching closely at every possible exit, determined that we should not evade them. We had carefully planned our escape. White House cars were of course dispensed with. Secretary Tumulty's black unobtrusive car awaited us by the South basement door. After the pictures had been taken and the family goodbyes said, we jumped into this waiting car and dashed through the West entrance of the White House. Photographers and newsmen were awaiting us; but two uniformed motorcyclists were waiting, too, to help us so far as they could. They slowed down our pursuers suffi-

ciently for us to take the next left-hand turn on two wheels and disappear around another corner before our pursuers could regain the
trail. Out to the Chain Bridge across the Potomac we sped; on the
Virginia shore hidden in the defile where the road turns sharply to
the right, and out of sight of the bridge another inconspicuous car
headed in the opposite direction was waiting. As we came alongside,
into this we jumped; and in a moment we were speeding back across
the Chain Bridge, into Washington, and then heading north for Baltimore. As we drove down Pennsylvania Avenue and passed the White
House we saw great crowds of people still lingering to catch glimpses
of the wedding activities. On we sped to Baltimore, where a warm
friend had moved out and put her house at our disposal. Here we remained hidden for two days, undetected and unmolested, although
the maid informed us that a telephone call had come reporting that
the "White House couple" were there and asking if it were not true.
"But what did you say?" we asked with considerable concern. "Oh,
I very frankly denied it," was her unhesitating reply.

The following Thursday morning was Thanksgiving Day. That
afternoon we unobtrusively drove back to Washington to share a
Thanksgiving family dinner in the White House. It was an unforget-
tably happy occasion.

Early the following morning Jessie and I took the train for New
York. Here we spent the night hidden in the modest apartment of a
friend; and on the following day we boarded the steamship *George
Washington* for Europe.

Again we eluded the reporters. As we reached the dock we saw
them lined up by the first-class gangway awaiting us. We quietly
boarded by the third-class gangway without any fuss or obstruction,
and were sitting in our stateroom when President and Mrs. Wilson
came to bid us goodbye. After the farewells were said and they had
disembarked, Jessie and I ascended to the top deck. There we were
greeted by the newsmen and posed for inevitable pictures.

In London we were guests for a month of Ambassador and Mrs.
Walter Hines Page. As I look back upon that happy honeymoon visit
it seems like a dream. "We are looking with the very greatest pleasure
to the coming of the White House couple," Ambassador Page had
written to his friend, Col. Edward M. House. "I've got two big dinners for them—Sir Edward [Grey], the Lord Chancellor [Haldane], a

duchess or two, some good folk, Ruth Bryan, a couple of ambassadors, etc., etc., etc. Then we'll take 'em to a literary speaking-feast or two, have 'em invited to a few great houses; then we'll give 'em another dinner, and then we'll get a guide for them to see all the reforming institutions in London, to their hearts' content—lots of fun."

That honeymoon month in London, arranged so generously and understandingly by our dear friends the Pages, gave us a wealth of memories. Lord Haldane who deeply charmed us and invited us to his house, Sir Edward Grey, Viscount Morley, Lady Scott, whose husband had lost his life in his recent South Polar trip, and a host of others of England's best, endeared England to us. Christmas we spent alone in a little hotel in Wales. That day we tried to climb Mount Snowdon, but halfway up were turned back by a snowstorm.

Following the Christmas holidays we spent ten days in Paris as the guests of Ambassador Myron T. Herrick. We were received by the President of France and entertained by other distinguished personages. But our thoughts turned increasingly to the little house awaiting us in Williamstown. In late January we sailed for home.

Our first week in America we spent with Jessie's family at the White House. We rejoiced to find all going well with them. We also learned that Jessie's sister Nell had become engaged to Secretary of the Treasury McAdoo. It was a happy homecoming. In early February Jessie and I departed for wintry Williamstown, where we were to live for the next three and a half years.

We were discovering that the real romance of true love begins only after marriage. Through the nineteen years that followed, our love kept growing and deepening and touching our expanding lives with a wand of enchantment. We faced happiness and discouragement and joy and sorrow, always together; and when at times the road seemed rough it was she who helped me through.

5

1914, End of an Era

In Williamstown President Garfield and all the faculty members and their wives welcomed us with open arms; we moved into the house of a professor absent on leave, and here we lived for the next half-year. Our home radiated happiness. After the excitement of Washington and New York we luxuriated in the simplicity and the quiet of Williamstown; and we rejoiced in the mountain country into which we could take leisurely walks and climbs or occasionally, in vacation time, go off for a two- or three-day walking trip into southern Vermont. Peace was everywhere, and no one dreamed of war.

My college duties were twofold. Part of the time I taught. I gave two courses: one in comparative government, with a survey and study of the different forms of foreign governments; and one in American municipal government. Later I introduced into the curriculum a course in international relations, which I taught as long as I remained at Williams. This was a new departure. Except for specialists in the field, American thinking in those days was innocent of the problems of international conflict or of international law; and nothing quite like this had been taught at Williams before. The rest of my time was devoted to my work as Assistant to the President; this took various forms and opened up many interesting opportunities.

Our home was brightened with frequent visitors and became the center of developing friendships. Here too on brief visits came my mother and my brother Nevin, who had been called to a church at Suffern, New York, and had asked my mother to live with him in the rectory.

Those quiet, peaceful days seem now to have been in another world. In Williamstown all but a very few of us still went about with horses and carriages, or else we walked; "horseless carriages" were few and far between. There were no traffic jams. No airplanes roared overhead; we read in the papers about the Wright brothers' experiments in flying at Kitty Hawk and wondered if centuries hence men would really be able to fly. We read of undersea boats and submarines; we wondered if they would ever become practical. There was no military conscription in the United States: it was considered undemocratic and quite unnecessary. Many felt that in the new age into which we were heading large-scale war was an impossibility: nations would go bankrupt if called upon to pay the excessive costs. In a period of supreme Victorian optimism we felt that we were moving inevitably onward toward "the Parliament of man, the Federation of the world."

After the June examinations Jessie and I journeyed to Harlakenden House in Cornish, where the Wilsons had invited us to spend the summer with them. They themselves had not yet arrived. Our visit there brought back a flood of happy memories of our engagement days.

On June 28 a shot rang out in distant Sarajevo. We read of it in the newspapers and were mildly interested. To us as to the majority of Americans it was merely an item of European news, of very little concern. But during July events took a graver turn. A crisis began to loom over Europe. The President could not leave Washington. And then at the beginning of August a desolating telegram from Mr. Wilson told of the grave illness of his beloved wife. All his life he had leaned heavily on her judgment and advice. She was the very heart of their closely knit family circle. Jessie and I took the first train to Washington.

On August 3 came the grim news that Germany had declared war and invaded France. That week Jessie and I were watching by the bedside of her mother, in the White House, dying. She breathed her last on August 6 without knowing of the heartbreaking ruin swiftly stalking across Europe.

To Mr. Wilson came double tragedy: the sudden loss of the loved companion of his life and, at the same time, the crashing outbreak of a war that spelled the breakup of the world he knew.

He moved about, stunned by the blow. His grief and loneliness were heartrending. His only relief lay in work—meeting the crushing responsibilities cast upon him by the European war. "It is amazing how one can continue to function in all ordinary, and some extraordinary, matters with a broken heart," he wrote to an intimate friend. "Now self is killed more pitilessly than ever—there is *nothing but the work* for me."

In September Jessie and I had to return to Williamstown. We moved into the "little gray house" on the edge of the small college town; and here for the next three years we worked and shared our happy lives. Here, too, came President Wilson for a short visit from November 25 to 27, seeking relief from loneliness and from the increasing pressures crowding upon him. It was his first Thanksgiving Day after his wife's death.

A month and a half later came the birth of our first son, Francis, Jr. Jessie and I and one or two close relatives had spent the Christmas holidays with President Wilson: he was still inexpressibly lonely. When I had to return to Williamstown at the end of December Jessie remained in Washington. About 4:00 A.M. on January 17 I was awakened by the ringing of the telephone; the connection was so bad that all I could get was a relayed message that Washington bade me come. I walked a mile to the railway station, caught an early train to Albany, and reached the White House at half-past eight that evening. Here I found the newborn child—the first born in the White House since Andrew Jackson's grandchild. Both the baby and his mother were doing splendidly, and for my restricted world all was well.

But in the great world around us all was not well. None of us at the time realized that we had reached the end of an era, and that the world which we were about to enter would be a changed and profoundly different one.

Before 1914 we believed that we had outlived the day of catastrophic wars. There might be border warfare, or "civil war," or uncivilized fighting between the "natives" in Asia or in Africa; but wholesale wars among the advanced nations of Europe and America were thought to be of the past. In the new, industrial age, with the

Jessie Woodrow Wilson, 1912

Davis & Sanford, New York

Jessie and Francis Sayre on their honeymoon, visiting Ambassador Page
in London, December 1913

development of mass production and the consequent growth of international trade and travel, with our amazing scientific progress, man was proving himself master of his fate; man was building and could build his own heaven—even, some believed, without the aid of a distant and little-felt God.

We failed to realize that the world we knew and took largely for granted was breaking up. We viewed the disaster in Europe rather as the tragic case of a single country which had gone amuck and askew, misled by a sordid group who were willing to wreck Europe in order to gain world mastery. It was militarism that we opposed; we were fighting a war to end war; and we were innocent enough to hope that, once we had downed these sordid gangsters who were misusing the German people for their selfish aims, we might end war and go forward on the same track as before.

Meanwhile, my college work at Williamstown continued its uninterrupted course. The "little gray house" was a joyous refuge; and our baby drew Jessie and me ever closer together. But we could not forget the profound loneliness of the man in the White House. Among my wife's letters is one from him, dated March 14, 1915:

My darling Jessie,

I am ashamed of myself when I think I have been so long acknowledging the dear letter from you that made me so happy, and touched me so deeply. You cannot know, I fear, what it meant to me to have you say that I had in some sort taken your incomparable mother's place when you were here! Ah! how little I knew how! And how impossible it was to do more than just let you feel, as well as I knew how, the infinite tenderness I felt and the longing that was at my heart to make up for what can never be made up for, neither to you, my sweet daughter, nor to me nor to anyone who ever had a chance to know how sweet and loving and infinitely rewarding she was. I cannot yet trust myself to speak much of her, even in writing. I felt so dumb when you were here, dear. I did not know how to *say* the things that were in my heart about you and the baby and all the crowding thoughts that made my heart ache with its fulness. I had to trust you to *see* them; and your dear letter makes me hope that you did. I can talk about most things but I always have been helpless about putting into words the things I feel most deeply, the things that mean most to me; and just now my heart is particularly voiceless. But I do love you and yours, my dear, more than words can say, and there *is* added to my love now the mother tenderness which I know the depths and beauties of in *her* heart. She was beyond comparison the deepest, truest, noblest lover I ever knew, or ever heard those who knew the human heart wish for!—It is delightful to hear how well everything goes with you. God bless you. . . . Nothing happens to the rest of us except daily crises in foreign affairs.

Love beyond measure from us all to you all.

Your loving
FATHER

President Garfield asked me that winter to interrupt my teaching long enough for an extensive speaking trip, visiting the various Williams alumni groups across the country. It was hard to leave Jessie for a full month during our first winter in the "little gray house"; but this was an opportunity to meet with Williams alumni all the way to California and to tell them something of college life and of President Garfield's plans for the future, and thus to stimulate alumni support. But I confess that when upon my return Mrs. Garfield asked me which part of the trip I enjoyed most I instantly and in all honesty replied: "The last mile and my arrival home."

The christening of Francis Bowes, Jr., took place in Williamstown on May 2, 1915. Happily President Wilson was able to join us, and with him and the other godparents and friends—my mother, my brother Nevin, Margaret Wilson, Agnes Winter, and Jessie's old college friend, Flora Robinson—we gathered at the little Episcopal Church on Park Street for the simple ceremony. To dip once again into our family life and share the simplicity of a college home seemed for a time to dispel something of the deep loneliness of the President.

As soon as the June examinations were over we bundled up the baby and took the train to Cornish to spend the summer with President Wilson at Harlakenden House. It was at Cornish that the President received the German reply to the second *Lusitania* note. This temporarily relieved the tenseness of German-American relationships, and enabled him to gain some sorely needed relaxation in the hills.

But, alas! the increasing gravity of the European conflict and the consequent pressure of responsibilities in Washington made it impossible for him to remain at Cornish except for brief intervals.

In September Jessie and I were back in Williamstown. It was becoming increasingly clear that in a war of such magnitude and involving moral issues of such intensity the genuine neutrality which at the beginning of the war we hoped to follow would soon be utterly impossible. We were learning that nineteenth century conditions were past; and that the inescapable interdependence of nations which had come with twentieth century commercial and scientific advance made neutrality for a great nation in a war of world-wide proportions no longer moral if indeed possible.

In the latter half of 1915 President Wilson found refuge for his lonely spirit. Our cousin, Miss Helen Bones, introduced him to Mrs. Edith Bolling Galt, living in Washington since her husband's death; and through her gracious and outgoing personality he began to find a new interest in life. She was possessed of wit and charm as well as beauty. But of even deeper importance was her utter devotion to Mr. Wilson, which gave great promise of happiness for them both. They were quietly married during the Christmas holidays while Jessie and I were with him; and all of us felt supremely happy that his days of grief and utter loneliness were over. Without her, I often wonder whether he could have borne the loneliness and carried on his work.

In March, 1916, a second baby came into our lives, whom we named after her loved grandmother, Ellen Axson.

President Wilson wrote to me in June:

> We think of you and Jessie and the little ones with the deepest love every day, and are always eager for news of you. I hope everything goes well with the little lady, now that she has gotten acclimated to her home. All join me in the deepest love to you both.

The summer of 1916 brought new anxieties and fresh separation. American relations with Mexico were badly strained; and American troops under the command of General Pershing were sent to Texas to police the Mexican border and prevent raids on American soil. At the request of the Government, eager to build and sustain the morale of the troops, the American Y.M.C.A. undertook social and religious work among the soldiers in lonely camps along the border. It was a new kind of venture for the "Y," and Dr. John R. Mott, directing the work, asked me to help.

Accordingly, soon after the completion of college duties in June I took a train south and spent most of the summer with the troops. It was stimulating work; and indeed for the "Y" the experience

proved invaluable when a year later it was asked to undertake similar work in France among our troops overseas.

In early September I returned to Williamstown to resume my
college duties. I found Jessie well and the babies growing fast.
We paid a brief visit to "Shadow Lawn" on the New Jersey coast,
where Mr. and Mrs. Wilson sought rest now and again by slipping
away from Washington. The end of his first term in the White House
was approaching; and the Republicans were making superhuman
efforts to return to power. Justice Charles E. Hughes had resigned
from the Supreme Court to lead the Republican fight. The outcome remained in very great uncertainty.

I spent the night of Election Day with the Wilsons at "Shadow
Lawn." It was a memorable evening. On every side excitement was
intense. Every few minutes telephone messages announced that
Mr. Hughes had forged ahead in this state or in that state, that Mr.
Wilson was holding his own in some critical district, that the Republicans or the Democrats in given areas were assured of victory.
Before me as I write is a memorandum in Mr. Wilson's own hand
which he worked out at the dinner table that evening, listing the
reasonably safe Democratic states other than the "solid South."
These totaled 103 votes. With the 114 votes from the South these
added up to 217; 266 votes were necessary for the election, so that for
victory 49 additional votes had to be secured. In two other columns
Mr. Wilson had listed possible states from which he might obtain the
necessary number.

Among all the people present that night the only calm, unruffled
person seemed to be Mr. Wilson.

After dinner the family went upstairs and, with Mr. Wilson,
played a quiet game of "Twenty Questions." I remember that when
I was the questioner the subject selected was Charlie Hughes, my
classmate at the Harvard Law School and the son of Justice Hughes.
Whether or not, in my twenty questions, I guessed the subject, I do
not recall; but I do remember the interest and amusement of all as I
probed toward discovery. More particularly, I remember the whole-
hearted way in which Mr. Wilson threw himself into the game, apparently unperturbed by the prospect that he might fail of reelection.
In fact, word came to us a little later that the news had been flashed
from the *New York Times* tower that Mr. Hughes's election was as-

sured. In his face was no shadow of disappointment or resentment; his deepest feeling seemed to be loving concern for Mrs. Wilson. Would she be as happy in retirement as he himself hoped and expected to be? He did not sit up that night to hear the late returns; all of us except his daughter, Margaret, retired early, believing that Mr. Hughes had been elected.

Next morning the tide had turned. Doubtful states, as the later returns came in, rallied to Mr. Wilson. The headlines in the morning papers indicated a probable Democratic victory; but there was still uncertainty, particularly in the Western states. California remained in doubt.

Almost immediately after the election President and Mrs. Wilson came to Williamstown for a few days of rest with Jessie and me; and it was in Williamstown that he learned of the definite final returns from California which made his election sure.

But in Mr. Wilson's demeanor that night there was almost nothing of elation. Apart from the infinite satisfaction of knowing that in spite of all the political slurs the majority of his countrymen understood him and believed in him, the drawn lines of his face revealed a keen understanding of the deepening tragedy and the well-nigh superhuman labors which lay ahead, perhaps even having to prepare the country to enter the war. When a group of townspeople, unannounced, gathered that evening to hail him and express their pleasure over his reelection, he stepped out onto the lawn, waved a greeting and smilingly and graciously acknowledged their welcome.

During this visit he took part as godparent in the christening on November 10 of our daughter Eleanor Axson. Also, on our lawn, that afternoon he planted a tree for Francis, Jr.

Through the following winter the war clouds grew blacker and blacker. American rights were daily more and more flagrantly violated. Continuing neutrality was no longer possible.

On April 2, 1917, Mr. Wilson recommended to a special session of Congress that "Congress declare the recent course of the Imperial German Government to be in fact nothing less than war against the government and people of the United States." And he stated:

The right is more precious than peace, and we shall fight for the things which we have always carried nearest our hearts,—for democracy, for the right of those who submit to authority to have a voice in their own governments, for the rights and liberties of small nations, for a universal dominion of right by such a concert of free peoples as shall bring peace and safety to all nations and make the world itself at last free. To such a task we can dedicate our lives and our fortunes, everything that we are and everything that we have, with the pride of those who know that the day has come when America is privileged to spend her blood and her might for the principles that gave her birth and happiness and the peace which she has treasured. God helping her, she can do no other.

On April 6 the President's proclamation declared war against Germany.

In our quiet college town the declaration of war was greeted with a waving of flags and patriotic fervor. But Jessie and I felt a profound sadness that war was at last upon us—realizing nevertheless that, in the light of existing facts and necessities, no other course was humanly possible. We must go through the tragedy with brave hearts and unfaltering courage.

On that day I wrote to Mr. Wilson:

Dearest Father,

War has just been declared; and I am wondering whether I should leave my work here, and where I could help most. The first to fill the army ranks should, I believe, be the unmarried men; but there are other countless ways (perhaps more effective) of helping America . . .

Jessie's and my hearts go out to you in these days, and we know how heavy must be your heart preparing for the terrible business of war. Love and reverence and high pride in all your leadership fill us every day. God bless you!

With deep love from the four of us,
                    Ever affectionately your son,
                              FRANK

In reply, he expressed the feeling that I should not abandon my family to enter the army, and that, in view of my relationship to him, I could not accept a Federal position.

Shortly thereafter Dr. John R. Mott pressed me to spend the summer in France helping to organize Y.M.C.A. recreational and religious activities among the American troops. Jessie and I agreed that I should go.

Our life in Williamstown was coming to an end. We were giving up the "little gray house." The Harvard Law School had asked me to accept appointment as the Ezra Ripley Thayer Teaching Fellow at the school, and I had agreed, beginning the following September. Jessie and the children were to spend the summer in a cottage at Siasconset on Nantucket Island.

At the end of June, 1917, after establishing my family at Siasconset, I therefore sailed for France as a member of the first group of Y.M.C.A. leaders to organize recreational and religious work among our soldiers in France. As I boarded the steamer the following telegram was handed to me: "Love. Affectionate goodbyes and good wishes from us all. You will be in our thoughts constantly. Woodrow Wilson."

On the way across the Atlantic we kept a wary eye against submarine attack. No lights were allowed after sundown; and several warm nights I slept curled up in a lifeboat on the upper deck under the stars.

Once in France we opened offices in Paris and plunged into the work. Few people today remember the extraordinary responsibilities placed by the Army on the "Y" in 1917. They included the setting up and maintenance of post canteens, the running of leave areas, providing entertainment for the troops, service to prisoners of war, the development of educational programs, and the conduct of hotels for the Army in Paris. It was an enormous assignment, and the undertaking was close to General Pershing's heart.

American troops were pouring into France. Back of the lines they were stationed in many little French villages where living conditions seemed at first intolerable—billeted in filthy barns, in filthier outhouses, wherever a roof could be found, sometimes with the cattle and pigs below them and the chickens above. They were eating their mess in the middle of the street and washing their clothes in neighboring streams. There might be no place in the whole village where they could write letters, or play games, or read; no books or magazines to be had at any price; no form of recreation or legitimate amusement of any kind. Our immediate task was to establish hundreds of centers, later known as "Y huts," where our troops could come for relaxation, for music, for entertainment, and where talks and addresses could be given. As troops were ordered to the front, we would establish posts at which they could obtain coffee and doughnuts on their way forward. At the huts we maintained close personal contacts. Often what the soldiers wanted most was to talk and let off steam.

The work of the Y.M.C.A. among the troops was under official sanction. Newton D. Baker, Secretary for War, well realized that organized activity was necessary to maintain the morale of the troops. Yet, as I have indicated, there was at that time no organized Army program on the non-fighting side of soldiering. At the very outset there was the question whether the "Y" workers should hold commissions in the Army and wear "shoulder straps." The Y.M.C.A. leaders quite properly decided against commissions.

In those days we were just beginning to learn how to meet war conditions, and it took time. Even under ideal circumstances caring for some thirteen hundred canteens and supervising the services of some eight thousand workers constituted no small task.

At every point we ran into difficulties—in securing supplies, in getting transport, in jurisdiction. The Red Cross was also at work, and it was natural that jurisdictional difficulties should arise. Who should do what? Army Order No. 26 of August 28, 1917, directed: "The Red Cross will provide for the relief work and the Y.M.C.A. will provide for the amusement and recreation of the troops by means of its usual program of social, educational and religious activities." A later order, of November 28, 1918, directed: "The Knights of Columbus and the Salvation Army will participate with the Y.M.C.A. in the activities prescribed it. The Y.W.C.A. and the Jewish Welfare will carry on their activities through the Y.M.C.A."

From Paris with two or three other "Y" leaders I motored back and forth, visiting the troops and when necessary going up to the front lines. Often, as we stopped, we could hear the big guns in the distance; they spoke of the great fight being waged for human freedom. Sometimes we were caught in shell fire and our car was hit by flying shrapnel; but we ourselves escaped injury. Some other workers were not so fortunate.

We visited, too, the British lines, and we stopped over at Rouen and again at Reims, at the time under desultory fire. The splendid work carried on by the British Y.M.C.A. gave us some conception of the magnitude of our own task. In the single small section which we visited of the long battle line across France there were massed one million men. As I wrote at the time:

What that means no one can grasp unless he has moved in and out among the lines some evening when a push is on and watched the endless movement to and fro—has seen the mile after mile of muddy camp-ground swarming with soldiers preparing to go up into the trenches, or has ridden past the acres of supplies, guns, ammunition, and horses. He must stand beside the road and watch the long line of traffic that goes on all night without cessation—the ceaseless columns of soldiers in khaki with their steel helmets on their heads, their gas-masks and kits slung across their backs, and their rifles on their shoulders, swinging by with grave, set faces; the huge guns ponderously lumbering over the roughly paved street; the trains of clattering ammunition-wagons; the great fleets of lorries loaded with unending supplies; the soup-kitchens; the empty ambulances—a great and endless stream of life surging forward to meet ruin and agony and death; and on the other side of the road, moving in the opposite direction, another endless stream of the broken and crushed, returning from the fighting—great trains of red-crossed motor-ambulances, carrying hundreds and hundreds of limp forms, wrapped in dirty, blood-soaked blankets, marching soldiers, dirty, disheveled, and dog-tired, returning from the trenches; disabled guns; empty lorries; broken wagons; and all that is worth bringing back after the touch of war. Or he must stand just back of the line at night and see the sky alight with the flashes of the great guns, not in one or two or three places, but the whole horizon aflame with that weird light as far as eye can reach; and he must feel the tremble of the very earth as the great guns hurl their tons of projectiles miles away into the enemy lines. It is vastness on a scale which the world never imagined before—vastness such as multiplies a hundred-fold the difficulties of any organization which undertakes to play a real part in the lives of those endless lines of soldiers, and to make its influence profoundly felt throughout that stupendous and gigantic array.

Under conditions such as these religion may come to mean something more vital, more compelling, than anything else in the world.

It was in the trenches in Flanders in 1917 that an English soldier wrote this poem:

We had forgotten You—or very nearly—
You did not seem to touch us very nearly;
  Of course we thought about You now and then,
Especially in any time of trouble
We knew that You were good in time of trouble,
  But we were very ordinary men.

And all the while in street or lane or byway,
In country lane, in city street, or byway,
  You walked among us, and we did not see;
Your feet were bleeding as You walked our pavements—
How did we miss Your footprints on our pavements?
  Can there be other folks as blind as we?

Now we remember over here in Flanders
(It isn't strange to think of You in Flanders)
  This hideous warfare seems to make things clear;
We never thought about You much in England,
But now that we are far away from England
  We have no doubts—we know that You are here.

You helped us pass the jest along the trenches—
Where, in cold blood, we waited in the trenches—
  You touched its ribaldry and made it fine.
You stood beside us in our pain and weakness;
We're glad to think You understand our weakness—
  Somehow it seems to help us not to whine.

We think about You kneeling in the garden—
O God! the agony of that dread garden.
  We know You prayed for us upon the cross.
If anything could make us glad to bear it
'Twould be the knowledge that You willed to bear it—
  Pain, death—the uttermost of human loss.

Though we forgot You—You will not forget us—
We feel so sure that You will not forget us
  But stay with us until this dream is past,
And so we ask for courage, strength, and pardon—
Especially, I think, we ask for pardon—
  And that You'll stand beside us to the last.

In those early days of the First World War there was no conscription or total mobilization, no all-out effort of the whole nation
for the supreme task in hand. Since by the end of the summer the
organization of "Y" activities among our troops was progressing
smoothly it seemed that I ought to return to my family responsibilities and take up my new work at the Harvard Law School. The
Thayer Teaching Fellow was appointed to take over the classes of
any Law School professor who might fall sick or have to absent himself from his classes during term time. The Fellow, however, was permitted to pursue graduate work so far as time allowed. I have always
considered myself beyond words fortunate that all the professors at
the school were blessed that year with excellent health. Not only could
I conceal my incapacity, but also I could devote my time uninterrupt-
edly to graduate law study for the S.J.D. degree—the Doctorate in
Jurisprudence.

I wanted this work particularly because Francis L. H. Pott, the
President of St. John's University in Shanghai, China, had already
asked whether I would be willing to come to China and organize and
head a law school as part of St. John's. To this Jessie and I were giving serious consideration. For it graduate law study would be necessary. Indeed one reason for accepting the Harvard teaching fellowship had been to prepare myself for Shanghai if we decided to go.
With the outbreak of war, however, the whole situation had changed.

Upon reaching Harvard in late September Jessie and I rented
an apartment at 39 Kirkland Street, not far from the Law School.
Once again I plunged into study, attending graduate courses in jurisprudence, Roman law, and international law. I was working more
intimately now with members of the faculty—particularly with Roscoe Pound. His course in jurisprudence was a landmark in the Law
School. The number of graduate students at Harvard was then small.
We had only about ten or a dozen students in these classes, and the
classwork was very much more intimate than in the undergraduate
courses.

Apart from the graduate work our minds were almost constantly
on the war. Profound changes in the democratic life were taking
place. Increasingly American people and resources became consecrated to the war effort. Education like all else must take second place.
Most of our soldiers were for the first time seeing Europe and learn-

ing European ways and attitudes; when they returned home new ideas were being poured into America. Civilians were finding it necessary to conform to innumerable war regulations.

In Boston, where Jessie and I were now centered, popular opinion as to America's entrance into the war was questioning and divided. Boston was largely an Irish Catholic community, and Irishmen were far from enthusiastic about going to war to assist and sustain England. Hence, Mr. Wilson's name was not too popular in Boston among the rank and file. Senator Henry Cabot Lodge, who depended in large part upon Boston's Irish vote, fought against him with intense personal bitterness. Different sections of the nation had often reflected in their feelings the countries from which they or their parents had emigrated; America's first great common war effort in 1917–1918 helped powerfully to unify and integrate the people of the country into a cohesive whole.

On January 8, 1918, President Wilson in a historic address to Congress outlined the fourteen points which in America's view must underlie the coming peace. It must be a peace of justice, he declared, and of justice to all—not a seizure by the victors of the spoils of war. It must help to create a new world order through international community of effort under which every people, great or small, might feel secure.

His Fourteenth Point was, "A general association of nations must be formed under specific covenants for the purpose of affording mutual guarantees of political independence and territorial integrity to great and small states alike." From this epochal statement came in time the League of Nations. And America, the victor, proved unwilling to join it!

The address was a very great statement of the kind of peace America was fighting for. Jessie, waiting in the hall of the White House to accompany her father to Congress where he was to give the address, wrote to me: "It is a momentous occasion. It is the risk of dice on which one may lose all or win all. God grant that the words will be winged words, charged with the grace and power of God for peace and justice." With the letter she enclosed Mr. Wilson's personal draft, with verbal corrections in his own hand.

In June, 1918, I received my Harvard doctorate of jurisprudence. Then Jessie and I proceeded once again to establish our family for the summer at Siasconset on Nantucket Island, "as near to France," we kept telling each other, "as it is possible to get." There President Wilson came for a brief visit before my departure; and there I left my mother and a Law School friend to watch over the beloved family during the summer while I was in France. In early July I set sail, once more to assist in the Y.M.C.A. work among our troops.

During the previous winter the "Y" work in France had splendidly grown. In spite of countless obstacles it was now achieving real results, not only among American troops but also, through the "foyers des soldats," among French troops. In early August I made a trip to Italy with Dr. John Kelman of Edinburgh and other officials of the British "Y" to help introduce "Y" work into the Italian Army. This was a task of exceeding delicacy in view of the strong Roman Catholic influence in Italy. Nevertheless, the war was on, and the need was great; and, with the loyal support of Roman Catholic as well as Protestant friends, we were successful in our efforts.

In the summer of 1918 much of the fighting in Italy was in the high mountains. I shall never forget one exciting occasion when we were ascending a mountain, suspended in the air astride a gun frame on an Italian *teleferica,* or air lift, used for hauling the guns up to the peaks. Halfway up, there was an ominous slowing down, a throbbing on the line, and finally a complete halt—while we dangled motionless and helpless, between earth and sky, wondering what the trouble was. Shortly afterwards Austrian shells began to sing past us. For twenty minutes we hung in the sky; every minute seemed an hour. Then finally we began haltingly to descend; and because of a broken engine we were pulled down by hand.

Later we travelled over splendid roads which the Italian soldiers were building up into the mountains, and saw the tunnels in solid rock through which guns were hauled and pointed down into the Austrian country on the other side far below. The Italians were at this time fighting valiantly. The Caporetto disaster came later.

When we returned to Paris in early September a sheaf of letters awaited me. One from Siasconset filled me with sadness. It seemed in keeping with the tragedy on every side. On August 15 my mother, living with Jessie at Siasconset, had suffered a stroke and had died. Henceforth the close companion of my boyhood days I would not see again.

Of all those exciting days the most thrilling was my homecoming. Having crossed the Atlantic in a troopship through a furious hurricane, which swept three men overboard, having landed in New York and made a public address, having reembarked on a steamer for New Bedford, Massachusetts, and there having caught a small island boat, I was approaching at last Nantucket. As we neared the dock I saw awaiting me a dear face which meant all the world to me, and trailing along beside her a little three-year-old boy. God does not give us in life many days like that!

By the autumn of 1918 the end of the war was in sight. Germany was exhausted and reeling. Her army was retreating.

Colonel Edward M. House organized a "Commission of Inquiry," composed of outstanding men in international law, to prepare for assisting in drafting the Peace Treaty. The Commission included David Hunter Miller, as legal expert, and Professor James T. Shotwell. Upon my return from France Colonel House invited me to become an unsalaried member of this group, and I gladly accepted. The Commission of Inquiry was housed in Columbia University; and Jessie and I engaged an apartment near by at 490 Riverside Drive, overlooking the Hudson River. From our apartment windows our children never tired of watching the camouflaged ships passing up and down the river.

The proposed association or league of nations occupied the center of my thoughts. I devoted my time in the Commission of Inquiry to running down the previous experiments tried out in international administration and studying the reasons for their success or failure.

For instance, there were the Universal Postal Union, the European Danube Commission, the Moroccan International Police, the Suez Canal Commission, the International Sanitary Councils, and, more important, the International Sugar Commission. When it came to the point of organizing a league of nations, could it function by majority vote, or must it follow the old unanimity rule of accepted diplomatic practice which would permit any single nation to veto and thus block any international proposal?

On this vital question I wrote:

The further progress of the world is coming to depend more and more upon concerted international arrangement and cooperative action;

and concerted international action presupposes of necessity a certain re-straint upon the exercise of individual sovereignty by each state. National sovereignty must thus yield to international demand; the right of the in-dividual state to stand out against the ordered progress of the world is open to serious question. . . .

The member states of any League of Nations will always have widely differing ideas and interests; if the League cannot act until all agree, it will never be capable of any but petty action.

On November 11 at last came the end of the war. The crowds in New York, as in every great city, went wild. The days of interna-tional warfare were over, and now we should go back to the delights of peace.

The Commission of Inquiry worked entirely apart from, and so far as I knew, independently of the Department of State. Therefore I hastened down to Washington in late November to confer with the Department of State as to my trip to Paris with the Commission of Inquiry. I reached the White House in time for breakfast and asked Ike Hoover, the White House usher, to make an appointment for me with Secretary of State Lansing. Immediately after breakfast I had a talk with Mr. Wilson and told him of my hope to go to Paris with the Commission of Inquiry.

"But, Frank," he exclaimed, "that is a government commission, with its expenses paid by the government. If a close member of my family should go to France as a government appointee or hold any official government position my enemies would surely blazon it abroad, and it would be used to hurt me."

Thus vanished in a moment my hope of playing a useful part in the making of the Peace Treaty. Nevertheless, Mr. Wilson was right. He always was most meticulous that no member of his family should hold any government office while he was in authority. I felt the more thankful that I had gone to France with the Y.M.C.A. and not at government expense.

There was no choice in the matter. Forthwith I cancelled my ap-pointment to see Mr. Lansing; and after an affectionate goodbye to Mr. Wilson I took the first train back to New York.

My disappointment came as a blow and left me in a sense stranded. With no possibility of a government appointment there seemed no practicable way of my helping in the shaping of the Peace Treaty or sharing in the work of building a new world.

The material which I had gathered for the Commission of Inquiry and embodied in a carefully prepared study, I gave to the Commission before its departure for Paris. This I now put into final shape and published in January, 1919, as my first book, *Experiments in International Administration*.

President Wilson sailed on the *George Washington* for Paris early in December. He realized the stupendous difficulties ahead and the reaction and intrigue which worked constantly against him. Just before his departure he exclaimed: "This trip will either be the greatest success or the supremest tragedy in all history; but I believe in a Divine Providence. If I did not have faith I should go crazy. If I thought that the direction of the affairs of this disordered world depended upon our finite intelligence, I should not know how to reason my way to sanity; but it is my faith that no body of men however they concert their power or their influence can defeat this great world enterprise, which after all is the enterprise of Divine mercy, peace and good will."

Jessie and I visited him and Mrs. Wilson in his cabin on the *George Washington* just before they sailed. It could not be a gay farewell, for the whole world was then hanging on his words and on his plans for the peace; and from the momentous issues which confronted him he could not even temporarily divorce his mind. Dr. Grayson stood beside him, shielding him from the insistent, unceasing demands to see him, so that he could have a quiet half-hour with Jessie and the children. As always with her he was his gentle affectionate self; but much of the old gayety with the children was gone. Earlier in the autumn he had visited us briefly in our apartment and now he wanted to know how we were faring in New York. He was interested in the children and asked about our Christmas plans. Then we took an affectionate farewell. Our last sight of him was on the bridge of the ship waving goodbye to the cheering crowds on shore.

6

Teaching at Harvard

Now that my decks were cleared I was available for other work, and when Dean Pound offered me an appointment on the Harvard Law School faculty I was happy to accept. We moved back to Cambridge and established ourselves in the comfortable house of Professor Wambaugh, absent on leave.

As if to add blessing to our new life a little newcomer joined our family on February 22, 1919. We named him Woodrow Wilson Sayre. President Wilson, returning from Washington to the Peace Conference at Versailles, stopped over a few hours to greet his namesake and to visit Jessie in the hospital at Philadelphia where Woodrow was born. His face was tense; we could feel something of the galling pressure under which he was working.

For the next fourteen years I was engrossed in my teaching, except for two years when I went to Siam. Younger men were then coming to the fore, and the Law School was expanding considerably in size, requiring a larger teaching staff. A new generation of teachers, working under the leadership of Dean Roscoe Pound, was molding the life of the School.

Zechariah Chafee, Jr., a recent appointee, was beginning a long and thoroughly respected life of teaching. He represented the younger, more liberal elements in the community. He became a stout and fearless defender of the American right of freedom of speech, and was generally admired for his forthright courage and sincerity. Felix Frankfurter had been appointed in 1914. He had a very keen and rapierlike mind, which was generally fixed on the human side of problems; he was unwilling to sacrifice human values to purely legalistic ones. His students admired his brilliancy, although they questioned sometimes the soundness of his judgments. One of Frankfurter's protégés was James M. Landis, who joined the faculty in 1926, and who after my departure took over my course in labor law. Landis, like Frankfurter, had a scintillating mind, keen and piercing. His brilliance seemed almost too burning for his years, and some wondered how he would mature. At the Law School perhaps he suffered a bit because of being regarded as Frankfurter's protégé. He later became chairman of the Securities and Exchange Commission at Washington and subsequently dean of the Harvard Law School.

Manley Hudson was beginning a long career as Professor of International Law. John Burns was appointed in 1928. A gifted and likable young man, he later became an associate justice of the Massachusetts Superior Court and after that the general counsel of the Securities and Exchange Commission in Washington. Calvert Magruder, appointed in 1920, was another young professor of marked intellectual quality. He was later appointed to the United States Circuit Court of Appeals. Austin Scott, who had begun to teach at the Law School just before my student days, was then forging forward with his outstanding work on trusts and was greatly looked up to. Sheldon Glueck was initiating his interesting and unique work in penology. Altogether, this new generation of Law School teachers was a brilliant and stimulating group of which I felt happy to be a part.

The principles of law expounded in the classes of these independent and outstanding personalities were naturally not always identical. But it was one of the cardinal principles of the Law School that each professor should have unquestioned independence within his own field. So far as I can remember, the correctness of the legal principles or doctrines I might be developing in my classes was never criticized or even questioned by the Dean or the faculty. The strong tradition at the Law School was for each professor to teach his subject in his own way without interference.

Once a week we gathered for a luncheon and faculty meeting.

There we had many clashes of opinion, sometimes tense. But they were over new faculty appointments or administrative issues—never over methods of teaching. I suppose faculty meetings are never serene. Ours were no exception. Among men of such independence and mental vigor there were bound to be very different points of view, and these were strongly debated and upheld.

During my first year on the faculty I took over Professor Wambaugh's course in constitutional law. Constitutional law is always a live subject. Exactly how are constitutional rights and liberties to be defined and safeguarded? The answer has varied markedly over the years with changing conditions and changing needs. The fight for freedom in America is constantly demanding fresh interpretation of constitutional rights.

Another of my courses was maritime law. This, developed from Roman law, was often in striking contrast to English common law principles; and it interested me particularly because of my love of the sea. I continued to teach it during all of my years at the Law School, and in 1929 published *A Selection of Cases on the Law of Admiralty,* dedicated "To Sir Wilfred T. Grenfell, with whom I first learned to love the sea."

During Dean Pound's absence on leave I took over for a year the teaching of his graduate course in Roman law; and I was glad to have this chance of working on Roman law so that I could obtain a better grasp of the underlying principles of maritime law.

Not long after my appointment, I permanently took over Professor Beale's course in criminal law. Later, in 1927, I published for my students a new *Selection of Cases on Criminal Law.* What I tried to bring home to them was the realization that crime—as I had learned in my work in the New York County District Attorney's office—is an intensely human problem. Herein criminal law differs sharply from other fields of law. In developing and shaping criminal law one must never lose sight of the human being.

In the country at large when I began teaching at the Law School revolutionary social changes were taking place. The Boston police strike and the national steel strike bore evidence of profound surging conflicts of opinion. In my own thinking many of the deep-rooted social problems of the day demanded fresh consideration and study by teachers and molders of the law. In the industrial field, for in-

stance, many of our courts were floundering and in conflict. Judges
were in the wildest disagreement whether or not workers had a legal
right to strike. Was picketing lawful? What about the legality of a
secondary boycott? And under what circumstances should courts issue injunctions in labor disputes? Different states were going different
ways in their decisions.

Although certain problems in the field of industrial relations
were incidentally touched upon in various courses, Harvard had no
course concentrating upon labor law and its underlying issues; nor,
I believe, was such a subject taught in other law schools. Yet here was
a field in which courts were every month handing down decisions of
crucial importance, which must affect vitally the lives of thousands of
people. I put the situation before the Harvard faculty, and it agreed
to include a course in labor law in the curriculum. I commenced
teaching it without any casebook, compiling one as we went along.
This was published in 1922. I wanted to get law students thinking
through these problems. The class was well attended and, I think,
was well received in the Law School. Later other law schools began
giving courses in labor law; and I believe it is taught in most law
schools today.

I opened the course with three or four lectures describing the
early English law. In England until 1825 it was unlawful for workmen to join a trade union or to agree to seek an advance of wages or
shorter working hours. Such efforts constituted criminal offenses.
After 1825 the law was gradually liberalized, but was still in a state
of considerable uncertainty. In the United States it was declared in
the Philadelphia Cordwainers' Case in 1806 that "a combination of
workmen to raise their wages may be considered in a twofold point
of view; one is to benefit themselves . . . the other is to injure those
who do not join the society. The rule of law condemns both." Although courts in the United States no longer followed such a ruling,
both state and federal courts were still seeking and wondering which
way to turn.

I threw at my students conflicting American decisions, and tried
to show something of the nineteenth century development of American law and the more liberal trend of twentieth century thinking,
all the while letting them argue back and forth as to which of various
conflicting decisions were the sounder.

Many of my students of twenty or thirty years ago are sitting on the bench today. I should like to think that my course in labor law had its part in shaping a sound growth in this field of the law.

Again and again I would find myself regretting that many of my students lacked a thorough grounding and training in sociology, upon which sound law must be built. As a consequence, too often they became immersed in legal technicalities and empty rules. The fault lay manifestly with the colleges, for no student was admitted to the Law School without a college degree; and in the crowded three years of the law course unhappily there was no time to teach the fundamentals of sociology or other social sciences.

In my teaching I always feared that I should drift too readily down the stream of the straight lecture system. It is far easier to do the talking oneself and let the students take copious notes than to draw constructive thinking out of them. A teacher's temptation is always to speak out his own mind and let the students lap up what he says. This is not true education at all. The real art of teaching is to make the student do the intellectual building. On the other hand, classroom discussion can degenerate into little more than loose talk by students who, without carefully thinking the problem through, toss off hasty, ill considered opinions. Law teaching at times seemed to me an impossible art.

Often I would leave the lecture hall with a feeling of utter futility. Then some student's chance remark would prove how impossible it is for a teacher to judge his own teaching. Sometimes at moments of discouragement a letter from a student would speak of his regret that the course was over, or express his appreciation. "Mr. Sayre has a knack of lifting the class out of musty legal mechanism," wrote one. "He has inspired me to aid in the fight." A letter from a practicing attorney who had been a student of mine seventeen years before spoke of his inspiration and of the "indelible impression" left upon him. Such letters, if they have the ring of sincerity, lift the teacher to new heights.

During the first summer after my appointment on the Law School faculty I was teaching at the summer session, organized to help the men freshly discharged from the Army. After a hard week of teaching in Cambridge I used to join Jessie and the children every week end at a delightful cottage which we had found on Martha's

Vineyard off Cape Cod. The cottage stood on a bluff, overlooking Vineyard Haven harbor and East Chop lighthouse and to the east the shimmering Atlantic Ocean. To it we returned summer after summer. It seemed like a bit of paradise where we could withdraw from the worries and the sophistications of a harrying world; and each member of our family grew to love it. Here we have gathered every summer when possible since then. Over twenty years later, when enemy forces hemmed us in at Corregidor in the Philippines and the hope of escape seemed small indeed, it was to Martha's Vineyard that again and again our thoughts and our memories turned.

Toward the end of that summer Jessie and I purchased a house at 26 Hubbard Park, just off Brattle Street, in Cambridge; and into this we moved in September and made it our home for the next fourteen years. Day by day I used to go back and forth between our house and the Law School, about a mile away. Sometimes I rode my bicycle; generally I walked. In later years I drove a Model T Ford back and forth; this saved time, but walking was better.

Our home offered a continual refreshment of soul, and our three growing children were a very integral part of it. Often we would play family games or indulge in family pranks. Nothing delighted the children more than when I would "Humpty-dumpty" Mother around the dining room. In other words, if the children and I got into the dining room before Mother, when she appeared I would sometimes suddenly pick her up and dance up and down around the dining room table amid her embarrassed cries: "Let me down. Let me down." It was a high occasion, and the children shouted in delight. We used to hold "family councils" for important plans and decisions; children and parents in turn would state their independent views, and in conclusion always we would reach common and generally unanimous decisions.

Often we would give students a touch of family life by inviting them to our home for dinner or an evening together. Among my letters is one from a former student who wrote in 1928 from Jesus College, Oxford:

As I look back over my last year at Harvard, I recall that my happiest day was Thanksgiving Day with you. It brought so much joy into a rather gloomy period, that on its approaching anniversary, I want to write to thank you again.

As the children grew older we sent them to day schools in Cambridge and Belmont. Early every morning I or another parent would drive the boys to the Belmont School. As their minds developed we used to discuss at mealtime issues of the day, and often I would throw at them various legal problems. The children were interested in law because of my teaching it. Often I would put law cases to them and draw out their opinions and conclusions. One case over which we used to have long arguments concerned an Arab, A, preparing to depart on a far journey across the desert. He had two bitter enemies, X and Y, each of whom was determined to kill him. Just before his departure X stole into his compound and secretly put poison into all the spare water jars, filled with water and waiting to be loaded onto the camels. After A and his party, including Y, had gone several days' journey, Y, ignorant that the water in the spare jars had been poisoned, emptied them so that A would die of thirst. When A opened the spare water jars on which he was depending and found them empty he died of thirst. Can X or Y be convicted of murder? Or can both? Who actually caused A's death? Over that our arguments waxed hot and long.

Our family made merry together throughout the year, particularly at Christmastide, when great doings were afoot. On Christmas Eve, after the candles were lighted in the windows, we would gather around the blazing fire while I read the loved story from St. Luke. Then from the "big red poetry book" would follow our favorite poems: "The Night Before Christmas," Alfred Domett's "A Christmas Hymn," "While Shepherds Watched Their Flocks by Night," Robert Louis Stevenson's "Christmas at Sea," "O Little Town of Bethlehem," and to the delight of the children, Eugene Field's "Father calls me William, Sister calls me Will, Mother calls me Willie, but the fellers call me Bill." In "The Night Before Christmas" I could always draw noisy protests when in order to tease the children and be very, very proper I would change the well-remembered lines and read of Santa Claus, "He had a broad face and a little round stomach, That shook, when he laughed, like a bowlful of hummack." "What's hummack?" would come disdainful protests. "Oh, a kind of Scotch pudding," I

would airily reply. Then each in turn would ask for his or her favorite: Tennyson's "Defence of Lucknow," "Sweet and Low," "The
Splendour Falls on Castle Walls," Sidney Lanier's "Ballad of the
Trees and the Master" or "The Marshes of Glynn," Alfred Noyes's
"The Highwayman," and so on. After that came the hanging of the
stockings, and a little later "the children were nestled all snug in
their beds."

On Christmas Eve, 1920, my brother wrote from a steamer
bound for Europe:

This is the time when all the candles will be lighted in the houses at
Cambridge, and when you and Jessie will be planning your Christmas for
Frankie and Eleanor and little Woodrow. I remember how dearly you
took me in for your Christmas last year when I had no place to go; and
that you wanted to take me in again this year. I am sorry I cannot be
with you; but any errand on which I can go to make hatred less and war
less in the world, gets the right of way in my life now. I have just been
reading Philip Gibbs's *Wounded Souls*. It simply adds to the conviction
which I have had and found growing all these last five years that war is
about the most unchristian thing on the face of God's earth at present,
and that the hour has come when true men and women must take every risk
in striking against it and refusing ever again to take part in it, that so it
may at last be put away even as chattel slavery was. And a war to end war
now seems to me the most chimerical of all false hopes.

Since that time my brother has spent his life as secretary of the
Fellowship of Reconciliation, fighting the evil of war as inconsistent
with the teachings of Christ. But so deep-rooted and far-reaching an
evil as war can be eradicated, so far as I am able to see, only by the
slow processes of building throughout the world sounder and more
Christian social and educational and political foundations; and during this long, slow process military force seems to me sometimes necessary to defend from attack and aggression the countries where gains
are being made and higher standards of civilization are being built.
But I profoundly respect my brother's convictions and the utter sincerity of his life. And I recognize that today the development of the
atom and the hydrogen bomb necessitates a complete rethinking of
the whole problem of war.

At the Law School, while I was developing my course on labor law, I naturally had frequent contacts which I always enjoyed with the Boston Central Labor Union. I used sometimes to attend the Union meetings, and I was proud when it later conferred upon me an honorary membership. "In the history of the Boston Central Labor Union," the Secretary wrote to me, "this is the first time an Honorary Membership has been bestowed upon any one." I also maintained contact with Samuel Gompers, who headed the labor world of that day, and with his successor, William Green.

In those post-War days we were living through a poignant period of American history. Throughout the country deep-rooted forces of conservatism were seeking to strangle the more liberal thinking growing out of the momentous War.

The Sacco-Vanzetti case, which took place during my teaching years, developed into a national issue and fired emotions to white heat. Even today no one knows whether these men were justly or unjustly condemned. Unhappily, once the issue of law and order was raised human values were largely brushed aside. After the defendants had been convicted their counsel, William G. Thompson, decided to appeal the case, and he asked whether I would serve as counsel representing them in the appeal. Thompson was a lawyer of standing and ability for whom I had a high regard, and I should have liked to serve. But, as a member of President Wilson's family and of the Harvard Law faculty, I concluded finally that I ought not to throw myself into this fight. It would have meant inescapable and unpleasant publicity; and this might have harmed all concerned.

My colleague, Professor Frankfurter, was greatly exercised over the trial. He wrote an article on the case for the *Atlantic Monthly* which was later expanded into a book. After the appeal was denied the defendants sought executive clemency from the Governor and there followed the hearing before the Governor's Committee, headed by President A. Lawrence Lowell of Harvard. Feeling ran high. My own view was that here was a case in which the wheels of justice ground in too mechanical a way, and that Mr. Lowell had a rare opportunity which he badly muffed. After the execution there were countless thousands who never forgot or forgave. Still today the blood of many runs hot as they read Vanzetti's masterly final statement before his execution.

Something of this same underlying struggle between the forces of extreme conservatism and those of liberalism was brought home to us in the Law School in the spring of 1921. Jacob Abrams, an alleged radical, had with others been convicted of conspiracy under the Espionage Act for distributing pamphlets protesting against American intervention in Russia, and Abrams had been sentenced to imprisonment for twenty years. Many felt that the ends of justice had been defeated. A petition had been circulated asking for executive clemency for the Abrams group; and Austen G. Fox of New York had prepared and circulated among some of the Harvard alumni a detailed statement charging that several Harvard Law professors had signed the petition and that it contained certain untrue statements misreporting the case. In addition, separate charges were made against Professor Chafee based upon his recent article about the Abrams case entitled "A Contemporary State Trial," which he had published in the Harvard Law Review.

President Lowell, feeling that alumni complaints as serious as these deserved careful consideration, arranged for a hearing and discussion of the case by the Harvard Law School Visiting Committee, who were charged with the duty of making periodic visits to the Law School to assure themselves that all there was well.

Zechariah Chafee was particularly suspect because he was the outspoken champion of freedom of speech, and he had signed the petition. So had Dean Pound. So had Felix Frankfurter. So had I. So had one or two other members of the faculty.

On May 11, 1921, a letter asked me to appear at the Harvard Club in Boston on Sunday morning May 22 to meet with the Visiting Committee and Austen G. Fox. This request sounded very much like a hearing and an examination of the offending professors to determine whether they were in fact Socialists or "Pinks." I replied that I should be glad to make the requested appearance, provided "I shall not be asked to submit to a cross-examination of my own personal beliefs and general opinions, religious, political or economic."

When we assembled that Sunday morning President Lowell, claiming freedom of speech for all Harvard professors, acted more or less as our attorney for the defense. At the outset of the hearing he showed that the statement charged to have been misleading was in fact not in the petition which we had signed but appeared in quite another document with which we had nothing to do.

This was devastating for the attack, and Fox was forced at once to withdraw the charge against us who had signed the petition. On the remaining charge against Chafee for his Law Review article, Chafee was called upon to testify at great length; in the end, the Committee by a majority vote concluded that Chafee was guilty of nothing blameworthy and the case was dropped.

I myself had to leave at noon and meet Mrs. Sayre to keep a luncheon appointment with Andrew J. Peters, Mayor of Boston, and his wife. I did not return to the meeting and was never informed of the outcome of the Committee's deliberations. Naturally the meeting was not mentioned in the public press.

The hearing was not strictly a trial. Nevertheless, it had the earmarks of one; and the whole proceeding seemed to me indefensible and indicative of the overcharged feeling of the times.

As a matter of fact President Harding later did grant to Abrams commutation of his sentence.

In the international field an even more savage conflict was raging between the forces of conservatism, fighting all innovation and change, and those of liberalism, seeking new avenues of progress to meet the changed conditions of the post-War world. Woodrow Wilson was the great prophet and champion of the latter. Leading the fight for a peace built upon justice for all nations, great and small, rather than upon increased material power for the victors, he was continuing in America the fight for "the common brotherhood of mankind" which he had launched at Versailles. The liberal thinking of the country was organizing behind a League of Nations, which the isolationists opposed. Throughout that spring and summer of 1919, opposition forces, led by Senator Henry Cabot Lodge, who nursed a personal hatred based apparently on wounded vanity, were increasing in power and in virulence. There could be no rest, no possible summer holiday, for the President.

On July 10, President Wilson presented to the United States Senate the peace treaty which had been signed at Versailles two weeks before. "The stage is set," he declared, "the destiny disclosed. It has come about by no plan of our conceiving, but by the hand of God who led us into this way. We cannot turn back. We can only go forward, with lifted eyes and freshened spirit, to follow the vision. It was of this that we dreamed at our birth. America shall in truth show the way. The light streams upon the path ahead, and nowhere else."

The opposition to the ratification of the treaty, developing in the Senate under the leadership of Senator Lodge, grew so menacing that Democratic Senators urged that the single way to secure ratification was for President Wilson to go directly to the people, on a trip that would involve making more than a hundred speeches between Washington and the Pacific coast. Against the advice of Dr. Grayson, his physician, he resolved to go, even though it might cost his life.

In those days the radio had not yet come into use as a means of political education. Had radio speeches been possible, perhaps Americans might have come to understand and history taken a very different course. Who can say?

Jessie and I, returning from our summer cottage at Martha's Vineyard, were just about to move into our permanent home in Cambridge when word came on September 26 that the President, who had spoken the previous evening at Pueblo, Colorado, had been stricken, was seriously ill, and was being rushed back to Washington. We dropped everything, quartered our children with an unselfish neighbor and took the first train for Washington.

Days of heartbreaking uncertainty followed. Shortly I had to return to my classes in Cambridge. Jessie remained for a time in Washington. Both of us spent the Christmas holidays of 1919 at the White House, doing what we could to help.

The treaty fight was lost. America repudiated the League of Nations. "We have torn up Wilsonism by the roots," Senator Lodge jubilantly declared.

President Wilson's body was broken, but not his lofty spirit. He still hoped that through a League of Nations we could go forward to build not only an enduring peace, but also common democracy and freedom around the world. He never gave up that hope. He never became embittered. Just before his death he told a friend: "I am not sorry I broke down. As it is coming now, the American people are thinking their way through and reaching their own decision, and that is the better way for it to come." "My clients," he said on another occasion, "are the children; my clients are the next generation."

Through most of the day he sat in a wheel chair, often in the sunny garden on the south side of the White House, with his wife,

Edith, beside him. She proved a tower of strength, both through her contacts with public officials seeking communication with him, and still more through her cheering presence and her personal ministrations.

The President's mind still was keen but did not function as rapidly as of old. His speech was sometimes slow. But his judgments were sound. His face was drawn, and the left side almost immobile. But he always smiled and had something cheery to say when Jessie or I approached. He could walk only with difficulty, leaning heavily on his cane.

The illness of the President lasting through a year and a quarter of his term of office created grave anxieties throughout the nation. Conflicting stories were spread as to his true condition. Many clamored for his resignation.

As far as concerned the conduct of the national government it was evident that normal procedures could not be carried out. Though Mr. Wilson's mind was clear his body could not endure the strains of normal Presidential activity. Ordinary administrative questions had to be handled by the Cabinet officers and other high officials. Cabinet meetings were rare and largely routine. The President had to confine himself mainly to matters of large import; and decisions might be based upon insufficient data. Often such issues were brought to Mrs. Wilson, and she, after talking with the President, would announce his decision.

Procedures such as these were always open to criticism and raised the serious question whether the President should resign, being now unable to carry on administrative duties in the ordinary way.

Unhappily resignation might have meant at that highly critical time in the nation's history throwing power into the hands of those who did not share his high vision of American leadership in a new world built upon a League or a United Nations. The isolationists were pressing for power and growing in strength. Later President Coolidge in his first Message to Congress was to declare that "the League of Nations is a closed incident." The undercurrents of the struggle between the isolationists seeking to build up the selfish power of America and the internationalists seeking to build a world peace upon justice and freedom for all peoples alike were running so deep that I always felt that President Wilson chose the right and the brave course not to resign during his last year of office. No question arose of seeking another term.

Nevertheless, one must admit that the grave illness of the President is bound to cause the nation inescapable injury as well as danger.

President Wilson was too far ahead of his time; and the American people in those days did not understand. Since earliest times isolationism and fear of entangling alliances in Europe had run in the very blood of all Americans. When it took as in the early days over a month to cross the Atlantic Ocean, when there were no airplanes and no ready international contacts, America, far apart from Europe and immersed in her own problems of developing growth and domestic economy, was bound to be isolationist. And the ingrained thinking of a whole people for one hundred and fifty years cannot be changed in a night.

But Woodrow Wilson never lost his faith in the ultimate triumph of what was right.

Up to the very end he fought. His last published writing was a cry for a more Christian civilization:

The "supreme task, which is nothing less than the salvation of civilization," he declared, "now faces democracy, insistent, imperative. There is no escaping it, unless everything we have built up is presently to fall in ruin about us; and the United States, as the greatest of democracies, must undertake it. . . .

"The sum of the whole matter is this, that our civilization cannot survive materially unless it be redeemed spiritually. It can be saved only by becoming permeated with the spirit of Christ and being made free and happy by the practices which spring out of that spirit. Only thus can discontent be driven out and all the shadows lifted from the road ahead."

Woodrow Wilson is often thought of as the President with a great dream who failed. It has cost us stupendous tragedy to understand that Woodrow Wilson was not a man of unpractical vision; he was the prophet of a new era. He was the first American statesman who appreciated the new sweep of world events, the need of world unity, and the changed part which America must henceforth play. His dreams are becoming the very warp and woof of international realities.

Deep in the heart of Woodrow Wilson profound religious convictions burned like fire. His vision came from his abiding faith in a God who rules human destiny.

This was the faith which he carried unwaveringly into the international field. This was the faith of our founding fathers. As nuclear science develops in the days ahead, if we are to survive, to this same faith America must be true.

7

Adviser to the King of Siam

During the spring of 1923 Dean Pound asked me whether I would be willing to go to the Far East as Adviser in Foreign Affairs to the King of Siam. It seemed like a bolt out of the blue and a far cry from our life at Harvard. Perhaps that was all the more reason for going.

Siam like other Asian countries had suffered under the nineteenth century aggressive advance of European strong-armed powers. Up to the close of the century France had bitten off parts of eastern Siam to add to her possessions in Indo-China, and Great Britain had added to Burma at the expense of Siamese southwestern territory. Siam sought help through foreign advisers; but when, following the counsel of a Belgian adviser, she informed the French government that certain French demands in Annam were preposterous—as indeed they were—and must be refused, France arbitrarily seized still further Siamese territory and demanded immediate evacuation by the Siamese and the payment of an indemnity. All these demands then became part of a humiliating treaty dictated to and perforce accepted by the Siamese government. Following this, however, Great Britain, glaring across Siamese territory at France and jealous of France's approach toward Burma and the Indian Empire, intervened; and a treaty between these two great powers in 1896 sought to avoid future conflict between them in this part of the world by guaranteeing the independence of Siam. After that it seemed clear to the Siamese government that it could rely upon neither French nor British advice in foreign affairs; henceforth Siam must turn to Americans.

The first American employed was Edward Henry Strobel, a graduate of the Harvard Law School. Strobel was of immense help to the government of Siam. When he left, his assistant, Jens I. Westengard, who was also a Harvard Law School graduate, was appointed Adviser to continue Strobel's work. When Westengard left to join the Harvard Law faculty, Eldon James, also of Harvard, went out as his successor. In seeking some one to succeed him, therefore, it was but natural that the Siamese government should turn to the dean of the Harvard Law School; and Dean Pound recommended me.

I had agreed to lecture on labor law at the summer, 1923, session of the University of Southern California; and I remember how at Los Angeles where I was lecturing, and at Santa Barbara where Jessie and I had taken a summer cottage, we debated, wondering whether or not we should move our home to Siam on the other side of the world. Our three children were then aged eight, seven, and four; and we had made it a practice to move them away from our Cambridge home as little as possible. Finally, by good fortune we discovered in Los Angeles a Presbyterian missionary who had lived and worked in Siam; and with her reassurances as to living conditions in Bangkok we decided to make the adventure, provided we should not be bound to remain in Bangkok longer than one year.

Filled with hopes and fears, we returned East at the end of the summer, and with our children spent several days with President Wilson at his house at 2340 S Street in Washington on a goodbye visit. It was the last time we were ever to see him. From Washington we returned to Cambridge to rent our house and to gather up our things. My outstanding memory of our few days in Cambridge was the warning given us by a lady who for a number of years had lived in Bangkok, and who now took the trouble to tell us of the deadly cobras which entered the houses there and the need to guard the children from snakes hanging from the trees.

A few days later, accompanied by Jessie's warm girlhood friend, Sally Scott from Princeton, to help with our three children, we took the night train to Montreal, where we spent a few pleasant days awaiting our ship's delayed departure for England.

From England we shipped southward on the *City of Paris* past Cape St. Vincent and Trafalgar and through the Strait of Gibraltar. Browning was in our thoughts:

> Nobly, nobly Cape Saint Vincent to the North-west died away;
> Sunset ran, one glorious blood-red, reeking into Cadiz Bay;
> Bluish 'mid the burning water, full in face Trafalgar lay;
> In the dimmest North-east distance dawn'd Gibraltar, grand and gray;
> "Here and here did England help me: how can I help England?"—say,
> Whoso turns as I, this evening, turn to God to praise and pray,
> While Jove's planet rises yonder, silent over Africa.

Jessie and I sat on the upper deck together in the full moonlight as we rounded Gibraltar and said goodbye to Europe.

Then on east through the Mediterranean, skirting North Africa, through the Suez Canal where we watched the camels trailing along the bank, south through the Red Sea and on into the Indian Ocean. Our first stop east of Suez was at Colombo in Ceylon. We arrived in the early evening; and that night we rode in rickshaws along narrow winding streets thronged with Singhalese to a Hindu temple where we watched strangely clad, half-naked figures advancing into the bright torchlight and retreating into black shadows, uttering cries and prayers in a language we could not understand. It was our first glimpse of the East and it will always live in my memory. We reached Singapore in early November and, after a few days at the Hotel Raffles, took a small steamer north into the Gulf of Siam and up the great Menam Chao Phya River to the city of Bangkok.

The Minister of Foreign Affairs in gay *penung,* accompanied by a large and motley throng of Siamese, was waiting on the dock to receive us and escort us to our quarters. We rubbed our eyes. Had we indeed fallen into some altogether different world?

Siam was still an ancient Oriental monarchy, for the most part untouched and untroubled by tourists; Bangkok was a city of color and of splendor. The King's Palace stood behind ancient white crenellated walls, and above the sacred enclosure, glistening in the tropical sunlight, rose the brilliantly colored tile roofs of mysterious royal quarters and ancient buildings, of temples and shrines, overtopped by tall, thin golden spires and phrachedis, reminiscent of Indian stupas. Throughout the city one's eyes lit upon golden spires and towers of fantastic temples and profusely adorned pagodas, their delicately curved roofs, one projecting below another with superbly ornamented gables. The temple called the Wat Benchamabophit, the Sala within the precincts of the Royal Palace, the Wat Po, were far more like Oriental dreams of splendor than marble realities. The teakwood temple doors, some carved with sitting Buddhas, others with intricate and rare designs, fascinated and beguiled. Color everywhere. Along the unpaved streets came rickshaws, or occasionally an elephant; for the most part they were thronged with men and short-haired women in blue or red or green *penungs* and *passims* (which took the place of European trousers and dresses), priests with clean-shaven heads and brilliant yellow cotton robes, naked children, some wearing broad-brimmed straw hats to shield them from the burning sun. But much of the transportation and movement was by water; for Bangkok, like Venice, is a city of waterways (*klongs*). In small boats on the *klongs* was carried on much of the marketing, the buying and selling; and thousands of Chinese with their babies and children and nondescript belongings had no home except the houseboats, crowded together in the waterways and lagoons.

Bangkok was a city of immense distances, some areas of which, still unclaimed by man, were filled with exuberant plants and foliage, tropical jungle, brown water grasses or exotic trees.

The day after our arrival, at the very outset of my work, a most delicate situation confronted me. The Secretary of the American Legation had committed a diplomatic *faux pas* in conversation with the Foreign Office, saying things which he never should have said. H.H. Prince Traidos, the Minister of Foreign Affairs, telling me of the matter, said he felt that an apology was due. It was not easy to extract an apology from a Western diplomat in the Far East. Nevertheless, I felt that the Foreign Minister was right, and that an apology ought to be given. What to do?

Without delay I betook myself to the Legation and had a long heart-to-heart talk with the American Minister. He rose to the occasion. The next day he proceeded to the Foreign Office and made a formal apology. The air cleared. The result was good for both sides.

Also, the Siamese saw from the very outset that I was sincere and very much in earnest—that I would not let them down. They began to feel confidence in me and placed more and more matters in my hands. I found genuine friendliness everywhere.

During the early part of our stay we were housed at the Royal Hotel on the Klong Satorn, not far from the American Legation. My small boy, Woodrow, busied himself in the hotel garden chasing the peacocks to their immense displeasure. To the Siamese, universally black-haired, his long golden locks were a wonderment and delight; many times I would see them stroking his head. My children enjoyed riding in the rickshaws and accepted with a lively interest this new world into which we had dropped. They always enjoyed our visits to the "cobra farm," maintained by the Pasteur Institute for treatment against cobra bites; there they used to watch the cobras swimming up and down the small waterways, sometimes with small frogs given them for food actually sitting on their backs, enjoying the ride. A month or two after our arrival the government put at our disposal the house formerly occupied by the Queen Mother on the Phya Thai Road.

Siam was an absolute monarchy. There existed no Parliament or legislative body; if the King wanted a law he had it reduced to writing and stamped it with his seal. Lawmaking was easy for those who had the friendship and confidence of the King. There was no constitution, and there were no constitutional restraints. The King acted as the father of his people; and that meant, too, that he felt a responsibility to his subjects to guard them from wrong and injustice and injury. King Rama VI, who was on the throne during my stay, worked tirelessly for his people; and the princes of the royal family must equally work for the welfare of his subjects. There was no middle class. The leading personages in the government were men of royal blood—often the sons or grandsons of Kings—and they served with a genuine sense of obligation. Although the King's rule was supreme, he did not abuse his power; the regime was in no sense a corrupt nobility ruling a suppressed people.

Nevertheless, the absolute nature of the monarchy meant unavoidable dangers. It was inevitable that ambitious, self-seeking men should try to win the King over to their designs, surround him with their own kind and cut him off from unselfish officials whose deep objective was the welfare of the people. Power acts like a magnet attracting sycophants. Now and again evil resulted.

My own contacts with the King were marked with utter friendliness. But since my official duties lay through the Minister of Foreign Affairs, it was only occasionally that I would have personal, informal talks with His Majesty.

Among the Siamese peasantry I found very little discontent. They tended their paddy fields and grew their rice as their fathers and grandfathers had done before them. Fundamentally they were a happy people. They accepted without question their King and his beneficent rule. Theirs not to meddle in the public affairs of their country. What took place in the government offices in Bangkok or among the princes and royal family was out of their world.

Among the royal princes were personalities one could thoroughly like and respect. Outstanding among these was H.R.H. Prince Damrong, who had served in the government as a powerful Minister of the Interior. He was a cultivated, able man, who had travelled in the West and still maintained many Western contacts, and yet who also maintained the ideals and the traditions of the East. The returned students or other young Easterners fired by the West, who want to establish Western forms of government overnight and to surrender or obliterate the culture and the traditions of the East, can do untold harm. The world will be the poorer if it loses altogether the ancient culture and fruitage of the East.

Prince Damrong was a man of character and could evaluate and combine the best of each. He set up a National Museum, where he displayed irreplaceable specimens of ancient art and many kinds of implements; he was a collector of the best. Nevertheless, he was a gentleman of the old school, and each of his several wives with their children lived in her separate house within his large compound. He was on intimate terms with the King and exercised considerable power. He had by different wives three able and outstanding daughters, well known in Bangkok. Many a pleasant and profitable evening I have spent in his house.

Later, when revolution came, he with all the other royal princes was driven out of the country. He lived with his daughters for some years in Penang in the Straits Settlements, and, I believe, finally died there. When I visited Bangkok in 1953 I was touched by his daughter speaking of his deep regard and fondness for me and presenting me with a cherished china jar which he had always kept on the table beside him.

The Siamese are a gentle and lovable race. Their rich and fertile rice fields give them food a plenty, and the tropical heat relieves them of problems of clothing and costly shelter. Economically they are well off; and perhaps that is one reason why they are on the whole easy-going and free from worry. Most of the aggressive, pushing business enterprise in Siam, as in other parts of the Far East, is carried on by Chinese. Most of the rice mills are owned by Chinese. Among both Siamese and Chinese one cannot but feel an ancient, centuries-old culture; but that of the Siamese seems more winning and full of charm. Often as I came to know them I felt like a crude interloper of the West.

My office occupied a building at the Sapan Yosé, and my staff consisted of three assistants and the necessary stenographers. I worked directly under Prince Traidos, the Minister of Foreign Affairs.

Service with the Foreign Adviser was considered excellent training; and I was fortunate thus to have assisting me young men of ability and of promise. One of these was Prince Vipulya, who later became Private Secretary to King Prajadhipok. Another was Prince Wan Waithayakon, a grandson of King Chulalongkorn, exceptionally able and attractive. I saw much of him during my days in Bangkok; often we talked together about the East and the West, about Buddhism and Christianity. I always enjoyed his brilliant mind. Years later Prince Wan, as he came to be called, was appointed Thai Ambassador to Washington, and took a leading part in the affairs of the United Nations in New York. In the United Nations we found ourselves once again working closely together. When Thailand was elected a member of the U.N. Trusteeship Council, he, representing Thailand, sat beside me, representing the United States, at the Council Table; and always we saw eye to eye. In fact, I do not remember a single occasion when he found he must oppose the position taken by the United States representatives. He left the Trusteeship Council in April, 1952, called home by his government to serve as the Minister of Foreign Affairs. Today he is filling that important post with distinction and ability. In 1956 he was unanimously elected President of the U.N. General Assembly.

In my office at Bangkok, as problems arose, my staff would translate the pertinent papers from Siamese into English and pass the bulky files to me; I would draft such reply or such memorandum of advice as seemed to be appropriate, and this, translated into Siamese, would be passed on to the Minister of Foreign Affairs. Were Royal approval necessary he would take it to the King.

Several other ministries had their own foreign advisers: Finance, Agriculture, and Justice. The Siamese government, being independent, was never ruled by its advisers, as were some governments in colonial possessions. It sized up its advisers and used them only if it found them dependable and the advice sound. In such cases the adviser exercised a great deal of influence and authority. On the other hand, if the government mistrusted the adviser's judgment, he would seldom be consulted. Indeed, some advisers in Bangkok were scarcely ever turned to.

As a professor, quite green in diplomacy, one of my early experiences puzzled and amused me. The British Adviser in Finance had lived in Bangkok for years and had come to be much relied on by the Siamese government. His was an enviable place. Upon my arrival he took the position that the Adviser in Finance, a long-time resident, outranked the Adviser in Foreign Affairs, a brash newcomer, and that I must therefore call on him before he would call on me. My first impulse was to call on him and have a good laugh. But on second thought I realized that this was not a purely personal issue between ourselves but a question of precedence between two offices, that of Foreign Affairs always in the past having outranked Finance. There was reason for this, and I felt it important for the smooth operation of government that the Adviser in Foreign Affairs should continue to outrank all other advisers. The position of all my successors was at stake. I consulted the Minister of Foreign Affairs. He in turn consulted the King. Things seemed to be getting serious.

To avoid royal and perhaps international embarrassment I one day cut the Gordian knot by rushing unceremoniously into the Financial Adviser's office without appointment to ask his advice about a current matter that had just arisen. Henceforth, I judged correctly, he would feel free to come to my office, I having called upon him first. Here, as I thought, was a happy termination of the grave incident— until some time later I heard that he was abstaining from a *social* call upon me until I should make a social call upon him. I gave up.

In my official work I was never troubled by internal politics and politicians. I was under a liberal and utterly honest Minister of Foreign Affairs, who, so far as I can remember, followed always my advice. He was straightforward in his ways, and the slant of his mind seemed Western rather than Eastern. I was politically unimpeded in my work. But, I am told, this was not true in all the other Ministries.

In Bangkok all of us got on together as a fairly happy family. I used to mingle and talk freely with officials in other ministries, many of whom became my warm friends. Formality and pomp were reserved for the great ceremonials. At the royal cremations, the most formal of all royal ceremonies, I had to appear in black knee breeches, silk stockings (my wife's), and a cocked hat adorned with a magnificent ostrich plume.

The houses had porches and great open windows to catch the slightest breeze or stirring of air. This meant that snakes and scorpions could also enter, so that we tried always to avoid going around the house in the dark. One of my missionary friends had a strange experience with a cobra. As she hastily opened a bureau drawer one evening to pull out a scarf she saw a cobra coiled in the drawer. It had crawled up inside the bureau and found a soft and comfortable nest. She had the presence of mind quickly to slam the drawer shut and run to the kitchen for a kettle of boiling water. Opening the drawer a crack, she poured this in and killed the cobra.

Another missionary friend had to get up in the middle of the night to give her baby a bottle and went in the dark to the back porch to get the bottle out of the refrigerator. All was well until next morning, when she found a cobra on the threshold of the back door with its back broken. It had started to enter the house when she was getting the milk but had been caught in the doorway when she shut the door.

The Pasteur Institute, prepared to treat cobra bites, was always a comfort. Indeed this saved the life of the wife of the foreign adviser who succeeded me.

Our fear was of the cobras and the kraits. The pythons or boas were not poisonous. But I did have a strange feeling shortly after Jessie and the children had departed for America, when it was discovered that a huge python had been making its home in our compound.

For house servants we had Chinese boys. They spoke little English, and one always wondered how much they understood. Our Number One boy would mechanically say "Yes, yes" to every order given. They took exclusive possession of the kitchen, which the house mistress could not afford to lose face by entering, so that one never knew what might be set on the table at dinner. The hostess for a dinner party might have been very particular in working out the menu and telling the boy what was wanted; but often no dinner guest could have been more surprised than she by the dishes which appeared. Dinner parties were at eight o'clock; and always before the guests took their seats at the table gaily colored bags (*sarongs*) were passed around into which one stepped before sitting down so as to protect ankles and legs against swarming mosquitoes.

Through the daytime not a mosquito was to be seen. They were asleep in dark corners and inaccessible spots around the room. But as soon as darkness fell they appeared in swarms, eager for the hunt. Always we slept under carefully draped mosquito nets in spite of their effectually cutting off any stray breezes or moving air.

The winters were hot and dry; April was the hottest month of all. After April the rains began; almost every day there was rain. "You bake all winter, and stew all summer," we used to say. Some of the rains were torrential. Every pit or depression would fill up with water. And the fact was stoutly vouched for by some of my friends who ought to know, that sometimes in summer swimming fish could be found in pools of water that had been dry pits through the wintertime.

They also told of fish which could and did climb trees. I never believed this until one day I actually saw them—small, queer-looking fish, their mouths bubbling, lodged in the low branches of trees near the waterside. These same strange tree-climbing fish we saw again during our visit to Western Samoa.

My relations with the King were always warm and cordial. Now and again I would communicate with him by personal letter. He would reply by letter written in his own hand, occasionally twelve or fifteen pages in length. He wrote in excellent English. In fact, dur-

ing his education in Cambridge he had gained a fondness for Shakespeare and hoped to translate some of the Shakespeare plays into
Siamese.

Not long after our arrival in Bangkok Jessie and I received an
invitation from His Majesty to dinner at court with him. To please
us he had arranged a dinner, not in his modern quarters but in the
old palace, where formal dinners were seldom given. During the
sumptuous dinner he turned and said: "Wouldn't you like to see
some of the old rooms in the palace interior?" We expressed an enthusiastic "Yes," and to our delight he personally took us to see the
former Royal living quarters. So far as I know Jessie was the first
white woman ever to visit them.

Later in the evening he asked if our children had ever ridden
on an elephant.

"No," we were forced to confess, "they never have."

"I'll send my elephant around for them to have a ride on tomor-
row morning," he exclaimed.

And so the next morning the King's white elephant, resplendent
in royal trappings, majestically appeared in front of our house. The
children were in seventh heaven; they have never forgotten their
ride that morning upon the King's elephant.

There were tigers in Siam, and I should have liked to have a
tiger hunt. But the Siamese are good Buddhists, and the taking of
life is not in accordance with Buddhist teaching. Also, I was too hard
at work and never had the time. In northern Siam were many tigers;
occasionally a prowling tiger would even enter a village and make
away with a child.

Happily, Siam was for the most part free from the crushing burden of hunger and abysmally low standards of living such as weigh
down great parts of Asia and Africa. Because of her abundant rice
production Siam's national economy was rich. Thailand produces
today an annual rice surplus of 1,500,000 to 2,000,000 tons. Neither
does the land tenure and ownership pattern give rise to a large dispossessed and disgruntled group of farmers. Thailand's agricultural
economy is based almost entirely on small-scale, peasant-type family
operations, with a majority of the farm operators holding title to
their land. I believe there has never been a popular uprising in the
history of the country.

The fight had to be waged against disease and ignorance. When I came, there were said to be 10,000 lepers in Siam, many of them wandering the streets, begging. When I selected house boys on moving into our new house on the Phya Thai Road, medical examination proved two of them to be lepers. In the fight against leprosy, however, splendid progress was being made by an outstanding missionary, Dr. James W. McKean, who had established a leper asylum at Chiengmai in northern Siam with some 250 patients. There he was pushing forward the scientific treatment of the disease, attaining excellent results through the use of chaulmoogra oil.

One morning in early February in my office a personal telegram from Washington was handed to me. It told of the death of President Wilson. I sped home to break the news to Jessie. She was heartbroken. Together we attended next day the memorial services in the English church, which was packed to the doors. It seemed hard that Jessie must bear this tragedy so far from family and friends.

My work kept me constantly absorbed. A great obstacle to Siam's progress in those days lay in the "unequal" treaties between her and the Western nations. They had been made in the middle of the nineteenth century when aggressive Western traders were pushing forward into the Far East to capture the lucrative Eastern trade, and exempted all subjects of the treaty powers from the jurisdiction of Siamese courts. They also held the Siamese import tariff down to 3 per cent. These "extraterritorial treaties" had been entered into when Siamese tribunals knew nothing of Western justice. The unhappy fact was that they contained no time limit and no provisions for alteration or denunciation; and the indefensible evil was that, now that Siamese tribunals had advanced to a point where they could and did administer justice according to Western standards, the Western nations refused to allow any alteration or modification of the treaties. Rights of extraterritoriality were demanded not only for European subjects living or travelling in Siam, but also for Asiatics coming from the Asiatic colonies of these European treaty nations and for protégés attached to their Legations. As a result, Siam found herself stripped of the right to try in her own country not only European but Asiatic residents—Cambodians, Annamites, Javanese, Malayans, Burmese, Tamils, and Indians born in European colonial possessions. These could be tried only in foreign consular courts. Furthermore, Siam was prevented by the treaty restriction on her tariff from financing needed reforms. And all these treaties were without time limit, irrevocable.

Soon I found myself running into insoluble problems of extraterritoriality. For instance, we were trying to enforce a General Education law requiring compulsory school attendance. Over my desk came a refusal to send two girls, good Mohammedans, to school during the sacred month of Ramadan. Because their grandfather had been born in the British Shan states to the north, they claimed rights of extraterritoriality. I went to the British Minister and asked for help. He refused, claiming their rights as sacred.

Following the lead of the League of Nations, Siam was carrying on an active campaign against the smuggling of opium. Much opium was smuggled in from China over the northern frontier. Again and again a man caught redhanded smuggling opium across the border would produce papers showing he was a protégé of some treaty power and hence exempt from the jurisdiction of Siamese courts.

Or, again, the defendant in some criminal case might claim to have been born in Java or Malaya or Burma. Unless it could be proved that he had been born within Siamese territory he must be released for trial in the foreign consular court.

One foreign minister who presided over his own consular court was a good friend of mine. One day in his office he showed me the opium which as judge he had confiscated. Its value ran into thousands of dollars. He himself was not a lawyer, and I was.

"You have no right to keep this opium," I said. "It belongs to the Siamese government." He disagreed. "Can you show me any law of your country," I went on, "specifically authorizing you to acquire title to this opium?" He could not. "Then," said I laughingly, "some dark night I'm coming around to take possession of it; and you can't object because you can't prove it yours." We laughed together over so preposterous a suggestion.

A few days later I appeared and proceeded to put the opium into my car, joking with him the while. "What are you doing?" he exclaimed, perturbed. But before serious objection could be made I was off with the opium.

I took it to the Siamese Ministry administering opium control and gave it to the Prince in charge, saying: "Here is a consignment of opium of considerable value. You are to receive it as belonging to the Siamese government. From whence it came you will not know. No questions of any kind are to be asked."

I was never asked about it again. But when I visited Bangkok thirty years later I was told that from that time on the minister had made it a practice to hand over to Siamese officials all opium confiscated in his consular court.

I remember, too, the difficulties which always confronted us in cases of law enforcement as to the defendant's true nationality. He could always claim to have been born in Java or Malaya or other neighboring area and thus to be entitled to exemption from the jurisdiction of Siamese courts. Shamefully I confess that sometimes the solution I sought lay through quite extralegal channels. With the same minister from whom I took the opium I used to play frequent games of tennis. Sometimes the question would arise between us as to whether a certain accused individual was or was not born, as he claimed, within a specified colonial area. Often the minister had no way of proving he was, and I had no way of proving that he was not. I have in mind one or two occasions when I jokingly proposed settling the question by a friendly game of tennis: the winner of the tennis match should have the man. I knew that when pushed I could always beat the minister. Thus Siam would get its man.

The Siam of that day was poised between the East and the West. King Rama VI had been sent by his father, the illustrious King Chulalongkorn, to Cambridge University in England, where he studied Shakespeare and the English classics. After his return he followed many of the Western practices, sometimes to the astonishment of the Siamese. Some years after his marriage to the Queen he fell in love with another girl. Polygamy was an accepted practice, and there was nothing to prevent his taking into the court a second wife. Instead he put his first wife aside and lived, following the practice of the West, solely with the second. That outraged the Siamese people. Their feeling was that under the sensible system of polygamy every wife as well as her children has legal protection and acknowledged rights in the household. It seemed to them highly immoral and outrageous under this barbarous Western custom to throw a wife aside and put a new woman in her place. Here was another example of how Western practices and customs, introduced into Far Eastern countries without time for proper assimilation, can make for hardship and suffering.

Siam is a Buddhist country, and in its life its yellow-robed priests play a vital part. In Siam and in Burma is to be found Buddhism perhaps at its best. Numbering over 200,000, the Buddhist priesthood is a highly influential and respected segment of Thai society. The Buddhist code of ethics is in many ways close to the Christian, and many of my friends were staunch Buddhists.

On one occasion I was dining in the home of Prince Traidos, whose little daughter lay critically ill upstairs. They did not know whether she would live.

"Have you prayed for her?" I asked my host.

"Oh, no! We do not pray," he replied. "Buddha taught that God is too high, too utterly incomprehensible, to be reached directly by human prayer."

"Then I as a Christian am going to pray for her," I replied. I did so. She later recovered.

Years afterwards, when as the wife of the Counsellor of the Siamese Embassy in Washington she was dining at our home, she told my wife and me that her father believed and had always told her that I was the man who saved her life.

During my stay in Bangkok I came to know and admire H.R.H. Prince Mahidol Songkla, another son of King Chulalongkorn, who had done so much during his long reign to open up Siam to the Western world and build the modern Kingdom. And because Prince Mahidol was one of Siam's best the telling of his story may not be out of place.

During his early years Prince Mahidol had been sent by his father to study in Germany, and he was slated to head the Siamese navy. At the German capital he used to see Kaiser Wilhelm and occasionally was entertained by the Kaiser at Potsdam. But as he matured he kept asking himself, "Why a Siamese navy?" As a result of his growing convictions and his belief that what Siam needed most was an understanding of how to fight disease he decided to abandon a naval career and to devote himself instead to the study of medicine and public health. So, with the King's permission, he came to Boston to study at the Harvard Medical School.

In Boston he fell in love with a Siamese girl who had been sent to America to study nursing—a commoner, without any royal blood. Prince Mahidol wrote to the King that he wanted to marry her. The King at first refused to hear of such a thing. But Prince Mahidol insisted and ended by marrying her.

Upon the completion of his medical course Prince Mahidol sought to become an interne in Chulalongkorn Hospital in Bangkok. But he was not permitted to do so because of his royal rank. Not many years had passed since it had been death even to touch the person of the King. How could a King's son be permitted to work in a hospital?

As I saw Prince Mahidol during my stay in Bangkok, winning in appearance, intelligent, straightforward in his gaze, I found him a rare young man—unassuming, intensely democratic, thoroughly modern in his outlook. In Bangkok he had little to do; and because he could not bear to be idle, a few years later he returned to Harvard with his wife for graduate study in public health and medicine. By then I also had left Bangkok and returned to Harvard, and in Boston I saw much of him. A substantial part of his princely revenues he was spending to send Siamese students to America for study; occasionally he even had to borrow money from me. He and his wife were living in the simplest and most democratic way without a maid in a Boston apartment. They did their own housework. His second child, Prince Phumiphon, was born in a hospital in Cambridge close by our home so that they could be near Jessie and me; and for a week after the baby was born they awaited a cable from the King in Bangkok giving the child his name.

During the summer Prince Mahidol rented a cottage close to ours on our beloved island of Martha's Vineyard, and we shared many afternoons and evenings together.

In April, 1928, Prince Mahidol fell seriously ill and was taken to a Boston hospital. Fearing the illness might prove fatal, he asked me to come and take down a dying statement touching upon the possibility of one of his children coming to the throne of Siam. In this he asked the King not to make either of them heir to the throne.

Happily he recovered his health; and in July he returned to Bangkok. Just before leaving he wrote me:

We are sailing next Sunday. I am therefore obliged to use this very unsatisfactory means of saying goodbye to you. Nevertheless, I want you to know that I am deeply grateful to you for all the world of good you and Mrs. Sayre have done us while we were here. . . . I will never forget your kindness. It has been the purest pleasure to have been associated with you and to have learned to know both of you. Thanks for ever! . . .

My wife joins me in sending our most affectionate regards to you and Mrs. Sayre and best love to the children.

MAHIDOL

From Bangkok, Prince Mahidol sent me a long letter dated February 27, 1929, in which he wrote:

I am still jobless. The idea of my entering into hospital service did not appeal to anybody. . . . Evidently they are bent on starting me into the already overcrowded career of general administration. I am of course quite prepared for this sort of disappointment. . . .

They pay more attention to things that are tangible, whereas health, education and spiritual and moral regeneration seem so remote that much money has not been given for such subjects. . . .

The energetic suppression of crime is another feature that seems to impress. But again, here, the efforts are directed towards catching thieves rather than investigation of the economic and moral causes of the condition.

We all send our best love to you and Mrs. Sayre.

A year or two later Prince Mahidol and his family, visiting in Switzerland, entered his two children at Jessie's and my suggestion in the little school at Chailly near Lausanne where we had placed our children; and in Lausanne the children were brought up, under their mother's care, attending school and later the university.

Prince Mahidol in the meantime returned to Bangkok and again asked the King's permission to work at Chulalongkorn Hospital. When this was refused he sought out my friend, Dr. E. C. Cort, a Presbyterian missionary running a mission hospital at Chiengmai in the north of Siam. Dr. Cort welcomed him with open arms; and there for several years he worked like any other doctor, never sparing himself, consecrated to his work. Not long after that he died, giving himself heroically, as he did all his life, to the people of Siam.

Shortly afterwards Dr. David L. Edsall, dean of the Harvard Medical School, where Prince Mahidol Songkla had studied, wrote to me:

I cannot forgo sending on to you a comment from an interesting friend of mine to whom I gave some letters to be presented on a trip in the Orient, among others a letter to Prince Songkla, whose death we all regret so deeply. Writing from Bangkok he makes the following comment:

"Americans are in very high favor but none equal to Mr. Sayre. As Dr. Ellis says, he could be King of Siam."

I thought perhaps you might want to prepare for that job.

I have been so very much impressed by the whole character of Songkla and all the fine feeling he left behind him here as well as wherever he went. . . . His extraordinary combination of gentleness, sweetness, intelligence and democracy in a person who came from such high position is one of the most striking things I have ever seen.

The sequel to his story lies in his children. When King Prajadhipok, the successor of King Rama VI, died leaving no children, Prince Mahidol's elder son, Prince Ananda, still at Lausanne attending the university, was chosen to the throne of Thailand. The young boy knew almost nothing of Thailand, nor did the Thai people know him. His mother wondered whether she could let him go. But the call was too strong; and to Bangkok he went and was crowned King. Not long afterwards he was found one morning in his room shot to death. Following his assassination his younger brother was chosen to be King. His mother, in Switzerland with him, wondered how she could possibly send her second son perhaps to his doom. Nevertheless, she bravely faced her duty and he too went to Bangkok.

Today, with a beautiful and gracious young wife, he sits on the throne of Thailand. Educated in the West, born of parents who for a time lived the democratic life in America and sacrificed much to prepare themselves for a life of service, King Phumiphon is a ruler whose reign augurs well for the future of modern Thailand. The Thai people are rallying loyally around him.

* * *

As spring approached in Bangkok, Jessie and I found the increasing heat almost unbearable. We had no air cooling, no artificial refrigeration, and even ice was precious. It was more than a week's journey to the nearest habitable hill station in Java or India; and the doctor advised that the children should not remain in Bangkok through April, the hottest month, or through the blistering summer. To guard the children's health the only way seemed to be for Jessie to take them back to America while I remained in Bangkok with the work I had undertaken. That almost broke our hearts.

When March arrived we all journeyed together down to Penang; and there I put Jessie and the children, our faithful friend and helper Sally Scott, and Billy Palmer, a missionary's little boy whom for a time we were taking into our family, on a ship for America. It felt like my own execution.

I tried my best to put on a brave face and struggled to keep back the tears until the goodbyes were said and the ship left the pier and steamed away. I watched it to the last.

I stayed on in Bangkok until September. It was a time of piercing loneliness. There was no airmail in those days; and every letter to America took four or five weeks.

I tried to lose myself in my work. After breaking up our home on the Phya Thai Road I took up bachelor quarters in the American Legation through the kindness of Mr. Brodie, the American Minister, and later in the Presbyterian Mission with one of the missionaries.

When the scorching summer heat was upon us the drive of work slackened. I sought relaxation in short trips away from Bangkok. With one or two friends I journeyed to Angkor Wat—in those days, before the railway was built, comparatively inaccessible. At Angkor have been uncovered the remains of stone palaces and temples built in the twelfth century and long ago overgrown by forest. The temple of Bayon is surmounted by fifty towers decorated with great quadruple faces of Brahma, built at intervals upon the galleries. The beauty of the temple of Angkor Wat, built without arches, lies in its exquisitely carved bas reliefs and stonework; its long passageways and galleries are crowded with intricate and rare carvings, perhaps executed by Indian craftsmen, but giving interesting pictures of Khmer life. It has been described as "one of the summits to which human genius has aspired in stone."

When hostile armies conquered the Khmer people and destroyed the city of Angkor the stone temples remained; but, overgrown with jungle in the centuries that followed, they were completely forgotten. Western travellers across Cambodia in the nineteenth century stumbled onto the ancient temple; and with the jungle now being cut away by French archaeologists, it stands out as one of the impressive sights of the Far East.

Today Angkor is easily accessible by railway, and even boasts of a comfortable hotel.

On another trip, into Java, I landed at Batavia and travelled up to Bandung, and thence to the ninth-century Barabudur Temple on its terraced mound, surrounded by stone galleries and crowned with exquisitely carved images of the Dhyāni-Buddhas. It stands today an unforgettable relic of Java's gloried past.

But these trips, in spite of their interest and fascination, could not dispel the aching loneliness; and I began counting the days until I could rejoin my family in America.

8

Breaking Siam's Nineteenth Century Shackles

My work in Siam seemed increasingly impeded by the shackles of the outworn treaties. As has been said, the exemption from the jurisdiction of Siamese courts not only of all Europeans dwelling in Siam, but also of all Asiatic subjects of European colonies in Asia, and even of foreign "protégés," barred progress and efficient administration again and again. So did the requirement under the treaties that no tariff above 3 per cent be levied on imports. Sorely needed improvements could not be financed. To me the continued insistence by the so-called Christian nations of the West upon these outworn treaty rights seemed intolerable.

But when I said, "These old unjust treaties must go," the King pointed out that the treaties contained no provisions for termination; and that whereas Japan, building up military and naval strength, had succeeded in ending the hated "unequal treaties" similarly imposed upon her, Siam possessed no substantial military power and had nothing to offer the West in return for giving up the treaties. Again and again, as he pointed out, the Siamese government had pressed for their termination by appealing to the resident representatives of the Western powers, only to be met by a blank refusal and an unyielding insistence upon the continuance of the profitable treaty rights.

I said that this was in its way understandable; that local representatives are not always broad-minded. I urged that the appeal be brought directly to the foreign offices of the ten European countries refusing to surrender the old treaty rights. Although Siam had nothing to offer in exchange I urged that once more the attempt be made, this time by strong appeal brought in a personal way directly to each of the ten European foreign ministers or heads of government.

I was taken aback by the King's reply: "Are you yourself willing to undertake such a task for Siam?" I was caught. How could I refuse?

Accordingly I prepared to sail from Bangkok in late September for Hong Kong, Japan, and the United States, pick up my family there and proceed to Europe on the arduous undertaking. Armed with a roving commission, I was to spend the ensuing year seeking to convince one after another of the foreign offices of Europe of the wisdom of giving up their existing rights in Siam.

Before my departure the Siamese Government graciously awarded to me the Grand Cross of the Crown of Siam. But what pleased me most was the King's conferring upon me a distinctive Siamese name and title: Phya Kalyan Maitri. "Phya" is a title of high nobility; and "Kalyan Maitri" means "the beautiful in friendship." By this name I am known throughout Thailand today.

I had grown very fond of the Siamese people; and when Phya Devesra, the Grand Chamberlain, asked me to take his young son Sivawongse to America with me to study there and become a part of my family, I gladly promised to do so. The boy had never been away from home. We sailed, the only passengers, in late September on a small two-cabined ship for Hong Kong; and when we were well out on the China Sea a raging typhoon struck us. It was a terrifying experience at best; it was appalling to a youngster who had just said goodbye to all he loved and who had never been to sea. The wind reached a velocity well over a hundred miles an hour; it screamed and howled, deluging our ship with great masses of driving water. Creaking and groaning, our boat labored heavily; no meals could be served; our trunks on the stateroom floors were wallowing in water. Could the little ship stand up in such a raging storm? I brought the terrified boy into my cabin and comforted him as best I could. We were not sure we would come out alive. Years later, when I had forgotten everything except the fury of the storm, to my astonishment he told me everything I had said to him that wild afternoon.

In the United States our train crossing the Rocky Mountains in Colorado ran into snow. He had never seen snow before. At one station I got out, picked up a handful of snow, and pressed it against his fingers. He jerked them back. "It's all cold," he cried excitedly.

"Of course it is," I replied. "You know that snow is cold."

"Yes, I know," he answered. "I've seen snow in American movies. But somehow I never quite realized before that it's biting-cold."

More is needed than the reading of books and the seeing of pictures to bring the West and the East into understanding unity and comprehension of each other.

But the radiant climax of the trip, which stands out all my life, was the intense moment when our train pulled into Boston. There on the station platform Jessie with shining face was running up the platform to meet me. With moist eyes we held each other close. With her and the children, I found, all was going well. They, too, had been counting the days until my return. The haunting loneliness fell away from my heart; once more our family was reunited.

From Prince Traidos, the Siamese Minister of Foreign Affairs, came a heart-warming letter of affectionate farewell:

> I cannot express to you adequately how sad and lonely I feel since your departure from this country. During the short time you were here, you have been to me not only an Official Adviser but also a true and loyal friend . . . How much I miss you no words can sufficiently describe.

He referred to new difficulties which had arisen in the French negotiations and the importance of early agreement,

> as the fate of all the other treaties depends upon the successful conclusion of this Treaty.
>
> As for the British Treaty, I have already telegraphed to you that the British Government had replied that they wished to negotiate in Bangkok. . . . Probably they will try to put off the negotiation as they have been doing in the past . . .
>
> Of all the foreign countries which still enjoy extraterritorial rights, Holland is the most troublesome and the most difficult to deal with . . . It is getting worse and worse since your departure.

He concluded by outlining unreasonable demands made by the Italian Minister in Bangkok and the difficulties to be expected in Rome.

When a month later I sailed with Jessie and the children to France for the treaty negotiations, I had to place Sivawongse in a Cambridge school where he could continue his studies. I remember how the tears streamed down his face the day I had to tell him good-bye. He would not see me again for months; and I was his last tie with home.

We sailed with mingled feelings, wondering what would be the outcome. To secure from ten different European foreign offices a reversal of policy and a voluntary relinquishment of valuable treaty rights with no offer of any compensating return seemed indeed no mean task.

Of all the Treaty Powers the United States alone had agreed to relinquish its treaty rights. In the First World War Siam had thrown in her lot with the Allies and declared war against Germany; she sent to France an expeditionary force with a substantial number of fliers. When the war was won Siam appealed to her allies gathered around the council table at Versailles.

"We have all been fighting," she said, "shoulder to shoulder for the rights of small nations and for the great cause of humanity. If, as so often proclaimed, we have in truth been fighting to protect the weak against the rapacious strong and to remove some of the old injustices that make for war, is it not right and fair that Siam should be freed from the outworn treaty restrictions of an earlier day which under the changed conditions in Siam have lost all reason for existence?"

The diplomats shifted in their chairs; a few fair words were spoken; but of all those present only one took definite action. President Wilson replied: "You are right. America will give to Siam a new treaty relinquishing the old extraterritorial rights; and she will give it as an act of justice, freely and without price." It was the new note in international diplomacy; justice and international right meant more than empty words.

In 1920 President Wilson gave to Siam the treaty which he had promised. Without compensation and without secret understanding of any sort, America, recognizing the efficient administration of justice which Siam had achieved, surrendered all rights of extraterritoriality, provided only that the American consul should have the right, up to five years after the promulgation of the last of the Siamese codes of law, to evoke out of the Siamese courts any case involving American citizens should this seem necessary in the interests of justice. Although as a matter of fact the right of evocation under the American treaty has never been exercised, this wise provision furnished to American citizens a guaranty against possible judicial abuse, one which Siam could gladly give because of her confidence in her own courts. Furthermore, the new treaty abrogated the earlier American treaty of 1856 in its entirety; and America, recognizing Siam's right to fiscal autonomy, agreed that Siam should have the right to impose any tariff she pleased against American goods, provided that all the other Treaty Powers agreed to similar provisions without compensation or price. The new treaty was made terminable after a ten-year period upon one year's notice by either party, and it was expressly provided that such termination would not revive the formal treaty. Through America led the path to freedom.

After the American treaty was signed, Siam asked Great Britain and France to follow America's lead. Favorable replies were given but little seemed to come of them. As a result of the war in which Siam had taken part, Germany and Austria had indeed lost their treaty rights; but unhappily there remained Great Britain, France, Italy, Holland, Belgium, Denmark, Norway, Sweden, Spain, and Portugal; and these countries refused to yield their old treaty rights. Finally, however, France had been prevailed upon to negotiate a new treaty in Bangkok, and negotiations were actually begun.

It had been my great hope that the French negotiations could be brought to a successful conclusion and the treaty signed before my departure from Bangkok; but as each difficulty was overcome new obstacles arose, and every new obstacle caused fresh delays. Nevertheless, by the end of the summer, general agreement had apparently been reached on the main provisions of the treaty draft. France was to renounce all the provisions of former treaties except those which concerned Indo-China, and to grant to Siam judicial autonomy subject to a limited right of evocation and fiscal autonomy on the same lines as in the American treaty. Most important of all, the new treaty was to be terminable after ten years by either party.

Upon reaching Paris early in December, 1924, however, to my dismay I found that new questions had arisen; the discussion of certain underlying principles revealed sharply diverging interpretations by the French and the Siamese governments; and to the French interpretation the Siamese government found itself quite unable to agree. Negotiations must be taken up afresh in Paris. We put our children into a French school and settled down to work. Several weeks of anxious, intensive effort followed. By the middle of January the French Foreign Office finally agreed to a formula satisfactory to Siam. After complete agreement on the treaty draft had been reached among ourselves, the text was laid before the French Cabinet and its consent won. Finally a date—January 31—was set for the signing. Success seemed at hand.

During the ten days' interval while the treaty text was being printed preparatory to the signing, I proceeded to The Hague to open negotiations for a new Dutch treaty. Three days before the date set for signing the French treaty, came a telegram from the French Foreign Office in Paris. It told of a murderous attack in Bangkok upon the wife of the French legal adviser and announced that the treaty therefore could not be signed. The news burst upon us like a bombshell.

I rushed back to Paris heavy of heart and cabled to Bangkok for a full report. For several critical days the outcome hung in the balance. What I most feared was a hostile campaign in the French press, which might easily kill the treaty. Bangkok's cabled reply, however, gave room for hope: the attack had been made without malice by an irresponsible individual too drunk to know what he was doing. Exactly similar attacks might have happened on the streets of Paris or New York.

But the difficult task remained of convincing the Foreign Office of the truth of these facts in the face of an adverse report from the French Chargé at Bangkok, and of getting action without incurring the long delays of a judicial trial. Until the French treaty was signed there was little hope of securing other treaties. It was not enough that the French Foreign Office finally agreed to ask for no indemnities.

For the sake of the other treaties France must be persuaded to sign the treaty forthwith in the face of this unhappy incident, and without additional demands or modifications. Fortunately the affair had so far been kept out of the French press; but the downfall of the Herriot Ministry was already threatened, and the Foreign Office feared that if the treaty were signed in complete disregard of such an incident the opposition press might still print an exaggerated version of the event and cause the overthrow of the government. Anxious days followed, filled with discussions, lengthy cable dispatches, persuasions, proposals, and counterproposals. For a week the outcome lay in the lap of the gods. We were fortunate in that M. Pila, the French Minister in Bangkok, who was liberal in his viewpoint and was a friend of mine, was in Paris for the talks and negotiations; he had first-hand knowledge of the progress being made in Siam and proved to be most helpful. In the end Siam's efforts prevailed. On February 14, at one o'clock, Premier Herriot as Minister of Foreign Affairs, and Prince Charoon, the Siamese Minister in Paris, attached their signatures to the document that meant so much for the future of Siam. Victory, after months of uncertainty and struggle, had come at last.

The delay in getting the French treaty signed prevented the opening of British negotiations until late in February. Our children were progressing well in their Paris school, and Jessie decided to remain with them while I crossed the Channel to open negotiations in London. The outlook was discouraging. The British Minister to Bangkok had been in London in conference with the Foreign Office and had just departed for Siam. The British Labor government, which had shown a friendly interest in Siam, had been overthrown and succeeded by a Conservative government. Furthermore, when, several months before, the Siamese Minister of Foreign Affairs had suggested a treaty revision, Great Britain had given a noncommittal reply, but requested that if conversations should be opened they should be carried on in Bangkok—a request which the Siamese Minister felt unable to refuse. Altogether the situation seemed far from hopeful.

Austen Chamberlain, in my opening interview at the Foreign Office, presented the British point of view with great frankness and fairness. The United States, he said, could afford to surrender existing treaty privileges in Siam, because American trade there was, comparatively speaking, non-existent. The British situation was very different. Over 80 per cent of the entire Siamese export trade was to British territory. If Siam should be released from the 3 per cent tariff restriction and should suddenly impose a heavy import tariff, great hardship would result to British merchants. For this reason, while Great Britain might agree to a moderate increase in the existing 3 per cent restriction, she could not justifiably grant to Siam complete tariff autonomy. Furthermore, British trade in Siam had assumed such substantial proportions that Great Britain could not afford to risk jeopardizing her commercial interests in Siamese law courts without adequate protection; the presence of European legal advisers in the Consular courts constituted the surest guaranty of such protection. For these reasons, Mr. Chamberlain felt that the time was premature to surrender the existing treaty privileges.

These arguments seemed, in the light of immediate interests, difficult to answer; nevertheless I could not but feel that in the long view it would be a mistake for Great Britain to hold to such a position. Mr. Chamberlain listened to the reasons I gave with an uncommonly open mind; and he attentively considered my suggestions for securing practical and adequate protection for British interests in Siam by methods framed to avoid infringing Siamese sovereignty or wounding her people's national pride.

At the end of an hour Mr. Chamberlain had convinced me of his sincerity and his fair-mindedness. "We had made up our minds to refuse the things you ask," he said. "But you have put a new light upon the situation. What you propose seems to me reasonable and fair. If you can convince the experts and heads of departments of the Foreign Office, of the Board of Trade and the Department of Overseas Trade, of the Colonial Office and of the Indian Office—if you can convince them as you have me, while I can't make any definite promises, I don't see why we shouldn't be able to enter upon negotiations along the line you propose." Siam had won her fighting chance!

A day in the following week was appointed for Siam to argue her case before the assembled representatives of the several ministries concerned. In the meantime my concrete written proposals were submitted to the various government departments, and were further

explained and urged in intimate personal conferences with those
who were particularly influential.

On the appointed day I met with the assemblage of British
representatives around a long table in the British Foreign Office.
Everything depended on the outcome. It was clear that, if Great
Britain refused to give Siam a new treaty, Italy would likewise refuse. Also Portugal and Spain, and probably Denmark, Norway, and
Sweden. We discussed the British position in Siam from almost every
angle; the British experts showed by searching questions how carefully they had studied my proposals and suggestions, and for a whole
afternoon, amid the rapid fire of question and answer, the tide of
battle hung uncertain. All forms of diplomacy had been dropped;
with utter frankness we sought to reach the fundamental truth. I
endeavored to explain the weak as well as the strong points of my
proposals; and the British representatives were equally frank and
aboveboard.

I kept emphasizing the importance from Great Britain's viewpoint of following a policy which would build up British trade in
Siam; and I pointed out that if Great Britain for her future trade
chose to depend upon treaty restrictions which impeded genuine
progress, and which therefore must stir up increasing Siamese irrita-
tion and ill will, Siam must turn to more liberal countries with a
consequent impairment of British trade. I urged that the strongest
and wisest trade policies were built upon a generous and a fair approach, and that the one-sided and outlived treaty provisions imposed upon Siam in the nineteenth century were neither generous
nor fair. At the end of the day we saw eye to eye, and the British
Foreign Office said, "We'll give you a treaty along the lines which you
propose."

Followed a month's intensive work of hammering out a draft
which would relieve Siam from the old, unjust restrictions and yet
would not leave British interests unprotected. It was agreed to wipe
away all the former treaties, and to replace them by a new general
treaty and a comprehensive commercial treaty framed in the new
spirit along the lines of my initial proposals. We held numerous
meetings with assembled representatives of various British offices and
found our minds clashing over many technical details and questions
of minor importance. Intricate legal problems arose over the rights

of children born in Siam whose parents were natives of Burma or of British protectorates; questions arose as to the probate of estates of British subjects dying in Siam. The position of India and the self-governing British Dominions with regard to treaty rights and privileges in Siam opened up fresh complications and problems. These and a hundred other questions furnished many contentious points; yet never once during the negotiations was there resort to subterfuge or concealment. We sought a common object, and in mutual whole-hearted confidence hurdled all obstacles.

By the end of March we had provisionally agreed upon drafts which embodied even more than I had originally planned to ask. Without compensation Great Britain agreed to surrender all existing treaty privileges in Siam and to recognize in terms precisely the same as those in the American treaty Siam's complete right to judicial and fiscal autonomy. The old treaties had been irrevocable and eternal; the new general and commercial treaties were made terminable after ten years by either party. Siam in return agreed not to impose any customs duty in excess of 5 per cent upon textiles, upon iron, steel, or manufactures thereof, or upon machinery manufactured in British territory and imported into Siam; but this undertaking was limited to ten years after the coming into force of the treaty, after which Siam's hands were free. In short, Great Britain agreed that henceforth British influence in Siam should be built upon Siamese good will rather than upon irritating and irrevocable treaty restrictions. It was a farseeing step for Britain to take. The provisional treaty drafts were mailed to Bangkok to receive the detailed consideration of the Siamese government and the comments of the British Minister; the five or six weeks which must elapse before cabled replies could come would afford me an opportunity to inaugurate negotiations in other countries.

During the work on the British treaty I had also been carrying on conversations with the Netherlands government; the night boat across the Channel made it possible often to spend alternate days in London and The Hague. The Netherlands' response to Siam's appeal was generous; friendly understanding and mutual confidence smoothed away all difficulties. The questions raised by the Netherlands treaty were far less complicated and fewer than those raised by the British; consequently, the draft of a new Dutch agreement progressed even more rapidly. By the time the British drafts were completed a new Netherlands treaty text had also been agreed upon, closely following the American model. The day following the dispatch of the British text the Netherlands draft was mailed to Bangkok. In the opening days of April I took the train to Italy.

At Rome I urged Siam's case first before individual, influential officials of the Foreign Office, and later before a formal group appointed to consider the question of a new treaty. Italian interests in Siam were comparatively small; and Italy saw little reason for changing the existing situation. The progress of the negotiations was so slow and uncertain that I arranged for a conference with Premier Mussolini; but illness prevented him from keeping the engagement. Time pressed; and, leaving Rome, I returned to Paris and took the *Sud Express* for Lisbon.

A new Portuguese treaty was of particular importance to Siam; for large numbers of Chinese residents claimed exemption as Portuguese protégés by virtue of alleged birth in the Portuguese colony of Macao near Hong Kong. Proof of the falsity of each claim by patient investigation failed to deter others from the same practice; apparently this was only one of the inevitable and incurable outgrowths of the system of extraterritoriality.

The political situation at Lisbon was peculiar. Ministry succeeded ministry with startling rapidity; the regularity of the process seemed to be broken only by revolution. A minister's hearty support might prove to be valueless with his removal a few weeks later. The frequent changing of cabinet positions concentrated power in the hands of the permanent officials. Yet these could not be reached except through their minister. Accordingly we first held conferences with Dr. Joaquim Martins, Minister of Foreign Affairs. After his support had been gained, no one could have been more gracious to us than he; yet, as I well knew, the real battle still lay ahead.

Of Dr. Antonio D. de Oliveira Soares, Director General of Commercial Affairs, I had been warned on several sides: if the path of our treaty led through his office, I was told, our quest would prove wellnigh impossible, for he was exceptionally difficult to win and, once having made a decision, adhered unwaveringly to it. Some called him stubborn. My hopes fell when I discovered that he headed one of the important divisions of the Foreign Office and no treaty could pass without his sanction. After conferences with several other heads of divisions varying in success, I secured an appointment with him on the last day of April.

With rather gloomy forebodings I walked down the long, highly ornamented corridors to the former bedchamber of the King, which with the coming of the Republic had been converted into an office. To my delight I found a man of brains and character who had studied and digested our proposed treaty draft, and was prepared to act. I entered into detailed discussions with him, and that very afternoon agreed to various modifications in the draft; and when we parted I realized that of all in Lisbon he best understood the point of view of Siam. He proved to be our staunchest friend; when seemingly insurmountable obstacles arose in other divisions of the Foreign Office, he championed our cause and overcame the opposition. Had it not been for him, Siam in all probability would not have won the treaty.

In the end the provisional consent of the various officials to a treaty closely following the American model, and also embodying a general arbitration clause, was won. The draft could not be finally approved, however, until it had gone before various bureaus and legislative committees. Our friends in the Foreign Office promised to expedite matters and to defend the draft if necessary; in the meantime negotiations could be opened in Spain.

In Madrid fortune favored us. On the day of my arrival the King was to attend the races; and the American Ambassador invited me to accompany him to the gala luncheon at the race course, where I was introduced to General Primo de Rivera, President of the Military Directorate, and to others close to His Majesty. That very afternoon, thanks to the American Ambassador, His Majesty heard about our Siamese treaty.

Next day there followed a conference with the all-powerful General Primo de Rivera; and, once his wholehearted consent had been won, success was assured. He promised us the treaty and appointed a commission to carry on the negotiations, placing at its head his nephew, Fernando Espinosa de los Monteros, the acting head of the Spanish Foreign Office. Every evening we gathered around a table at the Foreign Office in a large red room resplendent with fine old paintings; we modified only in quite unimportant details the original treaty draft which I had presented. In little more than a week the work was done, and Spain had agreed to surrender the old treaty and accept a new one closely following the lines of the American treaty. The commission good-naturedly laughed at my informality and my continual plea for speed. "You Americans would like to make a treaty over the telephone," they exclaimed.

From Madrid I returned by way of Paris to The Hague for the ceremonies attendant upon the signing of the treaty by the Netherlands, on June 8. That day disturbing news arrived from London. The Foreign Office wrote that the British Minister in Bangkok had raised serious objections to the draft of the new treaty. Apparently local British opposition in Bangkok was too strong. After further mature consideration in view of the Minister's cable, the Foreign Office must ask for certain additions and modifications to the draft. A glance at the changes asked made my heart sink. To certain of them Siam could not accede. Did this, then, spell the end of all our hopes?

I rushed back to London, realizing that the adverse report had made it necessary to fight again. A formal meeting was arranged with the experts and representatives of the Foreign Office, the Board of Trade, the Indian Office, and the Colonial Office, and with the former British Consul-General in Siam, who had been summoned for the occasion. For a whole afternoon the battle raged. I sought to explain why Siam could not accept certain of the proposed modifications, and why it would be a mistake for Great Britain to request them; why some of the demands were unnecessary and others could be satisfied in more practicable ways. It was one against many, and the battle never flagged. "You reminded me of Daniel in the lions' den," exclaimed one of the British representatives at the end of the afternoon. But, when the smoke of battle cleared away, the sun was shining. Great Britain had agreed to withdraw all the objectionable modifications, or to alter them to a quite unobjectionable form. The British treaty was won. During two more all-afternoon sessions such difficulties as remained were ironed out; and in individual conferences during the next ten days solutions were found for several highly technical but extremely difficult legalistic problems, and in addition a treaty of general arbitration was negotiated and agreed upon.

Some years later Prince Damrong of Siam wrote to me that he

had just been talking with Sir Austen Chamberlain in London about the treaty: "He told me frankly that the treaty with Siam was much opposed by British representatives in Bangkok. But he was so convinced by your explanation of the benefit of the revision that he overruled them."

By mid July the general and commercial treaties were ready for signature. I hurried down from Stockholm for the signing; and on the afternoon of July 14 Mr. Chamberlain and Phya Prabha Karavongse, the Siamese Minister to London, unostentatiously attached their signatures and seals to the documents of such vital importance to Siam. The new British treaty had come into being.

Shortly thereafter I was touched by a letter from Sydney Waterlow, the head of the Far Eastern Division of the Foreign Office and later British Minister to Siam, who had carried the brunt of British negotiations. After the signing of the treaty, I had heard of his personal bereavement and had sent him a short note of sympathy. He answered:

I was greatly touched—and helped—by your letter. This has indeed been a hard time—complicated by public anxieties—and nothing has done so much to ease it as the sympathy and the expressed goodness of friends, among whom I hope you will allow yourself to be numbered.

I don't know whether we shall ever meet again, but who can tell? Anyhow, to have met you and to have had dealings with you have been for me something on which I shall always look back with extreme pleasure and satisfaction. It was an oasis in the monotonous desert of official routine and official personalities, none the less welcome for the surprise of stumbling upon it. Whatever the eventual outcome of the Siamese business, thanks to you I go on my way heartened and encouraged.

I send you every good wish and my warmest thanks. Let us never despair!

In the meantime I had been turning my attention to the Scandinavian countries, Denmark, Norway, and Sweden, and to Italy. Should any one of these refuse to give up its existing rights, Siam must remain bound by the old 3 per cent tariff restriction on imports from all countries alike; for all the new treaties contained the provision that Siam should be free to raise its tariff only after every one of the nations holding irrevocable treaty rights had freely and without compensatory benefit agreed to surrender them. Quite apart, therefore, from the existence of considerable Scandinavian shipping interests in Bangkok, each one of these treaties was a matter of large importance to Siam.

In Copenhagen, in Stockholm, and in Oslo, again we encountered an open-mindedness, a sympathetic understanding for the plucky struggle of a small nation, and a readiness to translate sympathy into practical action which showed that, in spite of much that is said to the contrary, European foreign offices are not all closed to liberal sentiments. The three Scandinavian countries declared themselves ready to meet with Siam's desires and to give new treaties. In Denmark and Sweden, influential friends at court expedited negotiations, and final agreement was reached on the drafts of the treaties, which were to be signed in the early fall as soon as the parliamentary committees could formally signify their approval. Norway also promised a new treaty along the same general lines, and quickly agreed in principle to the draft proposed.

To Oslo came word from Lisbon that the Portuguese treaty had gone on the rocks. To protect her port and Madeira wine interests, Portugal insisted on a clause for the punishment of all who might sell wine labeled "Port" or "Madeira" that did not come from Portugal or the island of Madeira; in the Siamese treaty the formula had been considerably modified so as to avoid possible difficulties with British and French merchants selling these wines in Bangkok. The formula thus modified had run afoul in one of the Portuguese legislative committees; the treaty had therefore failed to pass and there seemed a not improbable chance of its total shipwreck.

During the four days' journey from Oslo I dispatched urgent cables to Bangkok and telegrams to Lisbon, so that by the time I reached the Portuguese capital the way had been opened to agreement on a new formula which would not endanger Siamese interests and yet would prove acceptable to the various groups in Portugal. In Lisbon, in intimate contact with Foreign Office officials who had become personal friends, it was not difficult to agree upon a formula; but a new difficulty then confronted us. The Minister of Foreign Affairs with whom we had negotiated in April had been succeeded by another; his successor had been deposed as a result of a revolution, and so far no Premier could be found able to control a majority of the chamber. As a result there was no existing Minister of Foreign Affairs by whom the treaty could be signed. We had, as it happened, come from Paris on the train with the man who it was hoped would be able to form a government. He ultimately succeeded in doing so; and one of the earliest acts of the newly appointed Minister of Foreign Affairs was, together with Phya Sanpakitch, the Siamese Minister to Italy, Spain, and Portugal, to sign the treaty with Siam.

It was then late in July; I paused a few days in Madrid to give to the draft of the Spanish treaty the final touches preparatory to signature, and hurried on to Rome, arriving the first week of August. The Italian treaty was the last one remaining, but it was still beset with difficulties. Would it be the one to wreck all our efforts?

Since April I had sent a succession of telegrams to the Italian Foreign Office urging the hastening of negotiations; but these had borne no fruit, and a bare three weeks remained before it was necessary for me to return to America. Rome was in the throes of intense summer heat, and the majority of Foreign Office officials were away on vacation. Apparently the only hope was to go straight to Premier Mussolini, convince him of the importance of Italy's not being the single nation to bar Siam's right to full fiscal autonomy, and urge top speed. With his aid it might be done: he worked with the speed and precision of a steam turbine, and by his compelling, dominant will drove the Italian machinery of state at a pace that it had never known before.

Marquis Paulucci di Calboli Barone, private secretary to Premier Mussolini, seemed to be impressed by my presentation and expressed the sincere wish that Italy might meet with Siam's desire and that the new treaty might be negotiated at once, especially since the Siamese government felt obliged to ask for the withdrawal of negotiations were the draft not agreed to before my departure. "But," he added, "unhappily we are blocked by physical impossibility. The Foreign Office officials are away on their holidays. There is no one in Rome competent to negotiate the treaty."

"But," I asked, "can they not be recalled?"

This was a question which only the Premier could decide. Marquis Paulucci promised to take it up with him immediately. For three days we waited, holding our breath; on the fourth, word came that telegrams had been sent to various Foreign Office officials calling them to Rome, that a Treaty Commission had been appointed and would meet with Siam's plenipotentiary on the following Wednesday, August 19. That gave just nine days before I had to leave Rome for America. Again the gods were favoring us and we had a fighting chance.

During the intervening days we got into personal touch with certain Italian representatives on the newly appointed Treaty Commission and talked over several of the more vital issues. None of the Commissioners thought it possible to conclude the negotiations within a week; yet I felt that if there was a will a way could be found, and we mapped out a program accordingly. The first clash came over the language to be used for the treaty text. The Italian Commissioners wanted it to be Italian. At the first meeting, however, they agreed to accept both an English and an Italian text, with the English one controlling; and we then proceeded to formulate a program of action for the ensuing week. Siam agreed to prepare and present to the Italian Foreign Office on the following day a treaty draft in English and Italian; the Italians were to study this and meet with us two days later to discuss counterproposals; and every day thereafter the Treaty Commission would sit with us until the work was completed.

Evidently Premier Mussolini had issued orders that things were to move, for this program was followed out to the letter. During the crowded days and nights—for there were times when the lights in the Siamese Legation burned till morning—there was never an hour wasted. The Treaty Commission, at considerable personal self-sacrifice, held long, protracted sessions with us, discussing our proposals, arguing against some of them, presenting counterproposals. I defended and maintained our draft in all the essential points, but yielded wherever possible on non-essentials. By the following Monday we had apparently come within sight of final agreement. The Italian Commission seemed to be ready to accept a text that was satisfactory to Siam, provided that Siam would agree to five demands, which Italy put forward as a *sine qua non* for the granting of the treaty. To these five demands I could not agree. For two days the debate raged. At last, on three of the points, the Italians agreed to accept modified formulas phrased in such a way as not to endanger

Siamese interests; but on the other two deadlock resulted. These were such as no self-respecting nation should agree to, and I felt unable to yield. They never should have been proposed. One included the right of the Italian Government to name one or more Italian advisers to the Government of Siam. In the end the only course open was to refer the impasse to Premier Mussolini. Only he could decide.

Accordingly I asked for a personal interview with the all-powerful Premier. Upon his decision everything depended. If he refused to yield on either one of the two Italian demands the treaty was lost; the only recourse in that event would be to bring Siam's plight before the League of Nations and seek its help. All our other treaty negotiations now hung upon the outcome of the Italian treaty.

The memorable interview with Signor Mussolini was fixed for the day before I had to depart for America. Our hopes were high. Success would mean a new era of economic independence for Siam. We refused to think of failure. Yet we realized that for us that day Mussolini held everything in his hand. Would he understand and fathom the truth that underlay our requests—that the Siamese people could never forgive Italy if by impossible demands it should be the single nation to stand in the way of Siam's economic independence and progress?

As we were ushered into the Premier's palatial office, resplendent with old Florentine paintings and adorned with rich red furnishings and curtains, the Premier rose from his large desk in the corner of the room, piled with papers, and walked over to greet us. His face was firm and strong, but kindly; his luminous eyes were gentle; his smile gave me hope. He was in military uniform; his figure was erect. But he walked across the room to receive us with no pose, no strut, no drama. He spoke in Italian; his aide interpreted to us as he spoke.

He began with generalities. Was I enjoying my visit in Rome in spite of the intense heat? Had I had time to get off into the country where it was cooler? Had I been in Rome before? I tried to give gracious and appreciative replies; but I was holding my breath. Would the answer be Yes or No?

Then, after what seemed an eternity, the Premier spoke of Italy's friendship for Siam, of how the Siamese people always struck a re-

sponsive chord among the Italians. He said that his government was
eager to continue that friendship, and that in token of it Italy was
prepared to withdraw its fourth and fifth demands.

He gave us a reassuring smile. Our hearts leaped; his words spelt
victory for Siam.

The last treaty, then, was won! After seventy years of extraterritoriality Siam was to be once more autonomous and free. I could
not forbear dispatching that day a cable to His Siamese Majesty:

As a result of successful completion of Italian treaty, all Treaty Powers
are now agreed to surrender old extraterritorial rights. Siam's complete
autonomy is now regained. I should like to be the first to congratulate Your
Majesty and I rejoice that [Siam] has now again come into her own.

There remained only the formalities of preparing the accepted
texts; and subsequent ratification was only a question of time.

With the ratifications of these new treaties the indefensible system of extraterritoriality in Siam became a thing of the past. At long
last Siam had regained her economic freedom and complete independence.

Fortunately, throughout the negotiations I had been able to act
with speed and precision because the Siamese government had generously given me complete confidence and trust. To no proposal or
formula which I suggested in the many negotiations did the government, so far as I can remember, refuse agreement. Red tape between
Siam and myself had been dispensed with. I was in a position to
argue Siam's case with complete independence; and I was able to
make provisional promises which the Siamese government always
accepted and honored.

Released from the shackles of extraterritoriality, Thailand has
not abused its new freedom; and for thirty years it has been making
steady progress and improving its economic position. Only good has
come of the surrender of the rights of extraterritoriality by the Western powers.

Some time later, after the story of the new treaties, together with
my comment, had been published in a Siamese newspaper, I received
a letter from "a Siamese who loves his country with an ardent love":

I have been so moved by a deep sense of gratitude that I have to write to tender you our humble thanks for the great services you and your justice-loving country have rendered to poor Siam. . . . One article from your pen has done more than years of diplomacy to tighten the bonds of friend-ship between the United States and Siam. Educated Siamese, from His Majesty down to His humblest subject, now learn to love two countries—their own and America.

In appreciation of my efforts for Siam His Majesty heaped high honors upon me, including permanent appointment as Minister Plenipotentiary for Siam and also as Siam's representative on the Hague Permanent Court of Arbitration. But perhaps it was the gratitude in the hearts of my many friends in Siam that I valued most.

* * *

Since the gaining of the new treaties thirty years have now passed —almost a generation. But the Siamese have not forgotten.

In 1953, when Mrs. Sayre and I were spending a year in Japan, the Thai Ambassador to Japan came one afternoon to our house in Tokyo. He brought a message from His Thai Majesty, King Phumiphon, the son of my old friend Prince Mahidol, graciously inviting us to come to Bangkok to share in his birthday celebrations as the guests of the government. We expressed our pleasure in accepting; and so it came about that in December, 1953, on our way home from Japan we flew from Hong Kong to Thailand. Circling high above emerald-green rice paddies glistening in the sun, we descended to Don Muang airport just north of Bangkok. As our plane landed, coming forth to meet us with garlands of flowers and bouquets of orchids were Prince Wan, the Minister of Foreign Affairs, Prince Kridakorn, and my boy, Sivawongse, now grown to manhood, together with a host of old friends whose faces brought a flood of memories. We were driven into Bangkok, down familiar streets crowded with Siamese in gaily colored native garments, past the crenellated walls of the Royal Palace enclosure with its graceful shining roofs, its golden towers and spires of Oriental splendor, and on past many well remembered places. How the experiences of thirty years ago surged back into my memory! Then on to the spacious "Pibultam Palace," which His Majesty had placed at our disposal—"under the watchful care of some twenty-six servants and two military aides," as Mrs. Sayre wrote home, "to whom our every wish is law and immediately attended to."

How can I describe the experiences of the next ten days, which seemed in quite another world?

A round of ceremonies, of sumptuous and official dinners in our honor—a Kingdom's touching appreciation of what had happened thirty years before—stirred our hearts. I had the chance to renew old friendships, to revisit many old haunts and memoried scenes, to relive some of the half-forgotten Bangkok days.

But the unique part of our visit was the chance it gave us to come to know His Majesty, to talk with him alone and feel his utter sincerity and determination to surmount his towering problems. The day after our arrival Mrs. Sayre and I were the only guests at an intimate luncheon with Their Majesties in their private suite in the Palace; we could not have had a more considerate host, and it gave us a chance to talk over many things together.

The birthday ceremonies, held in the gorgeous ceremonial hall in the Royal Palace grounds, were unforgettable. They marked the outpourings of the Kingdom's best to do honor to the King, following the colorful Siamese rites of ancient days. And we felt privileged beyond words that we, the only foreigners permitted to be present, thus had the chance to share intimately in this expression of honor and devotion to the King.

The morning of the King's birthday—December 5—we drove to the Palace at ten o'clock, signed our names in the King's book, and took our places in the ceremonial hall, crowded with Siamese nobility and high officialdom, the men in white uniforms bespangled with decorations, medals, and ribbons, and the ladies of the court, bejewelled in rich Thai silks woven with gold and silver thread.

I confess that although in heart and spirit I was one with those around me, in outward attire I was in sharpest contrast. When I arrived in Bangkok I was told that the proper court dress for me would be a black tailed evening coat with white tie. Years ago the Siamese court had perforce accepted for foreigners their Western formal dress of black tailed coat and white tie; they themselves, nevertheless, in view of the intense heat of Bangkok, adopted the far more sensible costume of white coat and *penung*. Consequently for formal court occasions foreigners appeared in black and Siamese in white. On this particular occasion, I as the only non-Siamese man in the company must be the single one to appear in a black evening coat. And unhappily I had none with me.

I blush to recall that I went to the American Ambassador, General Donovan, for help. He was exactly my size. He lent me his coat, and it fitted perfectly. Travelling without medals or decorations which I was supposed to wear, I was constrained to borrow from the Thai Foreign Office duplicates of those which had been conferred upon me, including the gorgeous sash of the Grand Cross of the White Elephant. It took my wife and both of my military aides— three people—to get me properly attired and in order! Thus arrayed in borrowed splendor, I made my appearance. But I, the only person in the hall in black, felt shockingly conspicuous.

As we awaited the King's appearance we had time to feast our eyes upon the resplendent interior. Massive, heavily gilded pillars, fifty or sixty feet high, formed a double row on either side of the hall. Deeply recessed windows with shutters of black and gold in rich design opened out into the sunlit courtyard; the ceiling was of gorgeous vermilion, ornamented with gold stars of rich red-gold set with little crystals that glittered like diamonds. It seemed as if everything in the hall shimmered or sparkled or glittered.

A few minutes later silence fell, and we heard the guns outside booming the royal salute. The heavy gold brocade curtains which had been closely drawn at one end of the room were parted and revealed a shining gold, boat-shaped altar and in front of it the King and Queen on their golden thrones. The King sat erect and reserved; the Queen, gracious and smiling, seemed the incarnation of loveliness. All made obeisance, many falling prostrate; and then followed the National Anthem. Thereupon with emotion the Prime Minister and another high official read heartfelt birthday messages from the people to His Majesty. The ceremony was simple but deeply affecting.

In the afternoon the continuing ceremonies took on a religious turn. As we entered again the glittering ceremonial hall we found seated on our left, cross-legged on broad seats, a group of the highest Buddhist priests, fifty or more, with shaven heads, all arrayed in their bright yellow robes. To our right were the members of the

King's family. In the center, where we had our seats, were the highest nobility and officers of the realm. The thrones had been moved to the left of a high altar; and as all fell silent the King and his gracious consort—the Queen smiling at Mrs. Sayre and me as she entered—took their seats. On a table in front of them were spread gifts for the priests—folded yellow satin robes, parchment scrolls, ivory-handled prayer screens, richly embroidered in gold and silver. The King, the head of the Buddhist religion in Siam, stepped forward and the priests, one by one, advanced to receive their gifts, along with various advancements and promotions. Following this, the King lit the candles on the high altar; and from these other candles were lighted. Then followed long Buddhist prayers by one priest after another asking blessing and happiness for Their Majesties. As the prayers were said the Chief Priest took a large ball of white yarn and, holding the end, passed it on to the next priest, and he to his neighbor and so on until the yarn ran directly from the Chief Priest into the hands of each of the others. This part of the ceremony was to signify unity of thought and prayer. When finally the chanting and prayers were ended, the long strand was passed back and rewound until it reached the hands of the senior priest.

At the conclusion two high honors were bestowed by His Majesty. I suddenly heard my Siamese name called, and I advanced and knelt before the King. Thereupon he conferred upon me the Royal Cypher medal, surmounted with the King's initials, all in diamonds. It was a rare mark of distinction, given to but few. Evidently His Majesty thus wanted to do honor to his father's friend.

My wife told me later how worried she had been lest I, so conspicuous in black, should do something wrong when suddenly my name was called—fail to kneel gracefully before the King, or betray my utter ignorance of Court etiquette. But after the crisis had passed she gave me an approving smile.

The ceremonies lasted until late in the afternoon and, indeed, were continued the next morning. Throughout the ten days of our visit we were honored at banquets, presented with gifts, touched wherever we went by deepfelt expressions of appreciation.

As my wife wrote home, commenting on the sumptuous banquet given us the evening before by the Prime Minister and Madame Pibulsonggram at the Government Residence:

All the chief officials of the Kingdom as well as many of Frank's old friends were gathered there. Speeches were exchanged and I can never forget some of the things they said about "Kalyan." In the middle of the dinner a Siamese chorus, accompanied by native stringed instruments, sang the song of welcome composed in our honor. A very rough translation from the Siamese runs something like this:

> "Elated is the Prime Minister
>   To welcome as a good omen
> The visit of Phya Kalyan Maitri
>   And charming Khun Ying to Thailand.
> Chao Khun with distinction served
>   Our Government in the past;
> The results greatly pleased His Majesty
>   And his memory will live forever.
>
> "Let us welcome today Chao Khun and Khun Ying,
>   Great friends of ours for many years past;
> May the Triple Gem protect them both,
>   And may they be blest with happiness and wealth.
> May no illness come in their way
>   And may their wishes be fulfilled always,
> May our two nations be closely drawn together
>   In 'Kalyan Maitri.' "

After dinner followed an exquisite performance of Siamese dancing in the old tradition to the music of ancient Siamese instruments, the dancers trained in the ancestral style and wearing old costumes of flaming color.

Our visit to Thailand thirty years after stands out as a unique memory of my life. It was like living in a fairy tale.

9

Teaching Again.
Sabbatical in India

After our exciting year in Europe negotiating the new Siamese treaties we returned to Cambridge in September, 1925, and settled down again to the quiet life of teaching at Harvard Law School.

Once back home I found my Siamese boy Sivawongse had been doing well in his Cambridge school; he rejoiced to see us, to enter our home again, and to become a part of our growing family. My own children also were happy to be back. In Europe they had had hard sledding for a time. When at the end of 1924 we had put them into a day school in Paris they did not know a word of French. It was like throwing a child who could not swim into a pool of water and, watching over him carefully, telling him to swim. For a time, uncomprehending, they floundered. Then two months later, when another American child entered the school, they found themselves explaining to the newcomer what the teacher was saying. By June they were rattling off French like French children; and for the summer, while I was all over Europe engaged in treaty negotiations, we had placed them in a delightful Swiss school, Champs Soleils, at Chailly near Lausanne. Now they rejoiced to be back in American schools again.

As I resumed my Law School teaching the developing work demanded my every waking minute. Advanced to a full professorship, I was now teaching classes in criminal law, in maritime law ("admiralty," as it was called), and in labor law. I had published a case book in labor law in 1922, and I was further organizing my work in this fast-developing field. What spare time I could muster was filled to overflowing with the writing of articles for law reviews and with an increasing number of outside lectures and addresses.

I could not forget Siam. Often in my mind I was still living in the Far East. In November, 1925, King Rama VI, whom I had known and worked with, died. He was succeeded by his half-brother Praja-dhipok; and King Prajadhipok expressed the strong desire to have me come back to Siam. Although I could not give up my work at Harvard, I visited Bangkok during the 1926 summer holidays at his request to confer with him and advise him as to some of the pressing demands for constitutional reforms.

The deep-rooted and far-reaching conflict between East and West was beginning to beset Siam. Students returning from England or France or America often were unhappy and disturbed, with half-baked ideas about democracy and human liberty; they wanted Siam to adopt Western forms almost overnight, as if these were but out-ward garments. Many felt that the Siamese culture was outdated, and their minds seethed with modern, Western ideas, often superficial and misunderstood. One of their outspoken demands was for a Par-liament and a modern Constitution.

Discussing these issues with His Majesty, I had to point out the inherent dangers. In Siam there was no middle class. The Siamese peasants took little or no interest in public affairs but lived their simple lives in secluded rural districts. To set up a legislature and clothe it with real power overnight without an educated electorate to control it would be likely, I suggested, to invite trouble and pos-sible corruption. Power uncontrolled was almost bound to breed corruption.

Other important issues upon which the King sought advice were how best to choose a successor to the throne, what changes if any should be made in the framework of government, whether or not to appoint a Premier. As I talked with him I felt the utter sincerity of the new monarch and his real desire to lead Siam into modern nation-hood.

Before I left Bangkok, once more the Siamese people gave evi-dence of their generosity. In the great Throne Hall, in the presence of all the court, His Majesty conferred upon me the unique honor of membership in the high Siamese order of Chula Chom Klao, in which, so far as I know, I was the only foreigner.

Six years later, in 1932, the discontent of the younger Siamese element seeking Western ways broke out in an organized *coup d'état,* with fresh demands for a legislative assembly. The King was constrained to yield rather than plunge the country into a bloody civil war. The King retained his throne, but henceforth governed under a constitution establishing universal suffrage and setting up a unicameral parliament with half its members elected and half appointed by the King, and a cabinet responsible to parliament. Fifteen years later came a second *coup d'état,* when Luang Pibulsonggram, the leader of the military party, became Prime Minister.

Today Thailand has a unique part to play in Southeast Asia. Will she be able to maintain her ideals of individual welfare and personal liberty and at the same time exercise a potent leadership in Southeastern Asia toward the ways that make for peace? Can she assimilate the best of Western civilization without being corrupted by its demoralizing forces? Can she overcome political corruption and successfully resist the pressures of Communism?

*   *   *

By the end of September, 1926, I was back in Cambridge, hard at work with my law students. Life was full, and at its center was our home at 26 Hubbard Park.

Into our home in 1929 we took another Siamese youngster— Debriddhi Devakul, the son of Prince Traidos Prabandh, the Minister of Foreign Affairs under whom I had worked during my year in Bangkok. "Tau" was an attractive boy and entered with zest into the life of Belmont School, which he attended with our two sons. Although he had never seen ice, he learned to skate, became captain of the hockey team and was lustily cheered by a great audience in the Boston arena when in the annual hockey match he led his school to victory over its hockey rival.

Today he is back in Bangkok, with an attractive Siamese wife, and playing a leading part in the life of Thailand. He wrote three years ago to my son Francis, now the Dean of the Episcopal Cathedral in Washington: "I have a son, now ten years old. Would you be willing to take him into your family in Washington as Father took me

and bring him up in exactly the same way as Father brought me up?"
Not always does the new generation follow so exactly in the footsteps
of the old. Tau's son, "Tri," is now a happy part of the family at
the Deanery in Washington.

During those years I was slowly gaining, I think, a deeper understanding of the power of Christianity. I felt increasingly the profound need of a more vital and biting Christianity in our own lives,
in that of America, in international life. In 1929, in an address on
"Religion and Life Today," I was saying:

If there is one thing this age seeks above all else, it is power—the power
to achieve material and tangible results, the power to control great interests,
the power to dominate. It is this lust for power which, I suspect, underlies
in large measure our growing lack of interest in religion.

The paradoxical tragedy is that religion, properly understood, is a very
dynamo of vitalizing force. . . .

The source of maximum power, said Christ, lies not in material force
but in spiritual appeal. And on that brave faith Christ dared to stake his
life.

He died a felon's death without a soldier to defend him—the very
negation of material force. Men called him a fool and proved to them
selves that his life was an utter failure. But in his life and in his death he
generated a spiritual force that has turned the world upside down. Never
before or since has the world felt power of such dynamic force as his—so
profound in its bearing upon all human life, so far-flung in its effects and
repercussions. . . .

How practically are we to understand and comprehend the fundamentals of Christ's teachings? So far as I know there is only one way—to
live with Christ. . . . The only way to understand Christ is to make him
your companion—when you walk along the city streets, alone among the
crowds, to walk with Christ; when you look up at the quiet stars at night,
to be thinking of him, of what he really was trying to accomplish, of what
he really meant when he talked about building the kingdom of God.

If one does dare to believe these revolutionary doctrines of Christ—
which are poles apart from the fundamental beliefs of our own time,
which are scoffed at and treated with contemptuous derision by the crowds
around us—if one dares to believe that what Christ said was true and to
put his faith to the test, what a thrilling adventure Christianity becomes!
It means no less than helping to save a civilization—which has in it very
much that is precious—by bringing to the profound problems of the day
a wisdom gained through knowledge of Christ and a vision caught from

his presence. What a fearful and thrilling task for those who, looking into Christ's face and taking his hand, are ready to walk with him and make the great adventure!

These quiet years of teaching were not all happy sailing. There came periods of discouragement now and again. Try my best to master and clarify the legal problems with which my students were wrestling, there would come days when I could not seem to arouse my classes or fire their minds—when the lectures became lifeless and little more than accumulated information. There were times when I wondered if ever I could become a really first-rate teacher.

Doubts now and again assailed me. And yet into the groove of teaching after my return from Siam my life seemed to be inescapably cast.

In 1930 Jessie and I availed ourselves of one of the privileges of academic life—to take a year off on sabbatical leave. In June we closed our house and with our three children sailed for France.

We spent that summer in the alluring countryside of Brittany, at the tiny seaside village of Beg-Meil within striking distance of Quimper. It was France at its best—free from tourists, unspoiled, simple, altogether charming. Here with the family I spent a solid month correcting "blue-books." In August I joined a group including Senator Alben Barkley and Reinhold Niebuhr under the leadership of Sherwood Eddy for a visit to Moscow. After talking with various of the Russian leaders there we journeyed off by ourselves to see some of the collective farm areas. From Russia I travelled to Prague as a delegate to the International Prison Congress, and after that rejoined my family in Brittany.

We left France in September for Switzerland to place our children in Swiss schools: our two boys at "Le Roset" near Geneva, and our daughter at "La Pelouse" at Bex, south of Lausanne. It was hard to leave them, but we knew it was right; and so in October, gripped once more by the lure of the East, Jessie and I set sail for India.

The British Simon Report on India had just been published. India was seething. New movements were afoot. I was eager to see and talk with leaders of the Indian people.

Rather, of the Indian peoples. India is a land of many races and of many tongues. Amongst the two hundred and twenty-two vernacular tongues spoken in India, no language has so wide a range as English. And the deep, abiding hatred between Hindu and Mohammedan still flames. Death to the unbeliever is still taught in the sacred books. Mohammedans, Hindus, Sikhs, Jains, and many other groups are irreconcilable and unyielding. Only about 2 per cent of the Indians are Christians.

From Bombay to Calcutta, from the Malabar Coast in the extreme South to the snows of Darjeeling and Kashmir we journeyed through the countryside talking with Indian leaders, visiting English residents, trying to learn something of India and its problems.

In late October, before the cold of winter froze the mountain country, we travelled up to Kashmir. From Rawalpindi we climbed by motorcar higher and ever higher into the northern mountains until we came at the end of the second day into the great Vale of Kashmir. Never in my life have I seen country of such matchless beauty. It was more like dream than reality. High, high above us, into the blue of the sky towered the great Himalaya Mountains, mantled in snow, now and again touched with soft blues and pinks and purples. Below them in the Vale, row upon row of Lombardy poplars, brilliant yellow in their autumn foliage, and on every side Persian chinar trees in their gorgeous autumn scarlet. In the immediate foreground a quiet lake reflecting many colors, and all around green fields filled with bright and many-hued flowers. So often the first sight of a far-famed place brings disappointment. But the many-splendored Vale of Kashmir outshone our imagination.

We spent a few days at Srinagar, which like Florence is the home of artist-craftsmen devoting their lives to the production of beauty. Here are made matchless shawls and textiles and exquisite gold and silver ware. From Srinagar we moved onto a houseboat for several days on the lake, the better to drink in the beauty which surrounded us on every side.

In early November we descended to the plains, visited Lahore, and spent several days at Agra, drinking in the peerless beauty of the Taj Mahal in its changing moods both by sunlight and by moonlight. From Agra we went on to Delhi, where we spent a week, wandering through the old Mogul capital and lunching in New Delhi with Lord Irwin, the Viceroy.

Christmas found us at the Residency in Trivandrum, Travancore, visiting the English Resident, Lieutenant Colonel H. R. N. Pritchard, Agent to the Governor General in the Madras States. In Travancore we found people, institutions, customs, utterly different from those of North India. And in Travancore as the guest of Her Highness the Maharani Regent, I was able to visit some of the wilder parts, and saw people living in houses in the trees to keep clear of marauding animals. Indeed on one occasion we suddenly came upon a herd of wild elephants.

By the kindness of the Maharani I was also given the privilege of a bison hunt. Accompanied by several Indian guides we managed to track down a herd of these magnificent animals in a dense part of the forest. But just as we reached the spot where they evidently had been bedding, and as we were maneuvering to catch sight of one and get a shot, suddenly a great crash close by broke the stillness, followed by the sounds of struggle and panting. A few moments and all was silence. A tiger, my Indians told me, had evidently preceded us and was making his kill. The jungle was so impenetrable and thick that I could see nothing; and since my accompanying Indians were unarmed I could not push further into the tangled jungle to get sight of the tiger. Since the herd of bison immediately scattered in every direction without our getting sight of them we had to return home empty-handed. But the excitement of that day's hunt was not soon forgotten.

Again and again throughout our Indian journey we touched upon the same profound problem which also confronts Siam: how to bring to an ancient civilization profit without harm from the modern West, how to reconcile the ancient East with the twentieth century demands of an ultramodern, aggressive Western world without producing discord, unrest, and growing hatreds.

"Can Western and Eastern civilizations be reconciled to the natural advantage of both?" I wrote in 1931 during our visit. "Or are the two fundamentally and eternally irreconcilable? In India Great Britain has been making an heroic attempt to harmonize the two. If she fails, will there be any solution other than an ultimate cataclysmic war movement of Eastern civilizations massed against Western ones? All the world has a stake in the outcome."

One of the outstanding men in India was Mahatma Gandhi. He was of unique spiritual power; and it is a tribute to his greatness that as long as he lived the problem of India could not be discussed without reference to him. His was a name to conjure with. An Indian friend of mine asked a group of villagers who Gandhi was. "He is a god," came the reply. "When he sits under a tree and it rains everywhere else, his tree is dry."

Both Jessie and I were anxious to meet and talk with him; and so, as we travelled north from Bombay toward Jaipur we stopped off for a day at Ahmadabad and spent an afternoon with him in his home.

The simple room where he entertained us was unpretentious and rather bare; while we sat beside him, Western style on chairs, he sat cross-legged on a cushion on the floor. He was in Indian homespun with a brown shawl thrown around his shoulders. His features were unusual and distinctive. He had a rounded face, bespectacled, with outstanding ears, a large mouth, and rather sparse hair. But, strangely enough and contrary to our expectation, to us he lacked the outstanding presence of a strong spiritual leader. What he said interested, but did not lift us; perhaps our own bluntness of vision prevented us from drawing inspiration from his presence.

We talked in English about India and the Indian hope of coming self-government. He believed in winning this through the Indian people's boycotting British goods and refusing to cooperate with the British government. He pointed to his spinning wheel in the corner of the room; through resort to the spinning wheel, he claimed, the Indian people could avoid the purchase of English textiles and thus prevent the British gaining an economic stranglehold on India. He said that moral force expressed in passive resistance against the British could be more effective even than physical force.

As we talked with him we could not but feel impressed by what he stood for. As a great religious mystic, he dared to place abiding faith in spiritual appeal as a mightier power than material force. By the sheer power of spirit, without a soldier to back him, without wealth, without family position or influence, without any of the things which this world regards as the source of strength, he made himself one of the great forces in India. At his call thousands and thousands of Indians were prepared to choose the pathway of suffering or imprisonment. Nevertheless, we could not agree with all of the economic or political views which he expressed that afternoon.

From the teachings of Christ Gandhi drew immeasurable power; at one time in his life, I am told, he seriously contemplated becoming a Christian. He never took this step, however, but maintained to the end his Hindu faith, which is inescapably based on a deadening fatalism.

The age-old system of caste on which Hinduism is built is a vast complicated network of religious, social, and economic privileges and taboos, enforced by the boycott in its most devastating forms. One's occupation is largely dependent upon caste, which is purely a matter of birth. Outcastes were held to pollute other Hindus by mere touch, and to defile all food or water. Ordinarily they could not use the village wells or tanks used by other castes; they were even denied entrance to Hindu temples. Gandhi sought manfully to alleviate their lot; but the evil caste system, he was bound as a good Hindu to accept.

From our afternoon with him we came away with a sense of disappointment and regret that so great a religious mystic was spending his major effort, not upon the timeless religious problems of India, but rather upon the political and economic issues then convulsing the country.

At New Delhi we were the luncheon guests of the Viceroy, Baron Irwin (now Earl of Halifax), Edward Frederick Lindley Wood. We were deeply impressed by his sincerity and his statesmanlike approach to the Indian problem. Of Gandhi, he said: "He seems to believe that all life can be reduced to one single, simple principle. I don't believe that. I believe that life is a mass of conflicting principles."

He saw that the end of British rule in India was fast approaching, but that India must first be taught the extremely difficult art of self-government. He was then hard at work Indianizing the Services. In the General Administration Department, of the 5,500 higher officials only some 630 were Europeans. In the judiciary out of a total of 2,500 only 230 were Europeans.

In the early days there was unquestionably unforgivable exploitation of Indians by the British. The East India Company was a trading company organized for profit, and all the world then thought of colonies in terms of profit. Unquestionably the interests of Lancashire textile workers influenced British Indian legislation. Nevertheless, India has profited immeasurably from British rule. Great Britain found in India a collection of native states, torn and impoverished by incessant warfare; and she established peace throughout the peninsula. She found arid districts where cultivation was impossible; by huge irrigation projects she substantially increased the food supply. She found a country periodically stricken with devastating famines; by building up effective transportation facilities she practically eliminated them. She found a country where the tyrannies of local officials were a byword; she established a civil service which came to be generally acknowledged as the best in the world. She gave to India law and order and a splendid administration of justice. These are the very foundations upon which all national progress must be built. One might wish that greater advances had been made in education, in training for self-government, in agriculture. Nevertheless, the balance in England's favor is very impressive. British rule made a united India possible; and it was conceptions of liberty and freedom taught by England which finally brought about the independence of India.

I found Lord Irwin singularly understanding of Indian thinking and sympathetic with much of it. During his term as Viceroy he continually sought under most difficult conditions to make future self-government possible. In November, 1929, with the full agreement of the Secretary of State for India, the Viceroy announced that the accepted goal toward which the British government was working was self-government for India with Dominion status.

In the meantime propagandists were hard at work, and anti-English opinion was being fanned into flame. At various places I was invited to speak. Before me lies a hand-written letter from one of the outstanding Indian leaders at Allahabad:

Probably you may like to know that most of us were deeply touched last night by your well chosen words of sympathy and plea for mutual understanding. You have the gift of speech and after listening to you we did not wonder at your success in the cause of Siam.

Personally I have small hope of mutual understanding. We are exceedingly sensitive and go looking for an inferiority complex where none is intended. The Englishman clothed in self-esteem and the excellence of his action troubles not to win the good opinion of others by talk. The extremists have done remarkably good propaganda work not only in India but on the continent and in America as well. The British government and the English people have done none. "Look at our acts and admire" has been their attitude. The situation would be more hopeful if a score of men like you were employed to talk to the educated Indians of sympathy and understanding.

As a result of our extended visit that winter, I felt that self-government should be given to India at the earliest possible moment. Delay seemed to me dangerous. As Jessie and I bade farewell to India and sailed west for Suez, I wrote:

Political reorganization will not of itself solve India's fundamental problems. But it may fire her imagination and generate other constructive and creative forces. Neither Hinduism with its deadening belief in caste nor Mohammedanism with its fatalistic teachings of Kismet has proved capable of lifting India out of its age-long poverty and ignorance, its religious hatreds and national disunity. Some new driving force is needed if Indian civilization is to be saved. Nineteenth century history teaches the irresistible power of freshly resurgent nationalistic movements. If such power can be utilized in India today to generate the forces that will lift her people to salvation, and if at such a time the West can help her forward instead of impeding her, it will be one of the memorable movements of world history.

10

Of Crime and Criminals

Upon our return from India Jessie and I spent a week in Egypt visiting Cairo and going up the Nile to Luxor, dipping into the very ancient past. From there we hurried back to Switzerland to see our children in their schools. They were well and happy, and we arranged to spend the Easter holidays all together in Rome and in Florence. In Rome we had a glad time together; but at Florence our boy Francis came down with the mumps and was threatened with serious complications. The doctor's advice was to take him out of school at once. That meant that Jessie must board an Italian steamer at Naples and take him home for a more thorough medical examination and treatment while I must remain in Switzerland until the completion of the school year in June and then bring Eleanor and Woodrow home.

It was a lonely May and June for me, living at Lausanne where I could keep a watchful eye on the children and, for relaxation, visiting briefly Munich and the Black Forest.

In time the end of school came; and, gathering up the two children and another youngster, a classmate and friend of Eleanor's, we boarded a steamer in France and sailed for home. At a family council in Switzerland, before Francis became sick, I had put the question, "Where shall we spend the summer?" All Europe lay before us, and I offered to take the family wherever they might choose. With one accord we voted for Martha's Vineyard; and so to our beloved cottage at Martha's Vineyard off Cape Cod we returned for the summer of 1931. I felt like a gentleman of leisure: I had no "blue-books" to correct.

By September, I was back at Harvard glad to resume my classes. Criminal law was attracting more and more of my attention. I planned to write a treatise on criminal law, and began by studies of particular problems, including *mens rea,* the criminal intent needed to constitute a crime, the necessary elements of "criminal conspiracy," and the features of a criminal "attempt." On each of these I published law review articles, which I hoped would ultimately become chapters in the treatise.

My Siamese boy, Sivawongse, had been developing a decided interest in art. Feeling that his own artistic talent against his inherited background of outstanding Siamese ancient art offered him a unique field of work, I had sent him for a year to the New York School of Fine Arts, where he did outstanding work. In 1931 I sent him to Paris to study in the School of Fine Arts there. In February, 1932, he wrote that his father wanted him to return to Siam, and told of his dissatisfaction with the Siamese students in Paris:

I feel sorry about this matter very much. Sorry because of these boys who some day will do many things to our own country and will set a very bad idea to our people who never once have seen the world. . . . Sometimes my tears drop. I want to be back in America; but at home they need me, in a way to speak. . . . I want to see you more and more. I want to talk to you, father. I feel very sad of not having anybody to understand things like you. . . . You are still my father. Always I smile when I think of those wonderful consolation and words and your teaching for the past seven years. What I will be, I will always be your son forever.

To carry forward our attack upon the problem of crime we set about organizing at the Law School an Institute of Criminal Law, hoping to work out a curriculum for correctional administrators and to prepare men of character and capacity for leadership in correctional work.

In early 1932 Governor Joseph Ely of Massachusetts appointed me to the Board of Trustees of the State Training Schools, which exercises supervision over the juvenile delinquents of Massachusetts.

This responsibility also brought home the vital need for the state to find more adequate and redemptive ways and means for coping with juvenile delinquency.

Finally, near the end of 1932, Governor Ely asked if I would accept appointment as State Commissioner of Correction. This would mean carrying full responsibility for the administration of state prisons and for the care of all state prisoners. Because of my deep interest in this field, I agreed to accept, at the same time continuing my full schedule of teaching. The Governor appointed me on December 21, 1932.

Then out of a clear sky, cataclysmic and devastating, came the crash that bade fair to wreck my life. Jessie died in the hospital as a result of a not too serious operation. The very foundations of my life seemed swept away. Black, utter despair loomed over me.

St. Paul's wonderful outcry of faith, which I asked to have read at the funeral service, kept echoing in my heart: "Who shall separate us from the love of Christ? shall tribulation, or distress, or persecution, or famine, or nakedness, or peril, or sword? . . . Nay, in all these things we are more than conquerors, through Him that loved us. For I am persuaded, that neither death, nor life, nor angels, nor principalities, nor powers, nor things present, nor things to come, nor height, nor depth, nor any other creature, shall be able to separate us from the love of God, which is in Christ Jesus our Lord."

Could I really through Christ conquer desolation and despair?

Again and again I repeated to myself the Twenty-third Psalm: "Yea, though I walk through the valley of the shadow of death, I will fear no evil: for Thou art with me; Thy rod and Thy staff they comfort me."

Could I rise to that?

At least I could with God's help make a brave attempt.

The children were left motherless. To God again and again I turned for help in gathering up the wreckage of my life and fitting myself to serve them now in a dual capacity.

At least I could rejoice in having had the past glory of knowing and sharing Jessie's life. Nothing could ever take that away from me. And I felt deeply grateful, too, that I, rather than she, was the one called upon to bear the suffering.

Letters poured in from all over the country. From a girl whom
Jessie had helped over many rough places came these quoted verses:

> You smiling lived, and smiling went away!
> Great heart, you would be sad were we to pay
> In tears our tribute. We would wreathe your grave
> With joy, and write the happiness you gave.
>
> The laughter of a little orphan lad
> You lifted from the wayside and made glad;
> The girl you started on the upward road;
> The toiler whom you helped to bear the load,
>
> .   .   .   .
>
> The counsels that you offered, thoughtful, wise;
> The kindliness that looked out from your eyes;
> The courage and the mighty power of good
> You taught to youth by your white womanhood—
>
> These pay you greater homage than our tears;
> These live beyond your own brief span of years.
> Dear friend, dear friend, the selfless path you trod
> Has marked for us the starlit trail to God.

Browning's words, I put upon her grave:

> Through such souls alone
> God stooping shows sufficient of His light
> For us i' the dark to rise by.

In the Women's Prison at Framingham, Massachusetts, in memory of Jessie I placed a stained-glass window picturing in brilliant
colors the life of St. Francis of Assisi, so that the inmates, starved
cruelly of the beauty of life, could every morning feel its radiance.
One of Jessie's classmates, whom I told about the window, wrote:

An "angel of light" is the one thought that keeps recurring, again
and again to me, for it typifies all she was to every human being whose life
she touched. I love to remember her influence—so unconscious—in college,
and the story I heard at the time of her engagement's being announced

of how the girls that worked in some factory had cut her picture out of the paper and pinned it up in their rooms where they could look often at her lovely face at the end of a tired day and keep up heart.

In time I began to comprehend something of the meaning of suffering. Somehow, mysteriously, suffering if borne constructively can be the pathway to a larger life. It was the pathway Christ chose. Without His having suffered as He did, would any one really care for Him or turn to Him today? Would He even be known? The suffering of the Cross, He turned into supreme victory.

As the days passed the three thoughts and growing realizations which helped me most were these:

First, that I must put out of mind the appalling question of how to live through the year stretching desolately ahead, or through the next month, or through the next week. One day at a time was all that life required. "Sufficient unto the day is the evil thereof." I could muster up courage for a single day; and each night I gave thanks for another day mastered.

Second, that I must struggle manfully and with all the strength I possessed to shift the center of my life from self to God. That took courage and eternal persistence. Complete, or even major, success did not come. But at least the sincere attempt brought help.

Third, that following Christ's teachings I must learn that suffering is something not just to bear but rather to use. I began to see that, if we once allow suffering to master us, unhappiness and tragedy result. But, if we are determined instead to master suffering, power is generated that can, in a way not at the time understood, make for some of the richest and noblest values in life. Suffering constructively borne draws other people to us, gives us new power to influence men's lives. Today I often think of my friend Maynard Hazen, who late in middle life was struck with blindness. He resolved not to let his tragic loss master him, but instead to carry on his work and life with courage and even gayety. As a result his life has become infinitely more meaningful and significant than ever before. He has uplifted and given courage to hosts of friends and admirers.

I wrote to him when blindness threatened not long after Jessie died:

One thing I have learned. To rebel or to repine drives the dagger in all the more cruelly. God can and does transmute suffering into the more precious values of life. Christ's own life was largely suffering. . . . Suffering nobly borne will be our great gift to God and we will learn to give it gladly and lovingly. . . . God will help you, as He has helped me, to bear the suffering. And so we need not be afraid.

Surely, suffering does not mean the failure of God's watchful love over us. Rather, it may mean His desire to deepen our understanding of life and to use us more effectively in winning other lives for Him.

But learning such lessons, as my frequent failures taught me, takes time and courage. Again and again would come relapses. So often I longed to die. Yet that, I also realized, was but a weak and selfish wish as long as the children needed me.

I learned, too, that love does not end with death. No physical barrier, nothing, could now ever separate Jessie and me, could bar our close communion. She now brought heaven, that once had seemed so far away, into daily life.

Months later in Washington I wrote:

I *know* that death is not the end. I know that I shall see Jessie again and that we will look back upon these waiting years that seem so long as but a memory. In the meantime I want to make life as great and crowd as much into it as I can.

The realization began to grow that I must launch out into a life of broader service. With an absolute trust in God's guidance and goodness could there be room for fear? In the words of Browning,

> Grow old along with me!
> The best is yet to be,
> The last of life, for which the first was made:
> Our times are in His hand
> Who saith "A whole I planned,
> Youth shows but half; trust God: see all, nor be afraid!"

In the meantime, work was my refuge. Into this I plunged to the limit of my endurance.

I now had two full-time jobs. I scheduled all my lectures at the Law School during the first two days of the week. The last four, I spent at the State House absorbed in the problems of prison administration. Incessant work crowded out from my mind broken-hearted thinking except in the evenings when, tired to death, I would crawl into bed, and sometimes in order to sleep be given a relaxing massage.

In Boston it was at first an uphill task to win the regard of the state officeholders and politicians. In fact, little love was lost between the politicians and Harvard professors. Neither quite understood the other. The officeholders regarded the professors as utterly impractical, ivory-tower critics.

It is true that the academic life is set apart. How can adequate research be done or treatises written except a man set himself apart for the task? On the other hand, the teacher gains immeasurably by plunging for a time into active field work. Study and field activity —theory and practice—are equally necessary for really constructive work. I now was moving in each. Perhaps that was why I never achieved my treatise on criminal law!

Yet in spite of the distrust between professors and politicians I never experienced at the State House any direct hostility because I was a Harvard professor. I was accepted and welcomed as a State House worker. But that did not mean, of course, the elimination of political intrigue in the office of the Commissioner of Correction.

During my undergraduate days there was little close contact between academic life and government. The change seemed to come during Woodrow Wilson's administration, as war activities multiplied. He himself, of course, stepped directly out of academic into political life. Also, by his time government had entered so many new fields of activity that it became almost necessary to attract into government many different types of trained thinkers. From his day on a significant stream of men flowed from academic life into government work.

Practical difficulties beset me as Commissioner of Correction at almost every turn. At the very outset I found that my principal assistant, responsible for a large part of the work and drawing a substantial salary, was utterly incompetent. But he had strong political influence. I called him into my office and told him that I could not continue him on my pay roll. He wept on my shoulder and told me he had a family and could secure no other means of support. When he found that unavailing he went to his political friends. I could not appoint another to his place without the consent of the Governor and his Council; and the Council was distinctly political in make-up and some of its members little more than political time-servers. It quietly gave me to understand that it would confirm the appointment of no new man. In other words, I could not replace the man with one of competence without a first-rate political upheaval; and in view of my other plans this was something I could not afford. So I had to retain on my pay roll and on my staff a man completely lacking in vision, from whom I could look for no real help in the fight against crime in Massachusetts.

As the work progressed, I began to discover the close and unholy alliance between politics and crime. For instance, the Commissioner of Correction had absolute power to transfer convicts from one prison to another. Now and again two or three ingratiating politicians would press me to transfer a friend, who had run into trouble in the institution where he was confined, to another. I remember on one occasion when two men of unsavory appearance requested such a transfer, how one of my loyal lieutenants refused to leave me alone with them after hours because of fear for my safety.

Six state prisons and penal institutions were under the exclusive control of the Department of Correction. In addition, it had general supervision over some fourteen county jails and houses of correction.

It soon became glaringly evident that, for an intelligent attack on crime in Massachusetts, we must have better planned prisons, and penal institutions more adequate for rehabilitative treatment. Charlestown, the principal State Prison, was medieval. Built a century and a half ago, it was designed primarily to cage degenerates and prevent their escape. "The outer walls are four, and the partition walls two, feet thick," reads an early report. "Each cell has two openings for the admission of air and light; each two feet in height and four inches wide. All the joints of the wall are cramped with iron." In this prehistoric institution men were caged like beasts and even fed in their cells. The cells had no toilet facilities and the bucket system was in operation. Charlestown then held over 900 prisoners.

Just at that time the Federal government stood prepared to aid in the construction of public works in the various states through the

National Recovery Act. I set to work organizing a building program for needed Massachusetts correctional institutions, with the hope of moving every prisoner out of Charlestown Prison and destroying it. At the head of this program I placed a keen young Dartmouth College graduate, John S. Dickey. He later served with me in the Department of State in Washington, and is now president of Dartmouth College.

In my Report as Commissioner of Correction dated November 22, 1933, I wrote:

> If a sound and constructive policy of prison administration is to be followed in Massachusetts, the State Prison at Charlestown must be eliminated. The plant is antiquated and entirely unsuited to modern needs. There is insufficient space. The buildings are old and impossible to renovate. The shops are inadequate and subject to serious fire hazard. The general plan of the institution makes it impossible to administer it along modern lines of penology.

If Charlestown Prison was to be torn down other institutions must be built properly to house and care for its 900 prisoners. The criminal population which Massachusetts had to house, feed, and maintain was then between 3,500 and 4,000. Other State penal institutions besides Charlestown required extensive alteration and replanning.

The Reformatory at Concord was another maximum security institution built in 1875 to replace Charlestown. But Charlestown was not torn down and the Concord institution, built to be a state prison, was soon turned into a "reformatory." It was utterly unsuited to rehabilitative work. In spite of its name records showed that almost 60 per cent of its inmates after their discharge were convicted of fresh crimes; and one can well doubt whether 10 per cent were ever really "reformed."

Prior to my appointment the state had constructed a State Prison Colony at Norfolk; and this was under the charge of Howard B. Gill, a man with progressive ideas but unfortunately often unable to secure the necessary support of legislative groups at the State House. They thought him impractical and viewed him with considerable misgiving. Gill was pioneering in his efforts to treat prisoners as individual personalities. His prime objective was redemptive. He sought to re-

habilitate warped lives and warped personalities, and realized that
stone walls and steel doors were not enough. But he was not always
too tactful; and his efforts often ran directly counter to well entrenched popular ideas.

The Reformatory for Women at Framingham was headed by
Miriam Van Waters, an exceptionally able and conscientious official.
Under considerable handicap Dr. Van Waters was doing a very constructive piece of work. Unhappily, some years after I had left, the
politicians prevailed upon the Governor in 1950 to retire her. Public
opinion rallied to her support; the Governor was forced to reinstate
her, and, I am glad to say, she still continues her constructive work
at Framingham.

The criminal insane were housed at the State Farm at Bridge-
water. There human tragedy seemed to reach a climax. The violent,
criminal insane cannot be allowed to live with others, cannot in some
cases even be allowed simple furniture in their cells. I remember one
time against the advice of the guards going into the cell of an inmate
to talk with him, an armed guard standing at my side to protect me.
A soft mattress on the floor was his only furniture. The criminal insane constitute perhaps the most difficult and tragic problem of correctional work.

Gradually, in the face of many difficulties, we began to clarify
the needs and to shape up a new State building program to be financed with the help of the National Recovery Administration.
Maximum security stone prisons are excessively costly both to build
and to operate. It became very clear to us that only a limited proportion of prisoners required housing in such costly institutions. For
some prisoners, whose personalities have become so hardened that
rehabilitation is out of the question, they are necessary. But for a very
substantial proportion of convicts they are not. Many short-term
prisoners can be safely housed in only medium security institutions;
some can safely be housed even without prison walls, behind lock
and key in rehabilitation centers planned primarily for rehabilitation, for the teaching of trades, for rural or farm training, or for
psychiatric treatment of one kind or another.

Our program looked toward tearing down Charlestown Prison
and using Concord Reformatory, enlarged with a farm dormitory,
for the more hopeless and hardened part of the prison population;

we would then transfer to the State Prison Colony at Norfolk all the better rehabilitative prospects. I also advocated a new institution with a capacity of 250, equipped with maximum security facilities, to receive all prisoners upon conviction by the courts, for study and classification; from it the more hopeful cases would be transferred to Norfolk, and the less hopeful to Concord.

As we analyzed the problem we inevitably concluded that only upon a comprehensive study of the personality and case history of each individual criminal could sound prison administration be built. Such a program, already inaugurated by my predecessor, Warren Stearns, was close to my heart; and fortunately we could press forward upon it without securing additional legislation. In charge of the all-important work of preparing individual case studies I placed Frank Loveland, who possessed outstanding ability. He carefully studied each incoming prisoner; and the man was classified and assigned to work according to his advice. Upon the resulting case studies rested the determination which of the several state institutions was most suitable for the prisoner; upon them, too, the Board of Parole came to base much of its work. Political influence in the handling of prisoners was thus considerably reduced.

My hope as Commissioner of Correction was to build prisons and institutions suited for handling different types of prisoners, to make a careful study of each convicted prisoner as he arrived, and then to commit him to whatever institution was best suited to his needs. We hoped, by substantially lowering the number of recidivists, materially to reduce the costs of crime to the Commonwealth of Massachusetts.

Not all the prison wardens and officials equally shared the ideas we were developing. In order to unify thinking, coordinate activities, and strengthen the common work I organized monthly staff meetings of all wardens and heads of institutions. These proved to be immensely useful and helped to stimulate an understanding intimacy among our group.

The fight against crime will always be an uphill fight. With all her brilliancy and progress, America's effort to cope with crime has been for the most part tragic failure. A committee of the American Bar Association to study existing conditions recently reported that "the criminal situation in the United States so far as crimes of violence are concerned is worse than in any other civilized country."

Crime costs in the United States are estimated at $10,000,000,000 to $20,000,000,000 a year. State and federal prisons hold 185,000 prisoners; and it is estimated that 100,000 additional persons are in jails and 40,000 in juvenile institutions. The cost alone of operating the state and federal institutions is about $225,000,000 a year. Prison population is increasing at a rate of some 4,500 a year, and the annual cost of new facilities to house this number is about $45,000,000.

Careful studies show that the proportion of criminals who are discharged from prison only to be returned again and again and again is appallingly high—probably considerably over two-thirds. Crime today, and particularly juvenile delinquency, is on the increase. And hard experience proves that punishment as an end and aim in itself yields surprisingly little social gain. Frequently it hardens the victim beyond all hope of redemption.

Unhappily in the public mind punishment is still the cure for crime. When Gill suggested putting curtains on the windows at Norfolk, the newspapers went after him like hounds on the trail of a hare; and the legislative groups did not forget it. In designing new institutions some of our architects asked: "Why make a prison so ugly? Why not let them have a few points of beauty, provided these do not lessen the security or increase the cost?" We agreed. The newspapers got hold of that and made much of it. The pressure of public opinion was so great that we had to instruct the architects to forget their ideas. We were well aware that legislators are strongly influenced by public opinion.

In my official Report as Commissioner, November 22, 1933, to the Senate and House of Representatives of the Commonwealth of Massachusetts I said:

The fruits of good prison administration must be looked for in the lives of the human beings confined within institution walls. . . . Almost all prisoners are discharged again into the community; and the real touchstone of success in sound prison administration depends upon the kind of lives prison inmates are compelled to live—upon whether their personalities are being hardened beyond redemption or won back to a point where social rehabilitation becomes a real possibility.

Twentieth century crime will never be successfully met with seventeenth and eighteenth century methods. . . . The barren objective of punishing evildoers must give way to the more practical one of protecting social interests. We must seek to impose not moral judgments but effective preventives.

Before all else we must realize that prisoners are no less and no more than human beings. The problem of crime is essentially a problem of human conduct. To prevent continued lives of crime means changing the motivating impulses of human beings. What will prove effective with some will be utterly unavailing with others. . . . The personality of the criminal and his life history can become really known only as a result of an intensive study made by trained caseworkers and psychiatrists. For this purpose felons upon conviction should be confined for one or two months in a receiving institution where mental and physical examinations may be made. . . . Upon these findings, carefully checked and verified, should depend the treatment to be accorded him.*

Just as we were getting under full steam in our challenging adventure the turn of events halted me in my tracks. Under the new Roosevelt administration I was asked to serve in the Department of State at Washington in a work of such importance that I felt unable to refuse. Accordingly my work in Boston ended rather abruptly in November, 1933.

When I resigned I was presented with the huge old key to Charlestown Prison, framed and under glass, which still hangs on my wall at home. Fastened to it is a parchment scroll, which recites:

This KEY
taken from the Arch
the oldest part of the
State Prison at Charlestown
built A.D. 1806, is presented
to Commissioner
FRANCIS B. SAYRE
on the eve of his departure
for National Service
as a symbol of his great
work in opening the way to
the abandonment of that
Ancient Prison
A.D. 1933
November 22

* *Annual Report for 1933 of the Commissioner of Correction, p. 3.*

After my departure the program lapsed. Charlestown Prison took on a new lease of life. For twenty years more this antiquated institution continued as the chief prison of Massachusetts.

Finally, fresh public interest was aroused by serious prison disturbances at Charlestown in early 1955. Riots were threatened. Governor Herter appointed a committee to submit recommendations for reorganizing the correctional system of the State. The committee reported to the Governor in the summer of 1955 that Charlestown Prison "has been a national disgrace for many, many years" and recommended its destruction. It further reported, confirming our findings of a score of years before: "In an acceptable correctional system classification is of first importance. . . . But there is no classification in a positive sense in Massachusetts."

As a result sweeping legislation was passed. Once again Massachusetts is conscious of the need to fight crime in more constructive ways.

I I

Assistant Secretary of State

My call to Washington came as a result of earlier contacts with Mr. Roosevelt as Governor of New York. In August, 1932, a letter from Raymond Moley, helping to organize Governor Roosevelt's Presidential campaign, had requested my advice and assistance in the campaign plans "particularly with reference to the general lines of his policy regarding foreign affairs. . . . I wonder if you could write down a few notes about what you think are wise policies for such a purpose."

Upon Mr. Roosevelt's invitation I visited him more than once at Hyde Park during September and October, and talked over with him the issues in the field of foreign policy which I felt he should stress in the campaign.

I wrote to Mr. Roosevelt on October 13:

I have come into contact with many quite influential people who say that they are going to vote for Hoover because you have failed to declare yourself in a progressive spirit on the problem of foreign relations and because of their feeling that the foreign problems are some of the most vital which America will have to face during the coming four years. They are continually bringing up the speech which you delivered before the New York Grange last spring. It seems to me that ideas such as these should be corrected and that a ringing declaration from you, showing the true slant of your mind on the foreign problem, would win the support of a large number of influential leaders and mean a great many votes.

I felt that Governor Roosevelt was underestimating the importance of foreign issues. He had a very ready and open mind, and was slowly shaping his policies in accordance with current developments. Of course he had no conception of what lay ahead. None of us did.

I had very definite ideas as to the kind of policies *I* felt were needed. Governor Roosevelt listened with real attention.

Three years before, in the *Atlantic Monthly,* I had written:

Seldom in her history has America seemed to enjoy such serene security as now. Prosperous beyond her dreams, conscious of a power to shape world destinies such as perhaps no nation has enjoyed before, she seems to sail the very crest of the waves. Yet seldom in her history have the undercurrents of danger been running as strongly as at present. The sharp reversal of American foreign policy which followed her rejection of the Versailles Treaty is hurrying America to a crisis of serious import. . . .

The solution of American problems of foreign policy may be sought through either one of two sharply divergent courses, and upon the course which America finally chooses during the next decade or two will depend very largely her future destiny. One course lies in the direction of the newer method which Europe has been trying to learn since the tragic breakdown of the old in 1914. *It is the method of seeking common understandings and of taking united action for the solution of international difficulties before they become acute.* . . . The alternative course is armed isolation. The logic of the situation in the minds of many compels such a policy.

Will America with all her youth and buoyancy, choose armed isolation, the old method which brought inevitably the world conflict of 1914? Or will she choose international cooperation and the effort to substitute law for war?

As Election Day approached, Mr. Roosevelt gave increasing support to the League of Nations and a policy based upon collective security.

Following his election in November I wrote of my delight; and on November 19 he replied:

Dear Frank,

It was grand to have your enthusiastic letter and you may be sure that such a word from you meant much to me.

I was also glad to have you write me frankly and freely of the foreign problems which are so much in your mind. I had not happened to hear of that vote for entrance into the League—as you say, highly significant in view of the part of the country from which it came.

I do not think I need tell you that I am anxious to have all shades of opinion and advice on this perplexing but imminent question. When I come back from Warm Springs, perhaps we can talk about it at some length.

After Mr. Roosevelt's inauguration now and again through 1933 I met men serving in the new administration. In the spring William Phillips of Beverly, Massachusetts, the new Undersecretary of State, invited me to lunch as he was passing through Boston. Early the following autumn I was invited to Washington for a talk with the Secretary of State, Cordell Hull, and Mr. Phillips. Mr. Hull, who was about to take off for the seventh Pan American conference at Montevideo, asked at the end of our talk if I would accept appointment as Assistant Secretary of State with the responsibility of handling all economic problems coming before the Department of State. In spite of my inexperience I did not see how I could well refuse.

Toward the end of October, on a visit to Williams College, I talked with President Harry A. Garfield, who told me in confidence that he was contemplating retirement and asked whether I would accept the presidency of Williams College if it were offered. I told him of my talk with Secretary Hull. Next morning the newspapers carried the announcement of my appointment. Shortly thereafter I received a cable from His Majesty, the King of Thailand, reading: "My sincere felicitations on your appointment to the post of Assistant Secretary of State. Prajadhipok R."

The new appointment meant resignation as Massachusetts Commissioner of Correction and also as professor at Harvard. At the time of my departure one of my criminal law students wrote me: "From all sides only regrets can be heard. . . . It is a wonderful inspiration to young men to see one whom they admire step into a position of great importance. I shall never forget the thrill that was mine when we stood and applauded as you left our class for the last time."

I was glad to be able to leave the empty home in Cambridge and enter new surroundings. My older boy, Francis, Jr., had entered Williams College in September. I decided to allow the younger children to complete the school year where they were. Accordingly Eleanor remained at the Winsor School in Boston to graduate in June, and Woodrow at the Belmont Hill School. The children, of course, came down to Washington to spend their Christmas and Easter holidays with me. The following autumn Eleanor entered Bryn Mawr College, to which I could make frequent visits from Washington, and Woodrow, living with me, entered St. Albans Cathedral School in Washington.

My heart was still broken; life had lost much of its meaning, and I was fighting a profound grief. At every turn I missed her who had so filled my life.

On November 25, our twentieth wedding anniversary, I said goodbye to Cambridge and to the happy life we had lived there. I boarded the train for Washington, to begin a new life in a lonely room at the Blackstone Hotel.

The next morning I commenced my work in the Department of State with considerable fear and trembling. I was not, in sober truth, too well trained in economics. My general background was rather in law. Nevertheless, I reflected, I had approached almost every one of my other jobs with similar fear and trembling. I had gone to Siam without training or experience in diplomacy, or knowledge of the Far East. I had accepted appointment as Commissioner of Correction although I was familiar only with the academic side of crime and knew nothing of political problems and conditions. But I believe that no one should refuse a task because it seems too big for him. A man should have the courage to accept and grow up to any job which is really worth while and which he is asked to swing.

Upon entering the Department of State I fell into the work that was nearest and dearest to the heart of Cordell Hull. From his earliest days in Congress and in the Senate he had sought the lowering of international trade barriers and the elimination of trade discriminations. And this far-reaching and critical program he now entrusted to me.

The group of men with whom I worked during the next five and a half years was an outstanding one. For sheer ability, singleness of purpose and, with a few exceptions, loyalty to the ideals of their leader, Cordell Hull, I have never seen its equal. The Democrats had just recently come into power. The New Deal was in the making. It was a creative period. No war was on the horizon. The State Department group in those days was still small and closely knit, working together almost like a family, dominated by the spirit of Cordell Hull. I was proud to be one of them.

Cordell Hull was not a professional diplomat. Quite the contrary. From humble beginnings on a farm in Tennessee he had made his way up, studied law, and by sheer force of will and integrity of character had won a Tennessee judgeship. Thereafter he served for many years in Congress, first in the House and later in the Senate, ever fighting for human rights against privileged groups. The lowering of international trade barriers, one of his most determined goals, was a natural outgrowth of his profound belief that true democracy could not be built upon privilege, nor lasting peace upon economic conflict. As he once wrote of his work in Congress: "From then on, to me, unhampered trade dovetailed with peace; high tariffs, trade barriers and unfair economic practices with war."

As I came to know him as a member of his working family, my respect and admiration for his sterling qualities grew. He was always simple in his ways and never could bring himself to insist upon strict diplomatic formalities. I think of him as I so often saw him in the old State, War, and Navy Building next to the White House, at the large flat-top desk, piled high with papers, under the southern windows of his comfortable spacious office. My own office as Assistant Secretary of State adjoined his anteroom, and I was in and out of his office two or three times a day. Generally as I entered he was thumbing through current telegrams selected for him out of the mass of cables coming in from every part of the world by his faithful office assistant, Harry McBride. Snow-white hair emphasized the piercing deep brown eyes—eyes that often lit up with quiet humor as he talked with his friends. I think of him always seated at his desk. He was not physically active or high-strung. His movements were like his mind —quiet, imperturbable, calm. His countenance was gentle, immobile —and rather belied the square cut of his jaw and straight firm mouth which revealed his fighting determination. His voice had the slow musical drawl of his native South.

Often several of us would be called in to help him formulate or polish some important speech. He did not have the agile, quick wit of an orator; often he groped for words, and sometimes he struggled painfully over his speeches.

He had a singular devotion to his ideals, and was firm as a rock in allegiance to his underlying principles. His long experience in Congress gave him strength on "the Hill"; in case of Congressional tangles he could always pick up the telephone and talk to his former associates in the intimacy of comradeship. Everywhere he was respected. He had high qualities of leadership and was recognized throughout the country as the strongest member of the Roosevelt Cabinet. Americans believed in him and trusted in him. He never sought praise or adulation. It was the work—positive achievement—that he cared about.

So far as I know he had no outside interests. He labored tirelessly and for long hours, including Saturday afternoons; and every Sunday morning he would walk down from the Carlton Hotel where he lived to his office to read the incoming cables and meet with a small coterie of office intimates. His only relaxation was occasional games of croquet, which he played with skill on the grounds behind Secretary Stimson's home with three or four of us from the Department in the late afternoon. Incessant work left him no time for social engagements; formal diplomatic entertaining, he left almost entirely to his Undersecretary of State.

I always admired Mrs. Hull for the calm strength, the understanding, and the unselfish loyalty with which she helped her husband to bear his load as Secretary of State. One evening she greeted us in her friendly way at the door of their apartment in the Carlton Hotel.

"Cordell is still at the Department," she told us. "I have been waiting dinner for him." As we sat down, she added with a smile: "You know, when Cordell comes home late like this, with his mind full of his work, I could put a dish of straw in front of him, and he would eat it unquestioningly. He really wouldn't know the difference."

The Undersecretary, William Phillips, was of an entirely different mold. Tall, slender, handsome, of New England and Harvard background, he had entered diplomacy in youth and knew the ropes. But he, too, was a man of high purpose and sensitive feelings, and he shared to the full the ideals and purposes of Secretary Hull. He befriended me when I came to Washington with an understanding heart, sensing my loneliness; and I have always remembered with gratitude his outreaching kindness to me during that hard time.

Next in rank to the Undersecretary were the four Assistant Secretaries: Wilbur J. Carr, in charge of the administrative, financial, and "housekeeping" work of the Department; Judge R. Walton Moore, an elderly, able, kindly man of whom I was very fond, to whom were assigned special tasks and problems; Sumner Welles (until recently ambassador to Cuba), concentrating upon Latin American affairs; and myself, in charge of the economic problems, which were now coming to play an ever increasing role in the making of our foreign policy.

The man upon whom I relied heavily for assistance in formulating trade and commercial policy was Harry C. Hawkins, who later became head of the Trade Agreements Division of the Department. He was a rare and splendid man whose whole heart and soul, like Secretary Hull's, were in this work of reducing excessive trade barriers. I suspect that, apart from Secretary Hull, the success of the trade agreements program was due more to Harry Hawkins than to any other single man. We were pioneering in new fields; and when I first came I turned largely to him for guidance and help.

I asked John Dickey to come down from Boston as my special assistant in "A–S" (Assistant Secretary—Sayre), as my office was called. I could always turn to him and know that he would never fail me.

Some extremely important problems confronted the new Administration in the field of economics. The Hawley-Smoot Law boosting American tariff rates to an unprecedented level, which in spite of the protests of more than a thousand leading American economists had been passed in 1930, lay like a dead hand on American international trade and threatened economic disaster. American exports fell to a third of their former value. Ruinous repercussions throughout our domestic economy followed. Great surpluses of cotton, wheat, flour, and other commodities, unsalable abroad, began to pile up.

To meet national economic problems such as these, and to centralize in a single agency supervision over all government action affecting exports and imports, there had been organized under the President's direction an interdepartmental Executive Committee on Commercial Policy, composed of representatives from the various departments concerned with foreign trade. William Phillips, the Undersecretary of State, was chosen chairman *pro tem* at the opening meeting late in November. When I arrived I was made chairman. Thereafter the committee assumed responsibility, of course always subject to the direction of the President, for the formulation of American foreign economic policy.

The committee met regularly twice a week. It was attended by top-ranking and capable men, and was not just a *pro forma* committee. From the Department of Agriculture generally came Secretary of Agriculture Henry Wallace or, when he was away, Rexford Tugwell or Leslie Wheeler. From the Department of Commerce came Assistant Secretary John Dickinson. Representing the Tariff Commission were its chairman, Robert Lincoln O'Brien, and Thomas Walker Page, both outstanding men. The Treasury Department generally sent Assistant Secretary Wayne Chatfield Taylor.

In this interdepartmental committee, representing widely different interests and points of view, it was heartening to find a group so single-minded in seeking to build sound economic foundations, so free from narrow political pettifogging and from departmental self-interest and jealousies. We kept the committee very informal and small.

Each of us felt deeply that we could never build a stable world peace until we secured better and sounder economic foundations, particularly in foreign trade. We realized that excessive American tariffs invited retaliation by other countries and could only result in serious injury to our country as a whole.

We therefore set to work formulating an adequate program and framing appropriate legislation to meet this deep-rooted problem.

There also came before the committee a succession of current trade problems. For instance, there was the problem of competing Japanese trade goods. Japanese cheap zippers, inferior electric light bulbs, tuna fish, and other products flooded the American market, and domestic producers with lessened sales protested, advocating

high trade and tariff barriers against such imports. Powerful lobbyists began to gather in Washington. To protect our market against
injury through cheap and poor-quality importations I worked out
with the Japanese Ambassador an informal "gentlemen's agreement"
whereby Japan agreed to place strict limits on the exportation to
America of specified inferior-quality goods.

The members of the Executive Committee on Commercial Policy
usually worked together in hearty agreement; but there was one dis-
senting voice. It was that of George Peek, whom President Roosevelt,
to our wonderment, had appointed as his Special Adviser on Foreign
Trade. Mr. Peek with his hearty manner and broad, winning smile
was personally most agreeable and easy to get along with; but his
fundamentally protectionist views were contrary to those of ourselves
and of Mr. Hull. His appointment and the failure of the White
House later to straighten out the resulting conflicts of policy are
perhaps illustrative of the way in which President Roosevelt often
worked. When fundamental disagreements arose among subordinates
he seldom entered the arena to settle the controversy. He seemed to
prefer to let the conflict ripen, even though it often meant two men
working at cross purposes or even at swords' points. The results were
sometimes tragic.

Raymond Moley was another example. In June, 1933, President
Roosevelt sent Mr. Hull to the London Economic Conference as
America's top representative; shortly after, he sent Mr. Moley as his
personal representative, regardless of the fact that the two held views
directly in conflict. Only shipwreck could result. For this and other
reasons the London Conference ended in failure. And yet for months
after that Mr. Moley continued to hold Mr. Roosevelt's confidence
and to act with his support.

All this meant heartache and sometimes tense conflict for Secretary Hull. A man of smaller stature, fearing he had lost the confidence
of the President, would have resigned. But Mr. Hull, steadfast and
unflinching, did not.

Later Mr. Moley dropped out of the Washington picture. So
did George Peek. But only after months of conflict. Unhappily there
were several other similar cases.

One must remember that Mr. Roosevelt was a many-sided man.
He enjoyed people of many different characters and hues and gath-

ered around him men of widely differing viewpoints. Perhaps this was due to his extraordinary breadth of vision.

I sided strongly with Mr. Hull, and against Mr. Peek and Mr. Moley. To me Mr. Hull's fundamental policy of seeking practicable ways to lower international trade barriers and to eliminate foreign trade discriminations was eternally sound.

I suppose that Mr. Hull sensed that I was absolutely loyal to him and to his policies. It was a constant surprise, nevertheless, during all my work as chairman of the Executive Committee on Commercial Policy and during the time we were hammering out the trade agreements program, how seldom Mr. Hull called me into his office to ask "How about this?" or "How about that?" However, he kept a watchful eye on all that we did and his queries not infrequently caused changes in our program. To the decisions of our Commercial Policy Committee he always gave full backing.

Our work in the Commercial Policy Committee continued unabated until my departure from Washington in 1939. I used to wonder whether any government interdepartmental committee with members representing such varied and differing interests ever worked more smoothly and cooperatively. It seems regrettable in many ways that the committee is now no longer in existence.

My individual responsibilities in the Department kept me steadily on the go. It was exciting and rewarding and altogether different from my academic life. The international economic problems which were constantly arising brought me into close touch with the ambassadors and ministers of many governments; and these stimulating contacts gave me an ever-widening variety of interests and friends.

All kinds of problems, some but slightly concerned with economic issues, came to my desk. Some were not economic at all.

I remember the fight in the United States Senate for ratification of the World Court treaty. There was every reason for America to become a member of the World Court set up under the League of Nations. Yet the isolationists stoutly opposed it. The President asked me to help line up our forces in the Senate for ratification of the necessary treaty. Senator Key Pittman, the chairman of the Committee on Foreign Relations, felt unable to lead our forces; Senator Joseph Robinson agreed to do so. He fought well. I was at his side the whole way through. Our forces were well organized and we expected to win.

But the final vote at the end of the week unhappily had to be deferred until the following Monday. Over the week end popular radio speakers, Will Rogers and Father Coughlin, spoke so persuasively against the Court that several senators who had been wavering voted against ratification, and we lost the fight. Will Rogers had a large place in the hearts of Americans and was of a kindly, winning nature, but he knew nothing of statecraft; and it always has seemed to me a shame that he should have ignorantly let the isolationists prostitute his popularity to block American entrance into the World Court.

One of the highly important issues that demanded increasing attention, was the United States' relationships with the Philippines. In 1934 Congress had passed the Philippine Independence Act setting up for a ten-year period the Philippine Commonwealth Government, and promising complete independence in 1946. The new and unique relationships between the two peoples growing out of this Act created many vital questions, and an increasing number of them came to my desk.

During 1937–1939 I was also asked to serve on the Board of Examiners for the Foreign Service and also on the Board of Foreign Service Personnel. This went to the very heart of the Department's work; for inevitably the character of the men chosen for the foreign field and the wise settlement of personnel problems must make or break the foreign service.

Such spare moments as I could muster had to be devoted to the preparation of speeches and addresses to build up popular backing for our objectives, and also to reading sheaves of incoming cables to keep abreast of current problems abroad. My "homework" never ceased.

During these driving years when I worked hard from early morning until late at night, I sought relaxation by taking a month off every summer during the intense August heat of Washington. In 1934 I took my daughter Eleanor on a steamer trip through the Baltic to Leningrad and back; and in 1935, while my two boys were at camp, I took her and her young friend across the Atlantic on a cargo boat and then on a walking trip through Ireland. That year we had taken into our family Helen Bell, the daughter of a missionary in India and a friend of Eleanor's; and in 1936, the two boys having returned to their summer camp, she and another friend of Eleanor's went with us on a bicycle trip through Normandy and Brittany. These trips helped to keep me in close contact with my daughter as well as to give refreshment of soul and renewed strength for the coming year's work.

All through these years I was fighting to regain my lost zest for life. I filled my thoughts with national and international concerns. I prayed with all my soul that God would help me walk bravely forward, and that He, and not chance, would shape my remaining years.

And then in 1937 came a wondrous answer. I met another rare and kindred spirit, Elizabeth Evans Graves. I could not doubt that God had sent her into my life. Her splendid husband, Ralph Graves, long in editorial work in Washington and on the staff of the National Geographic Society, had died shortly before my wife, and she too was wandering through dark valleys, lonely, looking to Him for help. We could not doubt God's hand in our meeting.

We saw each other first as guests of a friend at the Endless Caverns in Virginia. There we had gone for an all-morning walk together in the woods and been caught in a downpour of rain, which in no way dampened the delight of our walk. She was an artist; and since her husband's death she had conducted an art class in the Mount Vernon Seminary in addition to bringing up two attractive little sons, Ralph and Bill.

As we came to know each other in Washington we realized that there could be only one outcome. Although work did not permit us to meet too often, each of us knew. One day we went canoeing on the Potomac River and took Ralph and Bill along. When I called her, as I had come to do, by the name of "Betsy Sayre," a meaningful look passed between the two boys; and when we told them shortly thereafter Bill confessed that "on that day in the canoe Mr. Sayre had 'spilled the beans.'" Their delight was unmistakably genuine.

On June 28, 1937, we were quietly married in the presence of our families and a few intimate friends; and following our wedding we, the only two passengers, sailed from Boston on a freighter for London. From London we went to the Lake District, which Wordsworth had loved, and there took a walking trip; and after that, walking the trails together, we discovered and fell in love with Scotland. We sailed for home from Glasgow in early September.

Since then Betty has stood by my side through fair weather and through foul. Without her I wonder if I could have lived on.

Through my new life with her what was before a struggling belief on my part has turned into an absolute certainty. It is this: No matter how dark the world around us, no matter how black the sky, we need not fear, if only we have the soundness of mind to turn to God and put our hand in His. He loves each one of us with a tenderness far deeper than that of an earthly parent; and when out of the deep we call upon Him, somehow, as I have found, in unexpected ways He is close beside us, helping.

The supreme events in our lives, I have learned through the experience of many years, come not through chance but by His will and shaping.

Betty means to me and always will mean the irrefutable assurance of God's care and love in the shaping of our individual lives.

Through the beautiful, new companionship given us, as I know now, by Him, we have gone forward with happiness into new fields.

12

Breaking Down Trade Barriers

When Franklin Roosevelt took office in 1933 the United States faced a grave national emergency, due in part to the loss of foreign markets, which threatened disaster to our farmers and to our manufacturers. After the Hawley-Smoot Act of 1930 had raised American tariff rates to inordinately high levels, the value of American exports had fallen from $5,157,000,000 in 1929 to $1,647,000,000 in 1933. As a result great, unsalable surpluses piled up at home; and unsold surpluses, by glutting domestic markets, demoralized the prices received for that part of the product sold at home and thereby began to cause throughout the country economic dislocation and suffering.

Something had to be done.

This momentous problem stared us in the face when I assumed the chairmanship of the interdepartmental Executive Committee on Commercial Policy. Nor could we disregard the grave and far-reaching international repercussions. As the Economic Intelligence Service of the League of Nations pointed out in 1932:

The whole movement [toward higher tariffs] was undoubtedly accentuated both by the alarm and resentment felt in many countries as the discussions of the new Hawley-Smoot tariff dragged on in the United States Congress from May, 1929 to June, 1930, and by the real effects of that tariff when it went into operation. It was followed quickly by new tariffs in many other countries, among others, Canada, Cuba, Mexico, France, Italy, Spain, Australia, New Zealand. In the case of the British Dominions, higher general tariffs were accompanied by an increased measure of imperial preference, and the general idea of a more extensive system of preferential duties with the British Empire was appreciably advanced.

During the three-year period following the economic collapse of 1929 every industrial nation saw its foreign markets rapidly disappear as a result of mounting international trade barriers. Each nation entered into feverish competition to sell abroad a maximum and to buy from abroad a minimum. To protect against high excesses of imports over exports and the consequent outflow of gold, nations sought to cut down imports by intensive drives toward national "autarchy," or economic self-sufficiency. This movement was still further intensified by military considerations. New measures were devised arbitrarily to restrict imports. Through "quota" restrictions the importation of goods was cut to absolute, fixed amounts; and quotas varying from nation to nation came to be used as new economic weapons to discriminate against trade rivals and even to attain political ends. Other weapons were forged for similar purposes—exchange control restrictions, government trade monopolies, import-licensing requirements. Preferences and discriminations became the order of the day. Nation became pitted against nation in the parry and thrust of bitter trade rivalry. The trade highways of the world became blocked with impassable barriers.

Clearly some concerted program must be formulated and carried out if disaster was to be averted; and it fell to our Executive Committee on Commercial Policy to formulate such a program.

Our committee realized that in the modern, utterly interdependent world the standard of living of each industrialized nation was directly and inescapably dependent upon the import of raw materials and the export of finished products. No great industrial nation could possibly achieve complete economic self-sufficiency. Economic self-sufficiency was a policy of retrogression and ran counter to the entire course of civilization's advance. In spite of the strong and insistent demands of powerful protectionist groups, therefore, the committee reached the unanimous conclusion that legislation should be sought authorizing the President to enter into trade agreements with foreign nations reciprocally lowering trade barriers by agreement for the purpose of promoting foreign trade.

A few of us after considerable study drafted a proposed trade agreements bill for the consideration of the full committee. George Peek strongly objected, speaking from very practical experience: "That's too complicated a piece of legislative machinery. You'll never get Congress to agree to pass such a bill. You've got to simplify it and make the bill short." He was absolutely right. Beginning anew, we drafted a short, pithy, very simply phrased bill, which the committee in the end unanimously approved. It authorized the President to enter into executive agreements with foreign countries for reciprocal reduction of trade barriers, and in accordance with such agreements to reduce by as much as 50 per cent existing American tariff rates in exchange for foreign reductions. A highly significant provision directed the President, in the exercise of this power, to continue the traditional policy of the United States of "unconditional most-favored-nation" treatment—in other words, to treat all nations alike on a basis of equality and nondiscrimination so long as each nation accords the same treatment to us, and to refrain from exchanging preferential rates.

On February 28, 1934, the President called a White House conference to consider our draft bill. It was attended by Vice President Garner, Senator Robinson, Senator Harrison, Speaker Rainey, Representative Byrnes, Representative Doughton, Secretary Hull, Secretary Wallace, John Dickinson and Willard Thorp of the Department of Commerce, George Peek and myself.

We pointed out the disastrous consequences at home if the United States should lose its foreign markets. In agriculture, for instance, the loss of foreign markets would make it necessary to retire or find some other use for approximately 7,800,000 acres of wheat land, 15,600,000 acres of cotton land, 695,000 acres of tobacco land, and 5,700,000 acres of corn land needed primarily for raising hogs. Taking into consideration the land required to produce other important agricultural exports, seed, and food for work stock, we should have to retire or find some other use for 30,000,000 or 40,000,000 acres of farm land.

In the industrial field, the same kind of difficulties would have to be faced, although the workers might be somewhat more mobile.

The committee's draft won the approval of every one present at the White House conference, and on the following Friday, March 2, it was introduced into the House of Representatives with a strong message from the President urging adoption.

Enactment by Congress of the trade agreements bill required a very real struggle. It was a new step in American trade policy. We had to oppose powerful interests, strongly entrenched. We were proposing to give to the President the power by executive agreement, without Congressional or Senate approval, to reduce American tariffs in exchange for similar reductions by foreign nations. To authorize the cutting of tariffs is to arouse immediate determined opposition from vigorous and highly financed lobbies fighting for sectional interests and controlling many Congressional votes. If any one is bold enough to propose a reduction in the tariff, let us say, on cheese, at once he will have a powerful agricultural lobby on his back.

Our trade agreements often included agricultural products; in reality the farmers stood to profit heavily by the program. But, because certain sectional interests—for instance, cheese and milk producers—feared that their own sales might be lessened by undue tariff reductions, they would instruct their Congressional lobbyists to fight us tooth and nail. Again and again the agricultural lobby stood out against us.

The agricultural lobby was only one. There were many others.

The fight for passage of the bill began in early March with hearings before the powerful House Ways and Means Committee, of which Mr. Doughton was chairman. After several of us had presented the Administration's views and answered a heavy fire of questions and objections, other witnesses made their appearances. We were bitterly attacked by powerful sectional groups. It was a fight between the representatives of national interests—of the people as a whole—and the representatives of local or sectional interests. As so often happens, the national interests had few to fight for them; local or sectional interests were represented by highly paid, skillful advocates. Congressmen themselves necessarily must have regard for their constituencies and often find themselves on the side of local rather than national interests.

President Roosevelt, courageous and fearless, was always ready to back us up in the struggle. Later, when it came to making trade

agreements and we had satisfied ourselves with the text of an agreement, I would go to the White House to talk it over with him. Our
whole program was based upon finding places in the tariff wall where
reductions could be made without substantial injury to American
producers. Occasionally, however, a proposed cut might do local
hurt, and I would say to the President: "Here we must make a tariff
cut which might harm you politically. You may hear about this."
Almost always he would reply, "Well, Frank, if it's necessary, go
ahead, go ahead." He had confidence in us and did not hesitate to
follow through with our program.

In the final vote in the House Ways and Means Committee, the
members lined up almost solidly along party lines. The Republicans
attacked us bitterly; many of them were tied in with high tariff interests. Representative Harold Knutson fought hard to kill the bill.
But the Democrats stood loyally behind us. The real question was,
could we hold in line Representatives from states controlled by special interests?

It took hard work to marshal the support of all the Democrats.
It meant far more than laying a paper program before them. I was
on "the Hill" a good part of the time, conferring with leaders and
talking with members. Sometimes it would be necessary for the President to invite certain Representatives or Senators to the White
House.

Always I tried to present the issues and marshal the arguments
from the viewpoint, not of Democratic or Republican policies, but
of genuine American interests. As I said in the Congressional hearings in 1937:

Believe me, particularly you members on the right-hand side of this
bench, I am really addressing myself to Americans and not to partisans.
I think we have a real issue here which deeply concerns us all as Americans
and which does not depend upon policies which are Republican or Democratic. I think it goes too deep for partisan considerations.

My efforts brought often generous response even from the Republican side. Representative Woodruff declared in the course of
the hearings, "I want to thank you also for the very splendid way in
which you have handled the subject to which you have been addressing yourself."

In our partisan hard-fought struggle I valued particularly the comments of Republican leaders. My friend Robert Lincoln O'Brien, chairman of the United States Tariff Commission, wrote: "At a dinner at Mr. Treadway's the other night, when only Republicans happened to be present, Mr. Treadway stated that in all the years he had served on the Ways and Means Committee, he had never heard any subject so well and ably presented as that in which you had figured a few days before. His comments were superlative and unreserved."

In spite of sharp fire the bill stood up well under strong attack; and on March 17 the Committee on Ways and Means approved the bill.

Six days later it was debated on the floor of the House. It was considered, attacked, and defended from almost every angle—effect upon domestic producers, potential power to protect and increase American foreign trade, constitutionality, practicability, underlying policy. On March 29 it was passed by a vote of 274 to 111.

The bill next was debated before the Senate Finance Committee, headed by our friend Pat Harrison. Again we were hammered; again the bill stood up against all criticism and opposition. It was favorably reported to the Senate on May 2, 1934.

On May 17 the bill finally came up for debate in the Senate. For days the battle raged. On several occasions I was invited to sit beside our leader on the Senate floor so that we could fire off immediate answers to the questions with which the Republicans attacked us. It became a rough-and-tumble party fight—Republicans versus Democrats.

One of our friends, wanting to speak in favor of our bill, asked me through his secretary to draft a speech for him to deliver on the Senate floor. I said I should be delighted to. So I wrote a speech and sent it to his secretary. A few days later the Senator sent for me, said he wanted to speak in support of our bill, and would like to have my comment on the draft for his speech. Apparently he did not know, or in the stress of the fight had completely forgotten, where his proposed speech had originated. As he read it over, I waxed enthusiastic. "That part is wonderful," I exclaimed, or, "There you've hit the nail squarely on the head." The next day he delivered the speech before a crowded Senate.

The President and his leaders had whipped the Democrats into line, and one crippling Republican amendment after another was beaten down. Finally, on June 4 the final vote was taken. The bill passed by a vote of 57 to 33.

On the evening of June 12, in the presence of Senator Pat Harrison, Representative Doughton, Secretary Hull, and myself, the President attached his signature to the bill. The way now lay open for a constructive American program for economic advance.

We lost no time in proceeding with our program. The central foundation on which we built was most-favored-nation treatment, by which the United States must grant its lowest rates and most favorable treatment to every nation granting the same to it, both in tariffs and in other trade restrictions and barriers. There must in general be no trade discriminations or preferential treatment. Most-favored-nation treatment is the only possible way to build sound economic foundations for peace. Each of our trade agreements combined the exchange, each in favor of the other, of most-favored treatment, and the reciprocal lowering of specified tariffs.

To provide the machinery for making trade agreements we organized a group of workers heading up in the State Department. Originally the work had begun in my office ("A–S"). Now we set up in it a special section on trade agreements ("A–S–T"); and this in time grew into a separate Division of Trade Agreements in the Department of State. To organize and carry on the work I called in Henry Grady, dean of the College of Commerce of the University of California, and Alvin Hansen, professor of economics at the University of Minnesota.

The procedure in the making of trade agreements was worked out with the most meticulous care for the protection of all concerned. First of all we made a detailed study of the trade between the United States and the country under consideration in order to determine tentatively whether any of the country's exports could be admitted into the United States at a lower tariff rate without undue injury to American domestic producers. Many of these, of course, would be noncompetitive. Sometimes by careful reclassification tariffs could be lowered on noncompetitive or less competitive types of goods. Some commodities, like fruits or melons produced south of the Equator, where their summer is our winter, could be admitted freely during our non-producing season. Our program was based on confining our tariff cuts in the proposed trade agreement to those commodities of which the country was the chief source of supply to America, because under the most-favored-nation program we would grant similar cuts for the same products in favor of every nation which in return gave most-favored-nation treatment to American goods. By granting tariff reductions only with respect to commodities of which the other party to the trade agreement was the chief supplier to the United States, we could obtain in return the most advantageous reductions in foreign tariffs against American goods; for the chief supplier of those products was the nation which would pay the highest price for American cuts.

Our first step in the making of a trade agreement after exploratory talks with representatives of the foreign government concerned was to make public announcement of the intention to negotiate with a designated country and of the list of commodities as to which we were contemplating possible tariff reductions. This list was the result of a meticulous study to determine what tariff rates could perhaps be reduced or reclassified in a way to avoid injury to competing domestic producers.

So that we could tap in a practical way the vast reservoir of facts and information possessed by men in the actual mills of business and at the same time avoid undue hardship on domestic producers by affording any one an opportunity to present his views before the conclusion of any trade agreement, we set up what came to be known as the Committee for Reciprocity Information as a central point of contact between the American public and the trade agreements organization.

Numerous questions of whether, how much, and in what way, reductions in the American tariff might be made, and what we should seek from foreign countries in return, obviously required the nicest kind of balancing. Our basic consideration in every case was, "what will be best for the American people as a whole, for the consumer as well as for the producer?" The consumer had no high-paid lobbyist at his command.

Often the outcry at public hearings over the expected ruinous effects of proposed tariff cuts would be based on fear rather than fact; and whether the protests and objections were sound or merely based upon fear would be another nice question to be carefully weighed and considered.

Having made a careful study of each commodity in committee before the public hearings, we generally knew what the actual situation was and could probe deeper with questions of our own. The hearings were real—never superficial. We always were entirely ready to modify our original ideas as a result of these hearings. We were bent on doing an honest and sound piece of work.

Foreign trade exchanges are not always confined to two countries alone. The United States, for instance, sells goods to France. Then France sells goods, perhaps, to some South American country. The South American country in turn sells goods to the United States. Trade is often triangular or multilateral. All these factors enter into the picture, so that trade problems are often intricate, involved, and difficult.

The inauguration and establishment of the trade agreements program as an essential part of our American economic and foreign policy and the continuing fight for lowered trade barriers was of extraordinary delicacy and infinite difficulty. Eternal vigilance is the price not only of liberty but also of economic peace among nations. Unless those on the ramparts are vigilant, special lobbies will build up power for the interests of selfish groups. The people as a whole cannot devote time and effort to issues as complicated and technical as foreign trade. On the other hand, special, sectional interests are always on the alert to run up their prices whenever they can maintain a domestic monopoly and prevent foreign competition. Such monopolies mean, as a rule, that the American people as a whole pay the cost. It is all a part of our eternal fight for people's rights.

The Trade Agreements Act was an emergency piece of legislation. In 1934 economically we were slipping downhill fast. It was with this in mind that Secretary Hull and others framed the measure to continue in force only three years, thus increasing the chances for its passage through Congress. In 1937, when it was due to expire, it was reenacted for three years. By 1940 some of us hoped that the new Act might be made permanent; but Secretary Hull and others feared that this would be unwise. The legislation continued, therefore, to be reenacted by Democratic majorities for a period of three years, with many Republicans pushed by strong sectional interests seeking to kill it if they could. However, in 1949 the language of the Act characterizing it as emergency legislation was removed.

The passage of the Trade Agreements Act in 1934 was not an empty political victory. Through the years the program has brought positive benefit to the country as a whole. It has increased American foreign trade, benefited both agricultural and industrial workers, substantially lessened foreign trade discrimination, and helped to build sound economic foundations for peace. The results have proved even better than promised. Not only did we build up under its operation substantially increased American trade, American employment, and American export industries, but, as was shown in Congressional hearings through the years that followed, we did no serious injury to any substantial American industry competing against foreign imports.

Nevertheless, the program has continued subject to Republican attack. It is bitterly fought at each renewal time. Senator Vandenberg, who in 1934 opposed the trade agreements program, later shifted his views and came to our support.

Up to the time I left Washington in 1939 trade agreements had been concluded with nineteen countries, including some of the major commercial countries, accounting for 60 per cent of our total foreign trade. In the order of signing of trade agreements, these were Cuba, Brazil, Belgium, Haiti, Sweden, Colombia, Canada, Honduras, the Netherlands, Switzerland, Nicaragua, Guatemala, France and its colonies, Finland, Costa Rica, El Salvador, Czechoslovakia, Ecuador, the United Kingdom and the British Empire. By 1943 we had made 1,180 American tariff reductions in return for 5,000 or 6,000 reductions in foreign restrictions against American exports.

At the Congressional hearings of 1943 during which I laid before Congress the results of the program to date and the importance of continuing it, I said:

Trade constitutes the veritable lifeblood of nations in this interdependent world. Industrial nations, by selling processed products abroad in exchange for food stuffs and raw materials, have made possible the support of vastly increased populations. The population of Europe, which in 1650 was 100,000,000, increased to 140,000,000 in 1750, 266,000,000 in 1850, and 519,000,000 in 1933. Through foreign trade alone can modern industrial nations procure necessary food for their peoples, raw materials to keep their factories in operation, or the manifold goods which make present-day civilization and culture possible. Through foreign trade alone can they obtain large enough markets to keep their specialized industries going.

Industrialized nations must maintain access to necessary raw materials and necessary markets. If they are denied access to these they will feel forced to fight. If national frontiers bar them from the raw materials and markets they need for the maintenance of their populations, they will fight to destroy those frontiers. If goods can't cross national frontiers, armies will. . . .

What is clear and cannot be disproved is that the pathway of economic self-sufficiency leads as surely as the rising of the sun to growing unemployment and industrial break-down. It leads to economic chaos, international conflict and eventual war. On the other hand, the pathway of increased international trading leads with equal sureness to increased employment and heightened standards of living. It leads to lessened international strain and conflict. It constitutes one of the absolutely necessary foundations for lasting peace.

Since the Trade Agreements Act had never been passed as a permanent enactment, a serious question arose when the Republicans came into power in 1953. Would the Republican Administration seek renewal of the Act?

The highly successful operation of the Act for twenty years, and its essential soundness, could not be denied or disregarded. President Eisenhower bravely took his stand in support of its renewal. But unhappily he led a divided party. In 1955 Congress with strong Democratic support renewed the Trade Agreements Act, but with seriously crippling amendments and by an alarmingly narrow margin. The ultimate outcome remains uncertain.

Because of the success and fundamental soundness of the American trade agreements program it has now in broadened form become a world program. With multilateral agreements largely replacing the bilateral agreements of the American program, it was adopted as the basis for the General Agreement on Tariffs and Trade (GATT), signed at Geneva on October 30, 1947, by the United States and twenty-one other countries, providing for concessions on about 45,000 items, accounting for more than half of the world's imports. The GATT has been expanded to include thirty-four countries, whose international trade comprises about four-fifths of the world total. This multilateral agreement, like the earlier bilateral agreements under the American trade agreements program, is based squarely upon most-favored-nation treatment. In other words, the tremendous world program of GATT grew out of seeds originally nurtured and developed in our offices in the old State, Army, and Navy Building next to the White House.

Once the vital interdependence of nations is clearly realized, the nature of the economic foundations for a stable peace becomes clear. Today the standards of living, if not the very lives, of entire populations are dependent upon a steady flow of raw materials and foodstuffs at prices unenhanced by prohibitive economic barriers, and also upon a steady sale of surplus production in foreign markets for a remunerative return.

Men will fight rather than starve. They may also fight rather than see accustomed standards of living reduced to unbearable levels.

Furthermore, as President Eisenhower pointed out in his message of January 11, 1955, the trade agreements program is emphatically necessary at this time because economic strength among our allies is essential to our security.

The battle against the heightening of trade barriers and against foreign trade discriminations is an unceasing battle, for in every country sectional and privileged interests are engaged. It is a people's fight. Like the fight for democracy, it never will end. But it is a battle well worth the fighting for every American who seeks the welfare of his country and the peace of the world.

13

The Far East Calls Again

In late July, 1939, my wife was staying overnight in Providence, Rhode Island, on the way home from Martha's Vineyard, where she had rented a house for our family for the month of August. At the end of the evening, as she idly skimmed through the paper, her eye fell upon a familiar photograph on the back page, and the name, "SAYRE." Looking more closely, she turned back to page 1 and found the headline, "Sayre Assigned Philippine Post." In a daze she went to her room and put in a call to Washington. I was awakened to hear her voice, asking me, "What is this I see in the paper?"

"Well, Betsy, I guess, if the Senate should confirm me, you and I will be going to the Philippines. It will be a great adventure, won't it?"

For some time my work as Assistant Secretary of State had led me into Philippine problems. Ever since the passage in 1934 of the Philippine Independence Act providing for setting up a Philippine Commonwealth government and promising complete independence on July 4, 1946, countless delicate questions kept arising between Filipinos and Americans. All domestic legislation during the interim period before full independence was to be in the hands of the Commonwealth Legislature; but foreign affairs remained under the direct supervision and control of the United States, and "acts affecting currency, coinage, imports, exports and immigration shall not become

178

law until approved by the President of the United States." Manuel L. Quezon, who had outwitted and outmaneuvered every Filipino rival, the unquestioned political leader of the Philippines and one of the most colorful figures of the Far East, had been elected President of the new Commonwealth.

In order to meet our Philippine problems and coordinate our policies we had set up in Washington an Interdepartmental Committee on Philippine Affairs, composed of representatives of the Departments of State, War, Navy, Treasury, Agriculture, and Commerce and the Tariff Commission; and I had been asked to serve as chairman. One of the difficult issues facing us was Philippine trade after the date of independence.

As long as the Philippines remained under the jurisdiction of the United States Philippine goods imported into the United States came in free of duty. But once the Philippines became independent, full American tariff duties would naturally be collected. Philippine sugar, competing against American beet sugar, would no longer come in free.

Consequently, unless exceptional measures, such as preferential tariffs, were adopted, coming independence bade fair to wreck all Philippine producers who were dependent upon free American markets; yet every trade preference constitutes discrimination against all other nations.

In December, 1936, on the eve of relinquishing the post of High Commissioner, Frank Murphy came to Washington to discuss with President Roosevelt plans for a reconsideration of United States–Philippine relations. Shortly thereafter, President Quezon came to the United States and in February, 1937, took up residence in Washington. He well realized that unless some adjustment could be achieved, the coming independence might wreck the Philippine economy.

Resourceful and able on the political front, charming beyond words to those whom he set out to win, adroit, daring, astute, he presented himself at the White House. President Roosevelt requested him to take up the Philippine problems with me.

Thus President Quezon became a frequent visitor at my office. As I grew to know him I felt the charm of his restless spirit and his will to win. Our talks led to the setting up of a committee of American and Filipino experts, the Joint Preparatory Committee on Philippine Affairs. At the outset I was asked to act as temporary chairman; two months later Ambassador John MacMurray accepted the permanent chairmanship.

The problem was unique. Ever since 1909, subject only to minor restrictions, Philippine goods had entered the United States free. Inevitably Philippine producers had shifted to goods which they could sell advantageously in free American markets but, because of the costs of production, not against international competitors in world markets. In other words, while promising complete political independence, we had allowed the Philippines from 1909 on to become more and more dependent economically upon the United States. Now that we were granting independence, in my mind it seemed only fair to them to find some way to prevent economic wreckage.

Was there any possible way out?

For more than a year the Joint Preparatory Committee on Philippine Affairs wrestled with the problem. Public hearings were held, and intensive studies made. In the end a scheme of gradually increasing and progressive American duties was devised; and this solution was adopted by Congress in the Economic Adjustment Act in August, 1939.

This saved large numbers of Philippine workers, engaged in the production of cigars, scrap tobacco, coconut oil, pearl buttons, and embroideries from being thrown onto the scrapheap. It was a rich reward for our work.

Jurisdiction in the United States over Philippine affairs was exercised by the War Department's Bureau of Insular Affairs. The United States Army had a very real stake in the government of the Philippines. Furthermore, many army officers had served there, knew the Islands well, and understood their problems. On July 1, 1939, however, the President transferred Philippine affairs to the jurisdiction of the Department of the Interior, under Secretary Harold L. Ickes. Although the objective—placing the administration of the Islands under civilian rather than under military control—was sound, the results in practical administration seemed unfortunate. To the Army, to the Navy, and to the Department of Commerce, the Philippines was of vital concern. Also to the Department of Agriculture, for important agricultural products such as sugar, coconut oil and copra were coming out of the Philippines. But in the Interior there was a striking scarcity of men who had lived in the Philippines and knew Philippine problems.

That was one of the real difficulties which would confront the United States High Commissioner to the Philippines.

The work of the Interdepartmental Committee and of the Joint Preparatory Committee absorbed more and more of my time. Paul McNutt, who had succeeded Frank Murphy as High Commissioner, returned to the United States in May, 1939, to submit his resignation to the President. We had many conferences together.

During this period when Philippine problems had become of such importance President Roosevelt one day asked me if I would accept appointment as High Commissioner to succeed Paul McNutt. I had had most cordial relationships with President Quezon during his visit to Washington. In fact, he once told me that he had asked Mr. Roosevelt to send me out as High Commissioner. McNutt now urged me to accept the post.

Accordingly I promised to go if appointed and confirmed, although this must of course mean my resignation as Assistant Secretary of State and giving up my work on the trade agreements program.

On the morning of July 26, before any of this was generally known, my secretary rushed into my office with the report that the White House had just sent my name to the Senate for confirmation as United States High Commissioner to the Philippines. She was bubbling with excitement and asked if it could be true.

Three days later the Senate confirmed the appointment.

On August 8, 1939, in Secretary Ickes' office in the new Interior Building, before Betty and a large company of friends, I was sworn in by Justice Frank Murphy, my warm friend and predecessor as High Commissioner. A new chapter of my life had begun.

Shortly afterward came the news of Germany's invasion of Poland. The Second World War was upon us. We kept wondering what effect this portentous tragedy would have upon the Philippines.

Before my departure for Manila I talked over pending problems with Paul McNutt. During this time there developed, for reasons which were difficult to fathom, a coolness if not a hostility toward myself on the part of Harold Ickes. Was he really the "curmudgeon" that so many people called him? Possibly the coolness was due to my agreement with Paul McNutt in certain issues over which they were in disagreement. The ill feeling toward me boded no good, and I greatly regretted it. Possibly it was due to my relationships with the President. When the Philippines had been under the jurisdiction of the Bureau of Insular Affairs the High Commissioner had been responsible directly to the President. When the Department of the Interior took over Philippine affairs, did that alter the direct relationship and responsibility of the High Commissioner to the President? I continued, like my predecessors, to write directly to the President. The best advice I could get, as well as a study of the pertinent documents, seemed to confirm the correctness of this procedure. Perhaps Mr. Ickes felt otherwise and resented my doing so. The matter never was discussed between us. The President himself wrote to me on December 13, 1939, "Keep on writing me and I hope all goes well."

The question was authoritatively settled by President Roosevelt in an official letter dated May 17, 1940, written to me and circulated through the Interior and other Departments. That letter, in the course of defining the duties and responsibilities of the Department of the Interior under Reorganization Plan No. II, stated:

> You will note that there is no change with respect to your direct relationship in reporting to me. . . . Normally correspondence and reports on Philippine matters should clear through the Philippine Section of the Division of Territories and Island Possessions, Department of the Interior. . . . This will not, however, diminish your authority or materially affect your direct responsibility to me as defined in my previous communication of September 7th, and will not preclude direct communication with me whenever you deem it advisable.

I later heard that this letter of the President's was one Secretary Ickes never forgave; but whether this be true I do not know.

The days before departure were filled with countless arrangements for a long absence on the other side of the world. It was hard to say goodbye to my three children, who must remain in America for their work. Francis, who to my delight had chosen in 1935 to enter the ministry and had completed two years of study at Union Theological Seminary in New York, was passing through a stage of loving concern and complete disillusionment over his father's outdated and prehistoric theological and philosophic beliefs. Eleanor, having graduated from Bryn Mawr, was studying at the Fogg Museum of Art in Cambridge and was growing more and more absorbed in her work. Woodrow was a senior at Williams College. Helen Bell, the missionary's daughter who had been a member of our family since 1935, had entered Radcliffe College in Cambridge, and both my Siamese boys had returned to Siam. We would take along Betty's two boys, Ralph and Bill, aged fourteen and twelve, who would enter Brent School at Baguio in the Philippines. We regretted having to separate the children in this way, for they were all integrating so happily and wholeheartedly into our family life together; but no other course seemed possible.

On September 15 I received final instructions from the President.

The next evening at the Union Station in Washington Betty and I and the boys said goodbye to a group of our family and intimate friends, wondering when we would see them again. Travelling with us to San Francisco were Woodbury Willoughby, my administrative assistant, Mrs. Willoughby, George Gray, my general assistant, and Anna Belle Newcomb, my confidential secretary. Golden Bell, my legal adviser, retiring from the Department of Justice, and Mrs. Bell, joined the party at San Francisco.

After a few days' delay at San Francisco due to strike troubles, we sailed at last September 26 on the steamship *President Cleveland* for Manila. Ten days later we reached Japan, one of the loveliest spots in the Orient. Ambassador and Mrs. Joseph Grew, who had but just returned from home leave, entertained us at luncheon in the Embassy at Tokyo, and we had the pleasure of meeting a number of high Japanese officials. One of the most interesting was Admiral Nomura, tall and commanding, who had recently lost an eye in the Shanghai "incident."

From Japan we continued south to Shanghai. There a launch gleaming white and gold and flying an admiral's flag, darted through the maze of river traffic to our ship. Admiral Thomas C. Hart, commander-in-chief of the Asiatic Fleet, and Consul General Clarence E. Gauss boarded the ship to greet us and escort us into Shanghai.

Still bearing the tragic marks of the "Incident," Shanghai was an active center of Japanese aggression and penetration. We watched the dapper Japanese police at street intersections, standing beside the British police—tall and dignified, turbaned East Indians—each ignoring the other, and both directing traffic.

Shanghai was a city of amazing contrasts—a virtual war going on in one end of it while the other played about in a life of softness and luxury. A woman lay on the hard stone pavement curled up in her filthy rags to sleep for the night, while across the street rich merchants enjoyed American mattresses in a modern hotel where flowers, music, and perfume spoke the last word in luxury. In the early morning light one raised the blind to make out in the street below a child dead in the gutter, while early pedestrians hardened to the sight quite casually hurried on their way.

In the shopping district at noon a handsomely dressed European lady alighted daintily from her shiny brass-trimmed rickshaw and entered a shop whose alluring window was spread with silk, satin, crystal, jade, and silver; around the corner walked warily a fat, richly dressed Chinese with two bodyguards elbowing their way through the crowds. Upstairs in a busy newspaper office the editor lay face down, a knife sticking out between his shoulders, while the murderers quickly lost themselves in the churning street below. A city of life and sudden death, of easy luxury and sordid wretchedness, of peace and violence, of East and West, the rickshaw and the Rolls Royce, the barbed wire and the sunny flower gardens, the sandalwood incense and the stench of death.

Two days later our ship rounded the towering headlands and entered the dramatic port of Hong Kong. Here we were overnight guests of Governor Northcote at Government House. The Governor's aide, who came to the ship to greet us, took Betty aside and gravely explained that since Great Britain was now in a state of war the ladies would forbear wearing white gloves at the formal dinner to be given in our honor that night at Government House.

No one could have been more gracious than our hosts at Government House; and at the formal dinner that evening the traditional bottle of port passed round the table from hand to hand and toasts were drunk and speeches made by the Governor and myself betokening the very genuine friendship between our two peoples in this far part of the world. I was often to remember that scene in which the English bade us welcome to their world in the Far East—the great dining room with high ceiling, suspended revolving fans and crystal chandeliers, the large framed portraits of King George and Queen Mary at either end of the room, the long table with gleaming white cloth, on either side of which sat the invited guests in white dinner coats and formal evening gowns, the low English voices, the deft service, and the superficial gayety covering anxious hearts and worry for loved ones at war. Poignantly our memories went back to that night after war had finally let loose its fury upon Hong Kong.

The following day our hosts drove us to the top of "the Peak," and then around the beautiful island, which I had not seen since 1926 when I was returning from Siam. Once again as we looked down upon the bright blue water encircling picturesque islands and green jutting headlands we drank in the loveliness of the place. It seemed to us one of the most beautiful ports of the world.

Next day, as we steamed away from Hong Kong on the last lap of our journey, the captain of our ship pointed out to us the many gun emplacements dotting the hillside, overlooking the harbour. With the war in progress the British were much concerned, of course, with the protection of Hong Kong and the strengthening of its defenses. During my stay in the Philippines, more than once the British naval commander or other high officials came over to talk to us and confer with our army and navy officials.

Only a little more than two years later Hong Kong was in Japanese hands.

14

High Commissioner
to the Philippines

The day of our arrival in Manila—October 21—stands out as vivid in my mind as if it were yesterday. As the first faint light of dawn comes seeping into our stateroom, we hear the sound of roaring planes and then from the deck outside comes Bill's voice, shrill with excitement: "Hurry up, Dad, get dressed. The planes are zooming all around us!" We hastily throw on our clothes and step out onto the deck. An escort of United States airplanes and destroyers is circling around the ship, greeting the new United States High Commissioner.

Our ship is passing the green velvety slopes of Corregidor Island, just before entering Manila Bay. The water is like a sheet of glass, opalescent in the early morning light. Our vessel seems to float in space, gliding quietly toward the low shore line of Manila—the "Pearl of the Orient," as José Rizal called it—with its white buildings alight in the rosy dawn.

As the *President Cleveland* nears the city, a launch packed with people and gay with flags draws alongside, and American and Philippine officials board the ship to welcome us and to take us ashore. We clamber down the ship's ladder and take our places on the launch; and as it shoves off we look up the side of our suddenly enormous steamer and wave back to our shipmates crowding the rail.

As we approach the shore the open park along the waterfront

is crowded with thousands of people. The launch shrilly whistles three times; and the air resounds with answering blasts from the shore, culminating in the deep booming of a nineteen-gun salute. Then we hear the shouts and cheers of the people. The spontaneous friendliness of the ovation overpowers us.

As we step ashore the first to greet us are President and Mrs. Quezon. We are met also by Rear Admiral John M. Smeallie, Commandant of the Sixteenth Naval District; Major General Walter S. Grant, Commander of the Philippine Department, United States Army; Speaker of the National Assembly José Yulo; members of the Commonwealth Cabinet; and other ranking officials. As Mrs. Quezon talks with Betty, President Quezon takes me by the arm and leads me across the grass to a flower-bedecked pavillion. Bands strike up the music, and before us passes a guard of honor, composed of the United States Thirty-first Infantry Regiment and Philippine Army troops. Then as silence falls President Quezon, before the assembled throng, welcomes me with gracious words to the Philippines:

The new United States High Commissioner has arrived and we are here to greet and welcome him with hearts filled with gratitude; for no better choice could have been made by the President of the United States than the selection of His Excellency, Francis B. Sayre. . . . He knows the Philippines and the Filipino people. . . . He has spent the last three years studying the Philippine problem from all angles with the keen mind that he has and the great humanitarian heart that throbs within him. . . . For the last three years I had been hoping that His Excellency, Francis B. Sayre, might be appointed United States High Commissioner to succeed High Commissioner Paul V. McNutt, whose early return to the United States was anticipated. . . . Now he is here with us. He finds a people who know him as well as he knows them. We know his record as adviser to the Government of Siam—of his ability to treat with people of different race. We know of his deep interest in our welfare. We know that he is our friend, and we welcome him today with grateful hearts.

In reply I try to tell how deeply I appreciate the heartwarming reception:

I want to say to the Filipino people how happy and how proud I am that I have been given the chance to throw in my lot with you in helping

to work out the problems which lie before us. . . . The happy thing is
that the relationships between our two peoples rest not upon contest and
struggle and hostility but upon community of purpose and ideals. . . .
Our objectives and our fundamental interests are the same. Both peoples
alike believe in freedom, and they believe in a democracy based upon law.
. . . Until their independence is consummated the Filipino people are an
integral part of the American Nation. We are fellow Americans. As High
Commissioner I shall not lose sight of this central fact.

Entering a waiting car, with the High Commissioner's flag flying
from a short mast on the front left fender, we move slowly past the
milling pedestrians and pause before the monument of the patriot
José Rizal, where I place a wreath. Then on across the Luneta and
under a great arch decorated with flowers and flags, with a lettered
sign over the top:

> "Mabuhay! Excellency!
> U.S. High Commissioner
> Francis B. Sayre"

As we pass, the crowds peer into the car, wave and shout: "Mabuhay,
Commissioner Say-ree!"

Past throngs lining Dewey Boulevard we are then escorted to
our temporary residence by a detachment of the United States Army.
Within an hour President Quezon has come to make his first official
call.

Easily the outstanding figure in the Philippines of that day was
President Quezon. His was a unique personality. In stature he was
short—of average height for Filipinos; but in every other way he was
far from average. Filled with dynamic energy and restlessness, he
was always the center of movement and activity. His jaunty, bright-
eyed, expressive face one moment would be beaming with pleasure
and the next overspread with a quizzical or perhaps resentful expression. He had a birdlike way of cocking his head to observe the effect
of his words upon his hearers. His high-pitched voice was vibrant
with emotion. Even when racked with illness, his zest for life, his
energetic mind and responsive heart rose continually above his
physical weakness.

A man of marked ability, and a consummate politician, he made and broke other political figures at will. The Philippine Legislature was his creature and docilely rubber-stamped his wishes and decisions. Although he often spoke in glowing terms about democracy, real democracy was almost completely lacking in his political philosophy. He was a dictator, but happily a benevolent one. A man of impulses and moods, he was often insensitive to reason and logic. He was temperamental to the last degree—a prima donna of the first order. Always he was adroit and dramatic, and knew exactly how to play his cards to win his public.

Needless to say, throughout my work in Manila as High Commissioner I kept in intimate contact with the United States Army and Navy officials; and this intimacy deepened as the months went by and the world situation grew more critical. With both General Grant and Admiral Hart, I held frequent conferences in my office. In May, 1940, Major General George Grunert succeeded General Grant as Philippine Department Commander. Our habitual contacts ripened into warm friendship; many times they were our guests both in our Manila residence and at the summer capital in Baguio.

I felt peculiarly fortunate and happy in the aides assigned to me. Lieutenant William J. Priestley, tall, slender, and always smiling, was a joy to work with, loyal, efficient, and tactful. He became almost like one of our own family. My Naval aide, Lieutenant Commander Charles B. McVay, 3rd, was also outstanding in his winning personality and his ability. In July, 1940, he was replaced by Lieutenant Commander Thomas C. Parker, another man of rare personal charm who entered closely into our lives.

That first year in the Philippines was a singularly happy one. At every turn we felt the friendliness and the warmth of the people. The Filipinos, who then numbered some 16,000,000, are mostly of Malayan stock; but their more than sixty-five different dialects betray their widely different origins. Strong Spanish and Catholic influences had helped to unify the peoples in Luzon and the North. But among the Moros in the southern islands Spanish influences never had penetrated deeply. In addition to these Filipino peoples we found in the islands some 30,000 Japanese and 117,000 Chinese. In Luzon were almost 9,000 American civilians.

In Manila was an outstanding group of Americans, many of

them doing substantial business in the Philippines. Living in a far part of the world, often lonely, they drew closely together; and as problems developed we in the High Commissioner's Office felt we could always turn to them for friendly understanding and loyal support.

Life seemed less sophisticated and rigorous in the Philippines than in America, and simpler enjoyments prevailed. The tropical heat necessitated starting work each day at an early hour; but the noonday siesta lasted from twelve o'clock to three or four and always eased the daily strain.

Amidst these friendly, developing peoples life charmed and interested us. Also, my relationships with President Quezon were not only cordial, but at times intimate. I remember, for instance, the incident of All Souls' Night, not long after our arrival in Manila. On All Souls' Night, corresponding to our own All Saints' Day, Filipino families gather to visit the graves of their departed; and they make a happy night of it, feasting and living again with their dear ones. President Quezon, having lost one of his boys, went with his family to the grave. I went there, too, and brought him some flowers. There were tears in his eyes when he thanked me.

Often President Quezon would come to my residence, for official consultation or merely for a friendly talk; and our families were on warm, familiar terms. We spent the first Thanksgiving Day in Baguio at the "Mansion House," which President Quezon had generously placed at our disposal while the new High Commissioner's residence in Baguio was being built; and here, upon our invitation, Doña Aurora Quezon and their children shared our family Thanksgiving dinner during the President's absence in Manila. Later we spent a Sunday on the Quezon farm at Arayat. The three Quezon children were bright and attractive, and though older than our two boys were yet young enough to be altogether natural and friendly and quick to respond. The oldest daughter, named Aurora for her mother and nicknamed "Baby," was quick and keen, full of imagination and warm impulses like her father. The second daughter, Zenaida, an attractive girl in her early teens, seemed less dynamic, more quiet and domestic in her tastes. Nonong, the youngest, and the only son living, was shy and rather indrawn and studious. One of the tragedies in the Philippines after the war was the sudden death in Luzon at the hands of brigands of Mrs. Quezon and Aurora and Zenaida's young husband. Zenaida and Nonong alone survive today.

On January 6, 1940, I wrote to President Roosevelt:

> Everything continues to go smoothly and satisfactorily here. I continue to have informal and intimate talks with President Quezon about various matters and find him always cooperative and ready to play the game. Thus far he has accepted and loyally followed all my suggestions. I find him very loyal to you and to your ideals and, although he is impulsive and not always wise, I believe that his objectives and underlying motives are true. And these are combined with great executive force and driving ability.

During the first half-year, while the official residence of the High Commissioner was still in construction, Mrs. Sayre and I resided in a most comfortable private house off Dewey Boulevard near the bay. It was spacious and open to every breath of air, built by architects who knew the tropics.

In April, 1940, we moved into the new residence, on extensive filled-in grounds beside the bay. It was a modern concrete structure, built around a tropical patio. We had two spacious dining rooms, one for large state dinners and the other for the use of the family, and a beautiful two-storied ballroom with a gallery and great windows looking out over the harbor. From the large second-story porch in the late afternoon we used to watch the brilliant tropical sun setting over the rocky ridge of Mariveles on Bataan peninsula across the bay. In another wing were spacious offices for the High Commissioner and his staff. Behind the desk where I always sat hung two large silk flags: the one our Stars and Stripes; and the other, the High Commissioner's flag, which had come down from the time of Governor William Howard Taft. The upper half of this bore thirteen red and white vertical American stripes; the lower half, a white lion rampant with a curling dolphin's tail on a dark blue background. The lion was a relic of Spanish Governor General days.

The new residence was conceived in splendor, but designed by Treasury Department architects in Washington apparently unacquainted with the tropics and with Manila weather. The rooms were not planned to catch wandering breezes, but were enclosed and sealed, dependent upon air conditioning; and after we moved in,

Congress in a spasm of economy cut down the funds required for putting the place in order and for air conditioning. Without air conditioning the intense summer heat made the rooms at times unbearable. But the real trouble came when typhoons struck; then the immense glass windows of the ballroom leaked water by the bucketful; and our house boys spent hours and days mopping up and trying their best to stop the spouts and runnels of water that drove into the room.

We badly needed an appropriation to make the residence livable, and I even mentioned the matter in a letter to President Roosevelt. He replied with a chuckle, in a letter dated March 25, 1940:

> I am doing everything possible to have the money restored for the maintenance of the new Residence. Congress is in the funny frame of mind of being savagely interested in cutting out five or ten thousand dollars here or there from appropriations for minor items, like this one, and then the next day demanding $100,000,000 for additional river and harbor "pork-barrel" projects. Same old story.

The most pressing problems in the first two years were largely economic—particularly how to prevent independence from working undue hardship and strain upon the Philippine economy. I always believed in and strongly supported the grant of full Philippine independence at the end of the ten-year interim period. On the other hand, there were many, both in America and in the Philippines, who were pressing for a "reexamination" of the program for independence. In the Philippine National Assembly in September, 1939, José Romero, member from Negros Oriental, cried out, "Let us pause before we . . . crucify our nation upon the cross of an untimely independence." Was the ghost of William Jennings Bryan come to our shores? Other Filipino leaders who had spent the greater part of their lives struggling for independence, found it well-nigh impossible, now that it was at last in sight, to oppose it. Nevertheless business and other groups felt a growing uneasiness and fear lest independence entail economic disruption and possible disaster— even, it might be, conquest of the Philippines by an aggressor nation.

My own strong conviction was that we must not reverse the Philippine independence program but must bend every effort to prevent political independence from causing undue economic injury to the Philippine people. I wrote to President Roosevelt November 16, 1939:

I also discussed with President Quezon the issue regarding Philippine independence. He said to me that although there were governmental officials advocating "reexamination," in his own opinion the Filipino people will never consent to relinquishing or indefinitely postponing the idea of independence. He said that he did not consider the indefinite postponement idea from the viewpoint of practical politics at all practicable, and that he would continue to support the independence movement as provided for in the Tydings-McDuffie Act.

I believe that the position which I stated when I arrived in Manila is the only sound one for the American Government to take. It seems to me clear that the American Government is morally bound not to withdraw or substantially modify the program of independence adopted under the Tydings-McDuffie Act unless and until the Filipino people and the Commonwealth Government make a specific request. In that event, it will be for the United States to decide what course to follow, and this decision must be made in the light of the world situation as it exists at the time. What the world situation will be then, no one can foretell.

Do you not agree that this is the sound position for us to take?

President Roosevelt replied in a personal and confidential letter:

On the question of independence in 1945, it is best, so far as we all are concerned, to go through with our definitely chosen policy—chosen here and in the Philippines.

In matters touching upon foreign relationships President Quezon was generally helpful and cooperative. He had a generous spirit and wanted to lend the help of the Philippines wherever he could. One of his undertakings was the resettlement of 10,000 Jewish refugees from Germany in rural projects on Mindanao. That island contained rich possibilities of agricultural development, and President Quezon out of the generosity of his heart, responding to an appeal, offered them new homes there. Unfortunately most of the arriving refugees were urban dwellers who knew little and cared less for farming. Of the 521 Jewish refugees who were admitted up to the end of June, 1940, 68 reemigrated to the United States and other countries, and the others tended to congregate in Manila and other cities, competing with Filipinos. The project, therefore, could not be carried out as hoped and planned.

Although President Quezon and I were in full agreement in opposing the movement for reexamination of Philippine independence we did not see eye to eye in all matters. For instance, under laws passed in 1934, 1936, and 1938, the United States paid to the Philippine Government substantial sums collected in the United States in processing taxes upon Philippine coconut oil, which amounted to over $15,000,000 each year. This in effect constituted a gift from the American to the Filipino people for financing coming independence. The laws authorizing these payments restricted the use of the money to "meeting new or additional expenditures which will be necessary in adjusting Philippine economy to a position independent of trade preferences in the United States."

Shortly after my arrival I took up with President Quezon the use by the Commonwealth of these funds in conformity with American legislation. Knowing the heavy costs involved in the coming independence, I stressed the necessity of careful financial planning in order that the Philippines might achieve economic as well as political independence. "Perhaps you might even wish to put a substantial part of that money aside for use on a rainy day," I said. President Quezon on the contrary, centering his thoughts on the present, wanted to spend the full amount as it came in, sometimes for purposes in no way connected with the adjustment of the "Philippine economy to a position independent of trade preferences." While I carefully avoided trying to dictate the uses to which the money should be put, or playing a paternalistic role, I could not allow the Congressional statement of purpose for which the money was to be spent to become a dead letter. Upon this I insisted; and in the end we reached an agreement whereby expenditures of these funds were to be considered and approved by both President Quezon and myself before submission to the National Assembly for their authorization.

The preliminary draft budget which President Quezon first submitted to us was considerably in excess of the estimated collections for 1939, and some of the proposed expenditures failed entirely to conform to the provisions of the Congressional enactment. During the period of our negotiations seven draft budgets were prepared, considered, and revised.

An all-important item in the Philippine economy was sugar; and the problems connected with sugar production gave me considerable concern. In Pampanga, where great quantities of sugar cane were produced, thousands of Filipinos worked under disgraceful conditions and often for less than a living wage. They had to fight poverty all their lives, whereas the owners of the estates, living in Manila, grew inordinately rich and profited heavily from the free entry of their sugar into the United States. Here was a pernicious social problem—the indefensible and shocking contrast between the rich, lordly landowners living in Manila and the impoverished workers in Pampanga. The Huk troubles which arose after the war were part of the price which had to be paid for intolerable exploitation.

Nevertheless, this problem lay exclusively within the jurisdiction of the Commonwealth government, and under the Independence Act the High Commissioner had no right or authority to interfere. Always I must scrupulously guard against paternalism and concentrate upon the over-all policies and activities affecting distinctly American interests and international affairs.

Clashes now and again between Spanish or Roman Catholic influences and English-speaking or Protestant ones also were generally within the field of domestic jurisdiction and therefore beyond the scope of my responsibilities. Spanish and other forces were working assiduously to bring the Filipino orientation back under Spanish and Roman Catholic influence.

English and Spanish were the official languages of the Philippines. It lay in the mind of President Quezon to evolve from Tagalog a national language; and for this immensely difficult task he set up a commission. Inasmuch as Tagalog was known only to a minority of Filipinos, had no literature whatsoever and even lacked many words necessary for dealing with modern problems, and since there were no Tagalog schoolbooks, the effort to supplant English and Spanish in the Philippines with Tagalog seemed to us regrettable and most unwise. But here was another undertaking outside the area of American jurisdiction; and I was careful in no way to interfere or to express any official opinion on the undertaking.

During that first year in the Philippines neither President Quezon nor I allowed differences of viewpoint to sour our close intimacies. Nevertheless, there were fundamental differences between our points of view, our judgments, and our ideals; and I suppose that it was inevitable that, as public tensions increased, our close and cordial understanding should come to an end. Temperamentally he could not brook opposition, and many of his activities and policies seemed to me quite unwise.

His conception of democracy, for instance, was completely at variance with American thinking; our idea of a government chosen and really controlled by the people seemed almost lacking in this part of the world. Could we implant among the Filipinos our own understanding of what democracy means and a sense of its sacred value, and might there be a chance of such a plant, pathetically rare throughout the Far East, spreading into Asia?

On August 1, 1940, I wrote to President Roosevelt:

I want to write you about a matter which has been giving me considerable concern, namely, the pronounced drift here in the Philippines away from democracy and in the direction of totalitarianism or dictatorship. For some time the movement has been evident and has caused considerable comment. . . .

During a press conference in my office, I was asked whether I believed in a two-party system and I replied that I did. I was quoted as saying: "I believe the life of a democracy is stimulated by a vigorous expression of the views of the minority. Democracy is based on the determination of issues by popular opinion, and the way to determine issues, to get them over to the people, is through two parties." This statement immediately drew the following signed statement from President Quezon: "I am not surprised that High Commissioner Sayre disagrees with me on the need of a party system. That is the orthodox view. We, the Filipinos, have to do our own thinking and learn from the lessons of contemporary history or bust."

President Quezon's attitude reflects the extreme intolerance of himself and other political leaders here to criticism. . . .

Naturally I have sought, and shall continue to seek, to defend and stand for democracy so far as I can. My relationships with President Quezon thus far have been most friendly, cordial and even intimate. But the very situation which I have been describing means that as a result there is almost sure to come a growing difference of opinion and cleavage between the Commonwealth authorities and myself.

Often I tried to suggest, particularly to the younger generation, something of the meaning and the strength of American democracy. In a Commencement address on April 2, 1940, at the University of the Philippines, I said:

Democracy versus dictatorship. Admitting the shortcomings of democracy, does it follow that dictatorship is a superior form of government or better suited to Twentieth Century needs? Here is a crucial and fundamental question which you, building the new Philippine nation, will be called upon to determine. Will the enemies of democracy be able to captivate you with superficial arguments? Here is where education and intellectual training must serve to guard you against shallow judgment and emotional decision.

In the last analysis, democracy means government through processes of education; dictatorship means government through fear. . . .

Democracy is not a mere philosopher's theory. Our faith in democracy is the result of centuries of hard experience, evolved painfully by trial and error, bought with the blood of many of our noblest and our best. It is the forced recognition of the facts of history that the power and the strength of a nation ultimately rest and always must rest upon its people. Democracy has its roots in a belief in the slow processes of education and in the Christian teaching of human brotherhood. Experience has shown that the progress of civilization has gone hand in hand with advancing democracy and that conversely time after time tyranny and autocracy have stemmed human progress. . . .

Upon your ultimate conclusions must rest to no small extent the future history of the Filipino race. If you remain true to democracy, to human liberty and to the underlying principles of Christianity, you can face the future unafraid. These great principles will not save you from suffering or struggle. No one can foretell the future. But of one thing we can be sure. Ultimately these great principles must prove triumphant if the human race is to survive. Principles such as these are worth living and fighting and dying for. The fight for what you believe to be right, irrespective of victory or defeat, is what gives meaning to life and makes it truly worth the living. Remember always that, whatever time and chance may bring, "no evil can injure the really good man."

The apparently unfriendly attitude of Secretary Ickes of the Department of the Interior added to my difficulties. One particularly unfortunate incident bore evil results. The Philippine Constitution fixed the terms of the President and Vice President at six years without possibility of reelection. It was now proposed to amend the terms to four years with the right, however, to stand for reelection, provided that no one should hold office for more than eight consecutive years. A campaign for the amendment was vigorously pushed throughout the Philippines by President Quezon and other political leaders. The amendments were so written as to be applicable to President Quezon himself, and opponents charged that they were specifically designed to enable the President then in office to prolong his term and serve for eight instead of six years. Such a step would constitute a very dubious precedent.

This raised embarrassing questions, because every change in the Philippine Constitution must be referred to the President of the United States for approval, and it became my duty to advise President Roosevelt. At the time he himself was reported to be planning to run for a third term, although this of course involved no change in the United States Constitution. To my mind, it seemed exceedingly questionable whether he should approve changes in the Philippine Constitution extending the terms of President and Vice President, so phrased as to be applicable to men then in office, and in all honesty I so advised President Roosevelt in a letter of July 25, 1940:

The worst feature of this provision is that it is made applicable to the term of the President now in office. To change the constitutional provision regarding the tenure of office of the President in such a way that the term of the existing President can thereby be prolonged is to create a precedent of exceeding danger to democracy; for such a precedent opens the way for any strong President who desires to become a dictator to prolong his tenure of office indefinitely.

As a matter of fact President Roosevelt felt it wiser on the whole not to veto the Philippine constitutional amendment, and President Quezon was duly reelected for a second term under the newly adopted amendment.

Nevertheless my letter to the President had unfortunate effects; unhappily it came, I believe, into the hands of Secretary Ickes, and through his office, I am told, a copy came to the eyes of President Quezon. The result brought home to me afresh how extremely guarded all my communications to Washington must be, particularly if I felt critical of Philippine officials. The resultant blocking of intimate and frank communications with Washington increased immensely my task of zealously safeguarding American interests in the Philippines.

Incidents such as this almost inevitably cooled President Quezon's relationship with me. There was never an open break—we always remained on friendly terms; but the old intimacy was gone. In fact, it could hardly have been otherwise. His ideas of government often differed profoundly from my own; nor was I willing in those cases falling within the scope of my official duties to yield to proposals and desires that ran counter to American interests and American ideals.

During the intense heat of Manila, as often as work would permit, I used to motor with Betty up to Baguio, the summer capital, in the mountains at an elevation of some 5,200 feet. Here we drank in new life, as though ascended into another world. From the High Commissioner's residence on a spur that stood out far above great empty spaces below, we used to gaze across bottomless valleys toward range upon range of towering mountains to the north, fading away in the high distance, under the constant play of sunlight and shadow, of changing greens and blues, never two days the same, hauntingly beautiful, unforgettable. Sometimes with Betty I could stay a week at a time; sometimes only over the week end. But always the delicious coolness after the wilting heat of Manila and the entrancing views seemed to lift us and give us renewed strength for our work. Often we went with a picnic lunch exploring unfrequented Igorot trails through the woods and over the mountains; in Baguio we could forget our cares and many of our pressing anxieties.

Here also we would always see our two boys, Ralph and Bill, studying at the Brent School. They seemed to be entirely happy and well adjusted in this excellent school which had been conceived and founded by Bishop Brent in 1910. The school took in only American and foreign children; today, I am glad to say, Filipino children are included in the student body. Ralph graduated there in 1941 as valedictorian of his class; and as I was asked that year to give the Commencement address, we shared the stage together.

Two months later Ralph sailed to America in order to enter college in the autumn. With him we sent a small trunk packed with a few things which we did not need. Little did we realize that these would be almost the only belongings of ours in the Philippines saved from the destruction of war. Bill remained with us to complete his schooling at Brent.

In the meantime we continued to receive good news of our children in America. Francis, after two years at Union Seminary in New York, had graduated at the Episcopal Theological Seminary in Cambridge in 1940. Thereafter he became an assistant minister at Christ Church in Cambridge. Eleanor was still happily pursuing her art study at the Fogg Museum. Woodrow graduated from Williams College in 1940 and decided to take up graduate work in philosophy at Harvard. Our adopted daughter, Helen Bell, had entered Radcliffe College; so that all four were living in Cambridge in close touch with one another.

Part of my work was learning to know better the Filipino people and their problems. The seven thousand islands which make up the Philippine Archipelago are not peopled by one homogeneous race, but by many races, speaking many different languages, following different ways of life. I sought contact with these interesting peoples and their leaders whenever time and opportunity allowed, by inspection trips overland and by boat throughout the islands. Admiral Hart generously placed his naval yacht, the *Isabel,* at our disposal; and on this we had several happy trips.

The first inspection trip was in December, 1939, when I spent ten days on an American destroyer cruising through the Sulu Sea and visiting the Moro country of Mindanao and Jolo. Here were peoples converted in early days to Mohammedanism, whom Spanish Catholic missionaries were never able to win over, and whom the Spanish military were never able to conquer. There was no love lost between these Moros and the Christians of Luzon; in general, the Moros, stout fighters, disdained and even hated the Christians.

I remember on one occasion putting into a Moro port and receiving in audience a Moro *datu* (sultan). We talked together on the forward deck of the destroyer. He had been told, he said, of America's intention to create an independent Philippine nation: "If that be true, surely it would not be fair to include the southern islands and thus place them under the rule of Manila. For Spain never did conquer the Moro strongholds in the south; Spain could not therefore cede them in 1898 to another power. We have yielded to American troops, but never to the Christian Filipinos of the north. Surely you have no right, therefore, to place us under the Christian government of Manila." I tried to calm his fears and win his understanding. At the conclusion he sought to pay me high compliment: "Well, I have respect for you. Certainly you do not talk like a Christian." Before we sailed away he presented me with a beautiful lantaka—an old Moro brass cannon from one of the early strongholds.

Other visits were to spots subsequently made famous by mighty battles. In January, at Olongapo, I boarded the *Augusta* as the guest of Admiral Hart to witness naval maneuvers. In the same month, as the guest of General Grant, I watched the maneuvers of the American troops on the Bataan Peninsula. We were preparing—but with what lamentably small forces! The number of troops in the Philippine Department at the time of General MacArthur's appointment to head the United States Army Forces in the Far East was only about 10,000 regular Army and Air Corps men, supplemented by 12,000 Philippine scouts.

Early in March, with members of my staff, I motored to the northern end of Luzon, visiting places which even President Quezon had never reached. We stopped at provincial capitals and met local officials in Ilocos Norte, Cagayan, Isabela, Nueva Vizcaya and Nueva Ecija. Throughout the trip gay arches welcomed High Commissioner Sayre, and I spoke to large cordial crowds, planted innumerable commemorative trees, and greeted hosts of bright-eyed, excited school children.

The great island of Mindanao to the south, we visited about a year after my arrival in the Philippines. At Parang we were met by President Quezon. Together we proceeded by automobile over the newly constructed north-and-south highway across the interior, from the Cotabato-Davao road to Malaybalay in Bukidnon Province. This important highway was officially opened on September 2, and I felt immensely honored to have it named Sayre Highway. Some two years later, in Washington, I would read in the papers how the American troops fought the Japanese up and down the Sayre Highway.

The night after leaving Malaybalay we spent with President Quezon at the Del Monte pineapple plantation on the northern plateau. The country here was utterly unlike the lowlands of Luzon, and reminded me again and again of cattle country I had known in Montana. President Quezon, never too robust, felt fagged when we reached Del Monte; and when I suggested that he lie down and let me massage him he took off his piña shirt and lay on the couch in my room while I rubbed his back and we talked together. It seemed to help him and he felt grateful. Next day we sailed for Manila on his palatial yacht, the *Casiana*.

In January, 1941, I was off again—to Palawan and near-by islands on Admiral Hart's yacht, the *Isabel*. In Palawan we explored the famous subterranean river. For more than a mile, in a Navy flat-bottomed boat with a powerful searchlight, we ascended the river, winding through strange rock formations and caverns, bat-infested, spectacular, weird.

On the same trip we were most interested in the extensive leper colony at Culion. Here were lepers from all over the Philippines. Dr. H. Windsor Wade and his assistants in the laboratory and clinic were hard at work in an impressive effort to improve their lot. He pointed out to us the serious lack of water and also the very meager subsistence allowance granted by the Philippine Government. I promised to do what I could. Later when the war came the people of Culion were largely forgotten; and many of them fled.

Other trips were to wilder parts of the islands. Everywhere we went was outstanding beauty. I think of little-frequented roads in the southern islands, winding in and out through languorous groves of coconut palms of vivid green, skirting surf-fringed bays of gorgeous blue, every turn of the road revealing beauty such as all one's life one has imagined and never hoped to see. I think of the rice terraces at Bontoc, jewelled mountain sides of jade-green and intricate design, or of the hillsides of abacás at Davao, or of the great virgin forests of giant tropical growth in the interior of Mindanao, as untouched as in the days when the world was very young.

I have a lively memory of our trip by horseback and pack mule across the Zambales Mountains from Fort Stotsenburg to the China Sea, led by General Grunert and accompanied by General Wainwright, veteran cavalryman. We rode westward from Fort Stotsenburg, up through the Negrito country past the lower reaches of Mount Pinatubo, and down the westward slopes to the China Sea.

In many mountain fastnesses primitive peoples were still to be found almost untouched by modern ways. Deep in the interior of Luzon, far from roads or human habitations, I have chanced upon stray Negritos, shy as wild animals, half naked, hunting through the mountain forests with bow and arrow, sleeping on cold nights in the warm ashes of their campfires.

Revealing stories are told of them. One day soon after the outbreak of the Japanese war, a band of Negritos appeared at the office of Edward King, the commanding general at Fort Stotsenburg, carrying two tightly bound Japanese airmen. "We saw these men descending from the sky," they cried out excitedly. "Who are they?" They were told that the men were Japanese, and that Japan had declared war against the United States. The Negrito leader stepped forward. "Then I, King of the Negritos, declare war against Japan," he exclaimed. Thereupon at his request General King prepared a written statement in the form of a declaration of war. To this with great solemnity the Negrito leader affixed his thumbprint in lieu of signature and seal.

From the primitive Negritos, who numbered only a few thousands, or from the far more numerous warlike and fearless Moros of Jolo and Mindanao, or from the head-hunting tribes of northern Luzon, who still on occasion were said to revert to their ancient practices, it was a far cry to the dapper, white-suited students at the University of the Philippines or to the lordly sugar planters who occupied positions of commanding importance in Manila and in the provincial capitals.

Most American visitors to the Philippines carry away surface impressions of wealthy mestizo families in affluent Manila homes or of astute politicos who adroitly and smoothly manipulate national and local political machines or of the jostling, polyglot throngs in Manila streets or of enthusiasts who stake their money upon exciting games of jai alai.

But when all is said and done the destiny of the Philippines will not be determined by the sugar magnates or Manila-trained professionals or government officials. To understand the Philippines and get down to the heart of their problems, one must turn to the un-

tutored, poverty-ridden peasants who constitute the backbone of the
19,000,000 Filipinos now inhabiting the Islands. They live simply,
close to the land, cultivating with a lumbering carabao their bits of
rice or *camotes* or tobacco, happy-go-lucky, struggling to keep free
from debt but proving generally an easy prey to the landlord and
the money lender. The peasant's innate good nature shines in his
smiling face; and somehow in spite of poverty and simple surroundings one feels that he has learned the high art of distilling happiness
from life. His children, his wife, and the old parents are the core of
his life—and also his pigs and his carabao and his fighting cock, if
he has them.

Step into his simple grass or nipa shack on stilts above bare
ground in the average barrio, and you find generally eight or ten
children, one or more aged grandparents, and a hard-working young
wife—all underfed and often tubercular, but nevertheless smiling
and, in spite of biting poverty, apparently happy.

Has his life been really changed by forty years of American rule?
Perhaps not as fundamentally as many Americans would like to
think. But since the Americans came at least he has had uncontami-
nated water at the village well. He has been free from cholera and
plague and smallpox. He has been able to send his children to a
good barrio school where they could learn to read and write the
English language. Good roads and radios have exposed him to stimulating outside influences. The ferment of national independence is
in his soul. He thinks of America as a friend who has brought good
gifts.

His deep-rooted friendship for Americans and American ways,
and his fundamental qualities of steadfastness and goodness, offer a
firm foundation upon which to build. When the war broke and Japanese troops were hunting down their prey it was to him that many
a hard-pressed American or Filipino guerrilla turned for help and
shelter. Through those dark days his loyalty stood out, shining and
unforgettable. The future of the Philippines, he holds in his keeping.

Today under the bright promise of a new President, fresh hope
opens before him. Independence has come to the nation, and the
hope of a new freedom to him individually. He is no longer the
forgotten man; new blood stirs in his veins.

Throughout the months our thoughts were turning increasingly toward Japan. In December, 1939, President Roosevelt had written to me:

I think the Japanese actions will depend much on what Russia decides to do both in Europe and the Far East—especially in Europe. Later on I hope you will be able to take a little holiday in Japan and talk things over with Grew. [Nelson] Johnson, I take it, cannot get even to Hong Kong from Chungking, but I hope you will keep in touch with him and if he is able to get, say, to Saigon, you might run over there and see him.

Following out the President's suggestion I made a visit with Betty to Ambassador Grew in Tokyo in April, 1940. From Manila to Shanghai we travelled as the guests of Admiral Hart on the *Augusta*, flagship of the United States Asiatic Fleet, which was then changing station from Manila to Shanghai; and this we greatly enjoyed. As we approached Shanghai up the narrow river, the beauty of the approaching spring was all around us. In striking contrast to the hot seasonless tropics of Manila, it seemed incomprehensibly lovely. In Shanghai we conferred with various American officials; and then, accompanied by my Naval aide, Lieutenant Commander McVay, we proceeded to Tokyo, where Ambassador and Mrs. Grew welcomed us to the Embassy.

During our pleasant visit with the Grews I had several intimate talks with Hachiro Arita, Minister of Foreign Affairs. The bitter fighting between Japan and China was dragging wearily on, and I hoped that there might be some way to end it. Mr. Arita seemed more than interested in what I had to say and arranged to receive me in his own home. We had four successive meetings. Joe Grew shared my hopes, although he was not present at these conversations. Of course I kept him informed of everything that passed between Mr. Arita and myself.

I told Mr. Arita that, although I could not speak for my government, I felt personally that we must if possible overcome the current misunderstanding and unhappy relationships between Japan and the United States, and that to do so I ardently hoped that this might result from finding some way to terminate the protracted conflict between China and Japan. I said that it seemed to me apparent that sooner or later Japan would have to choose between throwing in her lot with the United States, Great Britain, and France or looking instead to Germany and perhaps Russia. I spoke of the deep cultural and ideological differences between these two groups of countries and of the need for Japan to make a wise decision between them. I also spoke of Japan's need for many raw materials, which the former group was certainly far better able to supply. Naturally it was for Japan, and for Japan alone, to choose what her future policy would be; but I added that if Japan, taking a long look ahead, should decide to throw in her lot with the United States and Great Britain it was manifestly to her interest now to smooth away any difficulties with these countries; and this would mean to find some practicable way of ending the fighting between herself and China. I asked whether it might not be possible to reconcile the differences between China and Japan. Mr. Arita answered that his mind in large measure went along with mine, but the real difficulty was to find terms which could be agreed to by both sides.

As I wrote to President Roosevelt on May 16, 1940, on my return from Japan:

The general impression which I gained from my conversations with the Japanese Minister for Foreign Affairs was that Japan is increasingly realizing the difficulties of carrying on her operations in China and that if a way could be found to retire gracefully and save her face she would not be averse to doing so, provided of course that she were given compensations in North China.

As a result of the conversations, perhaps the way lies open now, if and when the time becomes ripe to do so and if you should so desire, to extend American good offices or mediation in the effort to find some basis of reconciliation between Japan and China. Probably the time is not ripe at this moment, but it may be useful to know that such an avenue apparently lies open if and when you should want to use it.

These are tragic days, and I well realize the terrible strain and responsibilities resting upon your shoulders. God bless you and help to sustain you! I rejoice that you are at the helm. No other man in the country could carry the load as splendidly as you.

The year 1940 was one of worsening relations between the United States and Japan. Mr. Arita, in particular, was so cordial and friendly that I could not help feeling that he wanted to maintain peace with America, and that there was a distinct hope of averting war. But as the days passed the war party became the party of power in Japan.

I also talked with Admiral Kichisaburo Nomura, whom I had met in Tokyo on the way to Manila, and who was a leading figure. He also was distinctly friendly. (Later, it will be remembered, he was sent to Washington to represent Japan and carried on the historic conversations with Secretary Hull when the Japanese attack was made on Pearl Harbor.)

During our visit I was presented to the Emperor. Accompanied by Ambassador Grew I had a pleasant visit with him. In addition Betty and I were graciously received by the Empress. Our meeting, however, was essentially a formal one, and nothing of real consequence developed from our talk.

Although the atmosphere of Tokyo seemed tense, and the people resentful of foreigners, we experienced no discourtesy or unfriendly incidents. When the time came for our departure a number of high officials, following the Japanese custom, expressed their appreciation of our visit by presenting us with various personal gifts, including one or two beautiful ivories. I remember how pleased Betty was with the beautiful azalea bush which Mr. Arita gave us, grafted so that it bore blossoms of three colors upon a single bush. We planted it in the cool mountain air of our Baguio garden.

General Douglas MacArthur, after serving as Chief of Staff of the United States Army from 1930 to 1935, had entered the service of President Quezon as his military adviser to assist in the "establishment and development of a system of National Defense" for the Philippines. With his gracious wife and small son he occupied a spacious penthouse apartment at the top of the Manila Hotel when we reached Manila in 1939.

Tall, spare, with a thin face, receding dark hair, piercing eyes, and low, resonant voice, he gave the impression of drama in his bearing, his action, and his words. Sharp and observant though his glance, he seemed always indrawn and playing his part as a great actor. Although never seeming to lose himself in an emotional outburst, he was a skillful orator, conscious always of the effect upon his listeners. With his keen trenchant mind and his far-reaching knowledge of history and of military strategy as part of history, he could hold listeners spellbound.

Having lived in Manila several years before our arrival, he had a tight circle of loyal aides and admirers. As a man of strong, positive character, he naturally had enemies, too. To the average American in Manila who saw him always from the distance—for he held himself aloof from the crowd—he gave the effect of being inscrutable and enigmatic. His personality lacked the open, democratic, American approach.

In contrast the spontaneous warmth and genuine friendliness of his wife were of immense help to him. Americans and Filipinos alike were won by her charm and her soft, Southern voice. In their social life she knew well how to protect and uphold "the General," as she always called him even to intimate friends. They had married rather late in the General's life; and now with their three-year-old son, Arthur, their happiness seemed complete in their ivory tower atop the Manila Hotel.

Until his appointment as head of USAFFE my contacts with General MacArthur were social rather than official. One of his early communications was a very personal note delivered by an aide. At a large luncheon for ladies which my wife had given at the residence to the Red Cross volunteers, Mrs. MacArthur had not been seated with what the General considered to be a proper observance of her rank. Adverting to "recent circumstances," he set forth his understanding as to the proper rank which should be accorded to him and his wife. I sent back a note telling of my entire ignorance of the incident, adding that there was no intent to alter her rank and assuring him that his wife would always be accorded in my home all the honor due her. This the General immediately acknowledged with an appreciative and warmly expressed, hand-written reply.

Questions of rank in Manila often raised difficulties. The strict unquestioned protocol emanating from Washington was that the High Commissioner, representing the President of the United States in the Philippine Islands, should be "the Number One man" and should outrank the President of the Commonwealth. But very understandably it often irked the Filipinos to see their President Quezon take second place in the presence of the High Commissioner.

Because we sympathized with this very natural feeling and wanted to avoid hurting their sensibilities, sometimes Betty and I purposely absented ourselves from social functions attended by President Quezon so that he might make his appearance as the ranking figure.

President Quezon, as the months passed, had apparently lost confidence in the judgment of his military adviser, and more than once in a public address squarely contradicted previous positive declarations made by General MacArthur. Quezon, as I knew from personal experience, could be extremely temperamental. But his attitude toward the General, so far as one could see, was due more to fundamental loss of confidence than to superficial disagreements. To an exceedingly important conference held in Baguio between President Quezon, representing the Philippines, and myself representing the United States, to shape up general defense plans, I naturally invited General Grunert, in command of American forces in the Philippines, to be present and take a leading part in our discussions. I had expected that President Quezon would call in General MacArthur as his adviser; but to my surprise he did not do so and in our discussion the General was not referred to. According to the current talk of Manila, General MacArthur's star was rapidly descending and he was expected to drop out of the Philippine picture. His assistant and chief of staff, Colonel Dwight Eisenhower, whom we all liked and respected, had already asked for his transfer to Washington, and departed soon after our arrival.

However, all this was changed on July 26, 1941, when President Roosevelt ordered the incorporation of the Philippine armed forces in the United States Army and appointed General MacArthur Commander of the United States Armed Forces in the Far East. His appointment fell like a bombshell on Manila. From that time on President Quezon gave to General MacArthur loyal cooperation and support. General MacArthur at once set about a progressive incorporation of the reserve forces of the Philippine Army into the service of the United States.

15

The Coming of War

With the passing months the tragedy of the European war deepened and began to extend its ominous shadow over the Pacific. Japan had become an ally of Germany and, under the control of the war party, was concentrating upon military preparations. Indo-China, under constant menace, was not too distant from Philippine shores. The Japanese were driving deeper and deeper into the heart of China. General Grunert, Admiral Hart, and I held constant conferences to size up the changing military situation and to formulate plans.

As I wrote to President Roosevelt on November 13, 1940:

> Out here in the Far East the situation is growing more and more tense. I have the feeling that any day Japan may start moving southwards. Indeed, she is in a sense already on the way, and every day is strengthening her grip upon Indo-China.

In view of certain undercurrents of protest in Manila against the Philippines' being dragged into an "imperialistic war," it was important to keep the issues clear. In an address given in 1940 on the Fourth of July—a day in Manila when Americans drew closely together in deeply patriotic feeling—I said:

> The situation which confronts us today is a head-on conflict between two utterly conflicting philosophies or ways of life. On the one hand is

the philosophy of human brotherhood; the faith that the human personality is the supreme value of life; the belief that human rights and human freedom are paramount to all else. This was the faith which was boldly proclaimed 164 years ago today in ringing phrases by thirteen venturesome colonies; this was the faith embodied in the very heart of our Constitution; this was the foundation faith upon which our nation was built and has grown to power.

Opposing it is the philosophy of unrestrained force. We have been witnessing during the past terrible weeks the fruits of that philosophy. Battle and murder and sudden death, forced upon countries desiring only peace; neutral nations ruthlessly invaded; nonbelligerent ships bombed and submarined. Homes destroyed, women and children machine-gunned, families wiped out, cities blown to pieces, human suffering and agony indescribable. Wave after wave of fear and cruelty unloosed upon the world, spreading everywhere havoc and deterioration. . . .

In this stupendous battle for the defense of more than ten centuries of hard-won human progress, in this terrific struggle between the upbuilders and the wreckers of civilization, we must face the realities. I pray God that the United States will not be forced into the blazing conflagration; I hope profoundly that American soldiers will never again be compelled to cross the ocean to join in a European war or in any other war built upon racial hatreds. Yet some things are more precious than life itself. Without human freedom life is not worth living. Without faith life is not worth living. Without hope of a world secure for the peace-loving, life is not worth living. Burning as is our desire to remain at peace, we cannot watch the smashing of our civilization won through centuries of heroic sacrifice and struggle and see the blackout of the great principles upon which our nation fundamentally rests, and not lift a finger.

At an anniversary dinner in my honor on October 21, 1941, two years after my landing in the Philippines, I was saying:

Here in the Philippines, we stand at guard on the American frontier: and the whole future of the civilized world today hangs upon the strength and unity of groups like ourselves, devoted to a common cause. It is not a question of race or blood; it is a question of defending a way of life. . . .

It is a solemn hour. We know not when the call may come to redeem this pledge—with our lives and all that is precious to us. We stand ready. No wonder we feel strongly drawn together and one on a night like this.

All of us saw trouble ahead. In November, 1940, Admiral Hart in command of the Asiatic Fleet ordered all wives and children of naval personnel to be evacuated to the United States. The Asiatic Fleet, instead of going to North China waters as had been customary in April, remained in Philippine waters. In May, 1941, Army wives and dependents were also ordered home. I contemplated whether all American civilian women and children should be returned home, and raised the question with the State Department. The latter, however, feeling that such a move would only cause undue anxiety and excite fear, asked me not to follow out the suggestion. Many worried civilians kept asking me whether they should evacuate their families. I could only reply that none of us knew what lay ahead; their guess was perhaps as good as mine. I pointed out that both the Army and the Navy had evacuated their families, but that the Department of State had asked me not to advise the evacuation of civilian women and children. And I added that my wife and son were remaining in Manila.

I cannot better present the international picture as it looked to us at that time than by quoting from a personal letter written to me by President Roosevelt from the White House on New Year's Eve, December 31, 1940, a little less than a year before the attack finally came:

Dear Frank:

. . . We of course do not want to be drawn into a war with Japan —we do not want to be drawn into any war anywhere. There is, however, very close connection between the hostilities which have been going on for three and a half years in the Far East and those which have been going on for sixteen months in eastern Europe and the Mediterranean. For practical purposes, there is going on a world conflict, in which there are aligned on one side Japan, Germany and Italy, and on the other side, China, Great Britain and the United States. This country is not involved in the hostilities, but there is no doubt where we stand as regards the issues. Today, Japan and Germany and Italy are allies. Whatever any one of them gains or "wins" is a gain for their side and, conversely, a loss for the other side. Great Britain is on the defensive not alone in and around the British Isles, and not alone in and around the Mediterranean, but wherever there is a British possession or a British ship—and that means all over the world.

You say that you have the "feeling that any day Japan may start moving southwards." As you point out, we are faced with the danger of Japan's continuing her expansion in the Far East, especially toward the south, while the European issue remains in the balance. If Japan, moving further southward, should gain possession of the region of the Netherlands East Indies and the Malay Peninsula, would not the chances of Germany's defeating Great Britain be increased and the chances of England's winning be decreased thereby? I share your view that our strategy should be to render every assistance possible to Great Britain without ourselves entering the war, but would we be rendering every assistance possible to Great Britain were we to give our attention wholly and exclusively to the problems of the immediate defense of the British Isles and of Britain's control of the Atlantic? The British Isles, the British in those Isles, have been able to exist and to defend themselves not only because they have prepared strong local defenses but also because as the heart and the nerve of the British Empire they have been able to draw upon vast resources for their sustenance and to bring into operation against their enemies economic, military and naval pressures on a world-wide scale. They live by importing goods from all parts of the world and by utilizing large overseas financial resources. They are defended not only by measures of defense carried out locally but also by distant and widespread economic, military, and naval activities which both diminish the vital strength of their enemies and at the same time prevent those enemies from concentrating the full force of their armed power against the heart and the nerve center of the Empire.

The British need assistance along the lines of our generally established policies at many points, assistance which in the case of the Far East is certainly well within the realm of "possibility" so far as the capacity of the United States is concerned. Their defense strategy must in the nature of things be global. Our strategy of giving them assistance toward ensuring our own security must envisage both sending of supplies to England and helping to prevent a closing of channels of communication to and from various parts of the world, so that other important sources of supply and other theaters of action will not be denied to the British. We have no intention of being "sucked into" a war with Japan any more than we have of being "sucked into" a war with Germany. Whether there will come to us war with either or both of those countries will depend far more upon what they do than upon what we deliberately refrain from doing. . . .

With best wishes for a good New Year, I am

Very sincerely yours,

Franklin D. Roosevelt

By this letter the President made quite clear his understanding of our deep moral involvement in Britain's struggle and his determination to do everything in his power, short of a declaration of war, to help her, not only in the West but in the Far East, to which Britain's lifeline was staked. Like President Wilson before our entrance into the First World War, he felt our deep obligation to a nation which was fighting for its life—*and for our life, too!* But he drew back from the awesome declaration of war until our own people understood and saw clearly the issue and chose to enter the terrible conflict. Whether ourselves to take the initiative by declaration of war and attack or whether to await further the turn of events and a possible attack upon ourselves, as finally came about at Pearl Harbor, was a profoundly difficult and momentous decision.

We carried on in Manila as best we could, realizing that in the event of war we should be at a hopeless military disadvantage.

In July, 1940, several thousand refugees arrived from China, driven out by the Japanese fighting. This intensified my concern about "fifth column" activities in the Philippines and the need of a strong and effective staff of secret intelligence officers. As I wrote the President on July 2, the problem presented unique difficulties because, although under the Independence Act of 1934 "the Commonwealth Government is primarily responsible for the maintenance of law and order here, there are nevertheless vital United States defense interests whose protection we can hardly afford to entrust to Commonwealth officials. After various discussions, I have reached the conclusion that the Army and Navy should be empowered, through their intelligence work, to safeguard these vital American interests."

I therefore recommended that during the emergency the Army and Navy be authorized in so far as possible to handle general intelligence work in the Philippines and to expend such additional funds and employ such additional personnel as this might require.

The recommendation was carried out, and we came to rely increasingly upon the Army's "G-2" service.

As the war clouds gathered we were compelled to enter into many additional activities—financial and economic as well as diplomatic. The work of the High Commissioner's office was greatly increased. There were periods when we were working night and day. On May 1, 1940, the Secretary of the Treasury designated the United

States High Commissioner as his agent to carry out "freezing control" of funds within the Philippines. This included sweeping powers to control financial transactions by or on behalf of designated foreign countries or their nationals, and was inaugurated to prevent withdrawal of the funds of invaded countries and their nationals from the United States. As with the extension of the European war nations were added to the list of "blocked fund" countries, the work involved in our office became ever greater. The program was subsequently broadened and became a weapon of economic warfare against the Axis powers.

Another program undertaken by the High Commissioner's office was "Export Control." The Act of July 2, 1940, authorizing the President to prohibit the export of munitions and war supplies was unhappily not applicable to the Philippines. As the European War progressed and the demand for strategic war materials increased, it was evident that unless some governmental control could be imposed, the Axis countries would drain the Philippines dry of these.

The Commonwealth government expressed its entire readiness to cooperate to the fullest extent in a program of export control. The result was the passage on May 28, 1941, by the United States Congress of an Act extending the provisions of the Export Control Act to the Philippines; and the Secretary of State delegated to the High Commissioner authority to control by licensing the export from the Philippines of all articles named by the President of the United States.

By the early summer of 1941, however, the situation had grown still more acute. Far Eastern countries were tending to drain out of the Philippines stocks of commodities not listed in the Export Control Act. I sent an urgent cable to the President in July, and also wrote to him on July 31:

Perhaps still more pressing at the moment is the problem of maintaining Philippine stocks of food supplies and other necessities. If the shortage of bottoms becomes acute we will be extremely limited in what supplies we can get from the United States. Yet there is imminent danger that what we have will be drained away by being exported to neighboring Far Eastern countries where prices of supplies may be higher. We ought to control such exports; but how? The Export Control Act apparently is not broad enough to include foodstuffs and a number of other necessary commodities. Just now I'm wrestling with this problem also.

As a result, Washington decided to provide flexible control over exports from the Philippines by extending the list of commodities subject to export control to virtually all articles of necessity. This was done by proclamation of the President of the United States.

The carrying on of this export-control program involved extremely heavy work by our office. I placed Woodbury Willoughby, my financial adviser and able assistant, in charge of the program.

Finally, on September 15, 1941, I could write to President Roosevelt:

During the past two months our office has been working hard on export control and foreign funds control. Each of these has been functioning smoothly and well, and we have received full cooperation from the Commonwealth Government officials. Through them we have been enabled to build up effective economic armament in this part of the world.

My office staff was richly blessed with able and loyal helpers, tireless, unselfish, hard-working and uncomplaining, and I owe to them more than I can say. They were the bright spot as our skies slowly darkened; in the best traditions of American service, they rose to meet the ever increasing demands as war approached.

Defense problems were always in the background of our thought. Fortunately able men headed our armed forces in the Philippines, both military and naval.

Major General George Grunert, in command of the Philippine Department, pressed the work of preparation and reorganization and at the same time kept vigorously requesting additional supplies, ammunition, and equipment from Washington.

On June 18, 1941, I wrote to the President:

Pushing through defense measures of one kind or another has been occupying much of my time. I believe one of the most important military steps which should be taken here is the training of Philippine army officers and regular forces by our own army personnel, and to do this properly will cost over $27,000,000. In addition to this, aviation fields must be built and existing ones improved, roads must be built, existing Philippine army shelters and facilities must be expanded and communication facilities improved. All these run into money; and I believe the plan an excellent one to recommend to Congress the appropriation for Philippine defense needs of the $52,000,000 representing the sugar excise tax and dollar devaluation funds. At the outset I thought that President Quezon might resent the appropriation of these funds in a way which would place full control of expenditures in the hands of the United States Army and Navy authorities rather than of himself and the Commonwealth Government. But he is a realist and understands that only thus is Congress likely to be persuaded to appropriate the money; and I believe that he is now entirely agreeable to this form of appropriation.

General Grunert, in command of the Philippine Department, Admiral Bemis, in command of the Sixteenth Naval District, President Quezon and myself have reached full agreement on a program for the expenditure of these funds, and our joint recommendations, as you doubtless know, have been radioed to Washington. I know that you will do everything possible to speed the recommendation to be sent to Congress.

With the appointment on July 26 of General MacArthur to command the United States Armed Forces in the Far East, the whole situation was radically changed. All defense problems fell under his direction and command. From then on he had immense power. President Quezon, realizing that the defense of the Philippines now rested in his hands, assumed toward him an altogether different attitude; and the general, in a letter to President Quezon dated August 19, 1941, as published in the *Manila Bulletin*, congratulated him upon his unanimous nomination for a second term as President of the Commonwealth:

I feel the Philippines should be congratulated, the United States should be felicitated and the world in general gratified, at what has occurred. It is to you personally, however, in the bond of adopted brotherhood which has united us for so long a time, that I wish to express the thrilling elation that I feel. My love and affection for you is such that not even your immediate family can feel a greater surge of pride and happiness than that which animates me.

With his new responsibilities General MacArthur became exceedingly busy. In October General Grunert was relieved of his command and returned to duty in the United States.

The problem that gave me perhaps more concern than any other was civilian defense. Clearly the "active" military and naval defense of the islands lay within the responsibility of the United States Army,

Navy and Air Forces. On the other hand, it was evident that civilian agencies must assume responsibility for the "passive defense" of the civilian population, embracing measures for their general protection and welfare. The organizing and taking of adequate measures for civilian welfare and defense, such as ensuring adequate supplies of foodstuffs and fuel, preparing shelters and protection against air raids, strengthening and training the Constabulary, and organizing a home guard, lay largely within the jurisdiction and powers of the Commonwealth Government. Nevertheless, the problem could not be successfully met without the closest and most constant cooperation among Commonwealth Government officials, United States Army and Navy officers and representatives of the High Commissioner's Office.

Considerably more than a year before the attack on Pearl Harbor I inaugurated plans for the initiation of this work. In September, 1940, I asked President Quezon and General Grunert to meet in my office so that General Grunert could explain in detail the urgent need for collaboration in preparing for civilian defense. The following month President Quezon, General Grunert, and Admiral Smeallie, again meeting in my office, agreed to the creation of a Civilian Emergency Planning Board to formulate definite plans for civilian protection. This board, composed of representatives of the High Commissioner's office, the United States Army and Navy, the Commonwealth Government, the American Chamber of Commerce, and the Philippine Chamber of Commerce, held its first meeting in my office on October 28, with President Quezon and General Grunert attending. It at once set to work and, after four months of intensive activity under the constant inspiration and guidance of its chairman, Colonel Carswell, serving on my staff, submitted an excellent detailed report to President Quezon and myself on March 11, 1941.

On March 20, 1941, I again conferred with President Quezon and strongly urged that he set the machinery of the Commonwealth in motion to carry out the recommendations of the Planning Board. He agreed to do so; and on April 1 he set up for this purpose the Civilian Emergency Administration, headed by the Philippine Secretary of National Defense and operating through provincial, municipal, and city emergency committees. Through the weeks and months which followed I constantly sought to stimulate and hasten this work and placed at the disposal of the Administration all the facilities of my office.

On September 7 I sent to British Malaya and the Netherlands East Indies Major Cyril Q. Marron, who had succeeded Colonel Carswell as liaison officer of the United States Army attached to my staff, to observe the civilian welfare defense activities in those places. Major Marron made an able report on his observations, and I gave copies to President Quezon and to General MacArthur.

On the basis of this report I suggested to General MacArthur on September 30 the intensification of the work of the Civilian Emergency Administration, with a series of meetings between representatives of the military, the Commonwealth Government, and the High Commissioner's Office. General MacArthur replied on October 10 that he believed "little good would eventuate from the series of conferences you suggest." As to the sharp criticism of civilian defense preparations by visiting journalists, he commented:

Personally I think the effort toward civil preparation in these Islands has been admirable. I am fully cognizant of certain weaknesses of personnel, organization and accomplishment but I believe the criticisms, which have come primarily from itinerant journalists, have been not only unjust but harmful in the extreme. These critics, coming here from zones of actual combat, have used false standards of comparison and their ridicule and abuse of the effort being made here have unquestionably been colored by the desire for sensation and publicity. I especially criticise their charge of indifference and inertia on the part of the populace. I see neither one nor the other, only commendable poise and self-control.

In spite of General MacArthur's comment, I was far from satisfied with the progress made by the Commonwealth authorities.

Civilian defense in Manila was uniquely difficult. In the generally low-lying areas around Manila it was hard to keep water out of underground diggings and cellars, and beneath-ground bomb-proof shelters were largely impractical. There were not enough gas masks for general civilian use. Furthermore, evacuation problems were made exceedingly baffling by the impossibility of knowing in advance from which direction the enemy would come. For instance, immediately prior to the war, Baguio was chosen as one evacuation center; yet enemy planes appeared over Baguio early in the morning of the first day of the war. Similarly, Pagsanjan, which the Red Cross chose as an important evacuation center, proved to be in the very line of enemy advance from the southeast. This inescapable uncertainty made for considerable confusion in the minds of civilians.

Nevertheless, in spite of the difficulties, the work of civilian defense was steadily carried on and pushed forward. Practice blackouts were instituted, the first being in the Manila area on July 10. Air-raid alarm systems were set up, and air-raid warning services were organized. Rehearsal evacuations were carried out. Men and women were enrolled for emergency services. Volunteer guards were organized. Neighborhood district meetings were held to prepare for emergency needs. First-aid stations were set up, and hospital units organized. Large-scale evacuation transport and care were prepared for. Lists were made of Americans and others qualified for particular work; and a census of food and other necessary supplies was undertaken.

The Red Cross volunteer workers, both Filipino and American, threw themselves into the civilian welfare work. Many of the Red Cross meetings were held in the ballroom of the High Commissioner's residence, where for a year and a half before Pearl Harbor Betty stimulated and encouraged these activities. Here well attended training classes were conducted in first aid, in home nursing, and in canteen work. All this preparation and planning stood us in good stead when war finally came.

During November Saburo Kurusu, a high Japanese official whom I had met on our visit to Tokyo, stopped over in Manila on his way to Washington, and that evening in my study we had a long talk. I was deeply concerned at the time over the threatened breakdown of negotiations with Japan, which were dragging fruitlessly on in Washington. Mr. Kurusu told me that, although out of immediate touch with the current situation, he had been greatly surprised by a telephone call at two o'clock in the morning from the Japanese Foreign Office, which asked him to proceed at once by plane to Washington and join Ambassador Nomura in the conversations. From what he told me then I later felt convinced that he was ignorant of any plan to attack Pearl Harbor. The Japanese government, then in the hands of the war party, presumably chose him as emissary because of his complete ignorance of the plan to attack. Manifestly in diplomatic conversations such a person would be far more convincing.

As November drew to a close we grew more and more apprehensive of attack. General MacArthur, however, seemed to believe that war would not come before April. On November 27, less than two weeks before the catastrophe of Pearl Harbor, he, Admiral Hart, and I conferred in my office. Warnings of an approaching crisis had just arrived from Washington. Back and forth, back and forth, paced General MacArthur, smoking a black cigar and assuring Admiral Hart and myself in reassuring terms that the existing alignment and movement of Japanese troops convinced him that there would be no Japanese attack before the spring. Admiral Hart felt otherwise.

The danger of our position was constantly on our minds. For a long time our Army Intelligence officers had been preparing lists of suspects to be interned or arrested upon the outbreak of war. The movements of American merchant ships had been put under Navy control.

In early December Betty had gone to Baguio to attend a women's welfare conference; I was in Manila, expecting to follow her the next day to confer about civilian defense matters with President Quezon, who was then ill in Baguio. That night Betty had a strange dream, in which Leonard Wood, former Governor General of the Philippines, came to her and kept insisting that I should not be allowed to depart from Manila. "You must not let him leave Manila," he charged again and again. The dream was so vivid that when Betty awoke in the morning she actually went to the telephone to call me. Then she realized that her impulse was based only upon a dream, and she concluded not to call. I motored to Baguio that Saturday afternoon, conferred with President Quezon, and returned to Manila with Betty and Lieutenant Commander Parker on Sunday afternoon, December 7.

Early the following morning—which corresponded to December 7 on the American side of the International Date Line—I was awakened a little before four o'clock in the morning by the sound of stocking feet running down the passage way to my bedroom. Claude Buss, my executive assistant, burst in, bringing the first breathless news of the attack on Pearl Harbor. General Sutherland, chief of staff to General MacArthur, had telephoned him at his home and instructed him immediately to inform me.

Yet when war actually came, it did not seem real. We acted almost automatically, carrying out the plans carefully arranged during the preceding months. Fortunately, telephone wires had not been cut, and public utilities were functioning without interruption. I called my staff from their beds and set everyone to work. Public statements had to be issued, Commonwealth officials notified, civilian defense measures taken. I ordered the immediate closing of the Japanese banks in Manila, and the posting of guards around them.

The High Commissioner's residence had to be prepared for defense. Six months before, I had saved enough out of my annual appropriation to purchase bags and sand, emergency tools, first-aid materials, and the like. Now I assigned several of the staff to superintend the filling and piling of sandbags, and others to carry out carefully planned preparations to make the basement habitable as a splinterproof shelter. Against a possible siege, we bought quantities of food and supplies and numerous large garbage cans which were placed along the corridors for storing water in case the mains should be cut. We closed the gates of the compound, admitting visitors only by pass, and stationed heavy guards of Philippine Constabulary around the grounds and entrance hall.

All that Monday we worked feverishly. Word came of Japanese bombing attacks shortly after daybreak at Malalag in Davao Gulf. A group of Japanese planes struck Tuguegarao about 9:30 that morning, and another group about the same time attacked Baguio, where at the time President Quezon was staying. Instead of at once attacking Japanese flying fields and bases on Formosa and to the north, our fliers made only reconnaissance flights.

I was later told that General Brereton, the commander of our air forces, was unable to secure any authorization from General MacArthur to attack until about eleven o'clock in the morning of December 8, and that a strike against Formosa was then finally authorized to take place late that afternoon or on the following morning.

Many of our fliers, returning to Clark Field from the reconnaissance flights at noon for refueling, had gone into the mess to get lunch. Japanese planes, suddenly descending from the clouds, bombed our planes on the ground and destroyed them. It seemed incredible that this happened some seven or eight hours after word of Pearl Harbor had reached us. On this first day of the war, therefore, through the tragic blunder of failure to attack we were ignominiously stripped of the planes on which our defense heavily rested, and consequently were at the mercy of the Japanese. Our Far East Air Force had been eliminated as an effective fighting force. So far as our Philippine defenses were concerned it seemed as disastrous as Pearl Harbor.

We supposed that an official investigation would follow. But the war was on then, and minds were immersed in the immediate problems of resistance.

At the end of the afternoon I conferred with General MacArthur in his office. He was pacing the floor, and I could see from his face how grave the situation must be. He read to me the radio telling of the tragic losses at Pearl Harbor. Whereas our entire military strategy had been based on holding Corregidor and some territory on the Bataan peninsula against capture, and waiting for the American main fleet to fight its way west to our rescue, we now learned that there was no American fleet which could come. American troops were so few that we must depend—and depend for our very lives— upon Filipino troops, the majority of them raw, inexperienced, and but partially trained. When they began to see the terrible predicament and realize the dreadful odds, would they remain steadfast?

General MacArthur went on to tell of the destruction that noon of our planes at Clark Field. Our hearts were heavy, and it was hard to believe that we were not in some horrible nightmare from which we would awaken. Again and again the feeling returned—especially during the long watches of the night—that we were moving in a dream and that it could not be reality.

Beginning on the following day, December 9, the Manila area was frequently bombed. Nichols Airfield, near Manila, was bombed before dawn, but most of the bombing was by daylight. We were without adequate air defense. I hoped that it might be possible to evacuate civilians by sea and talked of this with Admiral Hart. The Japanese, however, from the outset held such mastery of both air and sea that the risk to civilians in evacuation by ship was considerably greater than that involved in their remaining in Manila. Also, naval vessels were engaged in intensive war operations, and none could be spared for civilian evacuation.

About noon on December 10, two days after the beginning of the war, looking up from the terrace of the High Commissioner's residence, I saw twenty-seven Japanese bombers approaching in perfect V formation. It looked as if our last hour had come; for the white concrete residence, standing on the shore of the bay in the center of large open grounds, offered the most beautiful target in Manila. However, the bombers passed over Manila, crossed the bay, and launched a smashing attack upon the naval base at Cavite. With slow deliberation they circled at a height of some twenty thousand feet and then dropped their bombs. For two hours the attack lasted. As at Clark and Nichols fields the opposition was feeble. Following the roar of explosions, great clouds of smoke and later leaping flames rose over the inferno. That afternoon small boats carrying mutilated human bodies came across the bay and landed their dreadful cargoes to be taken to Sternberg Hospital in Manila. Some five hundred men were killed or seriously wounded. Admiral Rockwell's house, the *Comandancia*, an exceedingly beautiful example of old Spanish architecture at its best, was burned to the ground, and he barely escaped with his life. All night flames lit up the sky above Cavite, and even next day the fires still raged. Cavite was a shambles and a gaping ruin.

Followed days of tense emotion and deepening tragedy. We slept in our clothes and, during the first few nights of the war, were up and down with air-raid warnings most of the night. Our basement, which was little more than a concrete-lined pit for the elevator shaft and the air-conditioning unit, lacked sufficient ventilation to be bearable by all the people of our household and staff longer than ten or fifteen minutes at a time. Later we improved matters by installing electric fans, a telephone, a writing table, chairs, first-aid materials, and emergency food and water.

The larger part of my staff moved to the residence for the nights, gathering there each afternoon before darkness. We improvised a ladies' and a men's dormitory behind sandbags along the center court, close to the stairway to the shelter. There under mosquito nettings rigged over mattresses on the floor, our staff spent fitful nights. No lights could be shown; and the residence had but one or two rooms which could be effectively blacked out. In these we tried to brighten an hour or two after an early supper by games of cards or by conversation before throwing ourselves, partially dressed, upon our mattresses to gain strength for another day.

My wife, Billy, and I slept on cots in the small study off the library. Each of us had a small suitcase, prepared to run for it in case the bombing got heavy.

As our troops, without air support, were forced to fall back toward Manila we could see developing a gigantic pincers movement with Japanese armies from the north and from the south aiming to meet at Manila and crack us to pieces. Without reinforcements there seemed to be no escape. Captain Priestley put up a map on the wall of the family dining room and marked each day's advance by the Japanese with colored pins.

Except for radio and cables we were completely cut off from the world. All mail communication had ceased. The telephone company, nevertheless, maintained local service and did a heroic job for which we felt everlastingly grateful.

On Saturday morning December 13 I sent a broadcast radio message to the United States:

Out here on the firing line we have come to grips with reality. . . . We are in the fight to stay. War enjoins upon us all action, action, action. Time is of the essence. Come on, America!

Throughout those early days we expected the Japanese to bomb and destroy the High Commissioner's residence; and although we were without shelters equipped to withstand bombing, we spent considerable time in the basement during air raids. But the Japanese, confident of capturing Manila, had determined to save the High Commissioner's residence for their own use.

Reports kept coming in of disaster after disaster. General MacArthur, with whom I kept in constant touch, told me of his plan, when Manila became untenable, to move to Corregidor, and set up a headquarters there. This seeming abandonment of the people of Manila was distasteful to me, and I wondered whether I should not remain and throw in my lot with them. General MacArthur, however, vigorously insisted that President Quezon and I accompany him to Corregidor when Manila became untenable. His idea was for us to take along a small nucleus of staff in order to maintain at least a semblance of government, which, he felt, would help the morale of the troops. To this President Quezon and I finally were forced to agree, and we promised to abide by General MacArthur's plan.

The days and nights that followed were crowded and memorable. The members of my staff, both American and Filipino, worked day and night under the most difficult and trying conditions. Their work suffered constant interruption from air raids and bombings. Throwing themselves wholeheartedly into whatever task or emergency arose, working through all the daylight hours and often doing guard duty at night, always dependable and faithful and careless of personal safety, they proved themselves through those grueling days a staff of which any country might be proud.

Each succeeding day brought darker and darker news. Reports reached us that a hundred enemy transports had appeared in the north. We could not believe that the Japanese would be able to make a successful landing—but they did; and soon we heard that Japanese troops were relentlessly pushing southward. Then came reports of landings to the south and the more or less rapid northward advance of these troops.

Shortly before Christmas a radio message from President Roose-velt directed me to gather for safe-keeping gold, valuables, securities, bank assets, negotiable paper, and the like, and, if in my judgment necessary, to destroy them to prevent their falling into enemy hands. Under this authorization, I proceeded through my ever-faithful staff officer, Woodbury Willoughby, to collect gold and valuables from the banks.

Others of my staff were at work removing from the files all secret or confidential documents which would have to be destroyed in event of flight.

The evening of December 23 we spent wrapping up Christmas packages of cigarettes and toilet articles which the Red Cross was to deliver to the men on the front line and also to the wounded, who filled to overflowing both regular and makeshift hospitals. We were also planning a daylight Christmas Eve gathering for the staff and for the members of the American consulate.

On the morning before Christmas came an urgent telephone message from General MacArthur. He informed me that the fall of Manila was imminent and requested me to leave within four hours for Corregidor with President Quezon, so that we could set up there a temporary seat of government. He promised to join us that evening.

We moved in a daze. I ordered the burning of all the confidential files into which had gone so many months and years of careful work. I removed the large American and High Commissioner's flags which had always hung over my desk in my office. These I took to Corregidor. I broke in two the High Commissioner's seal of office. I gave the order that my new, air-cooled automobile should be run off the dock and sunk in the bay.

In the ballroom of the residence, filled with tables and sewing machines, Betty was carrying on Red Cross work with the help of a nucleus of faithful volunteers. Calling her to the door I told her that we must leave within an hour for Corregidor, taking only such clothing and personal belongings as we could throw into a suitcase.

Under such circumstances one gains an entirely new sense of values. We had been the first occupants of the High Commissioner's residence, and during the preceding two years we had collected many works of art with which to beautify it—radiant old silks and Chinese brocades, carved ivories, Oriental screens, vases, paintings, silk rugs, as well as Moro brasses and bolos and *krisses* and a brass lantaka. All these had suddenly lost their value to us. We had to leave all behind. We never saw them again. There was not even time to go through bureau drawers and closets, and in any case we did not have the heart to do so. It was not the treasures, but the people we were leaving behind, that mattered now. Our minds and hearts were with the many friends, both American and Filipino, whom we must so unceremoniously leave. It might be many a long day before we would see them again—and who knew what might happen in the meantime?

Because of extremely limited accommodations on Corregidor, General MacArthur had informed me that I could take only nine of my staff, together with Betty and our fifteen-year-old boy, Billy Graves. Before the outbreak of the war I had assigned to my executive assistant, Claude Buss, the task of coordinating and assisting in the work of civilian welfare and defense. Now, characteristically, he requested permission to remain in Manila and look after the welfare and protection of the civilian population there. He had many times proved his outstanding ability and loyalty; and I thereupon placed him in charge of the High Commissioner's office in Manila during my enforced absence, directing him to take whatever action was necessary to protect and care for the civilian population, to look after the High Commissioner's staff remaining in Manila, and to care for the government property and buildings.

I took as staff to Corregidor Evett D. Hester, economic adviser, Woodbury Willoughby, financial adviser, and Mrs. Willoughby; Robert Huffcut, economic assistant; Cabot Coville, Foreign Service officer; James J. Saxon, Treasury expert; Miss Anna Belle Newcomb, my private secretary; Mrs. Janet White, clerk-stenographer; and Captain William Priestley, military liaison officer.

I also took four custodial employees to assist in the tunnel life on Corregidor: Carlos Tunay, veteran personal servant to American High Commissioners and Governors; Pablo Ortiz; Rickie Evangelista; and Lee Wong Kitt. Without question or protest, leaving families and homes behind, they took their places beside us on Corregidor.

As far as safety was concerned, there seemed to be little choice between Corregidor and Manila. Manila had no tunnel to resort to; but Corregidor promised to be the very center of Japanese attack, where life would be anything but safe or pleasant.

We were interrupted by the usual morning air raid. Bomb explosions sounded close at hand. The Japanese had commenced to bomb the port area and the harbor. At two o'clock in the afternoon the Japanese were still bombing ships in the bay. Shortly thereafter I called together the Filipino and Chinese servants to tell them that we had to leave and to say goodbye. Never have I had more true and loyal service than from these. Now we must leave them behind. Claude Buss stood by as we started to leave. I gripped him by the hand but could not speak.

The bombing stopped, and the all-clear sounded. We jumped into waiting automobiles and raced for the Presidential Pier, a quarter of a mile away. I could not help thinking back to the day when I had landed on this pier amid nineteen-gun salutes and waving flags, with zooming planes overhead, to be greeted by President Quezon and his cabinet. Now, two years later, he and I met again at the same pier, between bombing raids and in danger of our lives.

We boarded two waiting launches and sped to the *Mayon,* an inter-island steamer, lying outside the breakwater to take us to Corregidor, twenty-seven miles across the bay. With President Quezon were his wife and three children, Vice President Sergio Osmeña, and twenty or more of his staff and entourage.

On the *Mayon* we found that through some oversight the chief engineer and his first assistant had gone ashore, steam was not up, and the ship apparently was unable to move. We ordered the second engineer to get steam up immediately. At last we began to move. It was an exciting trip; but no Japanese planes appeared, and we reached Corregidor shortly before sundown.

"Japanese bombers were over Corregidor this afternoon," was the first word that reached us as we hurriedly disembarked.

We scarcely needed those words to alert us to the fact that we were entering a military outpost which promised to be the very hotbed of attack. On every side as we made our way up Malinta Hill we saw men in khaki, trucks, jeeps, all in feverish military activity. As we walked to the mouth of the tunnel which was to be our home for the next two months we asked ourselves what part our small civilian group could possibly play in the siege to come.

Out of the late afternoon sunlight we stepped into the dark tunnel, wondering what fate lay in store for us.

16

Corregidor—
Escape by Submarine

We went to sleep that Christmas Eve in cots jammed end-to-end along the sides of Malinta Tunnel, the men in one lateral and the women in another. All our possessions were in the suitcases under our cots. Life had been reduced to the elemental. On Christmas morning we went into khaki. There was no laundry, and no hot water; cold water was limited and, at times, not to be had.

One morning I met Joe Stevenot near Headquarters tunnel, and he was holding a glass less than half full of water. "What shall I do with this?" he asked, perplexed. "I drank a little of it, I shaved with some, I washed my face and brushed my teeth, and here's a whole half-glass left over!"

It seemed ironic that our first day in the Corregidor tunnel should mark the anniversary of the birth of the Prince of Peace. We could not even make believe in the Christmas spirit. Except for attending a short service read by one of the chaplains in the mess lateral, we tried to forget in the hot, foul tunnel air that it was Christmas Day and largely succeeded.

Corregidor, a high rocky island three and a half miles long, covered with dense vegetation, has rare natural beauty. Roads wind in and out and up and down through luxuriant tropical tangles and temperate forest growths. Birds are everywhere. High cliffs command views in every direction of blue, sparkling sea, studded with rocky islands. To the northeast lies the whole sweep of Manila Bay, and the white buildings of the city are visible on a clear day. To the north, across two miles of water, rise the green slopes of Mariveles Mountain on the Bataan Peninsula. Winds from the China Sea cool and freshen the air so that the island is free from much of the stifling tropical heat of the mainland. It is also one of the few places in the Philippines where one can sleep without a mosquito net. Before the Japanese attack commenced Corregidor had seemed to be the very incarnation of beauty and peace.

The stronghold of Corregidor unhappily was not in any sense a modern underground fortification. The Washington Naval Treaty of 1922 had prohibited both modernizing of fortifications and new construction. The defenses therefore were little different from what they had been before the development of military aviation in the 1920's. The guns were, for the most part, mounted on the surface. Corregidor had been fortified against attack by ships and naval guns but not against attack by air.

Malinta Tunnel, in which we took refuge, had been cut out of the rock and reenforced with concrete walls, floors, and overhead arches to furnish bombproof shelter for the hospital, headquarters staff, workshops and storerooms of the local garrison. It lacked adequate, modern ventilation as well as other conveniences. The food stocks were limited. In fact, we were soon down to two very simple meals a day.

In the lateral of the hospital tunnel where we lived, we gave up privacy along with the soft things of life. We ate in relays at a common mess in the tunnel, slept in the tunnel, and carried on there as long as the foul air and difficult working conditions permitted. I managed to secure two desks and make room for them at the end of the lateral. Here my staff and my secretary and stenographer faithfully did such work as was assigned to them, now and again resorting to the tunnel entrance whenever they could stand the tunnel air no longer.

In the Corregidor family Filipinos and Americans shared such accommodations as there were. President Quezon's cot was close to mine, and I could hear his racking cough through much of the night. He was a sick man, fighting his old enemy, tuberculosis, which finally took his life on August 1, 1944. Under the hard living conditions of

Corregidor his enemy was manifestly gaining the upper hand; but he fought on, dauntless as ever. All of us admired his pluck.

With him were Mrs. Quezon, their daughters Aurora and Zenaida, their young son, and a large entourage of servants and aides. For some of his servants he secured military commissions. Several days after our arrival his part-Chinese valet, an elderly man, appeared with lieutenant's bars on a khaki uniform.

"How come? Is he going out to fight?" queried our boy Bill. But he remained with us in the tunnel; and so far as we could see, the valet-lieutenant's duties continued unchanged.

The Quezon retinue included a Roman priest; and Mrs. Quezon set up an oratory or private chapel with candles in a corner of the tunnel.

General MacArthur was accompanied by his wife and small son. Jean MacArthur's tact and ever cheerful presence were assets to us all. Arthur MacArthur, the youngest member of the Corregidor family, was followed by his Chinese amah everywhere he went. In military cap he would now and again march through the tunnel, lustily singing the "Battle Hymn of the Republic," faithfully followed by his amah. Toward the end of our time on Corregidor we helped celebrate Arthur's fourth birthday by improvising a few presents and a cake and holding a party on the grass outside the tunnel. He was an attractive youngster, but was so dominated by his ever-present amah that he had little chance to speak for himself.

Vice President Osmeña was also one of our Corregidor family. Quiet, unassuming, kindly, always ready to help whenever called upon, he won the liking and the respect of us all.

With us also were Colonel Manuel Roxas, shrewd and brilliant, who had been Secretary of Finance; José Abad Santos, Chief Justice of the Supreme Court; General Basilio J. Valdes, Chief of Staff of the Philippine Army and Secretary of National Defense; Colonel Carlos Romulo, whose good humor and sparkling gifts as a writer and speaker were used by General MacArthur in the Voice of Freedom broadcast from our tunnel; and also Andrés Soriano, a naturalized citizen of Spanish birth, who had lived many years in the Philippines and acquired great wealth, later appointed by President Quezon Secretary of Finance.

The commanding general had placed at my disposal one of the

officers' houses a little less than a mile from the tunnel entrance. It was near one of the batteries and commanded a glorious view of Mariveles and Bataan. The morning after Christmas I went with my staff to look the place over and arrange a working office. We were interrupted by the drone of Japanese airplanes, and then by the explosions of bombs and the crack of anti-aircraft batteries around us. Each of us precipitately jumped for an open ditch by the side of the road and watched the fireworks. After that we all decided we preferred to work in the tunnel.

At the beginning of our stay the heaviest casualties were from the air. Disaster followed disaster. General Jonathan Wainwright was at the front on Bataan, holding the line as long as possible so that the Japanese could not plant guns there for the capture of Corregidor. We on Corregidor found ourselves practically without planes, almost at the mercy of the Japanese. Five days after our arrival a large fleet of planes circled overhead in full daylight and rained bombs upon "the Rock" for two and a half hours. The whole tunnel shook with the terrific explosions. "Topside," the upper level of the island, with the officers' quarters and the large hospital, was practically demolished. Our men were still so new to air attacks that casualties were heavy, and soon our hospital tunnel corridors were crowded with blood-soaked stretchers and dying men.

We watched the Army nurses, both American and Filipino, under grueling conditions in the hospital lateral, stanching blood, easing pain and giving of themselves unstintingly. We had heard how our nurses were asking to go over to the "tree hospital" on Bataan, where patients and nurses had no protection from shellfire or the elements save the branches of jungle trees. Out in the open, near the front, morale was better, and under the sky the air was fresh.

Near our own was the smaller Navy tunnel, where Admiral Rockwell and a nucleus of Navy staff who had survived the bombing of Cavite tried to set up a kind of base with supplies salvaged from the mainland. Indeed, no one did more gallant work in the defense of Corregidor than American sailors and marines. Often at sundown I saw them in twos or threes, actually whistling on the way to take lonely night posts on the beaches of Corregidor, alert against possible Japanese attack.

The harbor in front of us was soon filled with wrecked ships sunk by Japanese planes, including President Quezon's yacht, the *Casiana*. For several days divers worked at recovering Presidential supplies of fancy foods and drinks.

December 30, 1941, was marked by an impressive ceremony. Close to the entrance of Malinta Tunnel where all could take refuge in case of bombing attack, before a small group of Filipinos and Americans, President Quezon and Vice President Osmeña were inaugurated for their second terms of office. President Quezon gave a short inaugural address, followed by brief addresses by General MacArthur and myself. I said:

> The great days of any country's history are not the days of prosperity, but the days of adversity. It is when the odds are heavily against one and victory can be wrested out of defeat only through heroic action and unconquerable gallantry that a people writes the great pages of its history. . . .
>
> This afternoon, as spokesman for the American Government, I want to express America's gratitude and pride for the loyalty, the devotion, the gallantry, with which the Filipino people have entered this great struggle by America's side.

I concluded by reading a personal message from President Roosevelt. Seldom, I suspect, has an inauguration taken place under more unique and dramatic circumstances.

During the first week on Corregidor we kept in constant communication with Manila by military telephone and by small boats run at night. On New Year's Day I talked with Claude Buss for the last time. He reported that every member of the staff was well, and that the city was quiet. Manila had been declared an open city, and the Japanese were expected to enter late that night. He had no fear. I expressed deep and abiding appreciation of the loyalty and splendid service he and the other members of the staff remaining in Manila had shown, and we lingered a little over the goodbye. It was hard to say. I wondered if I should ever see him again.

The Japanese entered the city on the afternoon of January 2. Thereafter all except secret communication with Manila ceased.

From Army intelligence sources and from Filipinos who managed to cross the lines I learned that General Homma, the Japanese general in command, took over the High Commissioner's residence for his headquarters.

All Americans were ordered to register and to keep off the streets. With some exceptions, they were interned in the large buildings of Santo Tomás University on the outskirts of the city, where, crowded together under hard Japanese military discipline, they had a wretched existence, suffering, waiting and wondering. It was unofficially reported to us by men who ran the gantlet from Manila to the Rock in small boats at night that there had been little fighting in Manila, and that in general conditions were as good as could be expected. Nevertheless, internment means suffering, both physical and mental; and our thoughts were constantly with our Manila friends, now in the hands of the enemy.

One of my problems was how to dispose of the gold and other securities gathered during our last hectic days in Manila to prevent their falling into Japanese hands, and brought over to Corregidor by boat at night. The law authorized the High Commissioner to take whatever steps he deemed necessary to prevent such assets from falling into the hands of the enemy.

I thus found myself on Corregidor the unhappy possessor of some five and a half tons of gold, of $2,700,000 in American paper money, and of 28,000,000 Philippine pesos. Also, I had been given by the banks numerous boxes, filled with securities, paper assets, and valuables of various kinds.

What to do with them?

The American and Philippine paper money was no problem. After all, the paper was of no intrinsic value. If a careful record of it was made we could safely destroy it, to be reissued in Washington and, after the war, in Manila. This was the course we followed. After the great bundles of bills had been counted and carefully inventoried by the members of my staff I appointed a responsible committee to witness its destruction; and during the days that followed great stacks of American paper currency—five- and ten- and twenty- and hundred-dollar bills—were burned by the armful to the wonderment of the soldiers standing by. "Oh, boy," exclaimed one, "I never saw so much money in my life! But I wouldn't trade the whole lot of it for the chance of being back on my little old farm in Tennessee." My naval aide got the thrill of his life from nonchalantly lighting his cigarette with a rolled up $100 bill.

The gold presented a far more difficult problem. It could not be blown up or destroyed. It could be walled up in a secret hiding place—but might it not be found? It could be sunk in the harbor, the bearings of the spot being kept secret. But might not the Japanese, getting wind of it, torture the men who had sunk it until they revealed the spot? Many days and nights I puzzled over the problem. The metal was useless to us on Corregidor—a headache rather than an asset. There was also the problem of millions of dollars' worth of bonds and stock certificates and various paper securities. Was there a way by which these could be saved?

Finally, I sent a radio message to Admiral Hart, then in command of United States naval forces at Soerabaja in Java and operating submarines off the China coast, asking if he could put a submarine at our disposal to remove the gold. He replied that he would do his best to get one into Corregidor.

A submarine appeared during the dark night of February 3 and surfaced at one of the Corregidor landings. We carried down to the dock armloads of gold bricks with which to replace the ballast of the submarine. It was a slow, tedious job and the night was not long enough to complete the work. The submarine left an hour before dawn to lie on the bottom of Manila Bay all the ensuing day. When night came it reappeared, and we put aboard the remaining gold and cases of securities. With its golden ballast, the submarine made good its escape and proceeded to Honolulu—on its way, I am told, sinking two Japanese ships.

Each day we used to come out to the tunnel entrance and hang over the radio, hungry for news upon which to build our hopes. How soon could we get back to Manila? When might we expect to see American planes in the air? In the early days a conservative estimate was some time in February. Our hopes rose and fell with each day's news. As the tide of battle rolled southward and the Japanese effected one successful landing after another, our skies darkened.

We realized that deliverance depended upon a smashing defeat of the Japanese to the south of us. Hong Kong had fallen to them about Christmas time. We pinned our hopes on Singapore. We expected an Allied naval victory in Macassar Strait and believed that this would mark the turning of the tide. But the fall of Singapore compelled us to face the realities. As the Japanese continued to advance irresistibly southward we realized that American planes and troops could not reach us in February or even in March—might not arrive in time to save Corregidor—and that all we could do was fight on, defend our island fortress to the last man and force the Japanese to pay a terrible price. To face that realization with open eyes and stout hearts took more real courage than dodging bombs and shells. The great story of Corregidor and Bataan is that our troops, facing these realities, fought on with high spirit and unwavering determination. And Americans can never forget the loyalty and the faith of the Filipinos who there laid down their lives for the realization of American ideals. Our forty years of patient and understanding guardianship brought its supreme reward.

Over on Bataan American regiments of infantry, American marines, Philippine Scout troops, American bluejackets, and Filipino foot soldiers fresh from the fields fought shoulder to shoulder. The overwhelming majority were Filipinos. Day after day in their foxholes under the inspiring leadership of General Wainwright they stuck it out—with insufficient food, with dwindling stocks of munitions, with practically no airplanes, with medical supplies almost gone, with nothing ahead but death or defeat and the only consolation that the cause they were fighting for—human freedom—would at long last surely win.

It is a privilege to be one of a company of men like that. I fully expected to share their lot to the end. We had given up hope of seeing again—certainly for many long months—our children, our homes, the country we loved. Escape seemed completely cut off: no bomber could land at Corregidor, the Japanese had complete control of the air, and Japanese ships and planes commanded the seas for fifteen hundred to two thousand miles southward.

The Japanese seldom bombed us at night. The tunnel air was at times so overcharged with dust and germs that our youngster, Bill Graves, subject to asthma, developed a fever, was confined to a hospital bed, and could not seem to throw off the fever or regain his strength. Accordingly, Betty and I decided that danger from the germs and dust was worse than that from bombs, and slept for a time thereafter—except when air raids or shelling drove us back to the tunnel—with two or three other members of our staff in one of the officers' houses which was still left standing about a mile from the tunnel entrance. We used to steal away from the tunnel every afternoon an hour or two before sundown, walk up the dusty road to our haven of refuge, spread a blanket in front of the house, and stretch out on our backs, drinking in the fresh air and the beauty and serenity of the scene. Often we talked of home and of the peace of Martha's Vineyard where our cottage overlooks the sea. All of us were reaching out for peace in our hearts. We used to watch the stars coming out and wonder about the loved ones back in America who watched the same stars. How were they faring, and should we ever see them again? As darkness came on, invariably the artillery fire intensified on Bataan across the bay. We would see the flashes of gunfire followed by explosions. On many nights the whole sky would be alight with the flames from the shelling.

The future was a blank. We could not make plans. We were learning to take each day as it came.

When the gunfire was not too heavy we often spent the night in the house. After the Japanese had taken over Manila and Cavite and had trained their Cavite emplacements on Corregidor, we found the gunfire in some ways worse than the bombing. True, the shells came singly and did not often involve wholesale destruction. On the other hand, the drone of a bombing plane gave one time to take shelter or drop to the ground, while a shell gave no warning except its own scream—and then it was too late. Also, most of the shelling was at night. On the whole, I think we preferred the bombs.

If we were spending the night in our house of refuge, and if heavy artillery fire commenced, we would beat a hasty retreat to the tunnel. For this purpose we kept a small car ready, into which we could jump and drive like mad, hoping to reach the tunnel entrance before the shells got us.

It wasn't too happy an experience, yet day by day life went on. As we became accustomed to it, it did not seem too dreadful. Often, as I awoke in the morning, I would wonder whether I should be alive at the end of the day. I do not fear death. I think of it as a great awakening. What I feared then was the death or the wounding or crippling of my wife or our boy.

Perhaps the life was hardest on the youngster, just turned fifteen. Scenes of death around us, wounded and mangled soldiers being carried past us into the tunnel, lurid stories poured into his ears by the soldiers—these made him long to play his part as a man; yet he was still too young. Now, with him as with us, these are only memories: he has come through mentally and physically unscathed, and the dreadful experience has left no permanent ill effects. As a member of my staff remarked: "Well, Bill, when you get back to school and have to write themes, you'll have plenty of material."

There were occasions when one could be even amused by shell-fire. One afternoon General MacArthur and I were talking together outside the tunnel. Without any warning shells began to whine and whistle close over our heads. Military instructions were to drop flat on the ground when shells started coming our way, and almost unthinkingly I dropped. But not the General. He believed that death would take him only at the ordained time and was fearless of shell fire: he remained standing. Any one who saw us must have had a good laugh—at the General erect and at ease while the High Commissioner lay prone in the dust. I have often wondered whether he was as amused as I. In any event, his expression never changed.

We knew that life for us could never again be quite the same. In a world where organized hate and fury of people against people touched us hour by hour, we were impressed anew by the profound truth of Christian teaching and the inescapable need for it in the world. The utter futility of material objectives, the realization that happiness can be built only on spiritual foundations, came more and more into our consciousness. We began to weigh our lives. What were they worth? We deeply resolved, if we should be spared, to devote and consecrate ourselves to building for peace in the world.

Some afternoons Betty and I walked together among the trees in less frequented parts of the island. Occasionally we would see monkeys swinging and jumping among the branches—playing together as if war had not turned the world upside down. Then on a later day there were no more monkeys. Our soldiers were short of food and without fresh meat. War had caught up even with the monkey world on Corregidor.

In time war came to touch even the stray dogs. All American soldiers love dogs, especially in lonely places, and we saw strays adopted and befriended by the men even when it meant saving food for their pets out of their own meager rations. Later the medical officers had to take matters into their own hands; and one day we awoke to find no dogs on the island.

Out of a clear sky one February day a radio message from President Roosevelt suggested the evacuation of President Quezon and myself from Corregidor, adding that President Quezon and his Cabinet would be honored and welcomed in the United States. When I asked about my skeleton staff, President Roosevelt replied: "If conditions make it possible and there are sufficient accommodations you should evacuate your staff along with yourself and your family."

Did we dare risk the perilous trip? It was not a hard decision to make—for my wife and Bill and eight of my staff who were with me. The problems in the Philippines had come to be military and not civil, and I could do more for the war effort by laying the Philippine situation before the government in Washington than by undergoing capture. Evidently the President wanted us to come out if we could.

The unanimous decision was to take the risk.

Mindful of the submarine which had rescued our gold, I sent a radio message to Admiral Hart in Java asking if he could get another submarine to Corregidor for the evacuation. He radioed back, yes, he would try. In patience and hope we must wait.

President Quezon's health was visibly sinking under the rigors and hardships of tunnel life, and he asked to be sent first to Negros or another of the southern islands which had not yet fallen into Japanese hands, to recuperate and later proceed to the United States. Perhaps he wanted a little time in which to make the final hard decision whether to leave his people in the midst of war. Perhaps his racked body needed a little rest.

Some days later word came that a submarine had got through. When it appeared on the night of February 20, President Quezon was placed on board, and with him his wife and three children, Vice President Osmeña, Chief Justice Santos, General Valdes, and other members of his staff. The party reached one of the southern islands a day or two later; there they recuperated and made their preparations for their journey to the United States. Justice Santos, refusing to leave or to yield to Japanese domination, was martyred in Cebu City; and Colonel Roxas elected to go to Manila to see what he could do.

The submarine had been ordered to return for us after landing the Quezon party. Our rendezvous was fixed for a point in the bay just south of the Bataan peninsula. We kept wondering whether or not the submarine had been detected and perhaps sunk by the Japanese. Would it be able to return to Corregidor?

During that last day on Corregidor, February 23, we talked with many of our friends, unable for military reasons to tell them we were leaving, wondering if we should ever see them again. Some of them knew and gripped us in silent handclasps.

The sun had set when we walked to the entrance of the tunnel. There was a lull in the shelling. Our last goodbye in the tunnel was to ever faithful Carlos, stanch Filipino servant to Governors General and High Commissioners. He had left wife and children to come with us to Corregidor, and now we were compelled to leave him behind. His thought as we parted was only for our safety. "I am sorry, Mr. High Commissioner, that you have to go this way" were his last words.

General MacArthur was waiting and drove us swiftly down to the waterside. We could not linger over goodbyes: shelling might recommence at any moment. We pressed Admiral Rockwell's hand in parting. "You are going out on the *Swordfish* with one of our ace submarine skippers—the best," he said. I shall never forget General MacArthur's parting words: "When next you see daylight, it will be an altogether different kind of world." Nothing could have been more true.

Without our customary steel helmets and gas masks, we jumped into a waiting patrol boat, and seating ourselves on our suitcases we were off into the mysterious blackness.

As we left, Bill, to whom I had not yet dared reveal our plans or destination, renewed his questioning. "Where are we going, Dad?"

"We're going home!" I said with a choke in my throat. I could not believe my own words.

With me were Betty and Bill; Evett D. Hester, my economic adviser; Woodbury Willoughby, my financial expert, and Mrs. Willoughby; Cabot Coville, Foreign Service officer; James J. Saxon, Treasury expert; Miss Anna Belle Newcomb, my ever-faithful private secretary; and Mrs. Janet White, clerk-stenographer.

Robert Huffcut, my economic expert, dependable, loyal and unselfish as ever, being of military age, asked to be allowed to remain and fight. He did valiant service, was taken prisoner when Corregidor fell and was later wantonly shot by a Japanese guard at one of the prison camps. In America in later days those of us who knew and loved Bob helped to establish a scholarship in his name at Cornell, his alma mater, for Filipinos majoring in economics.

Lieutenant Commander Parker, Major Marron and Captain Priestley also chose to remain with the troops and fight. Captured and afterwards imprisoned in ancient Bilibid Prison at Manila, Captain Priestley lost his life near the end of the war as the ship in which he was being removed to Japan was attacked and sunk by American bombers. I am told that a Japanese officer shot and killed him after he had jumped into the water to save himself from the sinking ship. He was a gallant soldier.

As we steamed away, "the Rock," our home and our refuge for two months, loomed high in the darkness. Poignant thoughts of the friends we were leaving behind filled our minds; and we wondered what lay ahead. Would Japanese spies spread the news that the United States High Commissioner was on his way out from Corregidor? Could we escape detection? Months later I saw a translation of a Japanese report found on the body of a crashed Japanese airman, giving in exact detail the names of all our party on the submarine and the date of its leaving Corregidor.

We made our way across the bay, and under the black shadows of the rocky highland of Bataan lay to through the quiet evening, waiting, until the moon had set and the sky was black. Our rendezvous with the submarine had been fixed at three o'clock.

About half past two we noiselessly moved out into deep water to the point of rendezvous and waited. Three o'clock came and no submarine. Minute after minute passed. Only black water. A silent half-hour went by. Had our submarine, then, been discovered and sunk returning from the southern islands? All at once, as we peered into the blackness, something blacker seemed to emerge. Slowly on our starboard a huge ship lunged upwards out of the water. We made our way alongside. Hardly a word was spoken. Hands reached out to help us across a wet and narrow gangplank. Our suitcases were handed across. "Goodbye, and good luck!" they called under their breath to us. Commander Parker, who had come this far, pressed his class ring into Betty's hand. "Take this to Ruth for me," he said. "Give my love to her and to Johnnie and Tommy." We climbed down the small round hatchway, heard the muffled dogging of the hatch preparatory to diving, and the engines started.

We were off to a totally different world, but we could not forget. Experience had burned too deep. We had left behind a small army fighting a losing battle. Often I think of what those boys went through —Americans and Filipinos, living next to death, many of them thousands of miles from home, stripped of every comfort, filthy with sweat and dirt and blood. A very ordinary lot they were to the eye, some white-skinned and some brown, but with the stuff of heroes, unflinching, determined for their country's sake to stick it out to the end, and if need be to give up their lives. On Corregidor we had had a tunnel to run to when the shelling got hot or enemy planes came our way. Those boys on Bataan and many on Corregidor had no tunnel. They had only foxholes; and often they must stand by their guns and take it. A few got medals; the great majority, just as brave, went out in the dark and were never heard of again.

I think of our sailors on and above and under the sea. I remember the little flotilla of gunboats and surface craft, hovering around Corregidor and Bataan, whose crews faced death every time Japanese bombers swept over Corregidor or Japanese shells came screaming from Cavite. I shall never forget the thrilling battle one afternoon between a destroyer and a group of attacking Japanese airplanes. As the bombers each time reached the critical point where they could strike, the destroyer, with its crew gallantly standing alert at their posts, twisted and turned. In spite of the unequal odds, it outguessed and outmaneuvered the Japanese airmen every time so that their bombs missed and it made good its escape.

I think of the marines who bore the critical responsibility of guarding the shores and beaches of Corregidor. At their posts behind tangles of barbed wire night and day, cheerfully making the best of impossible living conditions, dependable unto death—never have I seen men of whom America had a right to be more proud.

When I talked to the American wounded their question always was: "How long before help comes? They do know what it's like out here, don't they?"

I answered as hopefully as I could; but underneath there was always the haunting doubt in their minds whether in the eyes of Washington we in the Philippines were "expendable." The battle of the Philippines in those early days was a brilliant exhibition of faith. Certainly it gave to the United States valuable breathing time in which to rally its forces and build up its fighting strength after the first murderous blow at Pearl Harbor.

*   *   *

Our course lay from Corregidor southward, past the southern islands of the Philippines, through the Sulu and Celebes seas, through Macassar Strait, and on to Soerabaja in Java, then the American submarine base. For hundreds of miles around us sea and land and air were completely in Japanese hands. For the entire length of our journey our course must be under water except at night when we rose to the surface to charge our batteries.

Our captain, Chester C. Smith, had been fifteen years in submarine service and, I believe, had more Japanese ships to his credit than any other American submarine commander. Young, earnest, rather pale-looking, with quiet assurance, he held the loyalty and confidence of all his crew; and we could see why Admiral Rockwell had chosen him to evacuate us from Corregidor. In the first days of our voyage we picked up a radio message telling that he had been awarded the Navy Cross for outstanding service in the Pacific.

Two weeks our submarine journey lasted. It was a new and exciting experience. Of course there are no real living quarters in submarines. The ship was a war machine. No one asked for comforts or soft accommodations. But, in a sense, it was a welcome change from the hard life of Corregidor. I was comfortable enough on a narrow bunk with the captain in his tiny cabin. We never saw the sunlight as we headed south through tropical waters infested by Japanese. Beneath the surface all day long, the temperature in the submarine ranged between 95° and 100°, and the air became so foul and stale by the end of the afternoon that it felt as if you could cut it with a knife. We were advised to lie still in our bunks most of the "daytime." We lived for that wonderful moment each evening when darkness had settled upon the waters above us and we dared to rise to the surface and could open our hatches and allow the fresh invigorating air to sweep through the ship. Since we never saw the sunlight, day and night were interchangeable. Officers and men not on watch turned in to sleep shortly after breakfast in the morning, and no lunch was served. Life began with the surfacing of the ship after sunset.

Through the daytime hours our ship continued an even course below the surface rising every twenty minutes to periscope depth for a careful look around and then again submerging.

But if the sight through the periscope revealed a destroyer or a plane then came a sudden crash dive down to immense depths. Every bit of machinery—even the electric fans—must be turned off because of the destroyer's very sensitive sound detecting apparatus. You hoped to heaven the enemy had not seen you, and in burning heat and deathly stillness you waited—minute after endless minute— to discover whether the enemy did sight or hear you and whether the depth bombs would begin to come—which might blow you into eternity. To us every minute of that deathly silence seemed an hour; and it was always a grueling experience. To the crew it was all in the day's work.

There was no doctor aboard, and I was in constant anxiety lest some member of my family or staff should fall sick. The Japanese were everywhere, and a forced landing would have been probably impossible. Sickness seemed in some ways a worse danger than depth bombs.

We crossed the equator in Macassar Strait, where a big naval battle had been fought shortly before. The waters were infested with enemy ships. At one time we sighted two large Japanese ships and two destroyers. One night a radio message told us that a sister submarine had picked up the survivors of a bombed British ship. How could they care for so many survivors in such a limited space?

While we were on the surface at night charging our batteries we could receive, but of course not send, radio messages. One evening in Macassar Strait we received the news that Soerabaja had been captured by the Japanese. Our destination, then, lay in Japanese hands. Japanese were landing also on Timor, Sumatra, and North Borneo. The Battle of the Java Sea was still raging. All that was left to us was to run south underneath the fighting and try to get through the chain of East Indian Islands which stretch eastward from Java toward Australia.

We decided to make a run for it through narrow, dangerous Sape Strait, which borders on Flores Island. Not one of our crew had ever been through Sape Strait before. There was insufficient water to submerge should we sight a Japanese destroyer. The charts were

sketchy, to say the least. We knew the Japanese were seeking to guard
all the straits. Nevertheless, it was our only chance, and we decided
to risk it in the blackness of the night. So we altered our course and
headed for Sape Strait.

I shall never forget the exciting night when we made the bold
run on the surface through the strait. It was touch and go. Would a
Japanese destroyer detect us and end everything? Could we navigate
the rocky, narrow passage in the black night? None of us could go on
deck: all we could do was wait through the night and pray. And by
the grace of God Captain Smith got us through.

What a skillful, gallant crew we had! Those fellows never turned
a hair. Living the life of the lone wolf, fired upon or bombed on sight,
not trying to escape danger but positively seeking it and hunting for
enemy ships that would blow them to kingdom come on sight, undergoing this inhuman existence uncomplainingly day after day and
week after week—only one who has lived with a submarine crew at
work can know what quiet, unassuming heroism really means.

After emerging in the early morning from Sape Strait we hit
southward for Fremantle near the southwestern tip of Australia, to
which the American submarine base had been moved. Then we were
in mortal fear of Australian planes, for apparently signals had not
yet been worked out to cover planes and submarines friendly to each
other. All planes were quick to bomb every periscope or ship seen
moving under water. We felt safer the second day as we got out into
the Indian Ocean. In the open sea far from land we could risk running on the surface part of the day; and we were encountering rough
seas and head winds. But, oh, the blessed fresh air blowing through
the straining ship! On the eleventh day we were allowed to go up on
deck, two at a time, for a brief glimpse of the sun. How glorious it
looked! And how our eyes feasted on the blue sky and the white-
capped sea! We were beginning to live again. Later we received a
radio report that a Japanese submarine had attacked one of ours in
the same general area that very afternoon.

Even in these waters, as we soon discovered, the sight of a plane
overhead, friend or foe, still meant a crash dive and a wait in deathly
silence to see if depth bombs would come.

Almost two weeks after our departure from Corregidor and after
a journey of three thousand miles, we turned east toward Fremantle.

Shortly before dawn on March 9 we picked up a patrol boat that escorted us through a deep, dripping fog into the harbor and to an anchorage. We clambered out onto our deck in the dark. Around us we could hear the welcome sounds of bell buoys, foghorns, and gulls. They were friendly sounds and did not portend death. It seemed strange and unearthly.

Then, as dawn came, we saw other ships—friendly ships—around us. As the sun slowly rose, shafts of bright sunlight lit up the sandy spits and the pine trees along the shore. Green hillsides began to appear. It seemed like a veritable glimpse into paradise.

Two hours later we caught sight of a small launch, heading directly toward us, buried in white foam and spray. On it was Rear Admiral Glassford, the American Admiral in command of our ships in southwest Australia, coming to take us ashore, to the near-by city of Perth. It was a joyful meeting. In Perth we spent the day and the following night.

It was a distinct shock suddenly to drop into peaceful human life again—to see people going about their ordinary, daily affairs, buying and selling, walking the city streets, driving cars, and not jumping into the nearest ditch or foxhole at the sound of a plane! It was, as General MacArthur had said when we parted, like entering an altogether different world.

Ever since December we had been under constant bombing and shell fire, living like rats underground, wondering each morning whether the night would find us still alive and with a whole body —caught in a world of terror and cataclysmic destruction and elemental passion, where might and brute force were rampant and overpowering. Then suddenly to step into a world where law was supreme, where civilization prevailed, where bright lights shone at night and automobiles filled busy streets and one could have hot water and food in abundance and enter into the precious, very ordinary, humdrum affairs of life—see children playing and hear careless laughter and drink in sunlight and fresh air—all this seemed like some beautiful dream.

That day Betty and I moved as in a daze. In the afternoon we walked outside Perth along a sandy beach in the sunshine. We watched the children playing and dogs romping, and when a plane appeared there was no need to jump.

Early the next morning a big American Navy bomber flew us eastward to Adelaide, where Betty and Bill and the members of my staff boarded a transport waiting to take them back to America. I continued with the bomber the next day to Melbourne and Sydney.

At that time the Japanese were still steadily advancing southward, and Australia lacked the necessary means of defense. Australians were asking, would America come with force to their rescue? And could American troops and guns and planes reach Australia in time?

At Sydney, Herbert Evatt, Minister for External Affairs, boarded our plane, bound for America to confer with President Roosevelt in Washington. The next night we were in the Fiji Islands, as guests at Government House of the Governor. There General Meade discussed the perilous situation, telling me that Fiji was entirely without adequate defense—that the Japanese might attack any day or night and, if they did, could capture Fiji with ease. He begged me to urge prompt American help—which he specified in terms of flying boats, fighters (pursuit), dive and torpedo bombers, and heavy bombers. Of course I could not predict what Washington's answer would be.

From Fiji we flew to Honolulu, arriving on March 16. There I visited the vaults where the gold and valuables from Corregidor were temporarily stored. Not an ounce of gold, not a single security, was missing. Careful audits later in the United States checked perfectly with the inventories which we had prepared on Corregidor. Every bit of gold and every security which the High Commissioner's office in Manila had taken over after the outbreak of war came through safely.

From San Francisco I indulged in the luxury of a sleeping car on a train, and arrived in Washington early on March 23. There on the station platform with glad smiles to meet me were my sons Francis and Woodrow, and my daughter Eleanor. It seemed almost unreal. We had not heard from each other since the capture of Manila; and I breathed a thanksgiving to God to learn that all was well with them. Woodrow, who was doing graduate work at Harvard, joyfully told me about Edith Chase of Boston; he had fallen in love with her during his days at Cambridge and their engagement had just been announced. When later I met and came to know Edith, I fell in love with her, too.

That noon I lunched with President Roosevelt at the White House, and had the privilege of presenting to him a sword taken from the body of a Japanese general on Bataan and sent him by General MacArthur. I tried to give a true and concise picture of the situation in the Philippines, telling of the heroism of the troops and the need of early help. Many things we talked over together.

In April the transport carrying Betty and my staff arrived at San Francisco, and a few days later the Sayres held a joyful family reunion in Washington. Once more we were a reunited, happy family.

General MacArthur and his wife and son had left Corregidor a few days after we did, on a small PT boat for one of the southern islands. There a plane was waiting to fly him directly to Australia; and here he took command of a new American army in formation.

President Quezon and his family, together with Vice President Osmeña and members of his staff, flew by bomber in late March from northern Mindanao to Australia, and proceeded by naval transport to San Francisco, arriving on May 8.

At the request of President Roosevelt I remained Philippine High Commissioner at Washington through the spring of 1942, with offices in the new Department of the Interior building. We struggled with the problem of getting relief to the civilian population interned in the Philippines, and held frequent conferences with the Department of State, the American Red Cross, and the Provost Marshal General. We sought to get in touch with the internees, to send a relief ship with food, medicines, and needed supplies, and if possible to arrange for the evacuation through exchange or otherwise of sick people, women, and children. But our efforts for the most part were unavailing due to the refusal of Japanese authorities to cooperate. We also set up a "Welfare Section," to give such information and help as we could to relatives and dependents in the United States of interned Americans.

The gallant defense of Bataan and Corregidor could not last indefinitely without reenforcement in men, ammunition, and supplies; and this proved to be impossible. Our troops under General Edward King were compelled to surrender Bataan on April 9. Corregidor held out another month under the plucky leadership of General Jonathan Wainwright, who had fought in the front lines from the first day of the war, but was compelled to surrender on May 6.

The defense of Bataan and Corregidor will go down in history as one of the great and heroic chapters of human courage and endurance. Those who died there will never be forgotten.

The majority of the defenders were Filipinos. After forty years of colonial administration, the acid test came when Japanese troops sweeping down from the north and promising them independence, sought to win the Filipinos over from America. The Filipinos stood firm. Their unflinching defense alongside the Americans of Bataan and Corregidor and the unwavering loyalty of the rank and file of peasants and townspeople, who during the Japanese occupation befriended American refugees and soldiers, pay high tribute to the character of the colonial administration which America had tried to give them during the preceding forty years.

Secretary Ickes remained true to form to the end of his life. On March 29, 1943, I wrote to President Roosevelt:

> When we fled from Manila to Corregidor, and when we escaped by submarine from Corregidor to Australia, among our very scanty belongings I carried out two silk flags which had always hung behind my desk in the High Commissioner's office in Manila. Both of these I brought to Washington. I think you can realize what it would mean to me to be given the right to keep one of these as my own, paying to the Government the value of the flag. May I have your permission, as my Commander-in-Chief, to do this?

A few days later President Roosevelt's secretary telephoned to say that the President had received my letter and wished me to keep the flag. The President felt an oral message was better than a written one, but, she said, it was a definite message from him.

The flag was then hanging in the office of Mr. Ickes. For some reason which I have never been able to understand, he declined to let me take it. He retained the flag as long as he was in office. After his retirement Oscar Chapman, his successor, promptly sent the High Commissioner's flag to my home, where it hangs today as one of my prized possessions.

Upon my arrival in Washington I had handed to the President the following letter of resignation:

My dear Mr. President:

In view of the present military situation which has caused the work of the High Commissioner's Office in the Philippines to be largely supplanted by military activity I should like to tender my resignation to take effect at your pleasure. I shall never lose my deep interest in the Filipinos nor my hope that our country may lead them wisely to the independence which we have promised them. But I am sure you will understand my desire in view of present circumstances to serve our country in a more pressing and active work.

With appreciation for the confidence which you have shown in me, believe me,

Ever sincerely yours,
FRANCIS B. SAYRE

At the end of June the President made the following reply:

Dear Frank:

In accepting your resignation as the United States High Commissioner to the Philippine Islands, effective as of today, I am complying with your urgent request which I have had before me for several weeks.

Your release from this post is merely a commutation since we have a mutual understanding that you are available for any call that is made on you in the war effort.

It is unnecessary for me to tell you of my appreciation for the fine and loyal service you have rendered.

I do want to see you just as soon as the pressure on me eases up a bit.

Very sincerely yours,
FRANKLIN D. ROOSEVELT

17

.

War's Aftermath and UNRRA

During the tragic days on Corregidor our hearts had often yearned for our children. And now that I had resigned from the High Commissionership we were free for a brief interval to turn once more to the peace and beauty of our island home on Martha's Vineyard and gather our children around us.

In May of 1942 all the family had flocked to Milton, Massachusetts, for the wedding of my son Woodrow Wilson to Edith Chase. The event was a cause of deep rejoicing for us all. After it they passed a radiant honeymoon in a little cottage on Martha's Vineyard—"up-island," high above the sea.

That summer on the Vineyard I was hard at work on my final Report to the President and Congress on the Philippines.* Frank, Jr., who was then serving as assistant rector at Christ Church in Cambridge and had volunteered as a chaplain in the Navy, came for a short stay. My most poignant memory of the summer was the sight of him at half-past six in the morning, on the deck of the island boat as it passed before our cottage, waving goodbye to us as he left to enter the Service.

When I returned to Washington in September, conditions in

* Sixth Annual Report of the United States High Commissioner to the Philippine Islands, 78th Congress, First Session, House Document No. 111.

Europe were growing more and more critical. With military demands mounting, available supplies for civilians of food and coal and other necessaries were growing shorter and shorter. The standards of living of millions of people were going down, down, down. Economic shortages, raw material shortages, food shortages, even starvation, threatened in many areas.

We were coming to realize ever more clearly that if the future peace was to be based upon secure foundations, relief and rehabilitation must play a more significant role. The problem was unprecedented. The Axis powers had overrun more than a score of nations, containing nearly one-fourth of the world's people. Before the end of the war whole nations were plundered of their resources and stripped of their means of livelihood. Factories lay in ruins. Commerce was paralyzed. Transport facilities were broken down. Fishing fleets were destroyed. Lack of fertilizer impaired the productivity of the soil. In Nazi-occupied Europe farmers lost about a fourth of their cattle and a third of their draft animals. In many areas Nazi forces cut the people's rations to less than 1,000 calories a day—to about a quarter of the ordinary American Army ration. There was fear of wholesale and ruthless destruction by Axis forces before they could be driven from the occupied territories. Already whole populations were in acute distress; never had the world known such immeasurable need. Prompt and effective help must be given if the breakdown of civilization in many parts of Europe and Asia was to be prevented.

In any realistic plan for peace the first step must be large-scale emergency relief. But how could this be effected?

In July, 1942, the United Kingdom formed the Middle East Relief and Refugee Administration to provide aid for refugees, including Poles, Greeks, and Yugoslavs.

A more important development took place later in that year, when the United States, launching out through uncharted seas, undertook to organize relief activities for Allied needs on a mammoth scale. On November 21, President Roosevelt asked Herbert H. Lehman to resign as Governor of New York State and undertake at Washington "the work of organizing American participation in the activities of the United Nations in furnishing relief and other assistance to victims of war in areas reoccupied by the forces of the United

Nations." For this purpose the Office of Foreign Relief and Rehabilitation Operations (OFRRO) was set up in the Department of State.

I told Governor Lehman of my interest in this undertaking. To bring help to the suffering people of the world through such international cooperation was in many ways the most constructive work I could see on the horizon. When Governor Lehman asked me to join him as Deputy Director I welcomed the proposal.

Offices were assigned to us in the State Department Building; and by the beginning of January, 1943 a competent preliminary staff was functioning.

Problems of exceeding difficulty confronted us. The needs were far-flung and immense. Never before had an attempt been made to procure and distribute food and relief supplies on so gigantic a scale. There was also the question of what specific objectives to pursue. Should OFRRO, for instance, include refugee work, children's relief work, wholesale economic relief where entire areas were in distress through economic disruption? Its precise functions were not, indeed, defined until March, 1943.

In April Governor Lehman went to London for conversations with Allied civilian and military authorities, including representatives of China and the U.S.S.R. looking toward the organization of international relief work on a world-wide scale. The realization was growing that, without civilian relief, certain Allied peoples could not continue fighting. In other words, vast appropriations were necessary, not only for armament and military purposes but also for civilian relief; and the brunt of these burdens must be borne by the United States. Would the American people understand and support such appropriations for the relief of peoples who were alien?

In addition to my responsibilities as Deputy Director of OFRRO I was carrying on the work of Special Assistant to the Secretary of State, by appointment of Secretary Hull after my resignation as Philippine High Commissioner. He had asked me to take over the responsibility of seeking the reenactment of the Trade Agreements Act, which was due to expire in 1943. Accordingly, I appeared with him at the hearings before the House Ways and Means Committee and the Senate Finance Committee during the spring of 1943 to present our case. The results of the trade agreements program as it had been carried on during nine years were so eminently satisfactory that the enactment had far easier sledding than in 1934, when the program was first proposed. Nevertheless, unhappily it remained a party issue; and we were glad to win its reenactment for another three years without crippling amendments.

In OFRRO we were pushing forward relief programs as rapidly as possible, concentrating in the winter of 1943 on North Africa, where there was heavy fighting preparatory to the invasion of Europe. One mounting difficulty was the baffling lack of coordination at Washington between government departments and agencies with overlapping responsibilities for civilian relief abroad. The White House took no action to resolve the growing conflicts. At the same time in London various governments in exile were bidding against one another for supplies needed for their peoples after the German troops should be driven out. It became increasingly clear that postwar relief could not be effectively carried on except through some form of international organization.

Building an international organization, however, involved negotiation with more than forty nations. In working out what was to become the basic United Nations agreement we consulted in Washington with the representatives of the United Kingdom, the U.S.S.R., and China. I remember particularly our talks with Andrei Gromyko, the U.S.S.R. Ambassador, youthful, black-haired, pleasant in demeanor. There was little evidence of the later effort of the U.S.S.R. to block constructive international cooperation. The Soviet Union in those days was, of course, eager for help. The Ukraine badly needed relief supplies. So did Poland. So did Yugoslavia.

After the four Great Powers had accepted a tentative agreement the draft was sent to the other Allied and Associated governments; and the draft, after modification to meet various differing viewpoints, became the final UNRRA agreement signed in November, 1943.

In the meantime Congress had to be kept informed of our developing plans and made to feel the need: without large appropriations we should have been blocked at the very outset. Before me is a memorandum I submitted to President Roosevelt, asking his assistance in keeping Congress informed and friendly. In the left margin are his answers, in his own hand; and each sheet bears his initials.

August 10, 1943

MEMORANDUM FOR THE PRESIDENT

The establishment of the United Nations Relief and Rehabilitation Administration is imperiled.

The Congress feels that it has not been adequately consulted. A survey of editorial reaction suggests that the public has not been adequately informed.

Immediate affirmative measures appear necessary. You may wish to authorize the Department to take the following steps:

1. If and when it seems wise in the light of current developments, to request appropriate Senate and House Committees to appoint representatives with whom the Department might confer from time to time concerning the nature and progress of UNRRA negotiations, and possible changes in the draft agreement.

2. To give positive assurances on your behalf that it is your intention to appoint Congressional representatives on the American delegation to the United Nations relief conference, should such a conference be held.

3. To give positive assurances on your behalf that after the UNRRA agreement has been negotiated and signed it is your intention to recommend the introduction of a bill authorizing the appropriation of funds as Congress may from time to time determine for United States participation in the relief and rehabilitation of foreign liberated areas in association with other nations. This will provide opportunity for full discussion by Congress of the entire United Nations relief plan.

4. To take immediate steps to inform both the public and the Congress as to the necessity for relief and rehabilitation, and to set forth the broad outlines of plans and policies for meeting this need.

On November 9, 1943, in the East Room of the White House representatives of all the United Nations met in a colorful ceremony for the signing of the UNRRA Agreement. It was just thirty years since I had attended another ceremonial in the East Room, and a flood of memories swept over me.

UNRRA was the first United Nations organization to come into existence, and the gathering was of historic importance. President Roosevelt sat at the center of a long table around which were grouped the other representatives, each about to affix his signature. The event was marked by short addresses from representatives of leading countries. "It is with a lift of hope," declared President Roosevelt as he signed for the United States, "that we look on the signing of this agreement by all of the United Nations as a means of joining them together still more firmly."

The agreement defined UNRRA's objective as being to "plan, coordinate, administer or arrange for the administration of measures for the relief of victims of war in any area under the control of any of the United Nations through the provision of food, fuel, clothing, shelter and other basic necessities, medical and other essential services."

As the Chinese representative at the opening Council session at Atlantic City put it:

> The rivers of China, the rivers of Russia, the streets of England, the fjords of Norway, the fields and cities of Belgium, of France, of Holland, the valleys of Yugoslavia and Greece, Pearl Harbor and the Coral Sea, have run with the blood and the tears of common men and women and children. We want the common man around the world who has felt this common suffering to know also a common healing and a common regeneration. . . . A great work lies ahead of us. Millions of freedom-loving people who suffered severely from aggression and hostilities look now to UNRRA with great hope.

The agreement provided for a Council, which was to be the policy-making body and to consist of one representative from each member government; a Central Committee, to make policy decisions between sessions of the Council and to consist of representatives of the United Kingdom, China, the U.S.S.R., and the United States; and a Director General to be appointed by the Council, clothed with exceptionally strong powers and authority for carrying out the relief operations.

Following the signing of the agreement in Washington we all

met at Atlantic City in the first Council session. This lasted from November 10 to December 1, 1943. On the opening day Herbert H. Lehman was chosen Director General. There could have been no better choice. A man of wide experience and proven ability, of deep integrity and large vision, his election was hailed with immense satisfaction all over the world.

The session immediately got down to the work of reaching fundamental decisions of policy. Two were outstanding.

One was the determination that our prime objective was "to help people to help themselves." It sought to reduce the need for supplies from outside by assisting people to produce their own basic essentials. For instance, UNRRA preferred sending seed potatoes in time for planting rather than shipping potatoes for distribution all through the succeeding year. A shipload of fertilizer for impoverished soil might make unnecessary a few months later half a dozen shiploads of food. A few mobile repair units, some replacement parts for machines, and a bit of expert advice might help to get a power plant or a gas works into operation and thus enable a whole community of workers to get back into production and become self-supporting.

A second fundamental decision was that no discrimination should be made in distributing relief supplies because of race, creed, or political belief. Relief supplies should at no time be used as a political weapon.

When UNRRA, a distinctively international organization, took over the work of OFRRO, obviously I had to choose between devoting myself henceforward to the service of UNRRA or remaining with the Department of State. The scope of the UNRRA work was so broad, and its power to help the suffering peoples of the world so potent, that my choice seemed clear. I therefore resigned as Special Assistant to the Secretary of State, and accepted appointment as Diplomatic Adviser to UNRRA—a post which I held from January, 1944, until February, 1947.

In an international organization such as UNRRA it was manifestly necessary to abstain from appointing too many Americans. We sought to find available, able men from as many different member states as possible. Sir Arthur Salter of the United Kingdom, Chairman of the Allied Maritime Executive in the First World War and a man of international vision and outstanding ability, was appointed Senior Deputy Director General. Dr. P. W. Kuo, Vice Minister of Finance in the Chinese government, was released to become Deputy Director General at the head of our Secretariat. Dr. Eduardo Santos, President of Colombia from 1938 to 1942, was appointed Deputy Director General for Liaison with American Republics. Mieczyslaw Sokolowski, former Permanent Secretary of State for Commerce in Poland, was appointed Financial Adviser. Many other nationals of wide experience and high ability joined the UNRRA staff, and my work with them proved to be a rich experience.

Naturally, the Soviet representatives waited upon Director General Lehman to ask that he name Russians to certain important positions. Their requests became virtual demands. Fencing resulted. In the end, he appointed as Deputy Director General heading the Bureau of Areas, Michail A. Menshikov, formerly a director of Arcos Trading Corporation and president of the All-Union Export Timber Organization at Moscow. Menshikov was personally likable and several times was a dinner guest in my home. As the UNRRA work progressed, however, we encountered more and more difficulties in getting papers beyond his desk. In time it became so difficult to transact business through his office that the Bureau of Areas was abolished in May, 1945, and the Bureau of Services took its place.

Whether or not the U.S.S.R. government purposefully sought to impede the work of UNRRA I have never been able to determine. As an invaded country the U.S.S.R. received huge shipments of relief supplies for the half-starving peoples of the Ukraine and Byelorussia. Yet from the very outset the Soviet government flatly refused to let UNRRA agents enter these territories and check on the distribution of relief as they did in every other country receiving relief. As an invaded country, the U.S.S.R. was not asked to contribute toward the purchase of UNRRA relief supplies; but even in the payment of the small amounts due for administrative expenses it fell down.

We of UNRRA were anxious to continue pleasant relationships and avoid any open break with the Soviets. Perhaps their peculiar behavior was due to diplomatic inexperience. I remember talking with a high official at the U.S.S.R. Embassy charged with UNRRA affairs, who kept telling me that he was an engineer and knew nothing of diplomacy. He possessed no diplomatic experience, no vision. "I'm sick of it all," he said. "I want to get back to my engineering work."

So thorny did relationships with the U.S.S.R. become that Governor Lehman decided on a visit to Moscow, to resolve the difficulties. His suggestion of a visit brought an evasive reply. When he pressed the matter he was told that he would be welcomed following the Montreal meeting of our UNRRA Council in September, 1944. Public announcement of his coming visit was made at the Council meeting. But later came word that the visit as planned was inopportune; and in the end Governor Lehman was forced to cancel the journey. He was never able to enter Russia to straighten out the UNRRA difficulties.

In setting up UNRRA we faced issues of extraordinary difficulty from the very outset. Fundamental was the problem of securing the enormous amounts of money with which to purchase the necessary relief supplies. Clearly they could not be financed by voluntary gifts of unspecified amounts from either private foundations or governments. At its first session at Atlantic City the UNRRA Council, estimating the total needs, resolved that each member government whose territory had not been occupied by the enemy should make a contribution equivalent to 1 per cent of its national income.

In accordance with this resolution the British Parliament, January 25, 1944, voted its first UNRRA contribution of £80,000,000. On March 28 the United States government authorized its first contribution to UNRRA, amounting to $1,350,000,000—equal to 1 per cent of its annual income. Canada followed suit on June 13, voting $77,000,000. As a matter of fact, the great bulk of UNRRA contributions came from the English-speaking countries.

An equally baffling problem was the securing of supplies. Starving people could not be fed with money. In many war-swept areas agricultural production had been reduced to a minimum. In some invaded countries it had stopped. In a world where military needs and demands always came first, the enormous quantities of food, raw materials, coal, and other relief supplies needed by civilians could not be had in the open market. Yet upon procuring them hung the entire effectiveness of UNRRA.

Shipping presented still another difficulty. If we obtained a million bushels of wheat, let us say, in the United States, how were we to transport it across the ocean to relief areas? Where were we to get the ships? The governments of the warring countries had taken over almost every ton of shipping, and war needs had to come first. Also, harbor approaches were still mined, channels obstructed, piers and port equipment wrecked, and roads and railways into the interior blocked.

Also, there was the problem of first-rate personnel. Again and again Governor Lehman would approach a government asking for the services of a man of competence and high ability. "Sorry," was the inevitable reply. "He is already tied in with such and such a war activity where he is indispensable." As a result, our organization had to appoint such persons as it could secure. And these were not always of first-rate ability.

Another UNRRA task was to assist in the care and repatriation of displaced persons. It was estimated then that there were in Europe twenty million people, in Asia perhaps twice as many, who had been driven from their homes by Axis tyranny or by the cruelties of war. Some were homeless and wandering; others, imprisoned in concentration camps; and still others, impressed in Axis slave gangs. It was a staggering problem of hunger, of disease, of human woe, against which UNRRA struggled manfully during the whole of its existence with a fair measure of success.

All in all, UNRRA brought help to suffering and dying people on an unprecedented scale. For this purpose a unique form of international organization was built up, upon which the later United Nations Charter was patterned. UNRRA made its mistakes—plenty of them. Little wonder, for it was venturing over unknown trails,—and time was of the essence. The urgency of the need brooked no delay. Yet whatever its mistakes and its shortcomings, it undertook with dauntless courage at a time when the world was torn with savagery to rescue and care for a despairing part of humanity.

18

Gathering Relief for Desperate Need

Adequate contribution of money and supplies was in a sense the mainspring of all the UNRRA work. Without this, it must cease; if contributions stopped coming it must fold up its work.

Unhappily many member governments were failing to make good on the Atlantic City agreement that each nation that had not been invaded should contribute 1 per cent of its national income.

The United States and most of the English-speaking countries had saved the day. But other countries were lagging. The Latin American states and the countries of the Middle East paid glowing tributes to UNRRA. But when it came to the paying over of hard cash or the delivering of supplies, a goodly number were not heard from.

So far as we could see in the summer of 1945, all available funds would be spent or obligated by the end of the year.

What could be done? The answer seemed clear. Written appeals and urgent communications had proved unavailing. There was no way of compelling governments to carry out the Atlantic City resolution. Only strong personal influence brought wisely to bear upon individual national officials and political leaders would produce the necessary lifeblood for UNRRA. That meant carefully planned visits and deft work in each of the countries which had not yet paid their 1 per cent contribution. And for this exceedingly delicate and difficult task eyes naturally turned toward UNRRA's Diplomatic Adviser. Obviously it was work which could not be delegated.

It was with some misgiving that I faced the task of visiting more than twenty different countries and by personal conferences with the heads of governments seeking to persuade them to commit their nations to substantial contributions, appealing to them simply on the grounds of common humanity and desperate need.

I set forth in the late spring of 1945, first for Egypt and then for India. Visits to four continents were involved: in Asia, to India, Iraq, and Iran; in Africa, to Egypt, the South African Union, and Southern Rhodesia; in Europe, to Belgium, Denmark, and Portugal; and in South America, to every country. The work was grueling by night and by day, without rest or letup. The travel was exhausting, often at unearthly hours. Two of my assistants were unable to stand the pace, and had to be left in hospitals along the way, one in Egypt and the other in Argentina.

We did not succeed in every country. Sometimes administrative officials seemed to let us down; sometimes, parliaments. There were times indeed when success seemed to be impossible. We could only put our best efforts to the test, and hope.

It is not possible to recount our adventures in all of the twenty-three countries which we visited. Each was altogether different and required different methods of approach. But perhaps some conception can be gained from our visits to two or three.

We flew from Washington on a June morning by way of Bermuda across the Atlantic and next day dropped into Casablanca. Awaiting me at the airport was my son, Lieutenant Woodrow Wilson Sayre of the ATC, whom I had not seen since he went overseas more than a year before. As we rode from the airport into the city the wind from the desert blew cool upon our cheeks. Casablanca is a strange jumble of the East and the West, of medieval and ultramodern, of Arab and French and English.

Early the next morning we took off into the rising sun, across North Africa over the route where early German triumph, led by Rommel, "the desert fox," had turned into disaster. Looking down from our plane, we could see the broken bridges, immense shell holes and in Tripoli harbor the sunken ships, grim evidence of the battle that had raged across North Africa.

Just before midnight we came to the lights of Cairo, meeting place of civilizations; a twenty-mile drive from the airport along the edge of the desert and through silent streets brought us to Shepheard's Hotel, where Rommel had engaged his rooms and planned to celebrate his triumph.

Egypt was our first destination, for Egypt had made but a small administrative contribution of $70,000 and UNRRA badly needed cotton and other Egyptian supplies. Our first call was upon the British Ambassador, Lord Killearn. We described our mission and asked his help. He promised to urge the Egyptian government to make a favorable reply; likewise the American Minister, Mr. Tuck, promised to press the Egyptian government on our behalf.

The following day Said Bey, who handled all UNRRA matters at the Foreign Office, received me with gracious and generous words; but I could get no concrete promises of payments either in cold cash or in supplies. In the afternoon I explained to a press conference the vital need of millions of people in distress and the part I hoped the Egyptian people would want to play in meeting it. As I reported to Governor Lehman, "I believe that since we will need pressure to move governmental circles here, it is well to have some popular backing."

Next we called upon Mahmoud Fahmy Nokrashy Pasha, the Prime Minister. We told him of UNRRA's work and present need. "UNRRA is the single United Nations organization which is actually functioning today," we told him, "and it seems clear that so important a state as Egypt should not be absent from this progressive United Nations movement." He was most friendly throughout and seemed to take a real interest in our mission. We next called upon the Minister of Finance, Makram Ebeid Pasha, who at the conclusion of our talk promised to back our UNRRA request for a 1 per cent contribution in the Council of Ministers. We also explained the situation to the Minister of Supply, Taha El Sebai Bey.

All these high ministers received us warmly; none could have been more gracious. They promised to take the question up at once in the Cabinet of Ministers and to introduce a bill in our behalf in the Parliament.

Time was pressing, and other countries were awaiting us. A

touch of fever delayed my departure a day or two. Then in high hopes we turned eastward, for India.

What could India's poverty-ridden 360,000,000 people, many themselves on the fringe of the subsistence level, do toward the needs of the suffering and destitute victims of war in Europe and Asia? That was the question for which we had come halfway across the world to find some practical answer.

Representatives of the government met us at New Delhi and invited the Mission to be guests of the government. For the next three weeks we worked night and day with Indian officials—in offices, in conference rooms, at dinner tables, at social gatherings.

I took three days off to visit the Viceroy, Lord Wavell, as his house guest at Simla, where he was presiding over the historic Round Table Conference to work out the terms of Indian independence. There, I had a ringside seat. It gave me the chance for long and intimate talks with Jawaharlal Nehru, with Jinnah, leader of the All-India Moslem League, and with Gandhi. I had long walks and talks with Lord Wavell, too. He was wrestling with India's problems with wisdom and sympathy and understanding. He had won the trust and confidence of the Indian leaders. Hope lay ahead.

Then back to crowded days of intensive work at New Delhi in the intense heat of India's summer. Thanks to the patience and unceasing kindness of Sir Azizul Huque, the head of the Department of Commerce, and of our Indian hosts, we found the answers to our problems. UNRRA badly needed bags for getting relief supplies to war-torn areas. That meant raw jute and jute manufactures. India promised to make available 10,000 tons of raw jute and double that quantity of jute manufactures. Together these ran in value to $8,000,000. Europe was in sore need of fats and oils. Peanut oil would help to save lives. India agreed to give some 70,000 tons of peanuts, valued at over $7,000,000. So on down the list of needed supplies of which India had surpluses—including cotton, linseed, tea, and pepper. By the end of our visit India had agreed to give UNRRA some $24,000,000 worth of badly needed supplies.

From those crowded and overflowing days certain unforgettable memories stand out: Kutb Minar, an amazing five-story tower of red and white masonry, utterly unlike anything else in the world, 238

feet high, built in the twelfth century when the Moslems swept across
northern India, mastering the known world with their military
power and engineering skill, leaving as a heritage to mankind buildings of unsurpassed beauty; dinner with the Secretary of Foreign
Affairs, followed by a midnight ride to an ancient capital a dozen
miles from New Delhi; driving up to the citadel fortress and in
through the old Mogul gateway, mysterious in the moonlight, then
wandering through the grass over to the silent mosque, deserted
for centuries but still lovely under the tropical stars; climbing up
the steep stairway of the library building where a Mogul Emperor
committed melancholy suicide.

It was with real regret that we said goodbye to our friends in
India. The call of human need had touched their hearts poignantly.
But time was pressing; we must make every day count.

We left Delhi on July 29 at dawn. We had planned to make
Baghdad the next port of call; but word came from Cairo that the
Egyptian negotiations had gone on the rocks. No UNRRA bill had
yet been presented to the parliament, and the session was drawing
to a close. Moreover, the newspapers reported that the cabinet had
voted a discouragingly small contribution to UNRRA—only £250,-
ooo Egyptian. Clearly decisive action was needed.

We made the long trip from Delhi to Cairo in a single day,
saw the American Minister a few hours after our arrival, and made
appointments to see Badawi Pasha, the Minister of Foreign Affairs,
and the British Ambassador the following morning. To the Minister
of Foreign Affairs we presented the appeal for humanity as elo-
quently and strongly as we could, pointing out that destitute people
in Europe and Asia were dying for want of relief supplies, some of
which Egypt possessed in surplus. It was an argument difficult to
withstand.

The Foreign Minister listened attentively. He seemed convinced; but the decision was not his to make. The Cabinet had already discussed the matter and had reached a decision. That decision was so disappointing that we asked for a reconsideration. The
British Ambassador and the American Minister both promised to
use such pressure as they could.

It was necessary to leave Cairo on Friday night August 3, in order to attend the Third UNRRA Council Meeting, which was to open in London early the following week. The Foreign Minister agreed to bring the question of the UNRRA appropriation before the Cabinet for reconsideration and to do his very best for us. The outcome rested in the lap of the gods. We held our breath, and left for London.

Cairo to London in a "bucket" plane! No rest for the weary! Seated on one of the two metal benches that ran the length of the plane without a back rest or even the chance to lean back, with apertures too small to see the countryside, and with the floor so covered by boxes and luggage that it was impossible even to stretch out full length there, we had to sit hour after hour, dozing now and again only to be jolted awake by bumpy air or by the admonition to fasten safety belts. Away from Payne Field at three-thirty Saturday morning, down at Athens at eight o'clock for a hasty snack, up again and past lofty Greek mountains overlooking the Ionian Sea, then across Italy with more bumpy air and down at Naples; off again in the early afternoon along the Tyrrhenian Sea, circling over the Colosseum and down at Rome; off again hitting boldly across the blue sea, high over Corsica, down at Marseilles at sundown for another snack; off in the dusk up the Rhone valley toward Paris; from midnight until two o'clock Sunday morning at the "snack bar" in Paris. Then off again through the black night, across the English Channel and down at London between three o'clock and four. One day after we had left Cairo we were in London walking along Hyde Park, at six o'clock in the morning, each carrying his bag, too early to secure a room assignment and with no place to go.

The next two weeks we spent at the Third UNRRA Council Meeting. The world picture had changed. Germany had surrendered in May. Nevertheless, the representatives from forty-four United Nations faced the critical problem of tiding destitute peoples over the coming winter and rebuilding their shattered economies. By the end of June, UNRRA had shipped abroad a million and a quarter tons of relief supplies, valued at over $280,000,000. Nevertheless, the desperate fact stared us in the face that by the end of the year UNRRA would have spent or obligated its total resources. There could be only one answer. UNRRA must go back to each of its member states for an additional contribution of 1 per cent of its annual income to see Europe through the critical winter of 1946 and to help China, the Philippines, Korea, and other parts of Asia back to their feet.

In the meantime good news had come from Mr. Tuck in Cairo. The Minister of Foreign Affairs had informed him that Egypt had increased its contribution to UNRRA to £1,000,000 Egyptian. Thanks to the able Bedawi Pasha and to the effective assistance of Lord Killearn, the British Ambassador, and Mr. Tuck, the cabinet had reconsidered and we had won. We felt like singing a *Jubilate*.

We hurried around to grasp the hand of Said Bey, Egypt's representative at the UNRRA Council session. I was anxious to secure a public commitment and roused his enthusiasm by suggesting that he make the announcement publicly before the UNRRA representatives gathered at London. He agreed to do so and asked me to draft some appropriate words. My draft seemed to please him. Then I suggested that his speech be given on an afternoon when the Council would not be under severe pressure of other work, and when the press representatives could be notified. He readily agreed.

On the appointed afternoon, when I reached the Council meeting I went to Said Bey and asked, "Are you all prepared?" He was agitated and replied, "I'm ashamed to say I forgot to bring my speech along, so I can't go through with it." His regret was extreme.

I pulled out of my pocket my somewhat rumpled carbon copy. "Here is a copy. Read that."

He was still further agitated and embarrassed. He had also forgotten his spectacles and therefore could not read the speech.

I pulled off my own. "Here. These are good ones. Read the speech with these."

He was nonplused. Others were watching. He could not well refuse. The unbelievable happened. He read to the Council through my glasses my carbon copy of his speech, to the gratification of all. He ended by publicly declaring:

"I have the pleasure to announce that the Egyptian government will present a resolution to meet its maximum contribution to the UNRRA fund at its next session of Parliament. This figure has been fixed at one million pounds sterling."

The Egyptian Foreign Minister had kept his word.

The sequel, several months later, was disappointing. When the

Egyptian Parliament convened, for one reason or another the appropriation was not made. The Parliament ultimately authorized a contribution, but only for £350,000 Egyptian ($1,446,667); and in spite of subsequent efforts on the part of UNRRA officials, no further Egyptian contribution could be secured.

While the UNRRA Council was in session, the atomic bomb burst at Hiroshima. Swiftly followed the end of the Japanese war. London went wild. For three nights Piccadilly, impassable to cars, packed with dense throngs of singing, happy people, celebrated as only Piccadilly can. London bobbies along the curb looked on good-humoredly, ready for action at need; but there was no rowdyism. Immense crowds in front of Buckingham Palace waited for a glimpse of the King and Queen, singing in the rain. On the first Sunday of the peace a great audience at St. Paul's, itself intact amidst blocks of rubble and gaping walls, packed it to the doors, singing with reverence and full hearts:

> "Now thank we all our God,
>   With heart and hands and voices,
>   Who wondrous things hath done,
>   In whom His world rejoices."

We left London in mid-August and on our way back to Cairo stopped over in Greece to see for ourselves something of the appalling need in mountain villages burned by the Germans. In the district which I visited, German demolition parties had deliberately burned and wrecked 50 out of 110 villages, to inspire the people with fear and terror. In many of the villages not one building was standing; nothing was left except twisted fragments and rubble. Sheer, wanton, barefaced evil, it seemed.

People cling desperately to their homes. As soon as the Germans had been driven out of Greece survivors returned and, living in crazy cellars and holes burrowed out of the rubble, wrestled against hunger and disease and cold and rain.

But they could not rebuild alone. They needed food—more than all Greece contained. They needed seeds, draft animals for the fields, clothing and shelter against the bitter cold of the approaching winter. Tragically they needed help. And UNRRA alone could bring it.

In the early days of September we flew to South Africa in search of coal and wool, arriving after four days at Pretoria, the capital of the South African Union, in all the beauty and the loveliness of a spring day, the sunshine fairly sparkling, the birds exultant in song.

Here General Jan Christiaan Smuts welcomed us as guests of the government. As we advanced to grasp his outstretched hand, we were at once won by the kindliness of his aging face. Slight of build and erect in bearing, with close-cropped white mustache and goatee, his eyes alert and piercing, he was clearly a man of strength of mind and resolute purpose. We felt that if only we could make him sense the need he would stand stanchly by us.

For three weeks in the government offices placed at our disposal, we met daily with officials, going over lists of needed supplies and explaining the deadly urgency of the situation. We spoke with utter frankness.

I could see that General Smuts understood. He would not let red tape interfere.

We could not wait in Pretoria until the Parliament met in January. We must press on with our world task. But before we left an official letter promised the introduction of a bill for an additional UNRRA appropriation of £3,475,000, so as to bring the South African contribution to a total of £4,500,000—1 per cent of the Union's national income.

While we were awaiting a decision we stole away one week-end to the Kruger National Park, perhaps the most interesting wild-game sanctuary in the world. Sunday morning we watched at a large water hole in open country while wild animals from far and near—wildebeests, herds of zebras, scores of impalas, warthogs, baboons, monkeys, kudus, two great towering giraffes, diminutive hartebeests—came to drink—driven into the neutral territory of the water hole by common necessity. Singly or by groups they would suddenly become apparent against the background of jungle; and then slowly and hesitantly, with constant watching, sniffing and stamping, always on their guard against lion, they would slowly work their way up to the edge of the water hole and, after a careful look around, stoop and drink their fill. I think I have never seen a more dramatic sight—unless it was on our way back that afternoon when, at a sharp turn in the wild and lonely, twisting road, our car ran full upon twelve great lionesses and a young cub in the middle of the road. We jammed on our brakes and came to a dead stop. They eyed us, motionless except for their slowly waving tails, and we in the closed car eyed them as motionless as they. Then they crept closer and, only a few yards away, ranged themselves around our car, wondering what manner of monsters we were. For twenty minutes we intently watched each other. But dusk was falling, and we had to catch the night train in order to reach Pretoria in time for Monday morning engagements, so we took reluctant leave.

General Smuts and his government proved as good as their word. In January they carried the necessary bill for an UNRRA appropriation through the Parliament, and turned over more than $18,000,000 worth of badly needed coal, wool, 43,000 cases of canned meat and vegetable rations, 120,000 cases of stewed steak, fish oil, smoked fish, canned vegetables, preserved fruit, blankets, cardigan jackets, flannel waistcoats, shirts, undergarments, waterproof capes, mosquito nets, tents, greatcoats, hides, mohair, seeds, agricultural hand tools, mules, horses, bulls, manganese ore, chrome ore, copper blister and asbestos.

We left Pretoria at dawn on Monday September 24. On that day the South African papers reported:

The UNRRA Mission to the Union, headed by Mr. Francis B. Sayre, Diplomatic Adviser to UNRRA and former United States Undersecretary of State, left South Africa this morning for Egypt en route to Iraq and Iran. . . . It is almost certain that the Union Parliament early in the coming session will be asked to approve the appropriation of £3,475,000 as the balance of the Union's first UNRRA contribution of £4,500,000 on the internationally agreed basis of one percent of the national income. . . .

The fact that General Smuts himself has been in close consultation with Mr. Sayre during the Mission's temporary sojourn at Union Buildings also suggests that the Government has no intention of "pulling its punches" in connection with the UNRRA appropriation. . . .

The success of the UNRRA mission's visit lies in the fact that its presence here has resulted in a keen "awareness" among responsible officials in the Union Buildings as to the urgency of relief for Europe and the fact that the Union can and is expected to play its important share in this international task of rehabilitation.

Next we were off on visits to Iraq and Iran, and it was not until October that we saw Washington again.

Once back in Washington our thoughts inevitably turned to South America. Few of the Latin American countries had yet rallied to the support of UNRRA. Such UNRRA missions as had already visited them had come back almost empty-handed. It seemed clear that I must devote the remainder of the autumn and the coming winter to making the Latin peoples realize the urgency of the world need.

Accordingly I set forth, visiting one after another of the countries of South America—some fourteen in all.

Many of the Latin-American states required two or sometimes three visits. After our press interviews and talks, following our arrival, with the editors of the most influential papers, after we had held numerous conferences with the President and top cabinet officials and secured a definite promise, in writing if possible, to press Parliament for an adequate and specific UNRRA contribution, there was too ready a tendency among leaders of these states to pay all honor to the visiting Mission, to make extravagant promises, to tender a sumptuous banquet the night before its departure, and then to allow these promises to be crowded out of remembrance by the ordinary demands of daily life.

Sometimes the most important part of our Mission's work, therefore, would be upon a return visit to confer with the Parliamentary leaders and make them understand something of the international need. This involved talks not only with the leaders of the majority party but, often of even greater importance, with the opposition leaders. Upon the passage of the bill as introduced, without opposition amendments, depended the entire success or failure of our Mission.

The results from many of these Latin-American visits were heart-warming. From Brazil, for instance, we secured the promise, subsequently fulfilled, not only of a $10,000,000 payment as part of Brazil's first contribution, but also a second contribution of $10,000,000. Something of the spirit which prompted such responses can be gleaned from the signed article in *El Tiempo* on the day of our departure from Bogotá, Colombia.

Mr. Sayre is right. Real and lasting peace cannot be maintained by means of physical force alone. It must be the outcome of human solidarity and it must be based upon justice and mercy.

Human brotherhood is sometimes a moral precept; now it is a very compelling need. Previously . . . the prosperity of one country was often built upon the suffering of another. In Spain, the Eastern peasants had a slogan for their coming harvests: "Rain, sunlight and war on Sevastopol."

Today we are far removed from the times of the Crimean War. But there can be no peace in the world while war goes on in Sevastopol. Europe can be saved only through brotherhood. And only upon brotherhood can a balanced and normal civilization be built.

In February we flew across the Atlantic for a hasty visit to Denmark. Although Denmark had been an invaded country and was herself struggling against shortages of cash and depletion of her stocks, she nevertheless gave us 10,000 splendid Danish horses, valued at $4,000,000, and also $1,000,000 worth of fish. The horses, UNRRA at once transported to Poland for the spring plowing; and thus we were able substantially to increase the Polish food supplies for the coming summer.

By early April, following visits to Brazil and to Uruguay, we reached Buenos Aires to open conversations with Argentina. Unfortunately Argentina had never joined the UNRRA ranks, and had declined a recent invitation to become an UNRRA member.

Colonel Perón, who had just been elected President, had not yet come into office. He was living on his ranch up country and was not accessible to visitors.

The day after my arrival I held a press conference attended by thirty or forty newspaper people. Argentina's refusal to join UNRRA was a "hot" subject and evoked lively interest. On the following morning front-page reports about UNRRA and the existing world food situation were prominently displayed.

Our first meeting was with Dr. Juan I. Cooke, the Foreign Minister, and the next day I called upon President Farrell at the Presidential Palace. I spoke of Argentina's splendid opportunity to win the gratitude of a starving world and suggested a three-point program for giving help. The President promised to call a special Cabinet meeting and lay my program before it.

Early on Wednesday afternoon I was informed that my three-point program was to be laid before the Cabinet the following morning. Still more important, word came that although Colonel Perón was seeing no one officially, the Minister of Foreign Affairs had made special arrangements for me to see him at his home.

That same afternoon, by invitation, I addressed a meeting of the important Instituto Agrario Argentino, whose membership included the leading grain growers of Argentina; and after the address they appointed a committee to organize help. Concrete results followed.

Early the following morning a close friend of Colonel Perón drove me to his ranch, about an hour and a half from Buenos Aires.

Colonel Perón welcomed me in his unpretentious ranch home with the greatest cordiality, and we talked together for an hour and a half. I laid before him, as before President Farrell, the dire need of Europe and the grave world situation. He was touched and, without hesitation, promised his utmost help. I told him of the program which I had urged upon President Farrell, and which the Cabinet was expected to consider that morning, and expressed the hope that he might be able to speak to the President before the Cabinet meeting. He at once called up the President on the long-distance telephone and asked him to push Argentine measures of relief in every way possible. Not only this. He also promised to take a personal part in the effort by speaking over the radio, probably on the following Tuesday or Wednesday evening, urging the Argentine people to economize in their consumption of food so that larger relief supplies might be made available; and he assured me that, as soon as he came into office, he would shoulder all the obligations assumed by the present government for our relief program. At his request I left with him a Spanish copy of my memorandum to the President setting forth my three-point program.

I was impressed by the simplicity and, so far as I could judge, by the sincerity of the man. There was no display of any kind, no attempt to make a show. He was his natural self in rather a humble home, very human, seemingly touched by the suffering of the world and anxious to do what he could to help. I saw no indication then of the later Perón. At that time, so far as I could see, he had not yet been corrupted by power or bent to the will of the glamorous Eva.

After our talk he took me out to see his chickens and turkeys, his tame ducks, his llamas, and his other pets. One could not but feel the warmth of his personality. The Vice President elect and the governor of the province, both important political figures, arrived while I was there; but Colonel Perón put them off until he had spent a full hour and a half with me on the relief problem.

On the following day I learned that, with only minor modifications, the Cabinet had adopted my program. The government agreed to deliver to UNRRA some 300,000 tons of wheat and to expedite in every way relief programs and shipments. The Argentine contribution figured up to some $7,800,000.

The battle of the Argentine had been won, but not without casualties. The pace of our Mission's work proved too strenuous for my faithful and valiant assistant, Torres Mazzoranna. Overfatigued by the intense, never-ceasing activity of our Mission he fell ill, and we had to move him to a sanatorium where he remained for a week. He had worked unceasingly throughout the Mission's crowded days in Brazil, Uruguay, and Argentina; and during our succeeding missions we sorely missed his effective help.

On Sunday morning, April 14 I left by plane, west across the Andes for Chile. The Sunday newspapers featured the Cabinet decision, and the Buenos Aires *Standard* carried the following editorial:

Mr. Sayre's Mission

By the time most of our readers are glancing at these columns, Mr. Francis B. Sayre, special envoy of the UNRRA to Argentina to secure vitally needed foodstuffs for the hunger-stricken people of Europe, will be en route to Chile, his mission to this country concluded.

Mr. Sayre has discharged his duties in Argentina in a highly successful twofold manner. Not only has he secured what he came for, but he has awakened this nation to the plight of millions of people overseas. The response to his appeal that is forthcoming from Argentina will go a long way toward endearing this country in the hearts of men, women and children throughout the world.

Few diplomats have come here with less fanfare and left with so much good will and understanding between them and the government and people of this nation.

The next two months were crowded with visits to Chile, Peru, Ecuador, Panama, Bolivia, Mexico, and Guatemala. Each visit had its own adventure, its excitement, its rising hopes, and for the most part its happy fulfillment. At last in May I turned homeward for a brief respite.

On June 8, 1946, we celebrated another happy family event. It was the culmination of a romance which began in the minds of Betty and myself in Manila, where we first met the attractive daughters of Admiral and Mrs. Hart. One night after our return from Manila we invited the Harts and their daughter Harriet to dine with us in our Washington home. My son Frank, who had then returned from his wartime chaplaincy on the cruiser *San Francisco*, at dinner that spring evening in 1945, quite unexpectedly met Harriet. It was love at first sight; and what followed seemed foreordained.

Now following my return from Latin America, both families gathered in Sharon, Connecticut, the home of the bride, to celebrate the wedding of Harriet and Frank. Dr. Henry Sloan Coffin performed the ceremony in the little Sharon church. Since that day Frank has gone steadily forward, and I rejoice in his present far-reaching work as Dean of the Episcopal Cathedral in Washington.

In July, a month after the wedding, I was off again, to Portugal and Belgium. Then followed another trip to South America to press to their conclusion several of our Latin-American contributions. By early 1947 the brunt of the work had been completed. The first postwar winter had been surmounted, and also that of 1946–1947. The European invaded countries were fast recovering economic stability. The food lines were shortening.

Meanwhile the United Nations had begun to function; and this seemed to be a work of even broader scope than UNRRA. When, therefore, the Department of State early in January offered me appointment as the first United States representative in the United Nations Trusteeship Council, shortly to be organized, I gladly accepted. That meant resignation from UNRRA on February 17, 1947, immediately after my return from Venezuela.

I was sorry to say goodbye to UNRRA. To it millions of people owed their lives. And, as I wrote to the Director General at the time of my resignation, UNRRA had "taught men and women of many different races and creeds and nations how to work unitedly together for the great ends of human brotherhood. Surely this must be the

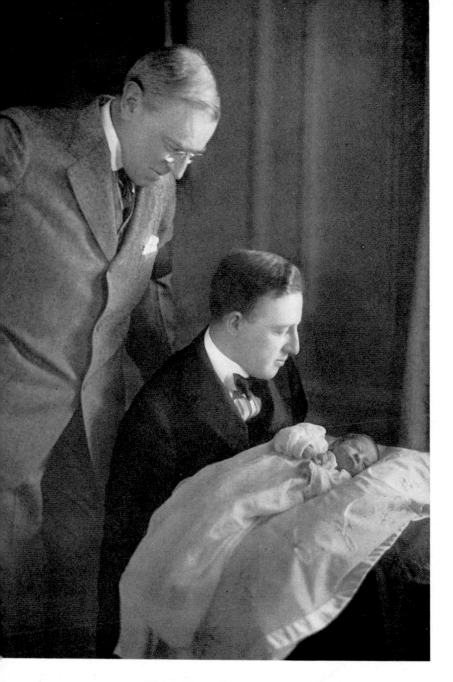

Three Generations:
President Wilson looks at his first grandchild, Francis, Jr.
The White House, 1915

Harris & Ewing, Washington

Adviser in Foreign Affairs to His Siamese Majesty, surrounded by his staff.
Bangkok, Siam, 1923

Narasingh Studio, Bangkok

foundation for any kind of practicable and stable world peace. UNRRA has blazed the path."

Herbert Lehman, who had resigned as Director General in March, 1946, wrote me a generous letter upon my return from one of our South American missions:

I understand that you are back in this country, and I want to tell you again what a fine job I think you did in Latin America. . . . You are in point of service, I think, about the oldest top man in OFRRO and UNRRA.

Our association of three and a half years was a most happy one and I certainly hope it will continue. Your devotion to duty, your unfailing cooperation and encouragement and your enthusiasm made a great contribution to the notable success which UNRRA was finally able to attain. I think you know how much I leaned on you and how much I have appreciated your constant assistance.

I also prize the letter written me by Major General Lowell W. Rooks, the Director General at the time of my resignation.

Dear Mr. Sayre:

It is with my genuine regret that you today leave UNRRA and I want, in this letter, to give you some idea of the deep personal appreciation I have for your magnificent effort on behalf of UNRRA. Yours has been an arduous and difficult assignment and I—as well as Governor Lehman and Mayor LaGuardia—am well aware of all the diplomacy and hard work which has been entailed in the achievement of so outstanding a result. . . .

I should like to have felt that we could all have remained together as a team until the day when UNRRA's mission was finally accomplished. A wonderful job has been done and a large part of the credit is due to you for your contribution to that success. The Administration was fortunate in having your loyal and devoted service and the benefit of your wide experience.

During the preceding year and a half, I had travelled some 98,000 miles heading missions to the four continents. And, as a result, we had secured for UNRRA almost $98,000,000. As it worked out, strangely enough, just about $1,000 to the mile!

Payment of the following contributions in money or needed supplies was secured as the result of our Missions:

Countries	Unpaid contributions which Mission helped to collect	New or lapsed contributions which would not have otherwise been obtained
India	$24,000,000	
Egypt		$ 1,446,667
South African Union	4,000,000	14,112,500
Southern Rhodesia		600,000
Iraq		
Iran		350,800
Cuba		5,261,473
Colombia		2,464,077
Dominican Republic	350,000	576,752
Denmark		5,356,660
Brazil	10,000,000	10,000,000
Uruguay		1,586,400
Argentina		7,800,000
Chile		3,089,916
Panama	266,666	
Mexico	1,200,000	1,200,000
Portugal		1,000,000
Belgium		1,572,000
Peru		1,000,000
Bolivia		77,738
Ecuador		150,000
Venezuela		
Guatemala		208,400
	$39,816,666	$57,853,383
		39,816,666
Total		$97,670,049

19

United Nations and Trusteeship Council

As the end of the Second World War approached, the hopes of a war-weary world centered more and more upon the organization of a strong United Nations. Instead of trying to balance peace, as in the nineteenth century, upon military alliances of self-seeking powers, each intent upon its own selfish gain, we were coming to realize that some form of strong international organization to build collectively for a lasting peace had become indeed the price of survival.

Assembling at San Francisco in the spring of 1945, the representatives of the Allied Powers had set about drafting the United Nations Charter; and one baffling problem was that of non-self-governing peoples. Some 200,000,000 people are at present non-self-governing; and some of these have the lowest living standards in the world.

But the problem of non-self-governing peoples is tormented today not only by rampant poverty and human need, but also by the deep resentment of these peoples, black and yellow and brown, against the entire white race. They cannot forget the way in which too often they were exploited by white colonial powers during the eighteenth and nineteenth centuries.

To meet this exceedingly complex problem of alien rule, the

framers of the United Nations Charter took a bold stand. They began with a ringing declaration in Article 73:

> Members of the United Nations which have or assume responsibilities
> for the administration of territories whose peoples have not yet attained
> a full measure of self-government recognize the principle that the interests
> of the inhabitants of these territories are paramount, and accept as a
> sacred trust the obligation to promote to the utmost, within the system of
> international peace and security established by the present Charter, the
> well-being of the inhabitants of these territories.

Then they proceeded to set up what was called the international trusteeship system, applicable to such mandated or other colonial areas as might be placed under it. Moreover, a strong United
Nations organ, the Trusteeship Council, was created to supervise
the administration or itself to administer such "trust territories."

Here were possibilities of tremendous import. If the new Trusteeship Council could be made a strong and effective organ to deal
decisively with this crucial problem of non-self-governing peoples,
rather than a debating society torn by conflict and endless wran-
gles between the colonial and the noncolonial powers, its contribution toward the peace of the world might be incalculable. But was
the idea practicable and could the Trusteeship Council be made to
function as a really effective organ?

Happily the framers of the Charter realized the dangers. They
set up the Trusteeship Council as one of "the principal organs of
the United Nations" (Article 7); and it is small enough (ten members at its first session) not to lose itself in endless debates. Its com-
position makes it powerful. Each of the five major powers with
permanent seats in the Security Council is a member. Half of its
membership is composed of all those states which administer trust
territories. The other half is made up of an equal number of non-
administering states. Sufficient non-administering states to maintain
the equal balance are elected by the General Assembly for three-
year terms.

By the late autumn of 1946 eight trust territories had been
created, in which lived some fifteen million people of different races
and with widely different problems. The approval by the General
Assembly of trusteeship agreements for each of these eight territo-

ries in December, 1946, made possible the organization of the Trusteeship Council in the spring of 1947.

Early in 1947 President Truman with the consent of the Senate appointed me the United States Representative in the United Nations Trusteeship Council. He wrote me that the work of the Council "will be entirely in your line and something which will do good for the world and the United States. I have every confidence in your ability to do it."

Later in the year came another gracious letter from President Truman conferring upon me the personal rank of Ambassador.

The Trusteeship Council assembled for its first meeting at Lake Success on March 26, 1947. Many curious eyes were turned upon it. Would it prove itself an effective working body? Would it be made up of men of character and drive or merely of diplomatic figureheads?

When the representatives, headed by Trygve Lie, the Secretary-General, filed into the Council Chamber at Lake Success and took their seats, that of the Soviet representative remained vacant. The U.S.S.R. had not replied to the United Nations invitation, and was boycotting the Trusteeship Council.

We lost no time in getting down to business. Mr. Lie said in his opening remarks:

> This is an occasion of historic significance. You meet here as one of the principal organs of the United Nations . . . For the first time in the world's history a permanent international body, whose membership is composed solely of official representatives of Governments, is assembled to deal exclusively with the problems of non-self-governing peoples.

The first official business was election of a President. To my great surprise, without any advance warning, the choice fell upon the representative of the United States, and I suddenly heard the Secretary-General asking me to take the chair.

My initial impromptu words, as recorded in the minutes, were a plea for unity in the work that lay before us:

> . . . As long as backward and depressed areas exist in Asia, Africa and elsewhere, filled with under-educated, under-nourished and unhappy people, we lack the foundations for a stable peace. To build solidly for

peace, we must remove the causes of war, and that is part of the high task of this Council. . .

I am going to ask that every member of the Council suppress all personal considerations, that we work together as a unit, intimately and strongly, for the achievement of our great task.

As we pushed forward with the work I was more and more deeply impressed with the caliber of the representatives at the Council table. They were not show fronts. They were not politicians. They were men of stature and of wide experience.*

One of my tasks as first President of the Council was to help shape from the very outset sound procedures for the Council's coming activities. I felt happy that we were building up a unity of purpose, that our efforts were not impaired by sharp cleavages between administering and non-administering states, between great and small powers, between liberals and conservatives. As a result we were able to evolve procedures that have stood the test; in fact, few changes have since been made either in the Rules of Procedure which we worked out and adopted during that first session or in the Council's objectives and method of work.

Only about 18,000,000 people live within trust territories today; nevertheless, if sound ways can be evolved to lift them to self-government or independence and enable them to shoulder its responsibilities, immeasurable gain can come for all non-self-governing peoples.

For this high task the Charter clothed the Council with stout powers. These included the power to require annually from each of the administering states written answers to a formidable ques-

* Government representatives sitting in the first session of the Trusteeship Council were:

Australia	Norman J. O. Makin, Ambassador to the United States
Belgium	Pierre Ryckmans, Honorary Governor-General of the Belgian Congo
China	Liu Chieh, Vice Minister of Foreign Affairs
France	Roger Garreau, Ambassador to Poland
Iraq	Ali Jawdat, Minister to the United States
	Awni Khalidy, Secretary of Embassy
Mexico	Dr. Luis Padilla Nervo
New Zealand	Sir Carl Berendsen, Minister to the United States
United Kingdom	Ivor Thomas, M.P., Parliamentary Under-Secretary of State for the Colonies
United States	Francis B. Sayre

tionnaire and also during the Council's examination of each trust territory oral answers to whatever questions relating to the trust territory the representatives at the Council table may choose to put. Also, the unique power to send to each trust territory Visiting Missions to explore on the spot actual existing conditions and report to the Council their findings. Also, the power to consider all petitions relating to a trust territory and personally to question petitioners. Also, the power to submit to the General Assembly carefully prepared Reports on each trust territory and to frame concrete recommendations for the advancement of the inhabitants.

During that first session of the Council we could not help feeling blest in the Soviet boycott. We were able to proceed rapidly and in cooperation. At the second session the U.S.S.R. apparently overcame its scruples; and since then its representative has regularly sat at the Council table. Fortunately, however, there is no right of veto in the Trusteeship Council; and much of the time the Soviet representative walks alone. Yet he is ever alert to foster and promote division wherever he can. We found, on the whole, that we could generally ignore his efforts and go forward with our business. But he could and often did cause harassing delay. He would make intolerably long speeches. We learned to let him talk and then vote him down.

The most interesting and important petition presented to the Council at its first session was signed by the leaders and representatives of Western Samoa, who had gathered together in a national *Fono* (Council) to consider the trusteeship agreement signed by the New Zealand Government to place Western Samoa under international trusteeship. The petition stated that the Western Samoans did not desire international trusteeship; instead, "we humbly beseech that Samoa be granted self-government."

After a discussion the Council resolved on April 24 to send a visiting mission to Western Samoa.

Our first session ended April 28, 1947, and at once we set to work organizing and preparing for the visiting mission to Western Samoa. As President of the Council I was asked to head it. Other members chosen for the mission were Pierre Ryckmans, the former governor of the Belgian Congo and Senator Eduardo Cruz-Coke of Chile, whom I had come to know during my UNRRA visit to Santiago. We also asked Felix Keesing, Professor of Anthropology at Stanford University and writer on Pacific peoples, to accompany the mission as an expert consultant. The New Zealand Government wrote that they would "be glad to give every assistance possible to the visiting Mission."

One night returning from a Council meeting to our New York hotel room, I said to my wife:

"Betsy, how would you like to visit Samoa, where Robert Louis Stevenson built his last house?"

Her eyes shone. "Stop teasing me!"

"No, it's all arranged for you to go as my guest. We're starting in June; so pack up your sketch box and your books on Stevenson, and get your things ready for a trip to Samoa."

In June, 1947, we flew from San Francisco to Auckland. There we met the other members of the mission, coming by different routes. It was bitter winter weather and we shivered with cold, and wondered what lay ahead. It was an entirely new course which we were charting in United Nations adventure.

20

Mission to Western Samoa

To most people Samoa spells romance, the charm of the South Seas, long white breakers booming over coral strands, lazy days and languid nights—the home of Robert Louis Stevenson. But in actual fact, Samoa for the past hundred years, in spite of its physical charm, has been a land of unhappiness, of problems and frustrations. Torn with factional struggle and rivalry between ruling families, Samoa seemed to Germany, Great Britain, and the United States—the three Great Powers fencing in the latter half of the nineteenth century for strong footholds in the Pacific—to be a rich and easy prize. Blood was spilt; and later a tragic war between the three imperial Powers was narrowly averted by the dramatic hurricane of 1889. With demoniacal fury it struck the German, American, and British warships anchored at Apia with guns trained on each other, and piled them high on the coral reefs. The struggle over Samoa ceased only in 1900, with a division of the spoils: Germany took Western Samoa, the United States took Eastern Samoa, and Great Britain received compensation elsewhere in the Pacific.

From that day onward Samoans were under foreign rule. But contentment did not come. From 1900 to the First World War Western Samoa was firmly ruled by Germany; it was captured in the war by New Zealand, which from 1920 administered it as a "C" class mandate under the League of Nations. Unhappy experiences followed, culminating in bloodshed in 1929. After the Second World War New Zealand signed a trusteeship agreement in 1946 placing Western Samoa within the United Nations trusteeship system.

And now in response to the Western Samoan petition and to discover the true conditions there we, members of the first U.N. Trusteeship Council visiting mission, accompanied by an international secretariat, met that wintry June in Auckland and from there flew to Wellington, the New Zealand capital, where we were welcomed by Peter Fraser, the Prime Minister. With him and other leaders in the New Zealand government I had long talks, both official and unofficial. The conferences with the Prime Minister filled me with hope. I felt his utter sincerity and integrity of character.

Accompanied by G. R. Laking as representative of the Prime Minister, the mission arrived by plane on the morning of July 4th at Apia, the capital of Western Samoa, where Colonel Voelcker, New Zealand Governor of Western Samoa, was waiting to receive us.

As we drove from the airport past a succession of little villages to Apia we received our first impressions of Samoan life. In each village grass houses, on mounds above the ground level, clustered about luscious green open plots of grass. The woven blinds which were the walls of the houses were rolled up, exposing intimate scenes of family life—Samoan mothers on mats nursing their babies; old men, cross-legged, twisting coconut fiber into sennit twine; old women braiding pandanus leaves into mats; children playing on the grass under great trees or bathing in the sea. The younger men were off in their dugouts, fishing. Already we could feel something of the charm and the outward serenity of Polynesian life; already we had gained our first glimpse of perhaps the handsomest of all the people of the South Pacific and understood something of their appeal to visitors like Stevenson.

Here was a languorous life amid unending natural beauty. It might be the ever-changing drama of sky, cloud, and sea, or the sun setting in a riot of color. We were reminded of the lady who exclaimed on first seeing one of Turner's impressionistic paintings of a sunset, "Well, I could not even *imagine* a sunset like that!" Turner replied, "Don't you wish you could, madam?" In Samoa you did not have to imagine; you had only to look—and then try to believe it was true.

For two weeks we plunged into almost continuous public and private conferences and interviews at Apia with New Zealand officials, Samoan chiefs, representative groups, heads of religious missions, and private individuals. After that we went on *malanga*, travelling by launch and on foot to the outlying districts and villages to reach the "grass-roots" opinion of the country.

Western Samoa is made up of two main islands,—Upolu, in which the capital town, Apia, is situated, and the more primitive Savaii. During the last week in July we practically encircled the island of Upolu, visiting the coastal villages; and in August we made our *malanga* through Savaii. Here we got away from motor roads and electric lights and twentieth century sophistication and dropped back a century or two into old Samoa before the Europeans came. Everywhere crowds turned out to do us honor. As we neared each village, our approach often announced by the beating of drums, the *matai* (chieftains) usually formed in a long line to receive us and lead us to the guest house, decorated and garlanded with flowers. As we sat in a circle with them there followed the colorful ceremony of drinking kava; and after that, offerings of food and gifts—whole roasted pigs, taro, and fruits, and in some cases historic fine mats—were laid reverently at our feet amid songs and ceremonial processions.

Through the rest of the afternoon before the assembled multitude there followed formal speeches, exchanged between Samoan orators and myself as head of the mission. Oratory in Samoa has become a fine art, and every village has its official orator. He carries a long staff as his "badge of office," on which he gracefully rests his right hand as he speaks. He also carries a short stick with tasselled hemp-string finely braided—which reminded us of the old-fashioned "fly-flicker." This hangs over his shoulder during his speech, with its tassels over his right shoulder blade. The lengthy flow of words was turned on at will, with no seeming fatigue to either orator or audience. The length of the speeches was, of course, greatly increased by pauses for translation. In spite of the crudity of my own approaches to oratory I was presented with an orator's

staff; and, leaning upon this, I would try to unfold to the people
something of the meaning of the United Nations and of the Trusteeship Council and of their concern for Samoa.

The speeches would be followed by ancient Samoan dances
and songs by the assembled villagers in our honor; and in the evening again we sat around the circle exchanging questions and answers with village and district chiefs as to self-government and what
it would mean and why it was wanted.

The fundamental problem which the mission faced was not an
easy one. The frustrations and unhappy contacts with foreigners
that the Samoans had lived through for three-quarters of a century
made their attitude not surprising. They wanted to be left to rule
their own country as they liked. They cared not for twentieth century economies or more efficient methods of production and increased revenues. Samoa was a land of easy living, where shelter
could be readily made of palm leaves and other local products,
where clothing was little needed, and where food in the form of
bananas and coconuts and breadfruit required a minimum of labor. Where needs were so few, Nature so bountiful, and idleness
so pleasant, why work all day to increase production? And why adopt
a European individualist economy, which left individuals often to
suffering and even hunger, whereas in their eyes the ancient Samoan
system of family organization and family ownership of land and
goods led to a far happier and more secure existence for all? Samoans, like many other peoples, wanted their own life and their
own family and village organization; and they wanted their own
government too.

Unhappily the coming during the nineteenth century of Western "civilization" meant inevitable change. Western sellers wanted
markets; Western traders wanted copra; Western imperialists
wanted a foothold in the Pacific. The simple Samoan economy of
earlier days could not withstand the inroads of driving Western
commercialism. Apia, the capital, became a rendezvous for Western
traders and adventurers, who in time demanded and obtained control of the port. During the latter half of the century, Germans and
British and Americans, competing for power, backed rival claimants
for the kingship. European armed forces were landed to make good
their demands. By the beginning of the twentieth century Samoa

was bound and shackled hand and foot to Western imperialism. This was the period of Robert Louis Stevenson's arrival in Samoa. Little wonder that he took up his pen in protest.

Now, with the setting up of the United Nations and the Trusteeship Council, organized to achieve human freedom, Samoan hopes rose.

The Samoan petition had referred to the way in which England acts "as protector and adviser" to the neighboring Kingdom of Tonga. For a more complete understanding of the Samoan ideas we flew to Tonga, where we were received by Queen Salote and entertained by the British Agent and Consul, C. W. T. Johnson. The night we arrived, we attended a great meeting of Tongans. Nineteenth century Christian missionaries had taught them to sing, and seldom have I heard such magnificent singing.

Later I learned of their own disillusionment about war. During the Second World War Allied troops had come in and taken possession; and when I visited the Tongan Legislature the next day, I noticed on the agenda the following proposed "Motion for 1947 (No. 14)":

That Her Majesty be requested to pass an Act which would forbid us from taking part in any future war abroad. Another great war is expected to be waged during this Century or in the next Century. Toward the end of this conflict God and His saints will descend on earth and will put an end to it with His great might (Zak. XIV, 1–5).

The Tongans felt that their peace had been disturbed and their life disrupted by foreigners for many years; and although Allied troops had come to guard and to protect them from seizure, they gravely decided to have no part in any future wars.

Our two days' visit was a delight. We drove to the beauty spots of the island and the interesting blowholes—open-topped caves through which the incoming tide shot high in the air like geysers. When we took our reluctant leave we felt that Tonga was a hidden paradise, far removed from the twentieth century world.

Back in Samoa we found many spots of charm and beauty to be visited too. One Sunday we climbed up the steep rocky volcanic ridge which forms the backbone of Upolu and from the crest gained memorable views of the blue Pacific and the encircling reefs. But

of chief interest was our visit to Vailima, the home of Robert Louis
Stevenson. The white frame mansion where for four years he lived
still stands, comfortable, commodious, in the heart of an estate six
or seven miles from Apia. Simple, of generous proportions, with
spacious verandas and red tin roofs, it is shielded from the hot sun
by handsome acacia trees, palms, bougainvillaea vines, and lush
shrubbery.

It is a well chosen spot six hundred feet above the sea with a
thickly wooded mountain at its back and a wide lawn, gently sloping
down to the road. Five streams flow through the property, giving it
its name Vailima ("five waters"). The air here is fresh and life-
giving, and one instantly responds to the charm and comfort of
this home about which Stevenson wrote so often.

Although the house has passed through several hands since
Fanny Stevenson sold it and moved back to California, it is substantially the same. It became, as its master prophesied, the home
of the Governors General; and here Governor Voelcker entertained
us. The much discussed fireplace, which Stevenson, yielding to a
touch of homesickness, insisted upon building in spite of the heat
of Samoa, is just as he built it, empty of anything save a ghost. From
the big dining room with Victorian rosewood panelling, the massive
dark stairway mounts with a grandeur which gives gracious dignity
to the first floor. Here the Stevensons loved to entertain. Here, with
Fanny and Belle as his sprightly hostesses, Stevenson gave joy to
many a visitor from far and wide, as well as to his devoted Samoan
friends.

From the house we strolled down to the running stream and
natural pool into which one can plunge for a refreshing swim; and
we followed the winding wooded path to the top of Mount Vaea,
thirteen hundred feet high, where a moss-covered stone marks Stevenson's last resting place. On the stone is a bronze tablet bearing
his unforgettable words:

> Under the wide and starry sky
> Dig the grave and let me lie.
> Glad did I live and gladly die,
>   And I laid me down with a will.
>
> This be the verse you grave for me:
> *Here he lies where he longed to be;*

> *Home is the sailor, home from sea,*
> *And the hunter home from the hill.*

On the opposite side another small bronze table bears the words he wrote about his wife, whose ashes are buried beside him:

> Teacher, tender comrade, wife,
> A fellow farer true through life;
> Heart whole and soul free
> The august Father gave to me.

We stood beside the tomb for a few minutes in silence. Directly below us were the red roofs of Vailima, and beyond the forest of trees Apia extended along the shore. Our eyes followed on out to the white breakers roaring across the coral reefs. How often Stevenson had gazed upon the beauty of that sight!

As we went about Samoa, met different groups, studied their problems, tried to follow their thought, and weighed various plans for political change, we began to realize the profound difficulties in the way of progress. Samoa had never achieved national unity. No effective central government had ever been freely accepted by the people as a whole. Constantly, two or three families have struggled and fought for the kingship; and in the opinion of many Europeans and Samoans who ought to know fighting among these families would inevitably follow if New Zealand withdrew today and turned over the full reins of government.

The Germans with an iron hand had forced the Samoans into unity. In 1912, after the abolition of the kingship and the death of the potential incumbent, Mata'afa Iosefa, Germans had created the Fautua, the highest Samoan title holders, Tamasese and Malietoa, representing the outstanding "royal" family lines of Samoan society; and in 1936, at the request of the Samoans, the holder of the Mata'afa title was appointed as a third Fautua. These three, appointed by the New Zealand Minister of Island Territories, served as "official advisers" to the New Zealand Administrator.

New Zealand, undertaking the administration of Western Samoa as a trust territory, faced very real problems with an intelligent and constructive approach. She was not exploiting Samoa. As a matter of fact Samoa cost her money. Some of her best civil servants—men like

Fred Grattan—were devoting their lives to building up a progressive Samoan administration. Nor was she neglecting social and welfare work. A government hospital had been built in Apia, staffed by able New Zealand doctors and by both New Zealand and Samoan nurses.

By the end of the summer the mission had reached unanimous conclusions. We recommended that immediate steps be taken to give to Samoans a substantially greater measure of self-government.

Nevertheless, in spite of the strong desire to give them the fullest self-government possible, the mission concluded that they were not yet "capable of assuming without assistance from outside the full responsibility of the Government of their country." Their nineteenth century history had proved that Samoans unaided could not withstand the aggressive attacks of Western adventurers nor maintain a satisfactory and unified government of their own. The mission found the Samoan people as a whole lacking in political technique and experience and in a popular understanding of national issues.

We also found the Samoans sadly deficient in education. Progress had lagged, and here again outside help would be needed for some time to come. "The level of mass education in Samoan schools does not reach beyond the lower primary grades, and a relatively small proportion of Samoans have finished even the Samoan type of primary education, which is two or three grades lower than New Zealand standards. Very few indeed have any secondary education, and almost none have done post-secondary study."

There was also the difficult problem of how to deal with Europeans resident in Apia. As a group these strongly felt that Samoa was their home and they should not be pushed arbitrarily aside in any new plan of government. Many believed that if full authority were handed over to the Samoans their own legitimate interests would be gravely and unfairly jeopardized.

In studying the problem of social advancement the mission found that the categories "Samoan" and "European" had come to connote a legal status, which depended strictly neither upon ancestry nor upon mode of living. The two groups had sharply different legal rights and limitations with respect to political representation, landholding, schooling, and court procedures. This legal dichot-

omy between Samoan and European residents, so obviously an artificial distinction, had created serious problems, especially for
many part-Samoans, and was an increasing source of strain. It was
resented greatly by the Samoans, especially in so far as it involved
social and other discrimination.

As our report to the Trusteeship Council stated:

> In the light of the mass of testimony presented to the Mission, the
> most deep-seated grievance, contributing perhaps more than anything
> else to the present state of mind, is the privileged situation accorded to
> Europeans. Again and again witnesses gave instances of Europeans being
> preferred over Samoans in matters of pay, in matters of advancement, in
> appointments, in treatment accorded in hospitals or schools. "The whites
> behave as masters and treat us as an inferior race, and this in our own
> country, Samoa," was the burden of many complaints.

As to this problem the mission made very definite recommendations:

> The distinction between "European" and "Samoan" seems unneces-
> sary, and is certainly unfortunate in its psychological repercussions . . .
> In principle, it is desirable to abolish this division as rapidly as possible.
> All *bona fide* permanent residents of the Territory should be placed on
> an equal legal footing as residents or citizens of Western Samoa.

Although it seemed clear that Samoans lacked sufficient trained
and experienced administrators to run an effective government of
their own, the mission urged that immediate steps be taken to give
Samoans a substantially greater measure of self-government:

> Even a limited degree of self-government involves risks which are
> not underestimated by the Mission. But these risks must be taken. The
> only way to promote education in self-government is to put political
> responsibility into the hands of the people to a degree where they can
> learn. Training in self-government can come only through actual ex-
> perience, sometimes costly. . . . Too parsimonious a measuring out of
> self-government would be worse than nothing. . . .
> It is essential as a basis for the development of self-government that
> the residents of Western Samoa should from now on feel that they are
> living under a government which is their own. . . . A "Government of

Western Samoa" should be established. This Government could develop its own distinctive symbols.

The mission then turned to definite and specific recommendations for setting up a new government of Western Samoa. The most striking was the creation of a legislature. At that time the New Zealand Administrator, "acting with the advice and consent of the Legislative Council of Western Samoa," made laws for the "peace, order and good government of the Territory." But this "Legislative Council," on which sat six official New Zealand department heads, two European members elected as representatives of the European community, and only four Samoans, and presided over by the Administrator, exercised little or no independent power.

The mission boldly recommended in place of the Legislative Council a genuine legislature: "The Mission believes that Samoan representation should have an absolute majority in the legislature. Any arrangement short of that would be quite unacceptable to the Samoan people, and would fall short of the objective of developing self-government."

Other mission recommendations were: creation of a "Council of State"; the development and constitutional recognition of an adequate system of popular local government, including the right of village governments to make local by-laws; the setting up of a city or town government for Apia; the grant of constitutional power to Samoan district judges or village councils to adjudicate matters arising out of traditional Samoan custom; improvement in the recruiting and training of a Samoan civil service; and the setting up of a Samoan Public Service Commission.

Throughout our visit we had tried to make real to the people of Western Samoa the genuine interest of the Trusteeship Council in their welfare and advancement. Our report concluded:

The leaders and representatives of the Samoan people afforded the Mission not only the highest honours and demonstrations of friendship, but also constant cooperation in its activities. Members of the European community, including individual missionaries, businessmen and planters, as well as the members of the European Citizens' Committee, also assisted the Mission in every way possible. The Mission's visit provided an impressive demonstration of the friendly cooperation among all groups, official and unofficial, Samoan and European, such as will be needed if Samoa is to make successful progress in self-government. It was also a heartening assurance of the possibilities of international cooperation to reach common objectives according to the principles of the Charter of the United Nations.

Through Mr. Laking I had kept in close and constant touch with the Prime Minister and the New Zealand authorities. Before we left, as chairman of the visiting mission, I showed to Mr. Laking the substance of the recommendations which we expected to make to the Trusteeship Council.

The day before our departure from Apia a statement by the New Zealand government in Parliament at Wellington outlined its plans for a new Government of Western Samoa. To the visiting mission it was of infinite satisfaction to learn that the proposals embodied substantially every one of our recommendations. Within the year the Samoan Amendment Act had been passed.

Our journey to Samoa had borne very real fruit.

We left Apia on August 28, 1947. All the way to the airstrip at Fale'olo, church bells were ringing, drums beating; and all the villagers turned out in their best tapa-cloth sarongs to bid us goodbye and garland us with fragrant leis of frangipani blossoms. At the little airport were crowds of people—the three Fautua and Samoans from all parts of Upolu, as well as New Zealanders and Europeans. They gave us a heart-warming farewell. One does not forget goodbyes like that.

21

New Hope for Dependent Peoples

The deeply significant role which the Trusteeship Council might play in building for world peace was becoming ever clearer. As I said at the opening of the second session on November 20, 1947: "Many non-self-governing territories contain valuable raw materials or offer rich markets; many command highly desirable shipping or aviation routes; still others constitute naval and military bases of strategic significance. Such territories frequently become sources of international rivalry or even conflict. Under the trusteeship system the attempt is being made to change such territories from possible international liabilities into assets."

The second session approved the report of the Visiting Mission to Western Samoa and voted that "the people of Western Samoa should be accorded such measures of self-government as indicated in the Report." Under the new Samoan Amendment Act passed by New Zealand, a High Commissioner was appointed, and plans were set in motion for assembling the new Samoan Legislative Assembly. In Apia at an impressive ceremony a Samoan flag was raised to a place beside the New Zealand flag.

The new Government of Western Samoa since then has been functioning well. Present plans are to grant it full self-government in 1957, with New Zealand retaining control only over defense, foreign policy, and the High Court. Western Samoa's star is rising.

From time to time new trust territories were formed. One of the most important was that of the Pacific Islands, formerly held by Japan under mandate.

At the end of the war, having driven the Japanese out of the islands at a fearful cost, the United States was in military occupation of the Marshalls, the Carolines, and the Marianas. Never again could we afford to permit these Pacific bastions to be held or fortified by any militaristic state.

But outright annexation was impossible. Again and again during the war we had declared, and sincerely declared, that we were fighting to gain not one single inch of foreign soil.

The alternative was to place the islands under the international trusteeship system, which the United Nations had set up with the strong backing and support of the United States. Accordingly, the United States submitted to the United Nations a "strategic trusteeship" agreement covering all the former Japanese mandated islands, with the United States as administering authority. This was approved by the Security Council in April, 1947, without a Soviet veto, and the Pacific Islands became the ninth trust territory to be brought within the trusteeship system.

The tenth trust territory was the island of Nauru. On November 1, 1947, the General Assembly approved a trusteeship agreement for this territory, which was to be administered by Australia on behalf of New Zealand, the United Kingdom, and itself. This isolated Pacific island is important for exceptionally rich deposits of phosphate, which cover four-fifths of its total land area.

In 1950 a solution of the vexed question of the Italian colonies was found by putting the former Italian colony of Somaliland under trusteeship for a ten-year period, as the eleventh trust territory.

Between meetings of the Trusteeship Council other responsibilities and demands crowded upon me. In a letter dated August 12, 1947, received in Western Samoa, General George Marshall, then Secretary of State, wrote to me:

In my letter of July 29, 1947, I informed you that the President, with the confirmation of the Senate, has appointed you to serve as a Representative of the United States in the Second Session of the General Assembly which is scheduled to convene in New York on September 16, 1947. . . .

In order to make possible early specialization within the Delegation, I am sending you the enclosed list of tentative assignments to the work of the General Assembly. . . .

Mr. Dulles is listed on Committee 4 because of his special interest in the subject arising from his work in the General Assembly sessions at London and New York. However, it is expected that he will concentrate a great deal of his time in Committee 1 and the Plenary Sessions. We shall look to you to carry a heavy burden of work on Trusteeship because of your position in the Trusteeship Council.

In the enclosed list of tentative assignments, John Foster Dulles and I were asked to represent the United States in the Fourth Committee, having to do with trusteeship.

Accordingly, with the convening of the second session of the General Assembly I took my place as one of the United States representatives and shouldered the responsibility for the Fourth Committee. Through the autumn we met at Lake Success almost every afternoon in the Assembly work, and my mornings were spent in New York at 2 Park Avenue, where our Delegation to the United Nations maintained its offices.

At the conclusion of the session Robert A. Lovett, Acting Secretary of State, wrote to me:

I cannot help feeling that your efforts were in large part responsible for the remarkable record of the Assembly in adopting acceptable resolutions on the handling of information regarding non-self-governing territories, in full accordance with the position of the United States, even after these resolutions had been drastically altered in the Fourth Committee. I have also been impressed with your success in securing the passage of thoroughly satisfactory resolutions regarding trusteeship problems in general.

Your services with the Delegation complement admirably your continuing and valuable contribution to the work of the Trusteeship Council.

From that time on I customarily sat as the United States representative in the General Assembly's Fourth Committee. I received official appointment as one of the eight United States representatives in the second (1947), the second special (1948) and the third (1948) sessions of the General Assembly; and after that, when, largely for political reasons, it became the custom to name to the

United States Delegation representatives from both political parties in Congress, I continued as an expert attached to the Delegation to handle trusteeship problems.

One thorny issue which arose to plague the second and subsequent sessions of the Assembly was Palestine. Hatred between Jew and Arab was flaming-hot; our utmost efforts were directed toward prevention of open warfare. When finally after long and heated debate the General Assembly voted for the partition of Palestine, Arab indignation knew no bounds. In a body all the Arab members arose and marched out of the Assembly.

How meet the burning issue of Jerusalem, the very core of controversy? After lengthy and fiery discussion, the Assembly voted on November 29, 1947, to place Jerusalem under a Special International Regime, set apart from both Jewish and Arab states. At the same time it assigned to the Trusteeship Council, in addition to its ordinary work, the uncommonly difficult task of framing and setting up a government for Jerusalem. It directed the Trusteeship Council to adopt a statute for the government of the city, to appoint a governor, and to administer the city on behalf of the United Nations for at least ten years.

The burden of organizing this work fell largely upon my shoulders as President of the Trusteeship Council. During February and March, 1948, the Council was hard at work drafting a statute for Jerusalem, which it transmitted in April to the General Assembly, asking for further instructions. None came.

The third session of the Trusteeship Council opened on June 16, 1948. Two weeks earlier Sir Carl Berendsen, the New Zealand representative, had written to me:

> With reference to the Presidency, as I have told you my instructions are to endeavour to have the rules altered to allow of your continuing in office. I would not wish to do this—nor would my Government—if you or your Government had any objections, and I wonder if you would let me—or Mr. Reid—know what your definite reactions are to this. Personally I am convinced it is the right thing to do if only because of the experience you have had and your undoubted success in the Chair.

However, it seemed wise to me to rotate the presidency of the Council each year, electing alternately a representative of an administering state and one of a non-administering state; and I resigned the presidency on the opening day of the session. Liu Chieh of China was elected to succeed me, and Sir Alan Burns of the United Kingdom was chosen Vice President. They held office until June, 1949. Liu Chieh was a warm friend of mine and continued the Council policies unchanged. Except for the Soviet representative the close personal intimacies built up in the small Trusteeship Council immensely increased its effectiveness, and stood out in sharp contrast to the relationships in some of the large committees of the General Assembly.

In the meantime, Jerusalem still hung fire, and the Trusteeship Council awaited final word from the Assembly. It was not until December, 1949, that the Assembly requested the Council to complete the preparation of a statute for Jerusalem, as previously requested in November, 1947. Accordingly, the Council, meeting in Geneva, Switzerland, spent the winter of 1950 upon the arduous task of putting the Jerusalem statute into final shape.

During this Geneva meeting Betty and I seized the opportunity to visit many of our old haunts. After a grueling week of debates and meetings, it was a delight to steal away for the week end and motor up to some ski resort in deep snow in the heart of the mountains or perhaps take the train to Interlaken and up to Wengen or occasionally to Chamonix for a tramp or a climb.

The Jerusalem statute, as finally proposed by the Trusteeship Council in April, 1950, after considerable acrimonious debate, seemed to me to be well framed for the task in hand. Under it the Council would be the administering authority. It gave to Moslems, Christians, and Jews absolute guarantees of freedom of religion and worship, language, education, speech and press, assembly and association, and petition. It provided for a legislative council, a governor, and also a police force recruited entirely from outside Palestine.

But the final result was highly disappointing. Determined opposition of both Arabs and Jews to the government of Jerusalem by an international organ made it manifest that to turn Jerusalem over to the Trusteeship Council must result in prolonged struggle and physical conflict. Consequently the General Assembly felt compelled to abandon the idea.

As soon as the Trusteeship Council completed its third (1948) session, Betty and I, together with my daughter Eleanor, in early August boarded the *American Flier,* a freighter bound for France. We and a French countess were the only passengers. After a relaxing and beautiful ten days at sea we landed in mid-August and proceeded to Switzerland. After a brief visit at Lausanne with Prince Mahidol's wife and younger son (the elder had been chosen King of Siam) we spent the balance of August hidden away far up in the Swiss mountains, at the little village of Evolène. From here we took long walks and climbs to the surrounding glaciers and isolated Alpine villages. Early September found us on the train for Paris to attend the third session (1948) of the General Assembly; and here Eleanor left us to return to her museum work in America.

Secretary of State George Marshall headed the American delegation, among the members of which were John Foster Dulles, Mrs. Eleanor Roosevelt, and myself. Foster Dulles' position was of peculiar interest. At the approaching American elections in November the Republicans were expected to sweep the country; and Foster Dulles was recognized by many, perhaps also by himself, as the incoming Secretary of State on January 1st. To each of his opinions was attached weighty importance. The news of the actual returns and of President Truman's reelection came in as we were sitting in the Council chamber attending a plenary session of the Assembly. Word passed from one delegate to another like a prairie fire. Supreme elation or bitter disappointment marked more than one face in the international gathering that day.

In the meantime the daily work of the session continued its even course. Early each morning our delegation would meet, presided over by General Marshall, to formulate plans and to talk over the day's program. Always wise, unperturbed, representative of the best in America, he proved an effective leader of our forces at the General Assembly. My own responsibility was, as before, to handle questions of trusteeship as the United States representative in the Fourth Committee.

We remained in Paris into December. Toward the end of the session I was asked to speak at the University of Heidelberg. In my address I said:

> The nineteenth century conceptions of absolute national sovereignty, of a balance of power dependent upon water-tight compartmentalized

nations, of a Triple Alliance pitted against a Triple Entente, must go
if Western civilization is to survive. We have reached an age when, whether
we like it or not, collaboration among peoples for the service of humanity
must take the place of power politics for selfish national ends. In the
face of modern technological development there simply is no other
way. . . .

I suspect the German people by reason of their experiences during
the past ten years are more acutely aware of the meaning and menace
of war—have more reason to hate war—than any other people. . . .

A unified Western Europe requires the constructive help of the German people. Here is a program of great promise and of great hope to
you and millions of others. If out of the tragedy and the suffering of
the past war the peoples of Western Europe can be welded together and
their ancient hostilities and deep-seated prejudices forgotten, the suffering inflicted by the war will not have been in vain.

After our return to New York the Trusteeship Council continued with its never-ending work, now constantly growing in vol-
ume. During 1949 it studied, considered, and debated annual reports on eight trust territories, examined forty-six petitions, and
considered the reports of visiting missions it had sent in 1948 to the
Belgian trust territory of Ruanda-Urundi and the British trust territory of Tanganyika. In October, 1949, another visiting mission was
sent to British and French Togoland and to British and French
Cameroons.

For me the outstanding memory of 1949 was a trip to the trust
territory of the Pacific Islands. The Council was scheduled to examine and debate in July the first annual report by the United States
on its trust territory; and in order to prepare for the debate, and
learn the facts so that I should be ready to answer attacks by the
Soviet representative, I decided to visit the islands in the spring and
see for myself existing conditions and problems. The United States
Navy was at that time responsible for the administration of the
territory and generously arranged for my trip. As soon as the Council had completed its winter session, therefore, I decided to spend
the month of May in the Pacific, after a visit at Honolulu with Admiral Radford, High Commissioner of the trust territory. I went
out with my fingers crossed; for, apart from the Philippines, the
United States had had but limited experience in the government
of dependent territories.

The problems of administering the trust territory of the Pacific Islands are formidable and unique. It stretches from latitude 1° to 20° north and from longitude 130° to 170° east—a region of some three million square miles. The distance from Tobi Island in the extreme west of the Carolines to Mili Island in the extreme east of the Marshalls is twenty-seven hundred miles. In this vast archipelago of two thousand islands and islets live in scattered settlements not more than fifty-four thousand people.

The outstanding difficulty, therefore, is one of immense distances. Problems of transport and communication assume unique importance. Upon assured means of transport for imports of living necessities and exports of copra and other products, standards of living directly depend. Without ready transport schools cannot be established and coordinated and educational progress maintained, adequate sanitary standards cannot be enforced or disease successfully fought.

We set out from Pearl Harbor in early May and travelled some eleven thousand miles by ship, flying boat, land plane, whaleboat, landing craft, and outrigger canoe. We visited islands of every kind and description: some extensive and supporting comparatively large populations; some uninhabited tiny coral atolls almost awash with surf; some "high" volcanic islands of mountain peaks and rugged scenery, and some "low" islands, spots of low-lying vivid green in the surrounding blue of the Pacific. We visited and talked with all manner of island people: tattooed native chiefs clad in loincloths and welcoming smiles, village councils assembled to greet and to exchange thoughts with us, magistrates and headmen, self-sacrificing missionaries, church groups dressed in their Sunday best, various officials titled and untitled, workers of every kind who desired to talk, groups of school children, and even inmates of local jails.

On the whole, I found the people happy, responsive and eager to learn more of American ways. Nowhere in the vast area did I find food shortages, epidemics, or cases of preventable human need. The indigenous population, judged by their own culture, are today well fed, well housed, and in good health.

Life for most of these attractive, brown-skinned Micronesians is simple and primitive. They have no literature. Few have any but the most elementary education. For centuries before the white man came they maintained a fairly happy existence, with a culture admirably adapted to the conditions under which they lived. Their subsistence economy was undisturbed by worries of buying and selling. Mother Nature was for the most part kindly. Coconuts, bananas, breadfruit, pandanus, taro, and fish were easily to be had; clothing presented no trouble—the less, the better; and shelter was easily furnished by the leaves of pandanus or palm. Sustained work was quite unnecessary. As in Samoa, a strongly developed communal family or clan system removed the fear of individual want or incapacity and promised care in time of sickness or old age.

Few of the people today are eager for change. Free from individual poverty or want, they prefer the idle, happy life which they have always known. They do not wish increased economic return at the price of hard work. Many of them regard their culture, indeed, as superior to our own.

The Micronesians are a likable people, tolerant of foreign ways, possessed of dignity and poise—and with a sense of humor, too. At Kwajalein I wanted to try a sail in an outrigger canoe when the wind was brisk and the sea choppy. The owner called the island governor aside: "Do I get him wet or keep him dry?" he gravely asked. I came back drenched. But I was convinced that the outrigger canoe is a considerably better and faster craft than any boat of comparable dimensions to be found in New England.

Everywhere I found friendliness. I wondered sometimes whether, dropping down from the sky as we did in our flying boat and anchoring in a lagoon circled by white breakers pounding on coral reefs, we should find islanders resentful of our intrusion into their quiet lives. Yet I never saw a scowling face. As we stepped from the canoes which brought us to shore, the leading men, assembled in a long line, would ceremoniously shake our hands; and back of them would be untitled men and frequently women and children to greet us. Often ceremonial dances were arranged for our entertainment; and not infrequently at departure time we were showered with gifts: tortoise-shell fans, small mats woven of coconut fiber, gay shells, toy outriggers, various pieces of native handicraft, and, on Yap, even pieces of the native shell money.

The immense distances separating these various island groups make for sharp diversities. The people differ markedly in appearance, in ways of living, in patterns of thought. At least eight distinct cultural groups have developed, each with its own language. Each island is a problem unto itself. Each has its local loyalties—as well as prejudices and jealousies. Into this archipelago of problems came American naval officials to fill the vacuum and take up the administrative tasks left by the 70,000 Japanese who had been killed or packed home. Their task was to build from the ground up.

Against this background of difficulty how much had the United States achieved in the two and a half short years since the Trusteeship Agreement had come into force?

In the political field considerable groundwork in democracy had already been laid. The task of organizing local municipalities, officered and run largely by the island people themselves, had been vigorously pushed by American officials. More than a hundred such organizations had thus far been constituted. Many democratic elections had been held; and the fact that approximately 80 per cent of the island inhabitants of voting age then enjoyed some form of suffrage was a clear indication of the progress in political education.

Political training and understanding, it is clear, must begin by being local rather than territory-wide. Until the diverse island peoples can be knit more closely together and unified in their activities and their thinking, the territory-wide political organization must wait.

In the economic field, the main problem is the export of copra—dried coconut meat, from which oil is extracted, used among other things for soap and for edible oils. To assist the people in getting their copra to world markets and bringing in such goods as they need, the Navy organized the Island Trading Company. All its profits were to go to the welfare and support of the island people. However, it was to be only an interim arrangement until such time as the inhabitants could be taught to carry on these functions on their own account.

In education our people had gone to work with a will. Nearly every inhabited island already had its elementary schools. Moreover, elementary education had been made compulsory. We found that one out of every six in the indigenous population was at school. This was no mean achievement. In every island, always I made for the school. Too often school was not in session, because of the holiday to honor the visiting Ambassador. But on a number of occasions I found the boys and girls in school and hard at work. After watching the teaching, I usually asked the children questions to test their English and their general knowledge. The answers were not always accurate, but their faces were always eager and alert. "Who is the President of the United States?" I asked the youngsters in a primary grade at Yap. Boys and girls scratched their heads. This was a hard one! Finally, an inspiration came to a small half-naked boy; he raised his hand. "Abraham Lincoln," came the triumphant reply.

As yet, the children had learned little of what lay beyond the white breakers encircling their islands. But they were avid to learn English, which all considered the highroad to advancement and the key to much of the magic and the mystery of America. It was taught throughout the territory, and would one day replace Japanese as the *lingua franca* of the islands.

Any system of compulsory elementary education must be based upon a good training school for teachers. It would be quite impractical to bring sufficient American teachers to man the elementary schools. An early step in the educational program was therefore to organize a first-rate training school. The Pacific Islands Teacher Training School ("PITTS") is now in full swing at Truk, where I talked with the trainees gathered from every part of the islands. I found them enthusiastic about their work; and as I saw schools on other islands taught by recent PITTS graduates I could understand why.

Finally, in the social field, particularly in public sanitation and health, notable progress had been made. Disease had been drastically reduced. I was told that when the Americans came, 90 per cent of the people of the islands were afflicted by yaws. Today there is almost none. Intestinal parasite diseases have been reduced dramatically. Tuberculosis remains a serious problem, in spite of earnest effort. All children under sixteen and most adults of the trust territory have been vaccinated against smallpox, tetanus, and typhoid fever.

One of the most imaginative projects in the health field was the U.S.S. *Whidbey,* equipped with X-ray, fluoroscope, and an epidemiological laboratory, which the Navy sent from island to island to make a medical examination and record of each inhabitant.

The heart of the program of public health lay in the training schools at Guam for medical assistants, dental assistants, and nurses. It was always a great occasion when a medical or dental assistant returned to his home island to take a professional part in the visiting medical officer's work or to preside over a local dispensary or health center.

When I turned homeward at the end of May, I felt a deep satisfaction in the groundwork the United States had built for what must constitute a long-time job.

I believe that the American colonial administration, first in the Philippines and now in the Pacific Islands, stands the test. True, we have been guilty of innumerable shortcomings and mistakes. We cannot afford to be complacent. Nevertheless, we have built and are building sound foundations.

The people of the Pacific Islands, on the whole, seemed to be genuinely appreciative of what the Americans were doing and had done for them. A recent petition to the Trusteeship Council from one of the islands asked for annexation to the United States, either as a state or as a territory.

The first examination and discussion by the Trusteeship Council of the trust territory of the Pacific Islands took place in July. I introduced Rear Admiral Leon S. Fiske, Deputy High Commissioner of the Trust Territory, and said, in opening the discussion:

All these island peoples have one general and common characteristic. They are likable. In spite of the succession of foreign rulers who have invaded their homes—Spanish, German, Japanese, and now Americans, each advancing new ideas of civilization—the people remain kindly, tolerant, patient of foreign ways, not resentful, but responsive and friendly. . . .

The United States administration in setting out upon the task in hand seeks no financial gain or advantage for itself or its nationals. Under the trusteeship system—and I am sure I voice the thought of all of us—there is no room for colonial exploitation. The United States is seeking in every practicable way possible to assist the inhabitants in achieving through their own efforts a self-respecting position in the world and individual lives of increased personal dignity and broader individual opportunity.

As we had expected, the Soviet representative bitterly attacked the United States' report. But at the conclusion of the debate he stood alone. The Council, by a vote of nine to one, adopted a Report which "commends the Administering Authority for the progress it has already made in the political, economic, social and educational advancement of the inhabitants." The Council's final vote of eight to none approved the entire Report containing this commendation.

The examination of annual reports should consist of helpful and constructive criticism. Unfortunately the Soviet representative regards the examination as if it were a trial, with the administering power a prisoner in the dock. With a debonair unconcern for the facts, he seeks by innuendo and cross-examination to show up "Western imperialism." And since the debate must be strictly confined to issues of trusteeship, no one is permitted to mention the fact that Soviet Russia has brought under its rule or dictation for purposes of self-aggrandizement or exploitation some 200,000,000 people in a dozen different countries by terrorism and fear. The Soviet Union is the arch-imperialist of the twentieth century. The six administering authorities, forced to defend themselves against often quite unjustified attack, find themselves too frequently compelled to vote together as a bloc.

The situation places the United States on the horns of a dilemma. On the one hand, Americans cannot forget the hopes and yearnings of dependent peoples. We were once ourselves a colony; and traditional American policy is to speed among dependent peoples the building of the necessary foundations for self-government. We should like to vote on the side of peoples seeking human freedom. On the other hand, we cannot close our eyes to the misrepresentations and propaganda of the Soviet representative against the administering powers. The United States is one of these; and it is to our vital interest to help defend Western powers against Soviet aggression. We cannot ignore the economic and other issues involved in cutting colonial ties. It is the tactic of the Soviet Union to magnify the cleavage between the administering and the non-administering groups, posing as the ardent champion of all downtrodden peoples, and branding the United States and the other administering authorities as imperialists.

But since in the Trusteeship Council there is no right of veto, the Soviet member can delay temporarily but cannot checkmate the work of the Council.

The real danger is of square and stubborn conflict between the

Elizabeth Evans Sayre
On the portico of the High Commissioner's Residence
Manila, 1940

A tense moment in the U.N. General Assembly:
Mrs. Roosevelt, Secretary of State Marshall, and the Author

Meeting of the Minds: U.N. Trusteeship Council, 1948.
Victor Hoo, Sir Carl Berendsen, Ralph Bunche, and the Author
Photos by Leo Rosenthal, PIX, Inc., New York

PRESIDENT

administering powers, which possess long experience and carry immense responsibilities for the welfare of the men and women in the trust territories, and the equal number of non-administering powers, which lack both experience in colonial rule and responsibility, and whose representatives too often are swayed by the immediate emotional impulse to increase the freedom of action of indigenous peoples.

Here lies a continuing danger. A tie vote means nothing done.

In the earlier days the Council had numerous tie votes. My unceasing effort as president and member of the Council was to develop understanding and cordial cooperation between these two separate groups, and help each to understand and appreciate the problems and desires of the other.

Such efforts have been largely successful. Representatives have learned to work more smoothly together.

Until the 1949 session of the Council the number of tie votes was on the increase, reaching a maximum of fourteen in the fourth session. In a later session the Council seemed to have learned better how to appraise and to judge. A majority was obtained in 71 votes; and during the entire session there were no tie votes. In the balloting the Soviet representative found himself frequently alone. Tensions, one can hope, are lessening; those seated around the Council table are learning with better understanding to work together.

Under prevailing twentieth century conditions the youthful and underdeveloped peoples of Asia and Africa will play an increasingly important part in the peace of the world. Surely it must be evident that leading underprivileged peoples out of ignorance and dire poverty and disease is emphatically a world task, requiring constant international coordination of effort. In this task of magnificent proportions the role of the Trusteeship Council is vital to future peace.

22

Can a Nation Be Ignorant
and Free?

The magnitude and importance of the Trusteeship Council's work grew year by year. During 1950 it examined the reports on ten trust territories, considered 361 petitions, and sent visiting missions to the trust territories of the Pacific Islands, New Guinea, Nauru, and Western Samoa.

As our work developed we felt increasingly the complexities and the dangers of colonialism, which today threaten to undermine much of the effort of free peoples to build for a stable world peace. The bitter revolt of our day against colonial rule grows out of three interrelated causes: desperately low standards of living among many colonial peoples, resentment bred by long years of exploitation and racial discrimination by the governing powers, and explosive nationalistic ambitions since the war. The Soviet Union is taking full advantage of the situation to stimulate revolt and hatred among these underdeveloped peoples. At a time as critical as this the Trusteeship Council can do much to study the problem and help find the pathway toward solution. Peace cannot be lasting except as it is based upon human freedom; and where there are desperate hunger and need, where racial hatreds and tensions are deep-rooted, and where peoples unprepared for the responsibilities of power acquire it suddenly, genuine freedom either for the individual or for a whole people is impossible.

Many peoples under alien rule are manifestly not yet ready for self-government. I think, for instance, of some of the primitive peoples in the South Pacific among whom the weird Cargo Cult still survives, with its belief in magic, in unholy spells, in the potency of the fetish. Struck by the utterly inexplicable power of foreigners to produce as from the skies inexhaustible supplies of ships and guns and food and kerosene stoves and machine monsters of indescribable power, certain South Pacific peoples under the spell of the Cargo Cult, perhaps touched by a misconception of sacrifice based on Christian teaching, will make a sudden decision to destroy everything they possess. They then tear down their houses, burn their pathetic belongings, chop down their trees and root up their gardens, in a fine gesture of faith and hope that their gods or ancestors will thus be induced to send them—as, they think, the foreign gods send to their followers—miraculous machines and a wealth of food.

Other non-self-governing peoples in equatorial Africa and in Asia, many of them illiterate and inexperienced although better versed in modern ways, clearly lack the training and the resources necessary for self-government in a twentieth century world. For them immediate independence would mean only internal chaos, the breakdown of domestic order and the inability to defend themselves against aggressor nations.

The function of the Trusteeship Council, as stated in Article 76 of the Charter, is "to promote the political, economic, social, and educational advancement of the inhabitants of the trust territories" so as to prepare them for self-government or independence. This is the constructive approach to the problem of colonialism; upon the success of such efforts depends in important measure future peace or war. The bitterness manifested in the General Assembly over Morocco, and France's consequent boycott of the Assembly in 1955 are fresh illustrations of the critical bearing of colonial issues upon the problem of world peace.

Since the end of the last war the great colonial powers, moved by a complex of motives and forces and hastened by the pressure of world opinion, have granted independence to more than 500,-000,000 people—a fifth of the population of the world.

Independence carries with it heavy responsibilities. Armed defense calls for huge outlays of money. Necessary buildings and public works cost heavily. So do adequate educational programs and public-health measures. Schools and hospitals and training institutions for schoolteachers and doctors and nurses cost money.

Take the case of the former Italian colony of Somaliland, which in 1950 by vote of the General Asssembly was placed under trusteeship with the promise of independence at the end of ten years. The civil expenditures in Somaliland in 1951 were almost double the receipts from the territory itself: local receipts totaled $4,616,850, while civil expenditures amounted to $8,463,140. The difference was made up by a direct contribution from Italy, the administering authority. Italy also assumed all obligations relating to the security corps; and it is worth noting that about 75 per cent of the direct and indirect taxes in Somaliland were paid by Italians.

Some experts have doubted whether Somaliland can ever be a viable state, supporting a high or even moderate level of government services. They have questioned whether it has sufficient natural resources or possibilities of industrial development ever to produce the revenues necessary for an adequately governed, self-sufficient state. In 1960, Italy, the administering power, steps out. What then?

Similar problems face us today in many underdeveloped areas. Men and women question the right of any nation to govern an alien people against its will; but they forget that the maintenance of independence and the development of economic and industrial resources cost money and require trained personnel. Where are these to come from? Surely the answer is not simple abandonment of the countries in question. Underdeveloped peoples cannot be left to live in ignorance and want even if they would. In many areas of Asia and Africa we today have perhaps our last opportunity to meet these problems with humane and Christian solutions. If we fail, can we be surprised if Communism moves in?

In these days when colonial rule—the government by a Great Power of an alien people—is often talked of as the cardinal international sin—and is so labeled by the communists—it is well to remember that in our aggressive Twentieth Century world political independence alone does not bring human freedom and democracy. Instead it is often the pathway to a cruel dictatorship or to totalitarian tyranny. Human freedom, if it is to last, can be built only upon sound political training and developed economic resources, upon widespread popular education and a heightening of social standards. And when Great Powers are berated for past colonial practices, many of them, it is true, quite unforgivable, let us not forget the practical assistance toward civilized advance, which also came from these Powers. The colonialism of the past was not all an unmixed evil; Australia, Canada, New Zealand and many other areas, products of the system, come to mind. Without previous colonial rule many peoples in far parts of the world today would be without parliamentary institutions, sound judicial procedures, governmental protection of minority rights and other bulwarks of human freedom.

As previously pointed out, the Trusteeship Council is composed of two groups: powers administering trust territories, struggling with colonial problems and bearing heavy responsibilities toward peoples under their rule, and non-administering powers which had never faced the problem of preparing an untrained people for independence and financing the necessary cost. Since the views of these two groups are often diametrically opposed to each other the United Nations Charter wisely provided that in the Trusteeship Council each group should have the same number of votes, so that neither could outvote the other.

But in the General Assembly unfortunately no such balances were set up. In the General Assembly sit representatives of eight administering states and more than fifty non-administering states. The latter can freely outvote the former. And the Trusteeship Council acts "under the authority" of the General Assembly, whose trusteeship work is handled by its Fourth Committee. The truth is that many members of that Committee have no conception of the real problems of underdeveloped peoples. They have no understanding of what Thomas Jefferson meant when he said: "If a nation expects to be ignorant and free, it expects what never was and never will be."

Unhappy consequences inevitably follow. Political intrigue begins to play its part in the Fourth Committee voting. In the meeting of that Committee in Paris in the autumn of 1951 trouble began with the passage of a resolution inviting to appear before it representatives of the Herero, Nama, and Damara tribes dwelling in the mandated territory of South-West Africa. This was bitterly resented and held unconstitutional under the Charter by the South African

Union government; in protest it withdrew its representative and boycotted the Fourth Committee for the rest of the session. Then came severe criticism by the Greek and Yemen representatives of British rule in Cyprus and in Aden. Strong British protests followed. Next came attacks by the Arab group on French rule in Morocco and on the "colonial" policies pursued by France. France, protesting that such attacks were flagrant violations of the Charter provisions, forthwith ordered its representative to boycott the Committee.

Dark clouds began to gather over the Fourth Committee. Would it split into irreconcilable groups? Intense emotions had been aroused; far-reaching issues were at stake.

As the animosities which developed in Paris made clear, there is ominous danger of a deepening cleavage in the councils of the world organization. On the one hand are the "colonial" or administering group—the United Kingdom, France, Belgium, the Netherlands, Denmark, Australia, and New Zealand—representing the culture of the Graeco-Roman world and of Western Europe, possessing great military strength and a wealth of strategic bases, and ripe in experience in dealing with indigenous and underdeveloped peoples. On the other hand are some fifty non-administering states, many of them newcomers to the family of nations, and most of them comparatively weak militarily and inexperienced in problems of colonial rule.

The resulting situation raises issues in many fields. It touches one of the monumental facts of our time—the progressive shift of power in world politics, from Europe to America and perhaps in coming years from America to Asia. The great nineteenth century arsenals of power—Great Britain and France, and with them Belgium and the Netherlands—are step by step being forced into second place. In such a time of transition there is need for the older ruling nations to be alert to swiftly changing conditions and to realize that they can no longer afford to base their policies and decisions upon outlived patterns or upon an assumed superiority of race which today is sharply questioned. Equally there is need for those peoples who have acquired newfound power to come to a more vivid realization of the responsibilities which world power imperiously demands.

In Paris the work of the 1951 General Assembly and of the Fourth Committee dragged on, and it proved impossible to complete it by the end of the year. On Christmas morning Betty and I caught a crowded train from Paris to Cannes to spend the week's holiday on the Riviera.

It was like a miracle after the damp and the cold of Paris to awaken in brilliant warm sunshine. We hired a car and drove eastward along the Mediterranean, feasting our eyes at every turn on the exhilarating beauty of gray rock and white surf and blue, blue sea. Past Juan-les-Pins and Cap d'Antibes we motored to Cagnes, and from there up into the countryside to the little village of St. Paul.

During the night Betty was taken sick. Happily I found by telephone a little English hospital; and to the well named Sunnybank Hospital at Cannes I rushed her next morning. There she found sympathetic care and welcome; it was as though the hand of God had guided us. Betty spent the remainder of our holiday in the hospital; and I lodged at a little French inn near by, passing the quiet days with her. By New Year's Day she was able to travel; and that evening we were back at our headquarters in the Hotel Crillon in Paris.

For three more weeks the Assembly was in session, and I was deep in the work of the Fourth Committee. Mrs. Roosevelt and I met privately with Dr. Donges, who was representing South Africa, in a vain effort to secure some improvement in the colonial policies pursued by the South African Union.

It was almost the end of January, 1952, when the Paris Assembly session came to a close. Thereupon Betty and I took plane to Munich to see our boy Bill, who had entered the Foreign Service and had been assigned to the consulate there. After a happy week with him, motoring into the Bavarian Alps, we flew to Barcelona and Tangier, where Betty's brother Colonel John Evans was stationed as military attaché.

From Tangier we drove through Spanish Morocco and into French Morocco, visiting medieval Fez, Meknes, the ancient Roman city of Volubilis and Xauen, the home of some of the former "Barbary pirates." Wandering through the crowded medinas and merging in the press and throng of Arab life, exactly as it has continued through the centuries, was like dipping back into the Middle Ages. Here we rubbed elbows with jostling Arabs, Berbers, Jews—a polyglot section of humanity, the great mass of them denied most of the good things of this world, burning with desires and hopes, struggling for a better life, highly charged with emotions and inflammatory feuds. It gave us a new picture of struggling humanity; and perhaps it helped make vivid some of the profound issues and problems fought over in the United Nations.

In February, Betty and I sailed on the *Constitution* from Gibraltar to New York for the winter meeting of the Trusteeship Council.

Amid the harassing pressure of the work, often through those years my thoughts turned, as they had on Corregidor, to the quiet peace and beauty and serenity of our summer home on Martha's Vineyard. Here every summer all the members of the family who could gathered for renewal of our family life and drinking in of health for the work of the coming year. Our cottage on a bluff overlooking the sea was the center of a never dull, but very simple, family life; here we could in large part forget the anxieties and the burdens of a struggling world.

The red Breton fisherman's blouse and trousers from France, in which I lived throughout our vacation, imparted to me perhaps a fisherman's placidity.

Every morning, after the household chores, we would gather in bathing suits on the beach for sun baths and family discussions and dips into the sea. Our afternoons were spent in various island activities—sailing, fishing, crabbing expeditions, hikes or walks, or in motoring or exploring trips to other parts of the island. Often in the afternoon we drove "up-island" to our South Beach stamping grounds, where the great white breakers rolled in from the Atlantic. Here we played with the children on the beach, had family picnics, and often played games seated around the campfire; and here we had a small, peripatetic bath house we ourselves had originally built—periodically carried away by end-of-the-summer hurricanes and, when found perched in some distant field, periodically hauled back and anchored in place. The memory of the lobster gorges on the South Beach still makes my mouth water; yet they, too, sometimes went awry, as when Ralph and Woodrow one afternoon piled

the fire with seaweed and lobsters to be roasted. Fifteen minutes later, pulling off the seaweed to uncover the roasted lobsters, they
found some of the unruly beasts crawling abroad, viciously resentful of their treatment. Most of our evenings were devoted to family
games or to music: Woodrow at the piano or with his accordion;
Frank, Jr., with his guitar; Eleanor with her flute or recorder; Bill
at the piano; and the rest of us singing—sometimes, I fear, boister-
ously.

Here as the summers passed we measured the progress of our
family. Frank, Jr., after his marriage to Harriet Hart had become
the rector of a church at Cleveland, his interests largely centering
in the industrial groups in that city; later he bought his own cottage, not far from ours, on Martha's Vineyard. Eleanor, devoted to
art, had worked for a term in the Fine Arts Museum at Providence,
Rhode Island, and was now happily settling down to her responsible work in the print room at the Boston Museum of Fine Arts.
Woodrow, irrepressible, unconventional, filled with a sparkling zest
for life, became a professor and was teaching philosophy at Pomona
College in Claremont, California. Ralph, who had served in New
Guinea during the war, studiously inclined and brilliant, successfully completed his university work at Harvard in 1948, and then
had entered journalism on the staff of *Life Magazine*. Soon thereafter he published his first novel. Bill after graduating from Harvard had successfully passed his examinations for the United States
Foreign Service, and after his assignment at Munich, he was transferred to Japan. Helen Bell in 1942 had married Robert Strider, the
son of Bishop Strider of West Virginia; he was entering upon a
promising teaching career, and would go far. Sivawongse and Tau,
my two Siamese boys, wrote us happy letters from Siam.

We felt very blest in our wonderful family. Each member was
developing an interesting and worth-while career. And now grandchildren were making their appearance—not ordinary babies, if
the truth must be told, but very exceptional, extraordinarily promising little personalities. And they, too, began to imbibe all uncon-
sciously a love for the Vineyard.

23

Return to the Far East

After the Paris General Assembly meeting in 1951, with its deep conflicts and struggles, my thoughts centered more and more upon the need, if we were ever to realize our dreams of an ordered world and a lasting peace, for something more profound than diplomatic and political efforts, vitally necessary as these were. We must go deeper into the heart of mankind.

How?

That was the insistent question that demanded more and more of my waking thoughts.

The sharp and profound reality of the present world is the basic conflict which divides nations and peoples. The world is torn today between two rival camps, based upon fundamentally conflicting philosophies, each spending a prodigious proportion of its energies and substance upon building up military power. One camp believes that the supreme values in the world depend upon material might, upon brute force, upon whatever will enable a determined group to crush its adversaries, with no holds barred. It brooks no moral restraints of any kind. It is supremely contemptuous of spiritual values. It laughs at religion, at any idea of God. To attain its end it preaches absolute dictatorship, ruthless killing, and liquidation of all opposition. Here is a typical expression of this philosophy, quoted from a Soviet encyclopedia:

Soviet patriotism is indissolubly connected with hatred toward the enemies of the Socialist Fatherland. "It is impossible to conquer the enemy without having learned to hate him with all the might of one's soul . . ." The teaching of hatred toward the enemies of the toilers enriches the conception of Socialistic humanism by distinguishing it from sugary and hypocritical "philanthropy."

The opposing camp builds on a fundamentally different philosophy. It believes that the most precious values in the world are individual human personalities—men and women and little children. The state exists to further their welfare and nothing else; human rights therefore transcend the claims even of state officials. It believes in peace, a peace not of armed might often resting upon national hatreds, but one of agreement, resting upon essential human brotherhood. It believes in a rule of law based upon morality and justice. Good faith and confidence must gradually replace national antipathies and distrust. The basic objectives of nations and of peoples must come to be not selfish national advantage, but the promotion of human welfare throughout the world.

The first of the two philosophies is a return to the primitive— a call back to savagery and the worst in man. The second is the outcome of centuries of upward striving and sacrificial effort, embodying perhaps the best of Hebraic revelation, of Greek and Roman civilization, of Christian teaching.

The future welfare of mankind hangs in the balance. If the former philosophy triumphs disaster looms ahead, and mankind must begin again its slow and toilful advance through the centuries. Upon what will the determination of the issue depend?

Surely not upon armed force and military strength alone. These are needed for defense against aggression; but the issue is too profound to be decided by military force. In the years following 1919 the total victory over German militarism did not end militarism in the world. The military conquest of Nazism and Fascism did not prevent the growth of something worse—Communism. A rooted philosophy can never be conquered by military force, only by ideas.

Nor can the present issue be determined by international organization, a United Nations, alone. A profound conflict of philosophies manifestly cannot be resolved by organized and collective political effort alone. This, like armed defense, is necessary; but it cannot settle. The issue goes too deep.

So far as I can see, the best hope for mankind is to build, particularly among peoples of growing influence and power, a profound belief in the superiority of spiritual values over purely material ones, a belief in the worth of individual human personalities as supreme over everything else in the world, a belief in a dominant God, overruling the earth. These were the central truths taught by Jesus Christ. This in its essence is Christianity. Although we of the Western world perhaps have no right to call our culture truly Christian, nevertheless it is basically founded upon Christian teachings, whereas the Communist philosophy is utterly and forever irreconcilable with Christian teaching.

The supreme tragedy of our time is that in many great areas of Asia Christianity is being eclipsed by Communism. And in Asia live well over half of the population of the world. Asia, so far as one can see, is the coming center of the drama of history.

The Soviet Union is like a great reservoir, piping out streams of contaminating Communism throughout the Asian continent. China with her 450,000,000 people has already become engulfed with it. In India, with its backbreaking problems of poverty and ignorance and religious hatreds, whether Christianity can within a measurable time prove a conquering force is still open to grave question. Of India's 360,000,000 people fewer than 9,000,000 are Christian. Most other Asian countries have a still smaller percentage. In some important areas of Asia the Christians number less than 1 per cent.

As I tried to think the appalling situation through, the thought of Japan, as perhaps one of the most critical key points in Asia today, grew ever stronger. Perhaps there lingered in my mind memories of Corregidor as we lay on the concrete floor of our tunnel under furious Japanese bombing, or at night under the stars watched the Japanese artillery blasting Bataan. Now the once powerful Japanese needed help.

Japan was emerging from a war of terrible disaster—her military forces smashed, her cities bombed, millions of her people killed, her countryside wrecked. Shintoism had taught the Japanese that they were a race apart, different from other men, descended from the gods, unconquerable. Now, disillusioned with their ancient Shinto teaching, they were groping, wondering.

Could the men and women of Japan be brought to believe in the great saving fundamentals of Christianity? Here seemed to me one of the supreme and vital questions confronting the world.

Gripped by thoughts such as these, I suppose the result was inevitable. The determination had been in the minds of many of us on Corregidor, daily facing death, to devote the remainder of our lives, if we survived, to building for peace and trying to dispel the tragic misunderstanding between the Japanese and the people of the West. To the Trusteeship Council I had now given of my best. It had become one of the strong agencies of the United Nations, and its work was well organized and running smoothly. Other men were now at hand to continue its work.

But our former enemy, Japan?

Was I prepared to resign my United Nations work and do what I might to strengthen the witness of Christianity and democracy among the Japanese? And was I fitted for such work?

In late February, 1952 I had a long talk in New York with my friend Bishop Henry K. Sherrill, then President of the National Council of the Churches of Christ and also Presiding Bishop of the Protestant Episcopal Church of America. I told him of my profound conviction that the increasing international conflict, which if unchecked threatened to destroy Western civilization, could be ended in no way other than through the basic principles taught by Jesus Christ. And I told him of my thoughts about Japan, as being the most challenging opportunity confronting Christianity today.

Bishop Sherrill eagerly welcomed my thought. He urged me to go as his personal representative, with a free hand to work there for Christ, unobstructed by denominational restrictions but with the backing and support of both the American and the independent Japanese Episcopal Churches. He wrote to me several days later:

I sincerely believe that you are the answer to our greatest need in the entire Church. . . . I pray that God will lead you to devote your great experience and talents to this cause. Mrs. Sayre and yourself can be towers of strength to Christianity in this strategic place in the world scene.

The possibilities of service were exciting, and I therefore tendered my resignation to President Truman as American representative on the Trusteeship Council on May 21, 1952. In a press statement the following day I said:

As one looks ahead into the next century will the Japanese people with other Asians be fighting *for* or *against* the civilization in which we believe?

In this present period of frustration and dizzy change, Japan needs help. But the kind of help she needs now cannot be confined to guns and armaments and material assistance. She needs a steadying hand in democratic and liberal thought, in Christian fundamentals, upon which our ideas of human freedom and democracy have been built. The time has come now for Americans to give Japan of their very best. That includes, at the very core, Christian ways of thinking.

I promised to give a year in Japan, and set my departure to follow the triennial convention of the Episcopal Church at Boston in September. In the address which I was asked to give there I said:

Christianity points the way forward. It is not a beautiful dream. It is not merely a hauntingly lovely poem of a fearless revolutionary who lived nineteen hundred years ago. It is not a way of escape. It is an intensely practical way of life for here and now. It is a unique and God-given revelation of the only possible foundation upon which human society can be built that will satisfy the eternal demands of the human heart and thus prove stable and permanent. . . .

If we believe, as Christ did, in a God who is actively at work in our world and profoundly concerned with humanity's advance, what a thrilling time is this twentieth century of ours in which to be alive! In our closely interknit world of today, national destinies are in the shaping on a scale never known before. And we can, if we will, be co-workers with God in the tremendous task at hand. For those who catch the vision, here is an adventure more exciting than any romance.

On October 10, a little group of family and friends assembled at the Union Station in Washington to bid Betty and me Godspeed and see us off on our new adventure. After reaching the Pacific coast we spent a day with Woodrow and Edith and their two little girls, Jennifer and Martha Nevin, on a picnic in the mountains near Pomona College; and the next day at San Francisco we boarded the freighter *China Transport* bound for Yokohama. Once again we sailed under the Golden Gate Bridge and into the open sea. Our memories went back to the afternoon thirteen years before when we had sailed for the Philippines. We kept wondering what would unfold in Japan, realizing that this would probably be the last great adventure of our lives.

The steamer was small, and the dozen passengers messed with the officers. It was the kind of ship that we liked, with no organized social or recreational activities. There was plenty of time to read and to talk and to stretch out in the sun. Most of the long voyage we devoted to a study of Japan—its present difficulties, the part it had played in earlier days in Asia, and particularly the tragic history of Christianity there.

Introduced by Francis Xavier in 1549, Christianity had flourished for a time. But unhappily many of the early missionaries became too closely identified with Western traders and adventurers and aroused a fear of Western imperialism. The Shogun, therefore, resolutely determined to stamp Christianity out of the country. Under the edict of 1614 the Shogun Ieyasu ordered the expulsion of all priests and the abjuration by all Japanese of the Christian faith. The persecution came to a climax twenty-three years later when 37,000 Christians in rebellion were slaughtered almost to a man. Over their severed heads was placed a sign: "So long as the sun warms the earth, let no Christian be so bold as to come to Japan."

The Tokugawa Shogunate made Christianity a capital offense, and all good Japanese were taught to fear "the evil sect." For two hundred years every Christian that could be found was ruthlessly killed. It was not until 1859, following Commodore Perry's visit to Japan and the signing of the Townsend Harris Treaty, that Christianity was reintroduced by Protestant missionaries. One of the first of these was Channing Williams.

The people were still strictly forbidden to believe in "the evil Christian religion," and the lingering fear of it was so strong that during his first twelve years in Japan Bishop Williams was able to secure the baptism of only ten Japanese. But five years after the Restoration of 1868 the prohibiting edicts were removed from the notice boards; and by the 1880's Japanese were flocking to Christian meetings. In 1887 was organized the independent Japanese Episcopal Church, the "Nippon Seikokai," in Osaka.

Unhappily the twentieth century brought fresh tragedy. With the taking over of Japan by a military totalitarianism before the Second World War came new persecution. In 1940, the Government sought to compel all foreign Christian Protestant churches to unite in a single Japanese church (the "Kyodan"), under its direction and control. Foreign missionaries were forbidden to hold any executive post in this Japanese church. A minority of the Seikokai leaders and members joined the new Japanese church; to some it seemed a possible pathway to the elimination of unhappy sectarianism which plagues missionary work, and to some it seemed the only way to survive. Others resolutely refused to subordinate their allegiance to Christ to any governmental officials, and accepted persecution.

The Seikokai had to go underground and was stripped of all official status during the war. Nevertheless, those who chose the pathway of suffering saved its life. At the end of the war, tragically crippled though it was, it still lived, and in the new freedom brought by the peace determined to go forward.

As a result of more than two hundred years of killing and persecution the Christians today in Japan, even a century after the reintroduction of Christianity, are pathetically few. As we learned from our steamer reading, less than half of 1 per cent of Japan's 87,000,000 people are Christian, including Roman Catholics, Protestants, and Orthodox. In all Japan there are today less than 30,000 active members of the Seikokai.

On October 31, exactly two weeks after we had left America, we were on deck shortly after dawn, approaching Yokohama. Towering in the sky to the west was Fujiyama, the perfect symmetry of its snowy slopes lit by the early morning sun. As one approaches Japan the sight of Fujiyama, which for days often hides itself in cloud, is known as a happy augury for the days ahead. Our hopes were lifted by its beauty, which we had not seen for some twelve years.

In Yokohama we were met by Bishop Makita of Tokyo and other friends; and three hours later we were in Tokyo, driving past the Emperor's palace, hidden from view by pine-clad slopes in the very heart of the city. The palace and its grounds are still surrounded by an ancient moat, above which rise gracefully sloping walls of hewn rock, gray-green with age. Here in the center of the driving, modern city lies the ancient past, seemingly untouched by modern sophistication.

Again and again in the days that followed I wondered whether Japan and its millions of farmers and fishermen, still secluded and in a sense walled in by their centuries-old civilization, so strikingly different from that of the West, could be won over to the fundamentals taught by Christ. Certainly Japanese Christianity might well assume a very different hue from that of America. Only as the great underlying concepts of the Christian faith are absorbed subjectively by the majority of the people so that they understand their values and weave them into their own lives and culture can Christianity win Japan.

The 87,000,000 Japanese, hard-working, simple-living, still conforming in large measure to traditions implanted centuries ago in a feudal and mediaeval world, are beginning to break away after a crushing, disastrous war and, as they face scarcely understood twentieth century demands, are wondering which way to turn.

The people sense the need of a new way forward. They remember 1868, when with the end of the Shogunate and the imperious demands of an insistent Western world it became necessary to build anew. The Restoration that followed was something of a miracle. In less than half a century Japan had transformed itself from a nation of 30,000,000, in a stage of economic development no more advanced than that of fifteenth century Europe, into a front-rank industrial and military power with its population more than doubled.

Can Japan today achieve a second Restoration?

24

Japan—Challenging Adventure

As we settled down into an entirely new life, we were greeted with friendliness on every side. I was privileged to meet outstanding Japanese leaders in different circles who were influencing Japanese thought; and through them I tried to learn something of Japanese problems and of Japanese thinking. Premier Yoshida in response to a letter invited me to his dwelling and offered to do anything within his power to help.

I was asked to speak in many places and to many different groups. Soon after our arrival, at a luncheon of the America-Japan Society attended by several hundred Japanese and American leaders whose influence could be far-reaching, I said in part:

I have resigned from every one of my official activities, cut myself loose from my former surroundings and come out here to Japan to share my life with the Japanese people. . . . Why?

Because I am convinced that Japan today in the long view is in many respects one of the most strategic and critical spots in the world. The concepts of democracy and human freedom are knocking insistently at Japan's gates and demanding revolutionary changes in her thinking, her ways of life, her international objectives. How will Japan respond? . . . Which way will Japan go? There lies one of the supreme questions of our generation.

The pressures to which the Japanese people are subjected are today terrific. Propaganda of every kind is flooding the country. Much of it is utterly false, but how are the masses of Japanese people to distinguish between the false and the true? . . .

We Americans, as part of the very fibre of our being, believe unwaveringly in the sacredness of every individual personality. Our fundamental thinking is based, therefore, upon democracy, upon the inalienable rights of man, upon human freedom. . . . Democracy, human freedom, peace based upon justice,—these are the great ideals upon which American policy is built and for which, if necessary, Americans are prepared to die.

Do the Japanese people understand these great human objectives and are these the ideals they are prepard to follow, shoulder to shoulder with the American people? If so, a bright road lies ahead. . . .

May I add one further word? These great objectives which inspire and shape the basic thinking of the free peoples of the world are essentially Christian objectives. Belief in the sacredness and the supreme value of each human personality, the elimination of every barrier of race or color or nationality that separates man from man, the protection of human rights by moral standards of conduct, the effort to supplant fighting by understanding and reconciliation, a deep concern for human progress everywhere,—all this is the very kernel of Christianity. True enough, we Americans have not always consistently followed Christian teaching. We are guilty of many shortcomings, of many lapses, of constant backsliding. Nevertheless, America was founded by God-fearing men, whose inmost being was bred of Christianity. . . .

Once an abiding faith in the fundamentals, taught by Jesus Christ, can grip the people and the leaders of Japan, the way forward is secure. The United States and Japan, moving into the twenty-first century, neighbors in the Pacific and leaders respectively in the Western world and in Asia, standing shoulder to shoulder and seeing eye to eye, will prove an irresistible force in the great forward march of humanity toward a better world.

I have great hope. . . . The Japanese people have proved in the Meiji Restoration their incredible power to build and shape anew. They are now on the threshold of another new period of high achievement. They are about to build a new Japan.

Under the leadership of God I have faith to believe that it will be a Christian Japan.

Life in Japan became to us a fascinating adventure. At first of course there were many difficulties, the greatest of which was the language. Driving a car through the densely thronged, narrow, winding Japanese streets and finding our way over the unnumbered and unlettered highways was always a baffling task. Most shops and houses were unnumbered, and small sketches and maps had to take the place of addresses. The American military had boldly lettered the streets and based their military maps on the lettered signs. But now that the military occupation was over, many of the lettered signs were coming down. To our frustration Japanese residents would blandly reply: "For centuries we Japanese have found our way around with no difficulty whatsoever." In time, we learned our way, but only through resorting again and again to the omnipresent police box, where officials trained in English replied with unfailing courtesy but not always with precise knowledge.

Much of our time we spent visiting various Christian institutions, learning to know their leading spirits and studying their problems. The work of pioneer Christian missionaries was in striking evidence. One of our earliest visits was to St. Paul's University (known to the Japanese as "Rikkyo") where we were to make our home. Often we visited St. Luke's Hospital in the heart of Tokyo and conferred there with the Mission medical staff. Always we enjoyed driving out into the country to beautiful St. Margaret's School in its attractive setting, where a thousand Japanese girls are taught what Christianity can mean in modern Japan. There was also the Seikokai Seminary, soon to move from ill suited buildings in the city to a very attractive new home twenty miles away. Now and again we motored to the new International Christian University. We had much to learn, and set about eagerly trying to understand and to plan.

Everywhere were surging crowds of Japanese. The local trains were sometimes so jammed that we could scarcely board them. The narrow streets were thronged with pedestrians and bicyclists. On every side and in most of the trains were troops of school children going and coming, the girls in attractive navy-blue skirts and white jumpers and the boys in blue, brass-buttoned uniforms of military appearance.

More and more we were struck with the extreme poverty and simplicity of Japanese life. In the piercing cold of winter men and women sitting on the floor would huddle over a tiny charcoal-filled *hibachi* (stove), hoping for spring. The native Japanese houses with sliding paper-screened walls had no such thing as central heating. Long hours and hard work filled the people's lives. Many of them did not have enough to eat.

Just before Christmas we moved from our temporary quarters in a friend's apartment into our home on the campus of St. Paul's University. It was a rich experience to begin Japanese life in our own home and to feel ourselves becoming a part of Tokyo life. Here each morning at half past six we would hear our Japanese houseboy, Sato-san, in slippered feet stealing into our cold bedroom to light the kerosene stove. Sato-san, then in his teens, had been forced to leave school to earn support for his parents and young sister. He had shining eyes, gleaming black hair, and a young, eager face. From early morning until we retired at night he was at work, keeping the house clean to a high degree of polish, the kerosene stoves filled and in order, and the garden and walkways gleaming wet and clean. Our household staff was indeed a very real part of our family, and always made us feel that they rejoiced in fulfilling our requests.

Our house was not Japanese but of New England style with white clapboards, wooden floors, and central heating. Unhappily during the war the Japanese, sadly lacking metal, had stripped all such houses of radiators, furnaces, and metal appliances; and we consequently shivered through the winter, heating the few rooms in which we lived with kerosene stoves and avoiding as far as possible the cold wide hallways which could not be heated at all.

We lived close to the Rikkyo Primary School. Every morning at eight o'clock the Japanese youngsters in neat gray shorts and jackets trooped past our front gate, dallying here and there, on their way to school. Their eager eyes were always alert; and one time, alas, some sparkling eye caught sight of the cap of the gasoline tank at the rear of our car, which stood on the gravelled walk. The devil whispered. Why not? Quickly the cap was unscrewed, and the tank filled with pebbles from the driveway. A little later we could hear the boys in the chapel, singing at the top of their cherub voices: "Yes, Jesus loves me; yes, Jesus loves me!" And as for us, we proceeded to the mundane and somewhat expensive task of having the pebbles removed and the gasoline tank fitted with a lock. Boys will be boys in every land.

Through the course of our year in Japan we journeyed far and near, making addresses, attending conferences, meeting with little groups and touching the lives of many. Sometimes we went at the suggestion of Bishop Yashiro, sometimes upon the invitation of lay leaders concerned with Christian movements. Among Japanese audiences the language barrier was readily overcome by skilled interpreters.

At every turn we found eager interest in what we had to say. And everywhere we went we found haunting beauty. Japan is a land of surpassing loveliness—a volcanic island thrown up out of the sea, with lofty mountains, snowy peaks, forests and pine-clad slopes, and, in the lowlands, green paddy fields glistening in the sun.

Our visits took us to Kyoto, the ancient capital and still the home of early, unsurpassed Japanese art; to Nikko, with its seventeenth century shrines half hidden in groves of magnificent cryptomeria trees against a superb background of mountains; to Kamakura, the capital of Japan from 1192 until 1333, with its revered bronze statue of the Great Buddha, cast seven hundred years ago, gazing with passionless calm over the gray tiled roofs at one of the loveliest bits of Japanese shore.

Several times our work took us to Japan's great northern island of Hokkaido, with its scenic mountains, its deep gorges and high waterfalls. Often Hokkaido reminded me of days in Labrador nearly fifty years ago. There also we had been busied in high adventure, seeking to make Christianity meaningful to a needy people through such practical help as we could bring.

Now and again during our visits we were gladdened by the sight of effective welfare work initiated in early days by Christian missionaries and later often taken over by the government for the outcasts of Japan—for the lepers, the blind, the mentally ill. I think of the National Leper Colony at Kusatsu. To the lepers gathered there came Christianity a generation ago through a faithful English missionary, Mary Helen Cornwall-Legh, who worked among them night and day "as their mother and saviour," sacrificing her life for them with wholehearted devotion. Through her effective ministrations six hundred of the eight hundred patients were converted to Christianity.

I was asked to address these lepers at a service of confirmation and, after that, to share in the Communion service. It was a poignant experience. I said to them that suffering was the pathway which Christ chose, and spoke of how through Him suffering could be used constructively, and even transmuted so as to gain many of the richer values of life. Many of those sitting on the floor before me were sightless; some lacked human features. Yet all seemed aglow with the happiness of sharing in this service and the breaking of bread together. Christ stood close beside us that morning.

Everywhere we went, on trains, on busses, at meetings, we found friendliness. Never once did we meet with rebuff. So far as I could judge, never has Japan been so receptive to America, so eager to drink in American ideas. And this only eight years after a crushing, terrible war! A different spirit is hovering over the new Japan. Will it take permanent hold? The rare present opportunity certainly will not last indefinitely.

So often our thoughts returned to the question, How best can Americans help Japan today? What would be Christ's answer?

Tokyo demanded much of my attention. Often I visited St. Luke's International Medical Center, built under the direction of Dr. Teusler, its lofty structure surmounted by a great cross dominating the lower part of the city. I had heard much of St. Luke's, given to the Japanese people by the American Episcopal Church and at one time the outstanding hospital in the Far East. It had been the greatest single contribution of any church to the social welfare of the Japanese and had great possibilities for lighting the fires of Christianity in Japan.

But when the war came the Japanese government seized it to care for wounded soldiers; and when the Americans captured Tokyo our Army took possession and still retained it even after the signing of the peace treaty.

The Mission staff, dispossessed, were trying to carry on in pitiful, woebegone quarters a stone's throw away from the great hospital built by Dr. Teusler for the care of Japanese. In the makeshift quarters I used to watch the endless lines of Japanese patients, crippled or suffering men and women, many holding babies with peaked faces, day after day crowding through the dressing rooms and hallways of the clinic, each patiently awaiting his or her turn in the doctors' constricted offices. Tragedy was written in their eyes; sometimes a look of hopeless despair told of the denial of hospital treatment which alone might give recovery to a patient fighting some mortal disease.

"Isn't it possible to find some way to meet this suffering?" I more than once asked Dr. Hashimoto, the able head of the hospital staff, pressed and driven, seeking to cope with one impossible situation after another.

"One cannot achieve results if stripped of his tools," he would answer with a shrug of his shoulders. "Once we had the best hospital in Tokyo, with several hundred beds, adequate wards, and the most up-to-date medical equipment in the city. Now, look at our quarters, with only a handful of beds and no wards at all. We lack the facilities even for a first-rate clinic. What can we do but carry on in these sorry quarters?"

The sights at the clinic prompted action. Furthermore, the plight of our St. Luke's College of Nursing, which before the war was generally recognized as the best nurses' training school in Japan, demanded attention. Temporarily housed with the Red Cross Hospital after the seizure of St. Luke's, it could no longer be accommodated there when I arrived in Japan; and now it was in danger of having to close its doors. St. Luke's staff was facing crisis.

Soon after our arrival I called on General Mark Clark, then head of the American Army in Japan, and pleaded for help.

"The Army simply cannot give up St. Luke's as long as the fighting in Korea continues," he said. "Nothing is too good for our men, wounded in the fighting there. Until that need is past you get St. Luke's back only over my dead body."

Nevertheless, he listened sympathetically. He saw our own critical need. Following my conferences with him and with other Army officers directly concerned, the Army agreed to vacate an entire block of temporary structures adjoining the hospital, which it had been occupying. These we took over, remodeled, and refitted; and in the late spring of 1953 we moved into a rejuvenated St. Luke's, with five wards containing 130 beds, and with beautiful new quarters for the College of Nursing. To the medical staff and the college came new life. And now in 1956 at last the Army is vacating the entire St. Luke's Hospital. The sky is alight. Christianity can sometimes be even more effectively taught in hospitals than in churches.

Living on the crowded campus of St. Paul's, I was constantly reminded of the potential of this great university for bringing Christianity to the youth of Japan.

Founded by the Seikokai in 1874, St. Paul's was moved in 1918 under the lofty vision and drive of Bishop Henry St. George Tucker to the extensive campus in Ikebukuro in the northern part of Tokyo. During the war the Japanese totalitarian government had done its best to drive Christianity out of the University. Furthermore St. Paul's was beset by problems of overrapid growth and lack of adequate financial means. Although the student body ran into the thousands, the chapel could seat only a few hundred. Lecture halls were jammed, and there was no auditorium capable of seating the whole student body.

The chief chaplain was Tetsuzo Takeda, a young-looking Japanese priest, sparkling-eyed, broad-shouldered, heavy-set, hurrying along with swinging vigorous step. He was an extrovert, outgoing in his thinking, frugal in his living, with a lovable Christian soul. His theology was summed up in his simple words: "Christianity is not mere philosophical logic, but the very reality of our daily life headed by our Lord Jesus." He had the rare faculty of seeing students' problems through students' eyes. He actually shared his modest living quarters with three undergraduates. As he said to me: "They get up early at six o'clock every morning and go to chapel with me to prepare for daily service. They are very grateful to live in my house with me and of course are very useful for the school evangelization. But I cannot accept more than three students." He also kept open house for all college men, so that he never seemed alone. Whenever I entered his quarters I would find him sitting with several students on the floor in animated discussion. Father Takeda in his simple ways brought Christianity into everything he touched.

Athletic prowess is a cult of Japanese student life no less than of American, and Father Takeda was a devotee. He attended all the St. Paul's contests, and he gathered around him a little coterie of devoted athletes. Every season after the close of the championship games Father Takeda would hold a service of his own in the University chapel, and would bless the trophies as they were brought forward by their various winners. "Last week quite a few students were baptized in the chapel," he recently wrote to me. "One of these was a good basketball champion of six feet, one inch, tall."

St. Paul's actively competed with the large government universities, which attracted perhaps the cream of Japanese students. Nevertheless, in its subtle Christian influence, St. Paul's possessed something rare which the great government universities lacked; and, more and more, that something was attracting students, and giving significance to their college life.

Only about half of the faculty were Christian: there were not enough Christian teachers of first-rate ability in Japan. Perhaps that in itself made the Christianity of men like Father Takeda all the more outstanding. But he was only one of a group of consecrated spirits who were making a strong Christian impress on the students. Junzo Sasaki, then President of St. Paul's, was a true Christian, reverent, devoted, deeply spiritual in his daily living and thinking.

Often I talked with leading trustees of St. Paul's. Their only answer to the pressing financial problems had been an ever larger enrollment of students for the sake of increased tuition receipts. The current enrollment was more than forty-seven hundred. Also on the St. Paul's campus were one of the best primary schools in Tokyo, a junior high school, and a senior high school; so that from kindergarten through college boys grew up under the influence of St. Paul's. The present total enrollment of all levels on the St. Paul's campus is close to seven thousand.

"May not the true objective of Rikkyo," I said to some of the trustees, "be the development of individual Christian character rather than the mass production of trained intellects? And, if this be true, will you not be wanting to devote concentrated thought and study as to how practically such an objective can best be achieved?"

A subsequent trustees' meeting reached vital decisions. The upbuilding of Christianity in Japan was to be the main objective. To this end the Christian forces were to be strengthened, and a new "Christian House," costing 5,000,000 yen, was to be built for Christian activities of every kind. (Up to this time the only central place for such work had been Chaplain Takeda's modest living quarters.) Moreover, since the existing university buildings were manifestly inadequate to meet the needs of a student population of some 4,700, the numbers were to be limited and a new building program inaugurated. A vigorous financial campaign was launched in Japan; and the unusually large Japanese contributions were supplemented by a gift of $100,000 from the American Episcopal Church.

The fruitage of the new seeds planted at Rikkyo cannot be measured by statistics. But revealing indications are that, whereas only about 10 per cent of the students entering Rikkyo are Christian, 40 or 50 per cent of the graduating classes have adopted Christianity. The real harvest of course can, be measured only in after years. Many non-Christian St. Paul's graduates, I am told, after returning to their home towns and marrying, enter into the activities of local Christian churches and, with their families, become baptized members.

Chaplain Takeda wrote to me in the winter of 1954, when the Freshman enrollment was limited to 1,000, that 10,000 applicants were on hand. "That means we select one out of ten applicants. . . . When I was a college boy in the school, we could not dream of such a thing. You should be happy to know our Episcopal university is so popular in this country." Later he wrote: "Yesterday we baptized thirty people, including professors. Our Christian family in the University is increasing constantly."

New campus buildings have now been completed, and the large Middle School building, the great Tucker auditorium, and, perhaps of even more strategic significance, the distinctive Christian House are in successful operation. Let us hope that dormitories will follow.

But perhaps even more important ground for the implanting of Christian seed in Japan were the five former Imperial Government universities. On their campuses, at Tokyo, Kyoto, Sendai, Sapporo, and Fukuoka, were gathered Japan's best in the student world—young men who will become leaders of political and social life, and whom it was all-important to reach. Organized Christianity had been practically barred from all five; but under the new dispensation interesting possibilities were opening up. It seemed high time to explore them.

The most auspicious of the five seemed to be Hokkaido University at Sapporo, the capital city of the large northern island. Hok-

kaido, with a population of 4,500,000, is a pioneering country—
men and women living in wide-open areas, opening up farms and
raising stock, cutting virgin forests for paper mills, harnessing water
for hydraulic power, building up the resources of a developing
countryside. As such it is filled with hope. Towns are growing fast,
and Christian influences were not touching them. Even some cities
of sixty and seventy thousand are without churches.

Although Hokkaido University through the efforts of Dr. W.
S. Clark had once been a strong center of Christianity, in later years
under the totalitarian government preceding the war the Christian
faith was fast losing ground. Now we found a new spirit. The university authorities were favorable to the idea of a student Christian
center immediately adjoining the campus.

Accordingly, we enthusiastically planned such a building and
won the generous help of the Church in America. In September
Bishop Sherrill, on his visit to Japan, flew with me to Sapporo. We
were welcomed by the university authorities and broke ground for
the new Christian center.

Today it has been completed and is playing an active part
in the building of Christianity among the Hokkaido students. Living in the center and jointly directing this vital work are an outstanding Japanese lay member of the University faculty, Hideyasu
Nakagawa, and the gifted young American missionary, William D.
Eddy. It is proving a splendid success. It is hoped to build similar
centers in the other four former Imperial Government universities.

Unhappily Christianity in Japan is a struggling faith beset with
poverty. There are not nearly enough church buildings. Church
groups lack money for building new churches or for keeping old
ones in repair. Church membership is drawn in the main from the
working classes, like that of the early Christian church in the days
of Rome.

I remember visiting Nagasaki, where the American atom bomb
had destroyed the Seikokai church in 1945. It still remains a pile of
unsightly rubble. The remnants of the congregation, with no minister to lead them, asked if I would be willing to meet with them.
We gathered in the small front room of a private home, all seated

on the floor, shivering in the cold, and held a service together. At the close of the service I asked, "What are your greatest needs?" They thought and talked with one another. I had no doubt that in this golden opportunity they would ask for a new church to replace the rubble pile of the old. Finally they reached agreement: "What we want most is first a full-time parish minister to lead us and help us again to build Christianity in Nagasaki. After that, a church to meet in."

Since then they have secured a minister. And in conversations at Washington with the Department of State shortly after my return to America I was able to secure the beautiful grounds of the American Consulate, which our government had decided to close, as their new church site to be purchased with American church funds.

As I travelled about Japan observing its needs and talking with its people very definite conclusions began to shape themselves in my mind. If Christianity was to win Japan two portentous needs must be somehow met: far more young men of valiant spirit must enter the ministry; and far more laymen must consecrate themselves to the building up of Christianity throughout the country.

The tragedy is that the Christian Church is not preparing and sending into the field anywhere near enough ministers to reach the millions and millions of farmers and fishermen, particularly in rural districts. One difficulty has been the meager salary paid to ministers in Japan—so small that in many places they are compelled to seek outside, secular work in order to support their families. How can brilliant young men be attracted into such a poverty-stricken life? Again, some seminaries admit only students who speak English, or fix the entrance requirements so high that only a picked few can attend. From the Central Seminary of the Seikokai, for instance, fewer than a dozen students are being graduated each year.

The second need—a greater number of consecrated laymen—seemed even more imperative. Yet, as I well realized, to build a strong laymen's movement in Japan would be far from easy. The confidence and support of the clergy must first be won. In Japan in church life, just as in political and in family life, it was to the elder statesmen, the older generation, that all eyes turned. In the Church the elder statesmen were the Bishops—saintly old men but too often lacking in vigor; and under them leadership belonged to the clergy, not to laymen.

Bishop Yanagihara of Osaka had sparked a laymen's movement in his own diocese. But his effort stood almost alone. The whole of Japan must be set aflame. And clearly, the flame must be lit not by foreigners, but by Japanese. If Japan was really to be gripped by Christianity, this surely must be a faith built upon Japanese thinking and tradition.

The thought of launching a great laymen's evangelical movement I brought before the Triennial Synod meeting of the Seikokai Church in the spring of 1953, when I said:

The longer I live the surer I become that the only thing that *really* matters in our lives is Jesus Christ . . .

The deep tragedy is that over 80,000,000 Japanese people know nothing of what Christ stood for . . . Instead they must turn to the Shintoists' vague undefined awe and fear of natural phenomena or to the Buddhists' philosophical search for the power in one's own mind to learn life's mystical meaning, or perhaps to the Confucian search for rewarding ethics. . . .

It is difficult to see how Christianity can be a really vital force in the building of the new Japan unless the Church launches out into a vigorous campaign for the winning of new members. With less than half of one per cent of the population Christian, not even one in two hundred of the Japanese people is today Christian. . . .

In the past Christian missionary activity has been concentrated largely among intellectuals and urban populations. Too little has been done to bring Christianity to the rural and to the laboring populations. It is imperative that these groups be reached if Christianity is to capture Japan. In view of the challenge which God presents to our Church today I should like, if I may, to lay before you for your consideration at this Synod this proposal: that the Seikokai undertake forthwith a strong laymen's evangelization movement. . . .

Our Church cannot blind its eyes to the world situation which we face today. Our generation is watching the spread of an ideology which is in irreconcilable conflict with the teachings of Christianity. . . .

Since the days of Rome was there ever such a challenge flung at the Christian Church?

The Synod reached a significant decision—that the fullness of time had come and that they would initiate a nation-wide laymen's evangelization movement. The work is now under way, and an intensive laymen's movement is spreading out into every corner of Japan.

It is too early to measure results. But in a recent letter I was told that at the National Laymen's Meeting of 1955 "over 500 men and women gathered from all over Japan. When the service started, no room was left in the Cathedral, and some fifty were standing outside."

As the Japanese slowly recover from the utter disaster of the war they stand on the threshold of a new era. Is it possible for a people so conservative in thinking, so self-controlled, so loyal to deeply implanted, traditional ideals, to shift their fundamental thinking from the primitive and nationalistic teachings of Shintoism and from the passive philosophy of Buddhism to the creative teachings of Christianity, on which much of Western civilization is being slowly built?

After a year of observation throughout Japan, I believe the answer is "Yes." Certainly the youth of Japan as a result of the war are of exploring mind, eager, open to some better philosophy or new faith upon which to build their lives. The Christian Church in Japan faces their inquiries, their searching minds and hearts. In this challenging hour only the best it has to give will suffice.

High Japanese leadership is needed. Among the creative leaders I think of Michael Yashiro, the Presiding Bishop of the Seikokai, the Japanese Episcopal Church. He would be an outstanding man in any country. When in the days preceding the war the totalitarian government tried to compel all Protestant churches to abandon their creeds and unite in a single, government-controlled, Japanese church, Michael Yashiro was one of the leaders who stoutly refused. He chose persecution rather than surrender of principle. During the war he was under the close surveillance of government agents. Ultimately, he made a convert of one of his guards. Humble in spirit, stout of heart, brave, wise, strong, here was a man whom one could not but admire and respect; and we grew to love him in his frequent overnight visits to our home in Tokyo.

Perhaps the greatest hope of Christianity in Japan today is centered in the little bands of devoted Christians, meeting under a few brave leaders here and there all over the country, building up their common faith and seeking to fire new groups.

Again and again I was reminded of those exciting days in the Roman Empire that followed the killing of Christ. Then, as now, the lust for empire and a belief in the supreme power of material force were rampant. Tiny groups of people began to meet in Jerusalem, in Corinth, in Asia Minor, in Antioch, in Rome itself. They, too, had been disillusioned by the materialism and the human exploitation everywhere around them. But they were excited by a new and strange teaching: that the world is actually ruled and history shaped by a God possessing supreme power who cares for individual men and women, who loves each of them more tenderly even than an earthly parent, and that the amazing man, Jesus, whom Roman soldiers had put to death was truly the Son of such a God! Could it be true? Could such a faith prevail?

Those few believers determined by God's help to make it prevail, no matter how preposterous the effort might seem.

Somehow or other this exciting and tremendous new faith—with God's help—did conquer Rome.

Small companies of consecrated Christians throughout Japan today are similarly determined, with God's help, to win Japan for this same tremendous faith.

Before we left we felt that in view of the help and friendliness the Japanese people had shown us, from the highest to the lowest, we should express our appreciation in a grateful farewell to the Emperor and Empress. We had been received by them before the war on our visit to Ambassador Grew in 1940. Then the strict formalities of the palace had been rigidly observed. In those days it was not the custom for the Emperor to receive ladies; therefore Betty, after having been presented with me to the Empress, had to remain in the reception room while Ambassador Grew and I were escorted into the Emperor's presence.

Now all was different. The main palace had been burned during the war, and the home where the Emperor Hirohito received us was a more modest building. It was in the midst of gardens, tended with such devoted care as only Japanese can give. Accompanied by Ambassador Allison, Betty and I were cordially welcomed at the palace and ushered into the reception room. A few moments later Their Majesties entered in Western dress and, as Mr. Allison introduced us, shook hands with entire informality. The low bows and curtsies, the extreme formalities of former days, had gone, and instead we all sat comfortably together in a semicircle for an hour, talking for the most part in English, in the simplest and friendliest way. We spoke of the Crown Prince's visit to America and of our happiness that he had so enjoyed it. Betty and I told of the happy year we had had in Japan, of our appreciation, and of our hope for a great future for the new Japan. Throughout the conversation we felt warm human hearts and a friendly interest in America and in ourselves.

Finally, in mid-November came our day of departure. A large group of American and Japanese friends motored from Tokyo to Yokohama to see us off. It seemed hard to have to say goodbye to those whom we might never see again.

But on board the *President Cleveland* as we came into the social hall, we were greeted by some twenty-five young Japanese boys and girls led by Francis Mitsui, the head of St. Michael's Christian School of Kamakura, and his beautiful wife. These friends had honored us by asking us at the time of their baptism several months before to become their godparents; and they had rejoiced our hearts by taking our own Christian names. Now they had brought their schoolchildren to Yokohama to board our ship and say goodbye. To the wonderment and delight of the American passengers, the Japanese boys and girls with bright, shining faces burst into their favorite hymns and songs as their goodbye to us. Mingled with the sound of their happy ringing voices were the sayonaras and goodbyes of our friends, who bowed low or pressed our hands when the ship's gong sounded and the visiting throng departed down the gangplank.

As our ship moved out of the harbor and gathered way to the open sea, deep in our hearts we were wondering: For Japan what would the future bring?

Two of the group who had come to say goodbye were particularly in our thoughts.

Before our departure our houseboy, Sato-san, had told us that he wanted to become a Christian like ourselves; and when Chaplain Takeda baptized him he too asked that he be given my Christian name. Francis Sato had come down to Yokohama to see us off with a full heart. Later he wrote to me in America: "I felt very badly because I had to say goodbye to you. It is only two months and a half, yet it seems like ten years, since you left. In a dream I met with you again. In my dream I was saying goodbye to you again and I wept. When I woke up tears had fallen on my pillow."

Our thoughts on shipboard were on the two Francises. One was a poor, uneducated, attractive young houseboy who had adopted Christianity as his way of life. The other was heir to a great name in Japan—Mitsui. A courageous Christian he must be to break with the traditions of one of the outstanding families of the old Japan, to be baptized in a new faith, and to give over his life and home to the building of a Christian school in the very heart of an ancient Buddhist city. Will other Japanese have the vision and the courage to follow such a lead?

Each Francis represents vital elements in the future of Japan— the one the old ruling families of influence, and the other the working youth by whose effort the new Japan must be built. Each group is of measureless importance in the critical days ahead. If Christianity is to win Japan both must be gripped.

25

The Path Ahead

As I look back over a life crowded with experiences among many peoples and in many distant parts of the earth, my most outstanding impression is the profound change which has swept across the world within the span of my own lifetime.

During my boyhood we of the West lived in utter Victorian complacency and smugness. I grew up in a privileged group feeling itself somehow divinely ordained as the class to which the good things of life belonged. My own family were waited on by three house-servants besides a nurse or later a governess, a coachman-gardener, and an assistant gardener. From early in the morning until late at night they served us; they had no holidays. I seldom saw my mother in the kitchen; and none of our privileged circle dug in the garden.

In the international world it was much the same. A few nations were the naturally ordained rulers of the world; some seven or eight Great Powers built up mighty armies—and a few, proud navies—to rule human destiny. Selfish national interests guided their steps. Into Asia or Africa they marched as they pleased; they built up colonial strength in the far corners of the world; and too often, by exploitation of "native" resources or even of "native" labor, they increased their own wealth for their own selfish purposes, seeking "a place in the sun." The Great Powers were the privileged of mankind; we took for granted that we should have the good things of life, and we realized very few responsibilities to the black- and brown- and yellow-skinned peoples of the earth. We had little or no consciousness of the oneness of the human race.

Today an entirely different world is in the making. We are slowly coming to realize that all men, whatever their background or the color of their skin, are of a single human family. Lasting peace and human progress, we are learning, can be built only upon human brotherhood. That is a stupendous realization. To believe it is one thing; but to put it into our lives takes time.

In the first half of the twentieth century, during my young manhood, we were learning this the hard way. We were discovering that, in a world knit ever more closely together by trade and intercommunication and scientific advance, the pathway of national self-seeking, of imperialism and nineteenth century colonialism, led inevitably to disaster. The monstrous tragedy of two world wars drove the lesson home by suffering and despair.

Today we are reaching out along other pathways. In 1919 President Woodrow Wilson, forward-looking and clear-visioned, declared before the International Law Society at Paris that "the future of mankind depends more upon the relations of nations to one another, more upon the realization of the common brotherhood of mankind, than upon the separate and selfish development of national systems of law."

Since then much has happened. The exciting fact is that the forward-looking nations in spite of constant failures and shortcomings are learning, as never before, to work together not for selfish national interests but for the common welfare of mankind. We are slowly learning to shift our objectives. Greater progress has been made along the lines of practical internationalism during the past thirty years than during the previous three hundred.

The United Nations, evolving from the League of Nations, is an outstanding example of that growth. Forty years ago collective effort through a world organization to build for peace did not exist. Today the United Nations, in spite of occasional failures, has gone far.

The Marshall Plan to rebuild economically nations wrecked by the Second World War was a tremendous and brilliantly successful undertaking, based on the new internationalism of brotherhood.

Such an undertaking would have been unthinkable fifty years before. So would the world program of UNRRA. So would our own "Point Four" program and the United Nations Technical Assistance Program. In place of nineteenth century forms of colonialism, we are developing an international trusteeship system whose basic objective is in the words of the Charter "to promote the political, economic, social, and educational advancement of the inhabitants of the trust territories, and their progressive development towards self-government or independence," and we have set up a Trusteeship Council with effective powers to see that these are not idle words. Ask the inhabitants of the Trust Territory of the Pacific Islands whether their lot has been improved or not by their shift from Japanese control based upon self-interest to supervision under the United Nations Trusteeship Council.

I think of the American adventure in the Philippines in sharp contrast to many colonial adventures elsewhere. In the main, the United States shaped a policy based upon human welfare rather than upon national self-interest. As a result, when in 1942 the storm broke and crisis came, the Filipinos stood by our side and against our enemies; and today the Philippines stand in the upset of Asia as a distinct asset to the Free World rather than a colonial liability.

As I said in an address in 1944:

> Never before has science and technological advance and new access to the earth's natural resources made possible so rich a life to mankind, *if only* we and other peoples can remember that our true interest lies in cooperation rather than in conflict, and *act upon that truth.*

Nevertheless, dark shadows overhang the world. How can brotherhood, how can the new internationalism, be extended across the Iron Curtain? How can Communists be brought to share in the new advance?

To me it is a question of time. Truth ultimately prevails. And I am convinced that the mass of Communists in the world cannot ultimately escape the truth. Russian Communism in the end can survive no more than could Nazism or Fascism. Its doom is sure. God cannot ultimately be defeated.

I am optimist enough to believe that we shall not destroy the world through the use of the atom or hydrogen bomb. In matters such as these I can only turn to experts, such as Vannevar Bush, the former head of the Carnegie Institution in Washington, who a short time ago declared that scientific effort "changed the very nature of war. And in fact it changed it so much, that war is now in a sense obsolete, in the sense that no one can now any more win a great war." He concluded that the destructive force of nuclear weapons could, in the long run, mean "an end to the great wars of the past three thousand years." With Dr. Bush many of the most brilliant minds of our day are in agreement. Sir Winston Churchill reached a similar conclusion.

The future is bright with promise if only we learn in time to shift our international objectives from purely selfish interests—gaining "a place in the sun"—to the welfare and the progress of all mankind. We stand today at a parting of the ways. Destiny awaits our choice.

The supreme question is whether henceforward we are to be governed by the belief that material power is the ultimate in this world, that exalted nationalism and self-interest are the pathways to the highest happiness, or rather by a faith in the principles of love and brotherhood and spiritual power. Will it be henceforth the philosophy of Communism or that based upon the teachings of Jesus Christ?

Will the principles taught by Christ really work in this twentieth century of materialism and cynicism and struggle? Are they, after all, weakening and disintegrating, certain in the end to undermine the real strength and manhood of any race in the competitive struggle for survival, as millions in the Communist world are coming to believe? Was Christ no more than a magnificent and winsome dreamer? Or was He a downright realist, laying down the only practical way of life which can ever permanently and ultimately satisfy and content both men and nations?

There, it seems to me, is the heart of the problem. Out of my own experiences in many countries of the world has grown the profound and unshakable conviction that human brotherhood as taught by Christ, belief in the conquering power of spiritual over physical and material forces, faith in a God of supreme power and yet of supreme love who actually rules human destiny,—these are the only possible bases upon which a human society can be built which will endure. All others fail. Christ's teaching was rock-ribbed truth. He was the greatest realist that the world has ever known.

In the background of my thoughts as I approach the end of my glad adventure is the part which America might play in the tremendous days ahead. Our country has today become the acknowledged leader of the West, the hope of all peoples who seek human freedom and democracy. America was founded in religious faith; the American venture was based upon Christian ideals. It is these ideals that have made the United States meaningful to other peoples. America now faces her supreme opportunity.

Lord of life and death,
We thank Thee for the great adventure of life,
With its untold possibilities,
Its incalculable chances,
Its mighty opportunities.

We thank Thee that—if we have Thee with us—
There is no monotony or weariness in the world;
But we go on—for ever exploring and adventuring,
Across new seas where ship has never sailed before;
Through trackless forests where human foot has never trodden.

We thank Thee that, for those who dwell with Thee,
Each day opens new a continent of vivid experience,
Each day shows new a world to conquer;
For Thy love is new every morning,
And life with Thee is daily born again from its beginning.
                                    —JOHN S. HOYLAND

Index

DATE DUE

GAYLORD			PRINTED IN U.S.A.